George Meredith

THE LAST SKETCH OF MEREDITH
by the French artist Noël Dorville

GEORGE
MEREDITH

his life and work by
JACK LINDSAY

London
THE BODLEY HEAD

First Published 1956

To Alick West
to whom I owe so much

Printed in Great Britain by
THE PITMAN PRESS, BATH
for JOHN LANE THE BODLEY HEAD LTD.
28 Little Russell Street, London, W.C.1

Contents

5

6 *Contents*

Foreword

My reason for writing this book is that I have failed to find any work seriously grappling with Meredith's ideas, his creative definition. At one time it was fashionable to write studies, uniformly superficial, on his attitudes to Nature and Women; but these studies never attempted to relate his attitudes on Nature or anything else to the clear and rich struggle in his life and work, and thus made him out as a thin-minded earnest intellectual of the type with no relevance to our perilous and bitter world, in which an inescapable crisis offers men the choice between the smoke of a final disintegration and a secure hold on Earth at long last.

So far, however, from being remote from this situation of crisis, Meredith of all our novelists developing after 1850 realised most deeply the way the world was going. Naturally he did not see its ultimate crisis in the precise form in which it has emerged; but he penetrated and defined the conflicts which have issued in that form.

Why then has he been so ignored, so little questioned, in the years after the 1914–18 War, when the relevance of his definition, if I am correct, has at last become fiercely obvious?

The answer to that question is what the whole of my book attempts. Here I shall make only one preliminary point. In 1931 an American critic (Chauncey Brewster Tinker) wrote, 'Disguise the matter as we may, the undeniable fact is that Meredith is a believer in Progress.' Simply, that is the explanation of his neglect and of the nonsense written about him. For he both grasped the essential nature of the conflict now issuing in the threat to life itself, and held a deep optimism which believed that despite all hells men—the masses—would master the threat and achieve a happy and harmonious life on earth.

Meredith has been ignored because of his profound relevance to the situation of our world.

He has his faults, which I think are not unduly evaded in this study; but it is his virtues that have told against him.

In my youth, reading uncritically all Great Novels I could lay hands on, I read *The Shaving of Shagpat*, *The Egoist*, and others of Meredith's works, and they left a respectful impression. But I did not return to him until I recently picked up *Beauchamp's Career*—one of the Great Novels I'd missed—and found how startling it was. I then read or reread through all Meredith's novels, and in due time arrived at the conclusions here set out.

While writing, I have asked all sorts of persons about their reaction to Meredith. Younger folk, almost without exception, had read none of his books, though they knew some of the poems; older ones were rather in my own position. They had read a few of his books many years ago and weren't at all sure why he had fallen from their minds. Pressed, they nearly all fell back on *The Egoist* as the one book remembered quite strongly; and as they talked of it, they found they were enthusiastic. *The Egoist* had affected them powerfully, but Meredith remained a rather dim figure, a believer in Progress and a psychologist who could analyse the most complex states of self-division. Like myself till I read *Beauchamp's Career*, they had not been driven to bring together those two aspects— the man with the Rapture of the Forward View, and the man with subtle insight into the divisions and the sharp-edged conflicts of the immediate moment.

A biographer meets the problem that there has never been an Authoritative Life. Perhaps the explanation lies in the fact that Meredith died in 1909, and that the 1914–18 war had the effect of obliterating his impact on the reading public. But whatever the cause, the materials about him exist in a very scattered way.

From Le Gallienne on to Priestley and the others there are many books of trivial gossip or literary chatter. Meredith stricken down with paralysis, an unwilling Grand Old Man, was haunted by journalists and admirers who hoped to write an essay on a Day with the Great. To the last he denied that he had any public, since the public he had, meant nothing to him. He wanted a different public, 'the vivid Many' of *Patience and Foresight*.

There are good bibliographies, that of M. B. Forman (with his *Meredithiana*: 1922 and 1924) and that of the Altschul Collection, by B. Coolidge, 1931. But the two volumes of Letters put out by his son are incomplete and feebly edited. S. M. Ellis's biography was amateurish, suppressed in its first edition for its swag of quotations; and the books by Sencourt and others are no better. The one writer on Meredith who gains respect is René Galland, but he cannot be expected to bear the whole burden on his French back.

The few works on Meredith during the 1930's, and the one study since the war (by Siegfried Sassoon), are as empty as their predecessors.* Perhaps

---

* Since I wrote my book, there has appeared *The Ordeal of George Meredith* by Professor Lionel Stevenson, an amiable and (within its limits) scholarly work, which does not affect the generalisations I have made.

the one significant tribute that his work gained between the wars was the belittling by T. S. Eliot and E. M. Forster, who realised, with whatever intellectual inadequacy, that Meredith stood for a way of life radically opposed to their own.

There seems then ample room and reason for a book on Meredith. I do not say 'another book,' for with such a dim vacancy in the field one feels a pioneer. Honesty has made me thus rude, with something of a Meredithian anger. I am aware that it will, and should, have the effect of making the reader approach my book in a critical mood, with a wish to pull it in turn to pieces. I think that it is rather a good way for him to approach my analysis, which is a challenging one.

Finally, I should like to thank Gyorgy Lukacs for some valuable counsel as to method.

JACK LINDSAY

by the same author

novels

ROME FOR SALE

CAESAR IS DEAD

THE STORMY VIOLENCE

1649

LOST BIRTHRIGHT

MEN OF FORTY-EIGHT

TIME TO LIVE

FIRES OF SMITHFIELD

THE PASSIONATE PASTORAL

BETRAYED SPRING

RISING TIDE

THE MOMENT OF CHOICE

biographical and critical

CATULIUS (LIFE AND POEMS)

MARC ANTONY

SONG OF A FALLING WORLD (350–650 A.D.)

JOHN BUNYAN

CHARLES DICKENS

BYZANTIUM INTO EUROPE

I

The Formative Years

1

The Portsmouth Family

About 1784 Melchizedek Meredith set up in Portsmouth as a naval outfitter at 73 High Street. He came from Portsea where in June 1763 he was baptized, son of John Meredith, and considered himself a cut above trade. He scorned the making of money as much as he liked the spending of it; kept horses and hunted; was accepted as guest in the country-house of many a squire of southeast Hants; practised gallantry; talked with a large ease, and prided himself on his aristocratic manners. A tall man with thin straight nose, big eyes, sensitive nostrils and short upper lip, with long hair and high white cravat.

He played his imposing part also in the town. In 1796 he joined the Phoenix masonic lodge as 'a gentleman,' and was churchwarden in the parish church, St Thomas's in the High, in 1801 and 1803–4. Retiring, with his fellow warden, he presented the church with two silver almsplates engraved with the donors' names. He jumped at the chance of a fine uniform on horseback, and in 1804 enlisted in the yeomanry: certainly not bothered that he was more likely to charge the discontented populace than any French invaders. On a Sunday in July 1814, aged 51, he died; and the *Hampshire Courier* recorded that he had 'for many years carried on a respectable trade in the Men's Mercery line.' He was laid out in yeomanry uniform with sword and towering helmet at his side.

The *Courier* would have been closer to the facts had it stated that the respectable trade was carried on by Mrs Meredith. Some ten years Melchizedek's senior she seems, Anne, the daughter of a Portsmouth lawyer Mitchell. An early portrait shows her with clear ruddy face, confident, with linen crossed over her throat; later she looks out at us as an energetic old woman with thin lips and slightly jutting chin. As her man grew more lavishly lax, she grew more grimly tenacious and honourably exact; she held the firm together and sent out the bills; and she kept her respect for the lordly and boisterous master of the house even when she had to carry him drunk up to his bed. In the intervals of running the shop and the household she bore two sons and five girls.

This pair were the grandparents of George Meredith; and though he had never known them, they left a strong impress on his life and work.

In *Evan Harrington* he set out the family-legend of them, and recreated the Great Mel with vivid force.

Melchizedek liked his odd name. To the confusion of parish clerks not strong in spelling he gave it to a son and a daughter, Charles and Caroline. Charles died young in 1794, but Caroline lived to marry a man with a dockyard post in 1809, dying four years later at 24. The eldest girl, Anne Elizabeth, also married in 1809, gaining a well-off banker and wholesale grocer in a big house across the street, Thomas Burbey. Burbey was Mayor in 1833, but Anne did not share his civic triumph; she died five months before Caroline, leaving a four-months daughter Mary.

The other three girls deserve more notice, since they appear as large as life, or larger, in *Evan Harrington*.

Louisa Mitchell at 18 married W. H. Read, who, born in 1775, served as a purser in the navy and then carried on consular work abroad. About 1832 he became Consul General in the Azores, ingratiated himself with Pedro Emperor of Brazil and sometime King of Portugal, and was dubbed Knight of the Order of the Tower and Sword. In Portugal the Reads held a high position in court circles, and their three sons and daughter settled down as Portuguese, themselves and their offspring swarming into army, navy, and diplomatic services. Luiza, the girl, met Antonio da Costa Cahral in the Azores, captivated and married him in 1834. From the rank of Judge he rose to that of Minister of Justice at Lisbon, and became Count, then Marquis de Thomar. In 1870 as Count he was appointed Portuguese Ambassador at Rome (where other countries had only legations). For a period he had been virtually dictator of Portugal.

Louisa and her girl Luiza had thus securely left behind them all hints of tailoring Portsmouth and reached a social level that the Great Mel would have acclaimed. Aunt Louisa's graces and laces, the scents of her fine condescending manners on her rare visits home to the bow-windowed parlour of High Street, all left a strong trace in the memories of a small boy, her nephew George; and her image was kept alive by gifts of strange fruits and sweets from Portugal where she settled after her husband's death in 1839. An early friend of his said that 'to her he was indebted for his manners and his courteous bearing towards women. He always spoke of her with respect and admiration.' However that may be, he wrote of her as a deadly essence of social falsity and personal unscrupulousness; as the Countess de Saldar she is depicted as without a single redeeming quality, the incarnation of snobbery and class-distinction.

Harriet Eustache, another daughter of the Great Mel, married in the same year as Louisa, 1811. Her husband was John Hellyer, brewer, of

Newington, Surrey; and the family provided the basis of the Cogglesbys in *Evan Harrington*.

Catherine Matilda, the youngest girl, was married in 1819, to Samuel Burdon Ellis, then Lieutenant in the Marines, later General and Knight Commander of the Bath, a man twelve years her senior. Ellis's great-grandfather had served under Marlborough, his grandfather lost an arm at Culloden, his father fought in Canada and the States, his uncle was killed at Bunker's Hill, three brothers served in the navy, and he himself took part in many sea-battles of the Napoleonic era, including Trafalgar. Later he fought in the war with China, 1840–2, and ended as Commandant of Woolwich, dying in 1865. His three sons carried on the naval tradition, though the eldest, George, who entered the navy at 15, was dissatisfied at the state of peace then briefly reigning, went to South Africa, and was killed at the age of 39 fighting for the slave-side in the American Civil War. Ellis of the Marines appears as the despicable Major Strike in *Evan*.

But besides the girls there was a second son, Augustus Urmston, born in 1797, who was 17 when his father died. He had been trained to despise trade and was going to be a doctor; but the Great Mel's death wrecked the family plans and Augustus reluctantly succumbed to his mother's pressure. Creditors had closed in—those mentioned in *Evan* are real tradesmen of the High—and Augustus had to carry on with his apprenticeship and shoulder all the debts, or face bankruptcy.

He too scorned money-making and wanted to cut a gentlemanly figure; but he lacked his father's robustness. Inclining to a mild melancholia, he blenched at heavy drinking and used to leave his guests to their wine; but he liked horses, chess, books, country-walks, and was a member of the Portsmouth Literary and Philosophical Society. A friend later described him as 'a smart, dapper little man, very quiet and reserved, a good sample of a self-respecting and courteous shopkeeper.' His son George put it more briefly: 'A muddler and a fool.'

With the last daughter off her hands, old Mrs Meredith decided it was time that Augustus settled down, and she married him off to a girl from round the corner, Jane Eliza, daughter of Macnamara the publican of the Vine in Broad Street, who had died in 1815. Jane's brother had given up pub for pulpit, and she was a refined and talented girl, about 17 when she married in 1819. She bore her one child, George, on 12 February 1828, and had him baptized in April. Then, on 28 November, old Mrs Meredith died. And her youngest girl took off her mouth the silver coin she had kept in her purse to seal her last breath.

In July 1833, when George was just over five years, his mother also died.

In later years he was rather secretive about his origins. When in March 1901 census papers had to be filled in, a guest offered to do the job for the crippled old man. Where had he been born? 'Is that necessary?' Meredith asked. 'Well, say near Petersfield'—about 20 miles off the mark. 'Don't call me Author,' he said. 'Put in "private means".'* Books of reference merely said he came from Hampshire. One daily in its obituary made a wild guess at Winchester as his home town. Not till S. M. Ellis, grandson of the officer of Marines, published his *Life* in 1919 were the facts known—though some of his close friends seem to have been in the secret.

His reticence, coupled with his fine presence, had begotten many rumours. He was a son of George IV or the sailor Duke later William IV, or at least some famous Admiral; he was of noble Welsh origin, or Bulwer Lytton's son. When it was found that Bulwer's son Robert used the pseudonym Owen Meredith the link seemed established.

But Blunt, citing Meynell gossip, was far from hitting the truth when he said that Meredith's 'tailoring parentage was the secret trouble of his life.' George was of tougher stuff than that. Still, it is of interest that Dickens, also born in Portsmouth, hid the facts of his childhood, while, like Meredith, using them extensively in his work. Forster's *Life* for the first time made clear, even to Dickens's wife and children, the autobiographical bases in his novels.

The ways in which George's position as the grandson of the Great Mel affected his early years will be followed out when we come to the struggle in his early novels, the opposition of genteel aspirations and of the rebel impulse to tear all veils away from a corrupt world.

George was always sure that he came of strong Welsh breed and that his mother had been pure Irish (though in fact her mother, Sara Dale, belonged to a family resident for generations in Portsmouth). For both these beliefs he had the evidence only of the names Meredith and Macnamara. No doubt the Merediths had once come from Wales, and the Macnamaras from Ireland, but there was no such close and immediate link as he fondly imagined.

In his notions of Race he was often at the mercy of the pseudo-science of his day, with its theories of fixed characteristics and its contrast of Saxon and Celt. He attributed a stolid and oppressive lack of imagination to the Saxons of England, and found in the Celts of Wales or Ireland virtues of sympathetic communion and emotional insight. Throughout his novels runs a series of Welshfolk admirably superior in moral fibre

---

* Rightly or wrongly, however, he seems to have thought his mother had gone to a farm owned by relatives of hers near Petersfield.

and humanist passion to the English with their rigid class-forms, hypo-crisy, egoism. But what we find here is essentially a social attitude, which is linked with the fundamental positions of his critique of the contemporary world. 'Passion, refused to the English,' says Galland, 'seems to be the privilege of races that they oppress or despise.' This acute observation goes to the root of the matter; and as we analyse Meredith's work its force will be better appreciated.

2

First Schooldays

DICKENS LEFT Portsmouth as a young child, and the place appears only briefly in *Nicholas Nickleby*; but Meredith was there till he was 13 or 14, and its scene sank deep into his mind. A centre of naval activities throughout the later 18th century, Portsmouth was a compact fortified town of ramparts, bastions, ditches, gates, barracks, admiralty offices, brothels and taverns. The gates were closed at fixed night-hours, the sentries demanded countersigns; mounted officers went the Grand Round; and press-gangs often prowled in the streets. The town,

> as it deserves to be, may be justly considered as the most regular and complete fortress in the British Isles. It serves likewise as an immense depot of all sorts of military and naval stores, vast quantities of which are laid up here, in such exact order that the workmen can find what tools they want in the dark. The rope house is nearly a quarter of a mile in length. (*Crossby's Pocket Gazetteer*, 1818.)

The High was mainly made up of shops, Broad Street of taverns with a neighbourhood of bawdy-houses. A low music-hall rollicked in St Mary's Street and many taverns also purveyed music.

The High Street, running at right angles to the sea and then curving round towards the Point, was the heart of civic life, with the Town Hall, repaired and enlarged in 1796, near its middle. Here

> also stands the white house, or town prison, having different apartments and cells for separating the prisoners into classes. The free school here is under the patronage of the dean and chapter of Christ Church, Oxford. This, it seems, is now become a sort of sinecure. Here is also an alms house of late endowment, a poor house, &c.
>
> That part of the harbour where the merchant ships lie, is a large bay between the gunwharf and Portsmouth Point, where is an excellent quay, and every requisite appendage. At the Point, and close to the mouth of the harbour, is a spacious and convenient bathing house. . . . The harbour is completely defended from all assaults by sea, by a great number of forts and batteries that defend the approach, and are almost level with the water's edge.

A snug fortress-town of the sort to stir a child's fancy.

No. 73 stood just before the curve, an old red-tiled house, on which a grafted stucco-front now masks the red bricks. The ground-floor was the shop, a door dividing two windows glazed with small panes; and at the back was the workshop, reaching back to the White Hart Road. The Premier Establishment of the town. 'We called at Meredith's, the tailor,' writes Marryat in *Peter Simple*, 'and he promised that, by next morning, we should be fitted complete.' He cut and stitched uniforms for the great sailors of the day, Nelson, Collingwood, Jervis, Rodney, and the others. Nelson's Hardy lodged there with Mel's widow; and his son, the Admiral, wrote to his brother in September 1827, 'I can give you a bed. I am at Meradith's [*sic*], the tailor, 73 High Street, opposite the Parade Coffee House.'

From the first floor George could see the thick masts of the harbour and the Isle of Wight across Battery Row; and to the left was the Grand Parade where for a July fortnight a free mart was held, an uproarious holiday suppressed in the 1840's. Richardson's had the best pitch by the Bank at the corner of the High, and nearby stood Wombwell's Menagery. Further, on Portsdown Hill a large fair was held on 28 July.

'I was a very timid and sensitive boy. I was frightened of everything; I could not endure to be left alone.' A portrait in a poor version of the fashionable style of the day shows him at the age of three, fine-featured with fair ringlets, elegant in a little white dress with blue ribbons. Bare-armed, he holds a whip and looks out with a clear wide-browed gaze, all too obviously a petted and precocious child.

James Brent Price, son of the printer and bookseller at No. 74, about two years older than George, brings the portrait to life for us. When some four years old, he was asked in to play. In the drawing-room he found George and his mother, but 'the boy did not seem to care much about playing with me, and I was rather shy.' Still, George brought out his toys and picture-books and impressed James, especially with a white horse-and-cart, very costly looking, with wheels that made music as George drew it along. 'Certainly a pretty child. I spent the afternoon with him, but we did not get on much together as he assumed a sort of superiority.'

Then in February 1832 or 1833 an invitation card came, 'Tea and Ball to keep the birthday of Master George Meredith.' Duly James with his two sisters and his elder brother turned up, the first arrivals, and James's brother made things worse by saying to the servant, 'Please, we are come!' They sat on a sofa while Mrs Meredith received the other guests. Then 'we were removed to a rout seat, many of these being round the room. Tea and coffee and cakes were handed round by servants.' The Prices were pleased to recognise a few neighbours out of the fifty odd guests, mostly grown-ups; but 'after tea the lady announced that the company were to go to the next room and that Mr Macnamara would be M.C. The musicians soon struck up, and a first set was announced.' James was made to dance with a grown lady 'and pushed through the figures,' but was such a failure that he had to sit out the rest of the evening, eating orange-quarters, almonds, raisins, and drinking weak negus, till he drowsed. At last 'supper was announced, and there was a rush to the front drawing-room. I got near my sisters and brother, and was pressed to partake of tarts and cakes.' Finally the lady said, 'It's time the children went home,' and so home they went. 'I was very glad.'

> At this birthday party George was, of course, made much of by everyone. He was then out of his frock-petticoat period. He and I often met after this, but we did not fraternise much. He used just to say, 'How de do,' and nod. I did the same.

It must have been soon after the party that his mother died after a brief illness, aged 31. He was too young to realise the loss; later he said that he merely wondered. His aunt Ellis or his cousin Mary Burbey came in now and then to tend him; but he had many lonely hours. His father, unsupported by mother or wife, was steadily worsening his business position, and he let part of the house, the drawing-room and the big room over the workshop, to an eccentric Irish baronet, Sir Edward Synge, first cousin of the poet Synge's grandfather.

Uncle Ellis's Diary in 1837 shows him walking with the Burbey ladies to their garden at Southsea, enjoying music and dancing after dinner, returning 'at a late hour' and sleeping 'at Mr Meredith's.' But Mr Meredith himself was growing milder and more melancholy; and this year, aged nine, George went to St Paul's day-school at Southsea, where he learned a little Latin and history. He was thus more than ever cut off from the neighbouring lads, who went to the humbler Frost's Academy in St Thomas's Street.

> The boys of St Paul's looked down upon us, Frost's boys, but George Meredith and I when we met always exchanged salutations: 'How de do, Price,' in his usual drawling, patronising way. He was certainly a good-looking youth, with bright blue or grey eyes, and a nice, light curly head of hair, and always well-dressed, much better than any of us boys all sons of tradespeople.

He didn't play with them at hoops, marbles, whip and pegtops, rounders, prisoner's base, or nickey-night (in which, when told to show your light, you struck flint and steel, a game for wintry eves); and so he was called Gentleman Georgy. And he didn't go with the other lads to watch the Convict Guard at the Guard House on the Parade drawing their cartridges and then to collect the powder for making up Devils (pyramids of spit-and-powder lighted at the top). But he sometimes hung about on the outskirts of all this jollity. 'It was in 1839 that I saw the last of George Meredith,' says James. The Frost boys had been running races on the Governor's Green and were chatting when George joined them opposite the Coffee House kept by Neale, who owned a racehorse. Joe Neale, son of the coffee-house keeper, was with them, and so George was very affable, remarking to Joe, 'I was at Stokes Bay races last week and I saw your father's horse come in second, but I think he is a grand horse. By George! he's got some blood in him.' James adds, 'N.B.—This young gentleman was at the most eleven years old!'

Still, if Frost's boys called him Gentleman Georgy, he probably didn't escape being called Son of Snip by some of the gentry at St Paul's.

In his isolated situation he early found solace in nature, stimulated by the walks on which he accompanied his father. He came to know and love the hinterland of shady pastures, thick hedgeways, hills overlooking the bright sea, wooded valleys, the pleasant flowered banks of the Test. And he must have enjoyed swimming, to judge from the importance of swimming imagery in his writings. He was also discovering the world of books, a new dimension of the spirit; and the work that had a supreme effect of stirring release was *The Arabian Nights*.

In 1838 came a crisis, when he was on the edge of puberty. A clothiers firm of Cheapside in November filed a petition of bankruptcy against Augustus, who was so hard up that the petitioner had to advance his expenses for attending the court. A rival tailor of the High took over the shop, and Augustus moved to London, where he found work as a journeyman tailor. In a place where no one knew him, he found courage to marry Matilda Buckett, who had been his young housekeeper (July 3, 1839); on the certificate he called himself 'gentleman.' Two years later on an affidavit he is mentioned as a tailor living in Tudor Street, between Thames and Ludgate Hill.

George was left behind in Hampshire among his better-off relations and seems to have gone to Petersfield, to the farm there. In his old age he told a friend that he went on to a boarding-school at Lowestoft. All we know is that he 'learned very little' and much admired the head-boy who kept all bullies down. His experiences provided the basis for the account of Rippenger's in *Harry Richmond*.

In that novel he relates his phases of adolescent growth: the movement of separation-out from his fellows in obscure and difficult pangs of self-consciousness, and the contrary impulsions towards new compacts of union. He defines the advent of a sense of inner conflict, of a self divided and bewildered, and the answering efforts to overcome the pressures of cleaving discord—with the changing attitudes to nature that arise out of this struggle. Into *Evan Harrington* he puts all the anguish of class-feeling in a lad torn between a sense of native worth and an inculcated fantasy of high-breeding; in *Harry Richmond* he deals with the temporary triumph of the fantasy and the struggle to defeat it, to break through into a stable awareness of reality. The first book covers the strenuous effort to find an honest ground of self-respect, to accept the world of work, to deny the lures and decoys of snob-values; the second explores the dreamworld of adolescence, the ways in which a true adaptation to reality is found despite all the divisive forces that tempt into the sphere of dream-satisfactions. Something of Augustus's attempts to educate his son and open up for him the boundless world of literature and history may have gone into the picture of Richmond Roy; but the main basis lies in the child's own awakening to the rich possibilities of life, helped and obstructed alike by the family-legend of the Great Mel and his swashbuckling enjoyment of all good things. It is perhaps premature here to cite these books in detail; but we need to glance at them to realise something of the tensions and conflicts which were at work in the lad George at this phase of his development.

One of Harry's turning-points arrives after an illness, when he feels sure he can read other people's thoughts—a conviction that accentuates his sense of difference, of superiority, and also, by bringing out the gap between what people say and what they do, stresses the self-divided nature of the world. That Meredith here drew on his own experience is proved by an 1862 letter when he writes about a similar conviction in his own son, 'I had the same faculty when I was young.'

The same letter tells how he early set himself against the religious exercises into which he was forced:

> I remember, at that age, how all love of the Apostles was belaboured out of me by three Sunday services of prodigious length and drowsiness. 'Corinthians' will forever be associated in my mind with rows of wax candles and a holy drone overhead, combined with the sensation that those who did not choose the road to Heaven, enjoyed by far the pleasantest way. I cannot hear of Genesis, or of the sins of amorous David, or of Hezekiah, without fidgeting in my chair, as if it had turned to the utterly unsympathetic Church-wood of yore.
>
> In despair, I used to begin a fresh chapter of the adventures of St George (a serial story, continued from Sunday to Sunday), and carry it on till the preacher's voice fell. Sometimes he deceived me (I hope, not voluntarily) and his voice bade St George go back into his box, and then ascended in renewed vigour once more; leaving me vacant of my comforting hero; who was not to be revived, after such treatment. I have known subsequent hours of ennui; but nothing to be compared with those early ones.

Harry has a bosom-friend Temple who shares his worship of an older schoolmate, Heriot. Heriot makes love to Julia, the Irish daughter of the headmaster, and plays the part generally that Steerforth plays in *David Copperfield*. He appears first as a dashing hero, the perfect type of army-officer; then he is exposed as a miserable philanderer rotten with vanity. No doubt Meredith is to some extent taking over the *Copperfield* pattern; but he is also expressing a disillusion, based in his own experience, with the admired types of Gentleman.

He seems also to follow closely his own pattern of growth in showing how Harry and Temple build up an attitude of pagan honour and courage in their resistance to the Christian idioms that rule the school—idioms that they identify with repression, the cash-nexus, stupefying pedantry.

Besides *The Arabian Nights*, Young's poems, the Ossianic epics, and *Telemachus* affected his young mind. Young's *Night Thoughts* helped to intensify both his feeling of inner division and aloneness, and his opposition to the corruptive world. 'I remember,' he wrote as late as 1902, 'how in my young time he sounded a bell in the night for me, and was Death's vision correcting our vanities—especially felt when we are under a disappointment. After seeing through him I conceived him as all humbug —always in error.' Ossian too had a lasting effect, rousing a desire for heroic action and a sense of union-with-nature through such action, yet blurring men's faces out under its thin wind of elemental imagery. How long Ossian continued to affect the youth is seen by a letter of Meredith's to his son Arthur in December 1871. Arthur in Germany has declared that he prefers Ossian to Homer, and George tries to convince him that Homer, concrete and realistic, is superior to Ossian with his intangible imagery. He admits, however, that the turning to Ossian 'represents a phase of thoughtful youth,' and tries to make Arthur see that what he likes in Ossian is

> the modern tone (under the guise of a weird, primeval, mystical melody and system of verse). . . . It has the same effect on the young as ruins of castles and abbeys seen by moonlight.

Telemachus, with its theme of the Quest for the Father, fitted in with his sense of social confusion, induced by his spoilt upbringing and the abrupt loss of family-life. It helped to lay the lines for such a book as *Harry Richmond* in which the father-quest becomes the search for the truth of things, the discovery of the real nature of the sanctions and authority that control society.

George had inherited a little money from mother and aunt; the trustee of his estate was charged with the arrangements for his education. George decided to go to the Moravian school at Neuwied on the Rhine. Perhaps a friend at the boarding-school had gone on to it, or had talked of it; but whatever the reason, he could not have chosen better. The story that in his determination he bearded the Lord Chancellor may be considered one of the fanciful embroideries he liked to weave in conversation in later years, merely expressive of his agitated wish to reach the Moravian school. In fact he had become a Chancery ward, with trustee-funds allotted to educate him 'for the profession of solicitor.'

3

Moravian Brotherhood

THE NEUWIED school had been founded in 1756 under Prince Alexander, a strong liberal of the epoch, who in 1762 proclaimed entire religious tolerance. He assisted local industry, and encouraged Lutherans, Calvinists, Catholics, Moravians (*Herrenhütte*), and Jews to live in amity. His town was set in the picturesque Coblenz-Cologne section of the Rhine, and had now a population of some 5,000. Swiss had come first to the new school, then Germans, and by 1832–42 the British were in a majority. There were houses, separate, for boys and girls, but many of the classes and the games were mixed. In the Friedrichstrasse about 140 boys were gathered, German, Dutch, French, British: divided into groups of twenty of about the same age. Over each group were set two Brothers who stayed with their charges, sleeping and waking.

Classes lasted an hour and consisted of boys of the same level of development. A pleasant communal life without rigours succeeded in producing a fraternal serenity in which the unceasing surveillance of the Brothers lost any effect of constriction, even in the dormitories where the beds almost touched one another and the windows were kept closed. The spirit was republican; and each group celebrated all the birthdays of its members, including those of its Brothers, so that there were 22 such festivals yearly. A Brother on his birthday was given a new pipe; and the afternoons were spent in excursions, with refreshments at some inn where the boys drank watered wine.

There were many other holidays. For Christmas the preparations began two or three months ahead, and everyone enjoyed making up the glittering candled Tree with the Christ babe in his manger shown below. On the last night of the year they went at 11 p.m. to the chapel for a sermon. At midnight's stroke the organ interrupted and the boys burst into the hymn of the New Year.

Nature-studies were encouraged. Pupils were helped to make collections of butterflies, insects, plants, minerals; and towards Pentecost excursions went on for days on end. Sack on back, staff in hand, the boys trudged out into the country, with donkeys for the youngest. They halted at towns to see the curiosities and sleep, but mostly lodged at hill-farms, eating in the big kitchens and sleeping in barns.

Henry Morley, a pupil shortly before George, kept happiest memories of the school. Fifty-five years later he edited the magazine linking scholars and old-boys of the various Moravian schools, and at a London meeting in 1889 he declared:

> No formal process of education had acted upon their lives so thoroughly or so much for their good as the little time they had spent at Neuwied. It had taken all the bitterness out of their lives, all envy and hatred and uncharitableness having been so thoroughly removed from them by contact with the gentle spirit of the old Moravians.

He wrote two essays on Neuwied. The secret of the school lay, he said, in the way the Brothers lived exemplary lives before the pupils with child-like simplicity of spirit and heart; they seemed incapable of understanding a lie and brought out the best in the children who were left full freedom of imagination; they deprecated all cramming methods and tried to develop their pupils' own faculties. The boys made up stories, especially the English who, stirred by the Rhineland, told of tower-flanked castles in Gower Street, or vast parks at the City's Gates; and the Brothers did not even smile. Morley himself once composed the tale of a mighty hunter; Brother Reuchlin found the copybook and seriously read it out to the others in translation.

George no doubt went from St Catherine's Docks to Rotterdam, then down the Rhine to Cologne, spending a night there and taking the early steamer to Coblenz. *Harry Richmond* describes the journey in a diligence, through pretty gardens, small green meadows, villages with clean children and folk who looked well-fed. After Bonn came the region of the seven mountains, rocks crumbling like ruined towns, towers topping dark ravines, mysterious forests with wrecks of Gothic chapels rambling to the river, vineyards on sunny slopes: the Rhineland of *Childe Harold's* third canto. Then a green isle, a big steep rock mounting guard one side and a town on the other, with castle, tree-avenues, new slated roofs, Neuwied.

Morley was met by a Brother cheerfully smoking his pipe and taken to the pension at the end of Friedrichstrasse, then was shown the town handsomely and regularly laid out, with pensionats, churches, a Museum of Roman Antiquities—Caesar crossed the Rhine here. The town was pervaded with warm plain-air freshened with smells of forest and river; and across the Rhine stood a village with square machicolated belfry, and, higher up, a monument raised by the Army of the Sambre and the Meuse to General Hoche, which evoked memories of the Year II of the Revolution. Three quarters of an hour's walk away was a fine park open to the public and much frequented in summer.

George felt at home. There was no doctrine of hell preached by the Brothers; all emphasis was laid on the Brotherhood of Man. Later he mentioned that as a boy he had a six-weeks spasm of religiosity when he made a nuisance of himself by asking everyone if they were saved. In a letter of 8 July 1844 to a schoolmate he utters the sense of fellowship gained at the school, though in religious terms that he rapidly outgrew:

> My dear Hill,—During the time that we've lived together, one feeling, whether in union, or shall I say enmity, no that is too harsh, has agitated our respective bosoms. It is fellowship. O may God grant that all may have the same feeling towards you to make your life happy. But true fellowship is not to be had without Christianity; not the name but the practice of it. I wish you the greatest of all things 'God's blessing,' which comprehends all I would or could otherwise say.—Yours, George Meredith.

But even this prim priggish note has a hint of his rationalist future: 'not the name but the practice of it.' The 'spasm of religion' last about six weeks. He said later, 'Never since have I swallowed the Christian fable.'

Of his activities at the school we know only that at a Public Exhibition on 10 April 1843 he delivered Uhland's *Death of William Tell* and a violin solo. His writings hold no reference to the Moravians—though the school lies behind the conclusion of *Lord Ormont*, and the lesson of the Brotherhood of Man had sunk deeply in.

His early knowledge of Germany helped to reinforce the German influences strong in the English culture of the 1840's. He read widely in the poets and romancers, and absorbed the themes of rebel brigands, villainous barons, revenging ghosts, vindicated heirs, and the folk-imagery with its sense of man's kinship with nature, talking birds and lovely undines, gnomes striking unseen bells. He learned the legends of the Rhine: Siegfried killing the Dragon on Drakenfels, elves dancing behind Hammerstein, Satan building bridges and cathedrals. And he was attracted by the chivalric attitude to women. In three works, *Farina*, *Feverel*, and *Harry Richmond* he describes powerfully a storm in Germany which merges with a spiritual crisis, a deep moment of change, in his characters.

What he responded to was the challenging and vigorous element in German romanticism, which extends from Goethe to Hegel, from Richter to Heine. Not the vague and yearning mysticism, the evasive idealism that sought to find recondite reasons for conforming to the State. Above all, he looked to Goethe, ignoring his weaknesses, concentrating on his strength—his effort to realise a high seriousness and sense of responsibility in art, his understanding that all true poetry was poetry of circumstance, his elimination of the wilful and pettily personal. His effort to achieve the integration of self within the historical process in which it played an active and socially-conscious part. And his effort to overcome the religious abstraction by defining the unity of natural process and man's organic place in nature. To show the ultimate unity of art and science, the fundamental principle of becoming, change, progress.

In these attitudes Goethe reveals himself an important link in the movement of thought that goes from Bruno and Spinoza to Hegel and Marx, in which pantheist sympathy and abstract notions of development steadily move away from otherworldly idealism towards a secure and entire basis in earthly life, in human society and its living relationship to nature. That Marx lifted the whole movement of thought on to a new decisive level does not remove the importance of the contributions made by his predecessors, and Meredith found his point of contact with the great movement in question. Having gained this basis on which to build, he went ahead with working-out his own application.

It is the radical German philosopher, von Karsteg, who pulls Harry Richmond up in his romantic meandering and forces him to face the question: what do you really want to make of life? He stresses the need to overcome the division of heart and head—one of the forms in which Meredith states the characteristic self-split in a divided society. In von Karsteg then Meredith summed up his debt to Germany, which before 1870 he felt as the land of Goethe rather than the land of the idealist conformer or the apologist for militarism. But it was Neuwied which made him thus concentrate on the vital and challenging elements in the Germany of 1800–50; for from Neuwied he drew the clear vision of fellowship which remained with him throughout life as the touchstone of virtue.*

By the time he left Neuwied, aged 16, he had gone through the two

---

* He stresses (*H.R.* xxxiv) the freedom of critical opinion in Germany as against the servile hatred of the British press for any criticism of established religion and its creed.

In April 1906 he wrote, 'I remember reading in my youth Otto Jahn's Memoir of the great Philologer Hermann and his indefatigable devotion to work, with a sigh of regret that he who had his rivals at home had so few if any among us. As for me, you ask of my readings of the formative kind. They were first the *Arabian Nights*, then Gibbon, Niebuhr, Walter Scott; then Molière, then the noble Goethe, the most enduring. All the poets, English, Weimar and Suabian and Austrian.'

Naturally M.'s reaction to Goethe in his youth was a simple one; but it is clear that at each phase of his own development of a philosophy of mans' unity with natural process he was indebted to Goethe. (The Goethe that Carlyle advocated was in part the Goethe with his feet on solid earth, but it was also Goethe as conformist: 'he has conquered his unbelief.' He sees Goethe's conflicts as with general ideas and emotions, Unbelief, Fear, Cant—not as expressions of a specific historical situation. Carlyles' attitudes to Goethe, then, closely parallel the typical contradictions and composions of the New Poets.

phases of experience which in their clash revealed to him the basic issues of his world. Portsmouth had deified the class-values of the Victorian middle-class, while overgilding them with vague aristocratic glamours of 18th-century leisured scorns. Neuwied set out a totally opposed system of values, in which the world's criteria of money and power had no meaning and all that mattered was the individual's intrinsic qualities, his readiness to work for the brotherhood of man. Between the two phases lay the money-crisis when the Portsmouth values had been shaken.

Out of the conflict thus set up in the boy's mind emerged in due time the poems and novels in which he attempted to face and resolve the contradictions, to penetrate to the full truth of his society. Not that the pattern of conflict remained at the level taken in 1844. Its very nature meant that it must change and extend its range, and that George as he continued to develop, would enrich his personal experience within the whole historical movement of his people between 1844 and 1900. But certain deep aspects had been clarified and the ground cleared for the struggle to come.

4

Into Literature and Love

W HEN HE arrived back in London, his father was working at his future career. In a Chancery application of March 15, 1844, Augustus, now a tailor at 16 King Street, Holborn, asked for permission to sell £400 of his son's annuities in order to apprentice him to John Williams, bookseller and publisher, of Paternoster Row. Williams proposed to take George out to Hong Kong, to carry on his booktrade there, 'together with the business of taking portraits, landscapes and other representative objects by the Photogenic System and of precipitating metals by Galvanic electricity.' The trustees had agreed and the son wanted to go.

Augustus lived near Williams and must have thought the Hong Kong job too good to miss. But perhaps George was not so 'desirous' as the application stated. He did not go to China, to the newly-extorted colony; and in February 1845 affidavits went in to Chancery for his articling to a young solicitor, Charnock, whose chambers were above Williams' shop. The court seems to have had some doubts about Charnock's fitness; but these were at last pacified. George himself was called before the court, and finally in December the arrangement was approved. On February 3, 1846, George was articled for five years. Augustus had become 'assistant' to a tailor, Mackie, in Southampton Row, with whom he was now partner.

Charnock, gaining £500, moved to Godliman Street. He was a big brown lean man with bearded goatish face, something of a buck and a bohemian, untidy and even slovenly, a great pipe-smoker and talker, keen on fishing and joking, a fantasist with claims to polyglot learning, who was one of the first on the books of the British Museum Reading Room in 1838, a member of the Arundel Club (with Dickens, Horne, and Lord John Manners, then associated with the Young England movement described in *Coningsby*), a rationalist and a cynic, who preferred Anacreon to Aeschylus and Hood to Tennyson. He soon gave up the law and lived unmarried, wandering over Europe and the Near East till his death at 84. Meredith summed him up as wanting in both business sense and morals.

In the years when Meredith was familiar with him he roamed over the

Harz (1848) and the Tyrol (1852–3) where he walked furiously through Styria and Carinthia.

George too was walking much, though not so far afield. His lithe figure, with its head of curly chestnut hair, was often to be seen striding through Brompton and Chelsea, then village-suburbs with pretty villas and market-gardens, on to the hills and heaths of Sussex. He thought nothing of a walk to Esher, doing thirty to forty miles a day; and there are tales that in paroxysms of suppressed energy he would run round the Park till he dropped. Tales that are at least emotionally true: his passion for exercise was a healthy thing, an aspect of his resistance to a fettering world; but it also had an element of desperation, of blind fear.

Preoccupied with poetic problems, he found in the jovial Charnock his perfect opposite, and gained much from the clash. He resisted Charnock's ruthless cynicism while absorbing something of his mockery of the creeds, his earthy scorn of nonsense and prejudice. For he was now growing fast, finding his kinship with the New Poetry of Bailey, Horne, Browning, Ebenezer Jones, which other young men were developing— Massey, Dobell, Alexander Smith. In his extreme sensibility, without a clear place in the world, he was torn between timidity and boldness, shrinking reserve and wild ambition. 'When I came to be eighteen, I looked round the world (as far as a youth of eighteen can look) and determined not to be afraid again. Since then I have had no fear of death.' Thus as an old man he stated this period, oversimplifying its struggle, but giving the essential truth. He felt lost, at home only with two or three friends, and found strength in Carlyle's work. Its reiterated advice to the young to close their Byron and open their Goethe chimed in with his mood. He felt the romantic rebellion had now run to seed and become an expense of spirit in a waste of shame; and he wanted to strive towards a Goethean ideal of personal sanity and social responsibility.

A poem of some fifty years later, *The Night-Walk*, defined the heady, confused, rich aspirations of this youthful moment. He and a friend walk among the hidden lives of the swarming darkness:

> *These busy people had our thanks*
> *For tickling sight and sound, but theme*
> *They were not more than breath we drew*
> *Delighted with our world's embrace:*
> *The moss-root smell where beeches grew,*
> *And watered grass in breezy space;*
> *The silken heights, of ghostly bloom*
> *Among the folds, by distance draped.*
> *'Twas Youth, rapacious to consume,*
> *That cried to have its chaos shaped;*

> *Absorbing, little noting, still*
> *Enriched, and thinking it bestowed;*
> *With wistful looks on each far hill*
> *For something hidden, something owed.*

Day had given Night 'the secret things we sought . . . which have no word, and yet are known.' The pair strode on, speaking of things seen, then of poets 'whom some view . . . evoked':

> *To speak the memorable, the true,*
> *The luminous as a moon uncloaked:*
> *For proof that there, among earth's dumb,*
> *A soul had passed and said our best . . .*
> *So royal, unuttered is youth's dream*
> *Of power within to strike without.*
> *But most the silences were sweet. . . .*

Thus subtly he expresses the bursting sense of potentiality in youth, which seems in the night's communing silence to gain a body but which cannot as yet transmute aspiration into action in the workaday world. The nature, the darkness, into which Meredith moves is not the nature-refuge of the Romantics; it is also a human space, in which the union of man and nature begets energies for the shaping of society.

Two early poems, published in 1851, embody his effort to bring out the struggle to change life which lies at the heart of the New Poetry. *The Sleeping City* uses imagery from *The Arabian Nights* describing an eastern princess in a city of the dead:

> *And saw in ghastly shapes of stone*
> *The sculptured life she breathed alone.*

She seems the sole 'child of change' in an arrested world: 'life's semblance but without its storm, and silence frosting every form.' Yet all the signs and shapes of past struggles are gathered in the enchanted scene. Similarly the poet sees in the midnight city 'the centre of the striving world' with man's fate entangled in its silence; and from it speak all the hidden aspirations, 'the language only known to dreams.' This is the moment when the unity of life, the brotherhood of man, the 'one common fountain,' is revealed under the distortions; and the forces that will transform society, reversing the existent system of relationships, are realised at work at the core of things:

> *While Poverty dispenses alms*
> *To outcasts, bread, and healing balms;*
> *While old Mammon knows himself*
> *The greatest beggar for his pelf;*

> *While noble things in darkness grope,*
> *The Statesman's aim, the Poet's hope;*
> *The Patriot's impulse gathers fire,*
> *And germs of future things aspire.*

Thus by the dialectical process that has driven him back into his own depths, into silence, into the opposite of the busy day of the cash-nexus,

> *A peopled hush, a Death not dead,*
> *But stricken with Medusa's head,*

the poet breaks through into a conviction of union with the forces making for a different sort of life, for liberated brotherhood.

In *London by Lamplight* he tells of a singer in the street of the night, who sings a ribald song to whores and outcasts. He sees through the present horror to the space of delighted innocence, of harmonious nature, from which the broken creatures have come; and feels sure that the song can beget the contrary movement which will regain love and happiness. So he accuses not only the agents who have twisted life into the ugly thing he sees, but also all who accept the result and do not fight it. The opposing movements, of deepened horror and redeeming revolt, clash and are one in the full reality, the whole meaning of the scene. Not only are degradation and misery present; there is also the transforming energy, which is the human essence and which therefore in last resort gives the scene its significance.

> *O, agony of grief! for who*
> *Less dainty than his race, will do*
> *Such battle for their human right,*
> *As shall awake this startled night?*
>
> *Proclaim this evil human page*
> *Will ever blot the Golden Age*
> *That poets dream and saints invite,*
> *If it be unredeemed this night?*
>
> *This night of deep solemnity,*
> *And verdurous serenity . . .*
> *Of starlight on the pebbly rills*
> *And twilight on the circling hills.*
>
> *This night! when from the paths of men*
> *Grey error steams as from a fen;*
> *As o'er this flaring City wreathes*
> *The black cloud-vapour that it breathes!*
>
> *This night from which a morn will spring*
> *Blooming on its orient wing;*
> *A morn to roll with many more*
> *Its ghostly foam on the twilight shore.*

Morn! when the fate of all mankind
Hangs poised in doubt, and man is blind.
His duties of the day will see
The fact of life, and mine the dream:

The dream will triumph: the lovers of earth will yet lie in redeemed sweetness in a garden from which the blight has been banished. *This night:* it is all there in the deep experience with its inner contradictions. The emphasis, *this night*, is what gives a note of imaginative greatness to the verses.

Despite some triteness of diction these poems show a deep and true poetic activity which hits the very centre of the social and artistic problems of the time. The midnight city is the deadly isolation that George feels as he reaches out to the union with his oppressed fellows, the detachment from the day of buying and selling which makes the union possible. And the street song, vulgarised as it may be, yet with its high spirits draws together the outcasts, and thus holds the pledge of the high poetry of struggle and aspiration that he seeks.

Meanwhile Charnock had made a useful suggestion. Let the unpublished young publish for themselves. And so a manuscript periodical *The Monthly Observer* was worked out, and a group brought together, no doubt mainly by Charnock. Each contributor was to take a three-monthly turn as editor, collecting material, circulating the issue, and setting out a considered criticism of each item. Everyone was expected to send in two essays, poems, or drawings monthly. Besides Charnock and George, the group consisted of Edward Gryffydh Peacock, son of Thomas Love Peacock, and his sister Mrs Mary Nicolls, with various amateurs, Snell, Cheltnam, Howes (of the Adjutant General's Office, Horse Guards), St Croix (of 4 Mincing Lane, City), and an artist, P. Austin Daniel, who worked in the Examiner's Office, East India House.

Ned Peacock was Welsh on his mother's side. He had gone young to sea, then became a clerk at East India House, and later a barrister. Interested in literature, cricket, rowing, he had professional boxers in his acquaintance; and one evening he, George and a boxer set out on foot for Brighton, arriving next morning. He lodged near the British Museum, with his sister Mary Ellen. In 1844 she had married a ship's officer, no doubt a friend of Ned's, who, two months later, was drowned at sea under her eyes. She bore a posthumous child, Edith, and the shock of the experience increased her emotional instability. A handsome round-faced blonde, with hair parted in the middle and arched eyebrows coming down to her small keen nose, with a fashionable cupid's-bow of an upper lip, she had big eyes that could be vivacious or dreamy:

Now, Madam's faulty feature is a glazed
And inaccessible eye, that has soft fires,
Wide gates, at love-time, only. (*Modern Love.*)

With a cultivated intelligence, she read Italian and French, and was accustomed to discuss freely all subjects, moral and political; she especially followed French events with interest and called herself *Citoyenne de la Grande République Française*. A mixture of feminine grace and cavalier decision, sharp malice and blue-stockinged seriousness. Holman Hunt called her 'a dashing horsewoman who attracted much attention from the bloods of the day,' and in *Marian* (1862) George set lightly out her contrasting elements. 'She can knit with cunning wit, and dress the homely dishes. . . . She can talk the talk of men, and touch with thrilling fingers,' a thing of soft compliance and lofting soaring, of dove-mildness and passionate adoring, 'steadfast as a star, and yet the maddest maiden: she can wage a gallant war, and give the peace of Eden.'

She thus appealed both to his strong romantic emotions and also to his anti-romantic femininism. In her, he felt, he would get the best of both worlds. If he had been more critical, he'd have noted some ominous signs of incompatibility. While he was breaking from all religious formulations, she inclined to a liberal protestantism, looking to Kingsley and the Christian Socialists, and, worse, a dim sentimental spiritualism. That she was half-Welsh, however, increased her attraction and threw a tint of wild freedoms over her confused instabilities.

At first he tried to fit his yet-vague aspirations to her sentimental religiosity, and wrote *Saint Thérèse*, Tennysonianly false, for the magazine:

Around her gloried form the air
Is stirred with falling snows
That cover all the convent bare
With symboll'd pure repose.
Above her halo'd head the sky
Is studded thick with spheres
All swimming to one blissful eye
Whose beam is bright with tears. . . .

That sort of prettification of ascetic attitudes he was soon to consider one of the worst degradations of art, a sensuous gilding of the ugly divisive forces in society; but for the moment, unsure of himself, he is partly dominated by Mary's intellectual pretensions.

Still, he moves steadily towards a more congenial artistic and political position, stirred by the revolutionary waves rising at home and abroad. A woman friend says that the names of Garibaldi, Kossuth and Mazzini were constantly on his lips and his conversation scared away his respectable acquaintances.

In 1848–9 he burns with the double idea that stirred the insurrections in Europe: the idea of nationhood and the socialist idea. In *Brotherhood* he deplores what man has made of the Lord's gifts, opposing the nay of his perverse will to the sweet calls of nature and humanity. (Galland.)

True, we know more of his attitude to the national-liberation movements on the Continent than to Chartism at home, but throughout his life he never shows any fear of mass-movements and his poem *Brotherhood* proves a strong response to Chartist ideas. Both in form and idiom it manifestly echoes the Chartist hymn; and I cite it in full for its biographical importance, since it has been ignored and is not available in any work on Meredith or any edition of his writings:

The Land is rich where'er we go
With Flowers and Fruits in clusters,
No little spot so poor and low
But some sweet tribute musters,
Abundance blesses—all things show
We should bless one another;
Take—says the Lord—but man says 'No'
—But these are mine—my Brother.

Strange is the difference which breeds
Dissention among creatures,
Which binds the slave to slavish greeds
And brands his godlike Features—
One Family are we, and Oh
The children of one Mother!—
Live—says the Lord but man says 'No'
Thy life is mine—my Brother—

The Treasures of the Earth how vast
Exhaustless and unnumbered!
Stored with the hivings of the past
Since first old Chaos slumbered—
And is there then no thankful glow
To knit us to each other?
Ah God when will this dreary 'No'
Melt at the name of Brother.

Religion is a war of sect,
And Fatherland of Factions;
Each deems himself the sole elect
But not thro' virtuous actions,
Not in the deeds whereby we know
The light no clay can smother—
Alas! to all things man says 'No'
And still denies his Brother.

Poems such as Ernest Jones's *Hymn for Lammas-Day* or Massey's *The Earth for all* make obvious the source of George's inspiration; there can therefore be no doubt that it is Chartism which decisively gives to the Moravian ideas of Brotherhood the political orientation that survives to the end of his days. And it is a pity that we lack the earlier numbers of the magazine; for Daniel's comment on *Brotherhood* suggests that it is milder than some of his previous contributions. Daniel sees the poem as:

> a return to Literature for its own sake, and real, practical, social purposes; things that were almost forgotten in the turbulent political ferment in which the Magazine found its birth, just twelve months ago.*

Charnock was the liveliest and most constant contributor. Each of the five extant issues has an essay signed Aretchid Kooez (A Wretched Goose), or, in more orientalised form, Alreschid Quooz. He writes with fanciful and slyly gross humour, pedantic and bitter, rambling into such disquisitions as that on the Prophet Elijah considered as a Cheesemonger that opens the account of his Harz tour. His *Gnothi Seauton* draws the editor Daniel to denounce his hostility to all ideas that don't conform to his pet systems, his scorn of all he rates as prejudice. Undaunted, Charnock describes man as inferior to the beasts in all but reason: how can he compare for strength with a flea that jumps sixteen times its height? The vulgar, he says, may accuse him of wanting to degrade the human race; but it can't be more degraded than it is, not even if one invents a million new religions and other forms of despotism, as is obvious to anyone who doesn't delude himself. And in another issue he sets out the *Neu Yorc Herald* of 1 July 3849, in which the news includes an interstellar space-flight, the driving of the British out of Canada after a two-hour's battle of huge slaughter, the annihilation of the British in India, and various inventions (suggested by the railway, the telegraph, the daguerreotype) which Charnock considers to show a lunatic movement into mechanisation. He signs from his Chateau, rue Diogène, No. 20.

> *Neu Yorc Herald, Munday July* 1. 3849. *Preis.* 3 *Farthings. Advertisements. For Sirius.* The fast mounter 'Daedalus' will start on Thursday morning at 12 for 12. Fares. 60 Dollars. Length of Transit. 70 hours. Only 10 lbs of luggage allowed.
>
> *For the Sun and Moon.* The 'Ærial' will start for these planets on Friday at 2 for 2. Passengers for the Sun will be allowed to stay 24 hours in the Moon. For further particulars apply to Mrssr. Mongolfier Rue Gas-sendi.

---

* In 1851 we find George writing to Kingsley, stirred by the element of social revolt in *Yeast*. 'I am driven with a spur to tell you the delight and admiration with which I read your last book *Yeast* and the positive "Education" I have derived from it. It was the very book I was in want of and likely to do me more good than any that I know.'

North Western Railway. Trains from Neu Yorc to Cape Prince of Wales in 80 minutes. Fares 120 florins. On the arrival of the Train the Electric ship will be in readiness to cross the Straits to the Coast of Asia. Length of passage 5 minutes. In correspondence with the Trains from East Cape to St. Petersburg —Moskau—Pekin and Bombay.

Patents which have passed the Great Seal. Thomas [Buxton *crossed out*] Lloyd of Rue Robespierre Charlestown for an improved magnet to attract Cannon Balls in War. This magnet possesses a repulsive power so that the material is sent back to the place from whence it came.

Asa Jones of Rue Lamartine Philadelphia Aurist for printing on paper by the sound of the human voice.

Foreign Nuz. India By Electric telegraf. Every Englishman has been driven into the Sea. Not one now remains in the whole of India.

George tries to satirise him in turn with jokes on his linguistic ambitions, while admitting his prompt fecundity as contributor; his bitterness, he says, perhaps proceeds from lack of appreciation.*

St Croix appears as a romantic poet of world-end dream and a vulgar economist with the fashionable thesis of emigration as cure for pauperism. Austin Daniel adds drawings of mother and children, a sombre Christ's head, and the like; and at Charnock's suggestion warns George of his reckless ambitions. A design of his shows a student with pipe and book at a desk, with Fame crowning him and a Dove bringing a money-box, while a crowd climbs up towards him; at the other side is a student in despair, with blown-out cape and book tumbled to earth, mocked-at by three Loves. George retorted by satirising Daniel's high-sounding titles for simple drawings.

Daniel as editor criticised George's writings. He finds his verse not yet firm in style, addicted to 'vague brightness' (a Tennysonian phrase, as he points out); and he picks holes in *Chillianwallah*, written on the battle of 13 January 1849, in which, on the banks of the Jhelum, the British lost 2,400 killed and wounded. This lament shows no awareness of the cause of the battle, which led to the annexation of Punjab, but Daniel does not attack it for political imbecility. He objects to the one imaginative line in its thin stanzas, which speaks of the wind in the strings of memory's harp. It isn't true, he says. So George substituted a conventional phrase, 'like a breeze through midnight harpstrings,' and sent the verses to

---

* He also attempted a theme set by Charnock, which he and everyone else found baffling: the Marriage of Bread and Butter. One of Charnock's philological jokes. Butter is Cow, Bread is *Brodt* and equated with Bull. The Marriage is a fertility-rite. Meredith sarcastically cites Festus, 'butter the thunder.' (We see here Charnock interested in ritual-myth, doubtless in terms of 'Aryan' research. He may well have given his clerk ideas and information useful for *Shagpat* and for the earth-heaven marriage which haunts his poems.) George makes a reference to Sinbad in no. 16: 'Thus in dark caverns the eyes of the lynx lead on to the light' (repeated *Egoist*, xxxvii; with a variant, viii).

Chambers Journal, where it was accepted. He then suggested a translation of a Life of Kossuth, abridged or complete. 'The accounts of the man now afloat are flimsy and unconnected.'

George was certainly developing in assurance through the magazine and Mary Nicholls too was trying to exercise her slight talent. In January 1849 she contributed in French *La Mort,* vaguely musing on death as birth and vaguely posing what she felt as the problem of her widowhood. 'Have the dead been taken from us for ever? do they pursue us with the same looks of affection that they lavished on us here below?' George is making love to her, and she worries about her dead husband. By March Ned and Howes ceased to contribute, and Mary's address was in Knightsbridge. That month she reviewed Kingsley's *Saint's Tragedy* and George inserted a sonnet, *Philosophy,* his last attempt to accommodate his idiom to Mary's religious views. He begins by attacking metaphysics:

> *Hateful are those false themes of speculation*
> *Goading the wise and harassing the weak—*
> *This world of ours—so lovely and unique*
> *Why is it subject to such sad vexation?—*
> *'Tis all for want of proper occupation*
> *'Philosophers' become so void and vain. . . .*

But instead of linking the religious abstraction with the metaphysical, he swings to a defence of intuition: the soul, 'sentient of its own salvation,' feels 'the great glory of its Future wings.' However, as he always later uses the Future to mean the earthly Future, the goal of human aspiration, we suspect that he is here equivocating with an idiom that can be taken either in a religious or a materialist sense.

Mary is said to have refused him six times, but with April and May he became ever more ardent. She was probably planning to leave London, as she did in June, and he wanted things settled. No longer a minor, he had come into a small sum and decided to leave Charnock and the law; and the fact that his father was going to emigrate must have made him feel more free, determined on decisive changes in his life. When he wrote in June to Chambers, he was on his own in Upper Ebury Street, Pimlico.

In June the magazine had Mary's poem *The Blackbird,* 'the true history of a blackbird known to me,' about a caged bird fed by a free one. She herself is the caged spirit offered the fruits of freedom. George, commenting, censures the 'slight touch of mysticism' at the poem's outset, but finds the rest 'delicious' and praises its vision of the organic universe. 'Yes! the Universe is a succession of links and we are all united—in nobility—and gentleness and love. All that is brutish is alien of kin—but gentle Love uniteth all.' Thus he generalises her meek little poem to give her the courage of its moral, and hopes for more of 'these true touches of Beauty.' In his proposals he suggests 'a philosophic examination of the Union of Poetry with general life and advancing science,' and names Mary as best suited to make it. A miscalculation, but showing his own mind's direction. He also suggests St Croix should write on:

> the inviolate claim of the Hungarian people to absolute independence and the Choice of Republican Government; with a glance at the chances and results of the present war and the resources of the country.

The shrunken July issue pretended nothing odd was happening. 'We are sorry to announce that Mrs Nicolls, being suddenly called on a journey to France, has been obliged to solicit our consideration this month—we expect to be favoured with two articles next month according to regulations.' In fact some crisis had intervened; Mary took George to her father at Lower Halliford. There her five-year-old daughter Edith surprised the lovers passionately embraced in the drawing-room; and when George went out, she clasped her mother, 'Mamma, I don't like that man!' In August, on the 9th, he and Mary were married by the curate at St George's Church, Hanover Square. He gave his address as Maddox Street, his father's profession as Esquire; the bride came from Devonshire Street; and her father signed the register.

Augustus meanwhile had tried to tailor on his own in St James's Street, in Clubland, and failed. He then had sailed in April for South Africa, where his nephew George Ellis had gone. He arrived at Cape Town on 23 June, and within a week had set up as Tailor and Professed Trouser Cutter in Short-market Street. 'N.B.—A.U.M. is not so bigoted in to his own style but that he willingly yields to Gentlemen's own peculiarities.'

5

Marriage and Poetry

THEY SOON left for a honeymoon on the Continent. Mary showed him
her dear France, and he carried her off down the Rhine. In *Pictures of the
Rhine* he merged memories of schoolboy excursions and honeymoon
raptures. 'Beauty renews itself in many ways.' He seeks to define a sense
of luxurious drifting on the river through the multiple perspectives of
ancient legend and present enjoyment. And in *Rhineland*, a dusk-poem,
he opposes 'the grey hawk-ruins' of feudalism with the embraced lovers,
yet links them in the song sung from the river-dark by 'a careless child
who sings an old tradition.'

By November they were back in London, at Peacock's place in John
Street, Adelphi. George sent 'four sheets' of his *Kossuth*, explaining
the delay as caused by his research. 'He was determined to ascertain if the
character of Kossuth was as fine' as he'd imagined. And said that the
editor could cut all passages not in accord with his journal's outlook. He
also suggested an account of the German scholar and humanist, Hermann,
who had died in 1848. But his opinions seem to have been suspect, and
Kossuth soon arrived in person to plead the Magyar cause. *Chambers*
then printed his speeches. Meanwhile the setback to George's plans for
articles had sent him back to verse.

The next three years were spent at Peacock's place, at lodgings or
boarding-houses in Surrey or by the sea, at Felixstowe or Seaforth. A
house where they liked staying was The Limes at Weybridge, some two
miles from Peacock at Lower Halliford. A pleasant house with large
garden, it was run by Mrs Macirone, widow of a colonel who'd been
A.D.C. to Murat King of Naples as well as a pioneer in aviation, a briga-
dier in the Columbian army and constructor of a 'steam road carriage.'
The two lovely daughters were more than half-Italian; and the elder,
Emilia, was an impulsive girl with a fine voice, who played an important
part in George's life. For she suggested the basis on which he developed
Sandra Belloni. That she was intimate with him is shown by the fact that
she later acted as intermediary between him and his dying wife. Brilliant-
eyed, with a skin of deep rich hue and a superb Italian head, she was
unconventional for the period. Like Sandra, she had a democratic feeling

for her audience; as Lady Hornby, on the voyage to the Crimea in
1855 she sang almost every evening to the soldiers and sailors; and at
Penn in Bucks she nightly at harvest-time entertained the reapers and
labourers in a barn.

The Limes had many literary boarders: Lytton, Horne, the journalist
Sam Lucas, and Eyre Crowe, A.R.A., who was Thackeray's secretary in
the early 1850's, Tom Taylor. Taylor was much liked by Meredith. He
taught at London University, turned to the bar, entered the Ministry of
Health, wrote Haydon's life as well as many comedies and burlesques,
and ended as editor of *Punch*. When he died in 1880 Meredith in a sonnet
paid tribute to his championship of 'the weaker by the wall,' and hailed
him as one of the spirits 'whose memory is our vital air, through the
great love of Earth they had.' Now at The Limes Taylor introduced the
young poet to the Duff-Gordons at their Weybridge cottage; and Janet
Duff-Gordon, about eight years old, used to call him her Poet and go for
journeys on his shoulder while he told her fairy-tales. Edith Nicolls, his
step-daughter, speaking of herself at about the same age, stresses what an
excellent companion he was for a child. 'We played cricket together; he
was a splendid playfellow.'

By far the most important literary acquaintance of these years was
R. H. Horne, who, after an adventurous youth at sea, had become a
leading poet and critic with the epic *Orion* and *The New Spirit of the Age*.
Already in March 1849 Meredith had written to him:

> You are a Poet and a Critic, and from certain of your writings I understand
> your sympathies in either phase to be with the young Poet. As this is a fact
> seldom found even among literary men, I have taken the liberty to address
> myself thus abruptly to you.
> I wish to lay before you certain Poems I have composed that I may obtain
> your opinion (in which I can trust) as to their merit—or more especially—the
> power of the Poetic Faculty in me.

They met and discussed Goethe; for in May Meredith wrote to say that
he had a copy of the *Minor Poems* for Horne, but isn't sure if he reads
German, though he thinks he must. 'Let me take this opportunity of
thanking you for the instruction you have already given me in the Art.
I believe that I am now *steadily* improving. I have but flickered heretofore.'
Discussion with Horne gave him the confidence for his first journalistic
efforts.

Marriage interrupted, but by late 1849 discussion was resumed.
George sent copies of verses on antique subjects and dedicated *Daphne* to
Horne in terms that warmly utter his respect. He asks Horne 'through
the simple picture' to 'see the winged fancy rising from the flower.'

Enough for himself to paint the flower in its natural hues and plant it: then its fate is with the sky.

> Happy is he whose last inspired desire
> Conquering its anguish shall have power to pluck
> The never fading laurel.

Round such a poet rays the dawnlight on the leaves. 'Therefore do we mark the strange foreshadowed crown of poet love.' Horne is type of supreme poet with a lyre

> Which sang of the giant bright whose starry limbs
> Still scale the midnight heavens and plant aloft
> Heroic footsteps up untravelled space!
> Long live and wear that constellated wreath.

A copy of the 1851 *Poems* was inscribed to Horne, 'by whose generous appreciation and trusty criticisms these poems were chiefly fostered.' And the volume cited *Orion* on its titlepage.

A comparison of the *Daphne* dedication with the poems of *The Monthly Observer* shows that Horne gave Meredith the secure basis, the concrete link between social struggle (Moravian brotherhood moving into Chartist demands) and poetic activity, from which arose all his later definitions of man's place on earth. Goethe had taught much the same lesson, but Horne revealed the contemporary quickening of the seed.

In *Orion*, sold at a farthing to reach a popular audience, he based his narrative on Hegelian ideas of development and attempted to show the stages in the evolutionary growth of man. Orion is both Worker and Poet: a conception that went far beyond Hegel, since it assumed the dialectical unity of art and productive activity. The epic is a splendid poem, not yet appreciated, with many rich and cogent passages of imagery which define the struggle in individual and society as new levels of mastery over nature are reached. The main weakness lies in the style, which imitates Keats' *Hyperion*, eloquently grave and subtly balanced, but unable to echo effectively the realisms of the basic concepts. And the stylistic flaw in turn exposes Horne's inability to advance more than intuitively beyond Hegel.

Orion is the work of primary poetic significance composed in the first post-Romantic generation. It strives consciously to overcome the contradictions, to clarify the confusions, of the Romantics. Its bias, despite its derivation from German idealism, is towards a materialist conception of history and art. Man is the child of nature, which he masters in art and labour-process, achieving his humanity in a linked series of forward-moving phases; and each of these phases develops its own inner contradictions, which must be overcome. The poem attempts to deepen the

consciousness of the rebellious energies expressed in the Romantic Movement, so that they may adequately grapple with the social situation of the
post-Romantic world. It draws much of its inspiration directly from the
Radical and Chartist struggles against the reactionary forces of the State.
Carlyle said of Horne, 'In this poet burns the fire of the skies,' praising
the poem's weakness; but in fact the gleam that mattered came from the
torches of Chartist struggle. And yet Carlyle was right in noting that in
the final analysis the fire of the skies, the stars of idealism, supplanted the
human hero; for Horne could not sustain the problem of defining simultaneously a materialist dialectic of development, the political conflict
in its deeper aspects, and the complex series of actions and reactions
from which was born the creative image of freedom. But the fact that he
was at all conscious, however confusedly and erratically, of the need to
compress such elements in a single definition shows the sturdy poetic
effort he had made.

Orion, simultaneously static and stately in form, and dynamic in aim and
idea, reveals by its contradictions a mixture of clarities and vaguenesses, a
strong impact of contemporary conflicts and the uncertainty as to the way
in which those conflicts were to be historically resolved. The form is thus
in the last resort the expression of the poet's unresolved tension. Still,
Orion was in many ways the key-work of the New Poetry, the post-
Romantic poetry of the period 1825–55—a position that it shared with the
feverish Festus of Bailey, in which a sense of immense new possibilities in
human life wrestles with a sense of doom and disaster.

The New Poetry—called in its later phase that of the Spasmodics—set
out to advance beyond the points defined by Byron, Shelley and Keats.
Byron, with his Cain, Don Juan and Manfred, dominated the epoch still to
a considerable extent and determined the lines of movement, the terms in
which the struggle was formulated; but there were efforts at the same
time to incorporate Shelley's revolt and his pantheist sense of unity with
the elements, as well as the Keatsian image of beauty, in which was felt to
be distilled the demand for the fullness of life on earth, the right to that
fullness and the entry into its realm of enjoyment. The New Poets sought
one way or another to bring these poetic elements together in a new
synthesis which clarified the place and destiny of man on earth, of poetry
in society—specifically in the society of expanding capitalist industrialism.

They therefore sought both to explore and overcome the contradictions
evident in the romantic achievement, to absorb the positive aspects and to
use them in grappling with the new situation of growing mass-struggle
and extending industrial forms. Their work, so far scarcely understood or
analysed at all in any serious way, was often extremely confused, unstable,

hectic and wild; yet it continually did make important advances and showed, at least in flashes, a deep penetration into what was happening to people, the shattering pangs and the great possibilities of delight and brotherhood in the new developments. The confusions all converge on the question as to *what kind of struggle*, what kind of personal and social development, can overcome the pang and make the possibilities come true.

These points are briefly and sharply put. As our purpose in this work is to follow out the conflict inside Meredith, which is rooted in its origins in the situation outlined above, we cannot spare the space for discussing how the problems affected other writers; but by our analysis of Meredith's development we have the means of checking, modifying, extending the tentative positions here set out.*

Roughly we may say that in the period between 1825 and 1850 there is a ceaseless mass-struggle in the economic and political spheres; people are aware of violent pressures, society is rapidly changing. From this period comes the great development of our Novel, as expressed in figures like Dickens, Gaskell, the Brontës, Thackeray, George Eliot (who belongs to the years in question, though she began writing her novels after it: just as Dickens carried on till 1869). In our poetry it is a period of intense storm and stress, when important new lines of potentiality are opened up by poets like Horne, Browning, Bailey, then Ebenezer Jones, Smith, Bigg, Dobell, Massey. In *Paracelsus* Browning shows his acute awareness of what is at stake, and is uncertain on which side to come down. Gradually he moves to the facilely pietistic side, expanding his psychological mechanism but narrowing the scope of his main ideas, his human perspective, his field of realisation; thus he ends by wielding a large analytic mechanism, from which the element that bites into life, gained from his period as a New Poet, keeps fading out. His system inbreeds indefinitely. Tennyson kept genteelly on the borderline, preening his sensibility out of the imagery-gains and techniques of the bolder spirits, till the time came when he could put his booty at the disposal of the full-fledged middle-class philistinism. His rôle begins to become clear with *The Princess* and *In Memoriam*; with *Maud* his abandonment of the ideals of the New Poetry is flagrantly announced. His fine pictorial powers, especially in landscape, with their harmonious expression in his verse-texture, reveal always his technical basis in the New Poetry; but the spiritual conflicts be sadly diluted or distorted.

---

* I am well aware how crudely simplified the comments on poetry are in this chapter. I, however, believe them justified, though I should need another book of detailed analysis to elaborate my points. That book, to be entitled *The Spasmodics*, I am at work on.

For definitions of the terms *idealism*, *materialism*, etc., see the Notes at the back.

Most of the young poets gave up the ghost, stopped writing or died, or drifted into futility (e.g. Massey). The dissident forces lost their broad basis after 1850; but certain aspects of revolt were carried on in limited ways—by the pre-Raphaelites, Swinburne, the Jesuit Hopkins. The only poet who squarely faced what was happening, and who resolutely tried through the bad second half of the century to carry on the tasks of the New Poetry, was Meredith—though Morris, especially in *The Pilgrims of Hope*, also made an important contribution along allied lines. This claim must be made at the outset, though only as we go on will its justice or its meaning be apparent.

Horne, sub-editing *Household Words*, introduced George to Dickens; and for six years many of the latter's poems appeared in Dickens's weekly, giving voice to his direct political ideas. Thus, *The League of Nations* hails a new era of peace and constructive work; war, born from man's irrational childhood, must yield to the spirit of world-brotherhood expressed in the Crystal Palace. *Britain* (November, 1851) declares that the nation must show a new way of progress; its great past will be as nothing to the future that must now be its goal. *A Wassail for the New Year*, in January 1852, makes extended prophecies of hope. *Force and his Master* depicts man's vastly enhanced control over the elements, but warns the British people of letting the new powers be made the instruments of 'revenge and greed.'

> Creation and Destruction now
> Are wrestling for the regal world.

One or other must conquer. According to the way Force is used, men will be 'blest, or most accurst.' If the nation lets it be used for death-purposes, 'Thou wilt be the first.'

In *The Olive Branch* of *Poems* he sees labour's hand as drilling 'the stubbornness of earth to shape.' The sea and its ships must be used for the union of men, not for war and privilege—'to join in far-off fellowship' the whole earth, to end 'the wrecking discords.'

> Now when the ark of human fate,
> Long baffled by the wayward wind,
> Is drifting with its peopled freight,
> Safe haven on the heights to find;
>
> Safe haven from the drowning slime
> Of evil deeds and Deluge wrath . . .
> 'Tis now the hour to prove the ground,
> To watch the Heaven, to speak the word,
> The fathoms of the deep to sound,
> And send abroad the missioned bird.

These are slight poems: Meredith himself some fifty years later called *The Olive Branch* 'dreadful.' But he was always hard on the 1851 volume; and he could correctly feel that such verses were, to use his own phrase, 'abstractly optimistic.' But he needed these plain statements, full as they are of the illusions of indefinite advance by some vague process of good-will or by the spontaneous pressure of economic expansion. They provided the basis on which the acids of his deeper analysis could get to work. He never lost the spirit of optimism they express; but he came to know that the earth of fellowship could be won only by the full working-out of social struggle and that the class-forces of evil went deep indeed.

Horne also introduced him to G. H. Lewes who, with T. Hunt, was preparing a weekly, *The Leader*, with a platform of positivist rationalism, a creed of world-brotherhood realised by the free development of our spiritual nature. The new journal appeared in March 1850 and soon had among its contributors Mazzini, Kingsley, Harriet Martineau, Newman. In October it published the manifesto on the organisation of democracy by the Democratic Committee of Central Europe.

Meredith reviewed several books for it, such as Mazzini's *Royalty and Republicanism in Italy*. Poems signed M. may be his, or Mary's; the only acknowledged verses were a translation, *Beauty Rohault*, and a sonnet to Alexander Smith. This sonnet has interest as showing that Meredith strongly felt himself one of the New Poets, of whom Smith was emerging as a new leader. A Glasgow weaver, in *A Life-Drama* and *City Poems* he was to tackle the post-Romantic problems I have discussed, and then to fade out under the Tennysonian pressures. Meanwhile, *The Critic* on 1 December 1850, attacking the New Poets, cited opprobriously Smith's sonnet on Fame; and Meredith took up the challenge.

To Alex. Smith, the 'Glasgow Poet' on his Sonnet to 'Fame'

> Not vainly doth the earnest voice of man
> Call for the thing that is his pure desire!
> Fame is the birthright of the living lyre!
> To noble impulse Nature puts no ban.
> Not vainly to the Sphinx thy voice was raised!
> Tho' all thy great emotions like a sea,
> Against her stony immortality,
> Shatter themselves unheeded and amazed.
> Time moves behind her in a blind eclipse:
> Yet if in her cold eyes the end of all
> Be visible, as on her larged closed lips
> Hangs dumb the awful riddle of the earth;—
> She sees, and she might speak, since that wild call,
> The mighty warning of a Poet's birth.

He is far from the equivocations of *The Monthly Observer*, but still not clear what poetry's action is. He is sure, however, that its meaning inheres in earthly life and that its work is not in vain—even though the poet shatters himself on the problem he invokes. There is thus still something of the romantic notion of the poet's doom here, but the emphasis is shifting. 'To noble impulse Nature puts no ban.'

George in fact was enjoying his country-life: the pines and birches through which he climbed St George's Hill, the view from the hilltop—northward the windings of Thames and the tower of Harrow rising from the Middlesex plain; southward the wandering Surrey hills. Broom-scent all round and birds singing through the year. Here he wrote or meditated many of the better poems collected in 1851, in particular *The Pastorals*.

The book came out in June 1851, with many misprints. It was dedicated to Peacock 'with the profound admiration and affectionate respect of his son-in-law, Weybridge, May.' Five hundred copies were printed at the poet's own cost, but only 100 bound. Later some 300 were destroyed and George lost £50 to £60 on the venture.

A sad failure, which found a few admirers. Charles Ollier, who had published Keats and Shelley and been the friend of Lamb and Leigh Hunt, praised it; and Meredith replied that the book would no doubt meet injustice and slights, but he was supported by knowing better was to come. The poems, he said, would probably die after making his name known to those ready to encourage young and earnest students of Nature, who were resolved to persevere till they won wisdom and true inspiration. To another friend he wrote that he wanted the poems to be taken as indications, not accomplishments, and that he had a firm if fond belief that he was a poet. He was anxious to know if he was on the right path, and he felt he had erred in putting together so many poems 'of so decidedly a sensuous and lyric tendency, as to mislead critics about the quality of my mind and muse.' It was all 'too young,' and he feared he wouldn't get the advice he needed, though 'Mr Tennyson, Mr Kingsley, and some others have written me words of very great encouragement.'

In speaking of the critics he must have had in mind *The Spectator*, which, saying that his book had more of promise than performance, accused him of involuntary imitations of Tennyson, Keats, the Brownings, found over-exuberant quaintness rather than originality, and insisted that the sensuous warmth must be tempered. And *The Guardian*, which also found Keats, Tennyson and the Brownings on every page, angrily declared that the poet

> must mend his morals and taste. Coarse sensuality is no proof of power . . .
> Ovid is bad enough, but *Daphne* and *The Rape of Aurora*, in this volume are

worse, for their studied and amplified voluptuousness. . . . Poetry must be protected from the incursions of the 'animalist' theory.

All things considered, however, he was better read than he should have expected. William Michael Rossetti in *The Critic* found 'various short-comings and crudities,' and unkindly added, 'We do not expect ever quite to enroll' him 'among the demi-gods or heroes.' But he found warmth of emotion, and, to a certain extent, of imagination. The author was certainly young (W.M.R. was two years older), but in *Love in the Valley* he had put passion enough, 'and of a sufficiently personal kind.' The poem:

> was purely and unaffectedly sensuous; and in its utterance as genuine a thing as can be. We hear a clear voice of Nature, with no falsetto notes at all; as spontaneous and intelligible as the wooing of a bird.

He too found elements from Keats, whom, however, he considered more objectively pictorial; Meredith was a sort of limited Keats.

Kingsley had promised a review, and included the book in *The Years Song Crop* in *Fraser's*. He writes sympathetically, but treats the poems as definitely minor, 'some of the most delicious little love-poems which we have seen born in England in the last few years.' They had a touch of Herrick, but a Herrick with more depth. The *Pastorals* were metrically careless, but 'honest landscape painting,' and 'only he who begins honestly ends greatly.' The poet should prune his adjectival luxury; *Daphne* had an overdone wealth of detail, outkeatsing Keats, and a stanza ill-suited to bring out the profundity of the myth—though there was something of Corregio's beauty of tone and feeling in it. Let the poet look at the Corregios in the National Gallery to see 'the severe scientific unity and harmonious gradation of painting . . . single glorious rainbows and precious stones,' unlike 'the jewelled hawk in the Great Exhibition, every separate atom of it beautiful, yet as a whole utterly hideous.'*

And what of the poems? *Love in the Valley* outstands, and Kingsley, Tennyson, the Rossettis recognised it as a poem out of the ordinary, though no one noted the debt of its lingering clashing melody to Darley's *Serenade of a Loyal Martyr*:

> *Sweet in her green cell the Flower of Beauty slumbers,*
> *Lulled by the faint breeze sighing thro' her hair;*

---

* *The Leader* sees only 'a certain charm . . . no depth or insight nor of feeling.' *The Athenaeum* found that the many negligences and set pieces betrayed the poet's youth, but he had some promise. Kingsley found *Love in the Valley* of 'instinctive melody.' But blamed M. for un-English adjectives (despite Keats) such as languourous, innumerous, and said he chose ambitious metres he couldn't handle. (Hardman argued with George about the lack of rhymes in *Pastorals* v, while they stood on the Hill of the poem, but 'I think he convinced me. . . .')

Sleeps she, and hears not the melancholy numbers
Breathed to my sad lute amid the lonely air.

In 1878 Meredith revised and extended the poem; but already in the first version we feel a new note. The girl and the various life of nature are merged so that each enhances the other. What is achieved is more than the use of nature as a decorative background. The penetration of the girl's beauty by the rich restless colours and forms of the valley is paired off with the intensification of the valley's colours and forms by her luminous presence; and the result is a dynamic and delighted fusion of girl and earth that owns a new rich fullness. Dante Rossetti said of the dawn-stanza that if white was the proper colour of poetry here was the veritable virginity of whiteness. The purity he perceived was born of the dynamic quality I have referred to.

Daphne, overwritten in the determination to bring out fully the effect of metamorphosis, has a fine dewy feeling of abundant nature thrusting ardently towards the moment of enrich change, of union with man.

> *In the twilight of the thickets*
> *Trees bend down their gnarled boughs,*
> *Wild green leaves and low curved branches*
> *Hold her hair and beat her brows. . . .*
>
> *Crowning her with amorous clusters;*
> *Pouring down her sloping back*
> *Fresh-born wine in glittering rillets,*
> *Following her in crimson tracks. . . .*

The *Pastorals* begin the effort to state Meredith's philosophy of earth: that we must enter into nature with full consciousness of what the acceptance of earthly life implies, what the active relation to nature means in social terms as well as personal. There are still trite phrases, lines like 'a whispering of old romance,' but these are being sloughed. Perhaps the new note comes out clearest in *South-West Wind in the Woodland*, with its eager mastery—from the picture of the hush before the storm, through the scurrying account of the tumult, on to the rapturous sense of union at the end:

> *The voice of nature is abroad*
> *This night; she fills the air with balm;*
> *Her mystery is o'er the land;*
> *And who that hears her now and yields*
> *His being to her yearning tones,*
> *And seats his soul upon her wings,*
> *And broadens o'er the wind-swept world*
> *With her, will gather in the flight*
> *More knowledge of her secret, more*

> Delight in her beneficence,
> Than hours of musing, or the lore
> That lives with men could ever give!
> Nor will it pass away when morn
> Shall look upon the lulling leaves,
> And woodland sunshine, Eden-sweet,
> Dreams o'er the paths of peaceful shade;—
> For every elemental power
> Is kindred of our hearts, and once
> Acknowledged, wedded, once embraced,
> Once taken to the unfettered sense,
> Once claspt into the naked life,
> The union is eternal.

Man's unity with nature is not through contemplation, reverie, or rapturous release; it is simply through struggle, through the recognition that man's strong life is one with the changing universe he helped to change.

At first glance the idiom may not seem to show much advance on that of Wordsworth or Shelley in their efforts to define a living relationship between men and nature. Indeed it is much less precise than, say, the finest passages of *The Prelude* or *The Ode to the West Wind*. But the ecstatic wish for union with the elements is passing over into a secure sense of man's definite place in nature. Nature is beginning to appear as something more than a healing source to which man returns, a great force with which he aspires to identify himself in moments of exalted outpouring. Man is a part of nature anyway; and the problem is to realise his place there, the way in which he is a part of nature and yet a part which has separated itself out. To realise all this and to build everything on the realisation. As we go on, we shall see how Meredith extends his realisation: *The union is eternal*—by discovering that man's relation to nature is an aspect of his social being, so that into it enters the forms of conflict in which he is enmeshed; and that the harmonious relation to nature involves the effort to transform her in the labour-process, in science and art, as well as the struggle to achieve world-brotherhood against all divisive forces. Only the dim beginning of this new orientation is as yet achieved; but in the light of the poet's later development we can recognise already the new perspective *The union is eternal*.

Not that Meredith is now, or ever, an equable and sustained poet. He has to fight too hard for the new centres of being which he is determined to grasp. And in this early book there are derivative poems, some weakly Tennysonian with false sentiment and idealist vagueness. But there is a clear vein of powerful originality; and the problem of poetry is definitely advanced. The young poet who could attain the lyric energy of *Love in* *the Valley* and the vision of man's alienation from his own essence in *The Sleeping City* was already a great innovator, whose innovations were based on a passionate insight into the real nature of struggle in his world.*

It is of interest to note how quickly Meredith drew away from Tennyson, flattered as he was by the latter's praise of *Love in the Valley*. Later he told how he had admired *Oenone* and the *Lotus Eaters* for their 'sensuous richness and imagery,' but failed to win Peacock or Jefferson Hogg to admit their merits. But by the early 1860's he had seen through to the pervasive falsity, human and artistic, of Tennyson's work.

> Have you heard that the Countess Guiccioli has two continuation cantos of *Don Juan* and means to publish them? Likewise more of Byron!—He's abused, so I take to him; and I'm a little sick of Tennysonian green Tea. I don't think Byron wholesome—exactly, but a drop or so—Eh? And he doesn't give limp, lackadaisical fishermen, and pander to the depraved sentimentalism of our drawing-rooms. I tell you that *Enoch Arden* is ill done, and that in twenty years' time it will be denounced as villainous weak, in spite of the fine (but too conscious) verse, and the rich insertions of tropical scenery.

Though he liked *Lucretius*, he continued to feel even more strongly that Tennyson was the arch-betrayer of all true cultural values:

> The *Holy Grail* is wonderful, isn't it? The lines are satin lengths, the figures Sèvres china. I have not the courage to offer to review it, I should say such things. To think:—it's in these days that the foremost poet of the country goes on fluting of creatures that have not a breath of vital humanity in them, and doles us out his regular five-feet with the old trick of the vowel endings—The Euphuist's tongue, the Exquisite's leg, the Curate's moral sentiments, the British matron and her daughter's purity of tone:—so he talks, so he walks, so he snuffles, so he appears divine.—I repeat with my Grannam,—to think!—and to hear the chorus of praise too! Why, this stuff is not the Muse, it's Musery. The man has got hold of the Muses' clothes-line and hung it with jewelry.
>
> But the *Lucretius* is grand. I can't say how much I admire it and hate the Sir Pandarus public which has corrupted this fine (natural) singer. In his degraded state I really believe he is useful, for he reflects as much as our Society chooses to show of itself. The English notion of passion, virtue, valour, is in his pages: and the air and the dress we assume are seen there.—I turn to Rabelais and Montaigne with relief. See what a gentleman Boccacio is in his narration! and always manly, always fresh.—Do you care to find the Holy Grail, Fred? Twenty years ago it would have excited me. This your foremost poet is twenty

---

* An early blank-verse poem, extant in manuscript, *Creed*, contrasts two brothers, one orthodoxly religious, the other a rebel. The latter says, 'Divide not men.' He wants sympathy with the life of nature, its flowers—'quickened by sinking thro' the beauty of the seasons—to die and to relive in deathless change.' And he wants good brotherly deeds. Any faith for the future must be based in reverence for the present.

This rather simple statement of revolt seems a half-way house between the wavering position in *The Monthly Observer* and the matured position that already appears in *Poems*.

years behind his time. Of course I expect a contrary opinion from you. But answer me—isn't there a scent of damned hypocrisy in all this lisping and vowelled purity of the Idylls? Well! just as you like. It's fashionable; it pleases the rose-pink ladies, it sells. (To Maxse, Dec. 19, 1869.)

To this viewpoint he remains steadfast, aware of some sad failure or betrayal in Tennyson, which has made that poet the mouthpiece of the egoist sentimentalism of his world. An anecdote of his shows what he thought of Tennyson's morose vanity. He managed humbly to meet the latter and they went for a walk. Tennyson was plunged in gloom; and after some miles he suddenly said, 'Apollodorus [Robert Gilfillan, the champion of Smith, Bigg, Massey: the New Poets] says I am not a great poet. A Scottish divine!' Meredith said something about not taking such opinions seriously. Tennyson retorted, 'But he oughtn't to say I am not a great poet.' Nothing else was said.

The tale shows Tennyson opposed to the latter phase of the movement from which he had in fact drawn his energies.

We get a glimpse both of Mary's sharp views and of George's in the comment she made to Hornby, the barrister who married Emilia Macirone, after he had declared Pope, Dryden, Goldsmith his favourites and had slighted the New Poets: 'You have a Manchester mind.'

Meredith retained the opinion, doubtless heightened by his later treatment at the hands of the critics, that *Poems* had been badly mauled. The critics fell 'upon his little volume of verse, like a body of barndoor hens on a stranger chick,' so that he was 'left with scarce a feather.' (And in *Diana*, Rhodes, a portrait of himself in youth, had 'recently taken a drubbing for venturing to show a peep of his head, like an early crocus, in the literary market.')

6

Peacocks and Duff-Gordons

ACROSS FROM Weybridge, close to the river, stood Peacock's one-storey villa—two cottages knocked together—with a huge elm dominating the pleasant garden. The river, skimmed by swallows and haunted by swans from Hampton Court, looked here like a lake, and there was pastoral charm in the horizon of low wooded hills and the bluish Surrey heights. Peacock had lived here some thirty years, driven into retreat by the distracted state of his wife, who died in 1852. Like J. S. Mill and Lamb, he worked in the East India House. He went to and fro by train, hurrying back to garden and library, where (he told Thackeray in 1846) he read only Greek.

He was now in the later sixties, closely shaved, with the high collar and white cravat of the earlier century: his thin lips compressed with disdain, his eyes sharp under thick brows, his white hair flying off thickly from his forehead. He had begun as a romantic idealist, musing on Solitude and a Greece that never was on sea or land; the admired friend of Shelley. But he soon decided Romanticism was a malady to be cured. His betrothed, five months after their separation, married another suitor, and he sought systematically to kill his aching sensibility with a bitter exercise of intellectual discipline, an ethic of moderation. He liked a country stroll and a chat with other learned reactionaries; he read Homer and Aristophanes, holding Nonnus' *Dionysiacs* the world's best poem after *The Iliad*, and discussed good wine and food. He turned his keen disillusion on anything that seemed to him smacking of system-making, abstract ideology, or romantic excess; he despised equally the Wordsworthian return to Nature and any political attempts at reform; and yet the displaced passion of his being found expression in his defence of the Enlightenment, of rationalists like Voltaire or Montaigne, Buffon or Monboddo. He held that the love and the clear perception of the truth were necessary to good comic writing; and he felt the world's lunacies resisting the acids of his contemptuous humour. He had written *Melincourt* in 1819, dealing with the dangers of luxury, paper money, Malthus, the obscurity of German philosophy, love's inanities; and he found such fads of the world unaffected. His scorn of civilisation and of returns-to-nature alike he had expressed in his picture of the monkey-man, Sir Oran Haut-ton, which follows Monboddo in an anticipation of the thesis of human evolution.

His trick was to set opposite positions into a clash which brought out the nonsense underlying them both. Not to resolve the oppositions in a discovery of the truth, but to insist on the one basic idea, that of human folly, from which one cleansed oneself by laughter, not by tears. And yet the Voltairean rationalist was merged to some extent with the Rousseauish libertarian; and for all his efforts to attain a lucid detachment he turned to the periods that his persistent Romanticism could imagine as healthily free from the contemporary blights: the woodlands of Robin Hood and the hills of the Welsh bardic past. In the same way of self-contradiction the man who spent so much time among the Greek Antiquities of the British Museum and despised modernity did much to help the introduction of iron steamships into the trade with India; and his scorn of a corrupted world did not prevent him from putting up a very capable defence of the East India Company against the charges of Silk Buckingham.

Meredith found much to admire, much to resist, in his father-in-law. He liked his partisanship of the Enlightenment, his mockery of religious otherworldiness and romantic delusions, his enjoyment of the humorous earthy writers. He could not help being fascinated by his conversation with its classical reminiscences, its unpredictable twists, its ingenious paradox directed against most contemporary trends: the progress of machinery, the spread of London, youth's extravagances. But he was repelled by the narrow inability to grasp the vast new potentialities of the modern world, whether in the growth of productive capacities or in the aspirations of the New Poetry. And so, doing his best to argue politely, he gained much from both his admiration and his revulsion.

> If he won't forget to make his heroes eat and indicate to us, discreetly, the physiology of his characters, if Mrs Berry tells the young lovers that kisses won't last but cooking will, if the description of heroic repasts, the praise of generous wines, abound in his work to the end, it is right we should render homage for all this to his father-in-law and the dignity he conferred on the restorative function. (Galland.)

And he owed also a deeper debt. The Peacockian paradox stimulated him to build his own dialectic of opposites-in-clash. But where Peacock halted at the exposure of irreconcilable absurdities, Meredith sought to show the resolution of opposites in the vital truth of man, the total social movement, the struggle from which progress derives. Not that he evolved his dialectic easily or in a single piece; he faltered at times over the idea of reconciled-opposites or paused at the bitter impasse; but generally from his first story in 1855 to his last novel in 1895 he attempted to relate the clash of characters and ideas to the basic pattern of social conflict, from which they drew meaning, and in terms of which they fell back or developed with deepened coherence.

The other intimacy of this period which had important effects on his work was that with the Duff-Gordons. Lady D.-G.'s mother was Sarah Taylor of Norwich, an early devotee of Goethe, whom Carlyle admired. Her *Characteristics of Goethe* opened the series of books culminating in Lewes's *Life*. She married John Austen who taught jurisprudence at London University and whom Macaulay thought the best talker he'd ever met; and their London house was the meeting-place of men like Carlyle, Mill, Sydney Smith. Lucy, their daughter, was educated in France and Germany as well as England. At thirteen she dined at Boulogne with Heine, who dedicated verses to her; and she was Carlyle's Lucykin. At nineteen she married Sir Alexander Cornewall Duff-Gordon, to whom she bore Janet, Maurice and Urania. They travelled and spent some years at Paris, where she knew men like Guizot, Tocqueville, de Vigny, Léon de Weilly (whose novel *Stella et Vanessa* she translated). Her husband was a Treasury Official, who later acted as secretary to a cousin, Chancellor of the Exchequer.

Her parents had retired to Weybridge: that was why it was there when she first met Meredith. Her circle was one of artists, musicians, travellers, whereas her mother's had been political and philosophic. She was much attracted by the East. Kinglake, Layard of Nineveh, Haxthausen who wrote on Russia, were among her friends—as well as Dickens, Thackeray, Taylor, Watts, Millais.

She appears as Lady Jocelyn in *Evan Harrington*, Lady Gosstre in *Sandra*, Lady Dunstance in *Diana*. Tennyson took her as prototype of his Princess. Kinglake, commenting on her classic features, her nobly poised head, her stately height, her pure complexion, said that 'she was so intellectual, so keen, so autocratic, sometimes even so impassioned in speech, that nobody feeling her powers, could feebly compare her to a mere Queen or Empress.' A confirmed cigar-smoker, she preferred the company of men, whom she treated with genial equality. Meredith admired her tact, her direct humour, her level-minded authority, her aristocratic certitude which could assume a democratic pose of taking people on their merits.

> Her humour was a mouthpiece of nature. She inherited from her father the authority and composure of a judicial mind. Hers was the charity which is perceptive and embracing—a singular union of the balanced intellect with the lively heart. Her aim was at practical measures for help; she doubted the uses of sentimentality, and had an innate bent for exactitude.

So he wrote in 1902, when she was long dead. She helped him to overcome his nerves and gain social aplomb; and she did much to direct his attention to France and French literature. On the death of her father her health declined; she went to the Cape, then to Egypt, where she died in July 1869, aged 48, after having dictated the telegram that announced her death.

Among her friends was the poetess Mrs Norton, granddaughter of Sheridan and original of *Diana of the Crossways*, now past forty, a mature beauty with dark sleek hair, long-lashed eyes, straight nose, mobile mouth and fine teeth, unaffected though well aware of her opulent charms and Irish wit. In 1850–1 she was working on *Stuart of Dunleath*, a veiled account of her relations with her ignoble husband, from whom for some fifteen years she had demanded a divorce or the right to live alone. London society was divided: and Lady D.-G. was her chief champion, treating her as a sister and refusing to visit houses that excluded her. The children called her Aunt Carrie.

Stimulated by old Peacock, George and Mary set up as gastronomes and tried to compile a treatise based on 'the finest Epicurean principles of indulging the Palate, as far as can be done without injury or offence to the stomach, and forbidding nothing but what is absolutely unfriendly to Health.' For 'Economy in a wife is the most certain Charm to ensure the affection and industry of a husband,' and so husbands should praise wives, since 'to cherish the desire of pleasing in them you must show them that you are pleased.' But only fragments were written, and Mary's Cookery Book never got beyond a revision of Kitchener's standard work which *Feverel* mentions. She did, however, try a more ambitious essay in *Gastronomy and Civilisation*, printed in *Fraser's*, December 1851.

Her father's influence and her husband's aid are evident. She lightly relates social conditions and the cooking art. A Greek section eulogises Epicureanism; the Romans and Germans are rebuked for orgies and sharpsweet sauces; *The Thousand and One Nights* are praised for elegant meals with flower scents as necessary as food; in England we glance at Chaucer and characters from Elizabethan drama, and scan an East India Company menu of 1622. The English tend to neglect the charms of social intercourse; the worst political system for a proper use and appreciation of food is the monarchical, while

> We have recorded, on historical evidence, that the most incorruptible republicans were austere and abstemious; but it is still a question whether they could have exerted a more beneficial influence and have been better men, if they had moistened their throats with Madeira and enlarged their sympathies with grouse. Solitary habits take away many means of forming correct

opinions, and prevent opportunity of removing prejudices. The student in his
cabinet is an impartial spectator, and may be a wise judge, but he is never a
good governor. Austerity, as Plato says, is the companion of solitude. It is
problematical whether Coriolanus would not have gained the consulship, and
thereby have saved his country from war, and himself from disgrace, if he had
been conciliating and social, instead of isolated and overbearing. If Robespierre
had held companionship with others, he might have exercised in public the
tenderness that characterised him at home, where it was never believed that he
had committed the severities that distinguished his career. 'Il était si doux' was
the invariable reply of the girl where he lodged, to every accusation that was
brought against his memory.

Meredith and Peacock would equally endorse the plea against hermit
philosophers; and this passage may then serve to define the common
ground between them, here precariously maintained by the imitative
Mary.

From The Limes the Merediths moved to a red-brick cottage near the
Weybridge parish school, then in 1853 joined the widowed Peacock.
Their son, Arthur Gryffydh, was born on 13 June at Lower Halliford.
S. M. Ellis oddly remarks, 'Several children had been born to the Merediths earlier, and died as infants; this was the only child of the marriage
who survived to any age.' As they had been married only four years, it
is hard to fit the 'several children' in; but if there had been miscarriages
or stillbirths, it would help to explain the mounting tension between
husband and wife.

Peacock, irritable man, did not get on with George, who hummed as
he strode restlessly about and fidgeted with ornaments. He didn't even
feel safe in his long low-ceilinged sitting-room; for George was a keen
smoker and Peacock was so scared of fire that he permitted only a few
matches in the house at a time. Edith says that he 'could not stand' his
son-in-law.

So he took a near house for the couple, the small Vine Cottage across
the Green. In its little front-room George finished Shagpat, 'with duns at
the door,' and gave readings to friends in London. These must have been
the years of which he said later, 'In youth I looked out from under a hail of
blows,' and 'when I was young, had there been given to me a little sun-
shine of encouragement, what an impetus to better work would have
been mine.' A lawsuit over his inheritance did not help to ease the
situation. However, he enjoyed his walks and his games of cricket with
Edith and the village children; and at the close of 1855 Chapman and Hall
published The Shaving of Shagpat, so that he at least had the pleasure of
reading his words in print. Like Poems, the book sold badly and is said
to have been remaindered.

Another person who did not like George was Jefferson Hogg, also once the friend of Shelley. He came visiting in the summers and at first called Meredith the Son of Song, then George the Fifth, then the Dyspeptic. His letters to Mary try to offer tactful sympathy.

> I would that the Patient were well placed in E.I.H. [East India House] or elsewhere; how can we help him? . . .
> How is George the Fifth; is he less dyspeptic? Not to digest your delicate meats is to insult your art.

He had now emerged from his formative period. Though he continued to develop till the end of his days, in *Shagpat* he has found his characteristic position. He sees into the heart of the contemporary struggle and he realises where that struggle is leading; he achieves faith by grasping how searching and strenuous the fight, how deeply entrenched the forces of evil.

II

Ordeal

7

The Shaving of Shagpat

HE TURNED to prose allegory as a halfway-house between poetry and the novel on contemporary life. Deeply stirred by what he intuited and analysed of his epoch's basic conflicts, he wanted to set out a full vision of the great moment of crisis in which he felt caught up. He wanted to show the relentless pressures of evil and to define the hero who led the difficult way into an earth of brotherhood. Thus he needed a form of more extended realism than he could put into a poem, but he could not yet conceive a story of everyday life large enough in scope and significance. He still felt unsure of the way to tackle the daily scene and wanted to pack his sense of a tumultuous crucial struggle all at once into a tale. So he drew on memories of *The Arabian Nights* for a fable adequate to express the entangled conflicts and the driving-force of revolutionary activity in 1848–9.

An immediate stimulus had come from a story told by Haxthausen at the Duff-Gordon's. The traveller claimed to have fought the Queen of Serpents in a burning valley, till, attacked by hordes of infuriated snakes, he fled with the crown from the Queen's head. This prize he kept in a little gold box inside a red silk bag hung from his neck; and he showed it to the company. 'Meredith never took his eyes off M. de Haxthausen,' says Janet D.-G., 'while he told this weird tale, and when next he brought me home he told me a marvellous story about the Queen of Serpents, which afterwards developed into Bhanavar the Beautiful in *The Shaving of Shagpat*.'

The book's core was thus the Bhanavar episode, a romantic tale of the *femme-fatale*, the girl led by vanity into becoming a sort of vampire that feeds on the lives of men for the renewal of her charms. Bhanavar, against her own will, after lusting for the snake-jewel of fascinating powers, becomes the creature of doom, in turn dooming her lovers.

But this kind of theme ran counter to all Meredith's maturing creed of man's power to direct his life with a rational consciousness that overcame all the old divisions and dooms, and so he gave the episode a subsidiary rôle in the completed narrative, where it represents the sort of love-relationship that must be discarded. Still, it is of interest to see that he still had enough of the romantic mood to start from a fate-conception, though he then went on to build up a story which moved in a diametrically opposite direction.

Shibli Bagarag, a barber, is wandering hungry and rejected when he meets a hag who bids him confront the hairy Shagpat. He does as told, and is hunted, beaten. The hag returns and encourages him. She asks if she is beautiful. 'Thou art that thou art,' he says, and she answers, 'Not so, but that I shall be.' (An answer with the core of Meredith's philosophy of struggle, of purposeful transformation.)

She tells him that he'll be Master of the Event if he weds her. He hesitates, agrees, kisses her; and she lights up, growing younger. They go to the Vizier, and Shibli is again to be beaten. But the Vizier admits his jealousy of the supremely-hairy Shagpat, and inclines to favour Shibli's aim. (Here is inserted the long sub-story of Bhanavar.)

The woman, now a lovely girl, is Noorna. He betroths her, and she tells him that Shagpat demands her. If he is to shave Shagpat and end the spell of the evil dispensation represented by his hairiness, he must gain the water of a certain well, the hairs of a magic horse, the lily of light. Then he will be able to claim the Sword of Aklis, which alone can shear Shagpat. She calls up an evil genie Karaz whom she controls, and the three tasks are carried out. Despite failures and temptations through vanity, headstrong impulse, he finds the waters of vision (which produce the conscious and active union with nature), the horse-hairs of elemental energy, the light-lily of realised love: these necessary objects are won.

Noorna now tells Shibli her tale. She was lost in the desert as a child, rescued by a chief, and befriended by a genie through an act of charity in Oolb. She fought against a princess who has spelled many men, including Noorna's own father; and learned Karaz's secret plans to destroy or enslave men. Then she stole from Karaz the Identical, the Hair that is his Life-object and in her desperate effort to escape him, dropped it into Shagpat's head. Hence the latter's place of power among men.

Shibli sets out for Aklis, but has first to pass the realm of Rabesquarat, another version of the fatal-woman, but wholly evil, without Bahanavar's inner struggle and devotions. She fetters Shibli for a while and sets Noorna amid the furies of the sea; but he uses the waters of vision to show her in her true shape of evil; and goes on with the dwarf Abarak. He meets more trials and temptations, and, falling into power-lust, gets a crown fixed on his head. Through the weight of this crown, he is almost lost when crossing the bridge over the devouring Roc. However, he wins through to Aklis, though he cannot gain the respect of the Sons there till he gets rid of his crown. At last, girded with the Sword, he sets off on his return journey, rescuing Noorna from her dangers.

He is almost destroyed at the last moment by flashing the Sword at the Veiled Figure who rows him across the dividing waters. For he sees that the Figure is Rabesqurat, the pleasure-queen now realised as the void, death. He falls into a swoon, from which he is saved only by sleeping on the bosom of his beloved Noorna.

His uncle, another barber, is used to distract Karaz, who has taken the form of a flea; and then Shibli himself, in a series of vast apocalyptic world-convulsions, cuts the Identical, removes the spell and force of Shagpat's rule, and inaugurates a new epoch of constructive labour, in which women lose their disabilities and the laws are such that

> Were men once clad in them, we should create
> A race, not following, but commanding, fate.

Even from this cramped summary the carefully worked-out allegory of struggle and liberation is obvious. But Meredith was so disgusted by the total failure of everyone to see what he was getting at, that he later ironically deprecated any inner meaning at all. The second edition of 1865 had a note that 'one who had no fear of Allegories on the banks of the Nile' (Lucy Duff-Gordon?) took Shagpat for Humbug and Noorna for the Seasons and Shibli for Circumstance, which the Seasons guide 'towards our ultimate release from bondage.' But 'the Allegory must be rejected altogether.' The wording is ambiguous. He does not make clear if any inner meaning or the given interpretation is to be rejected. Certainly the Humbug-Seasons-Circumstance tags, with their suggestion of a process operating outside human will, are about as far from Meredith's creed as they well could be. He adds bitterly that allegories must be clear if they are to be of any value, and, if clear, they repel.

In 1892 he replied to a correspondent with deliberate obtuseness:

> Wonderful to hear that there is a woman who can read of Shagpat! I suppose he does wear a sort of allegory. But it is not as a dress-suit; rather as a dressing-gown, very loosely. And they say it signifies Humbug, and its attractiveness, while Noorna is the spiritual truth. Poor Sh. Bagarag being the ball between the two. I think I once knew more about them and the meaning, but have forgotten, and am glad to forget, seeing how abused I have been for having written the book.

And in 1906 he wrote to one McKechnie who had essayed an analysis:

> An Allegory is hateful to the English, and I gave it clothing to conceal its frame. But neither that nor the signification availed. Very few even of my

friends have cared to read the book, and of those I can count but two who have said a word in favour of it.

McKechnie had seen enough of the book's point to make the blank denial of 1892 impossible, but not enough to bring Meredith wholly out of his shell. He generalises the episodes: the first three quests become the winning of Insight, Enthusiasm, Idealism. And Shibli is 'a conservative reformer.' And 'to remove an abuse whether in Church, State or village community is to shave Shagpat. All that is demanded is that it be an objective evil, something that hurts the world.' That last sentence is good, and McKechnie adds:

> Not that the Allegory does not take recognition—it takes very ample recognition—of the existence of, the necessity for shaving inward Shagpats, those Shagpats that abide in and blight the soul of man. None the less it will have no direct tinkering with the soul, for of such tinkering spiritual hypochondria, worse evils come.

But the general trend of the interpretation is to make it all amiably harmless. The passion and anger of the book, which is an account of the tests and trials of the revolutionary hero in his movement to victory, derive from Meredith's responses to 1848–9. The tale is of the Pilgrim's Progress, divested of its religious transpositions, with the goal of a free fraternal Earth put in place of the Heavenly Jerusalem.

Shagpat sets out in concise and powerful form what is the main theme of all Meredith's work, and is therefore important to understand. Here I can deal only with some of its principal points, though in fact there is nothing in its rich exposition which is not poetically and politically realised.*

Meredith has in mind both Horne's *Orion* and Carlyle's *Sartor Resartus*. Like Orion, Shibli is both worker and poet, revolutionary and creator, whose struggle changes life at the root. But whereas Horne attempted a direct mythical statement of human development in its various stages of struggle and resolution, *Shagpat* uses a method of entwined grotesqueness and lyricism; and here Meredith draws on *Sartor*. That book could not but strike home to one who was so sensitively the son-of-a-snip. For it uses Clothes as emblems of the veiling element in life, the divisive force,

---

* How close much of *Shagpat* was to contemporary political satire of a radical kind can be seen by taking *H.R. a Satire of Present Evils, with Indications towards Future Good: or, Work for the Modern Hercules*, by J. B. Ruach (Manchester, 1857) which, dealing with the need for a Hercules to clean the Augean Stables of Victorian society, has a Vision of insignia'd Apes and Hermaphrodites. 'Those which bear the forms of apes are they who seek for themselves power, titles, gold, as ends of life. The hermaphrodites are those who seek these things as means to some good which they propose to do mankind at some future time.' Science and 'the humanising influence of Art,' says Ruach, together make 'true men.'

and at the same time, in its idealist idiom, manipulates them into symbols
of the 'manifestation of form.' But Meredith makes concrete and realistic
what is paradoxical and mystical in Carlyle. The Barber, who clears away
human excrescences and bares the truth, is in fact the anti-Sartor, he is
plainly worker and poet, without any overtones of pathetic irony or
burlesque contrasts between man-the-spirit and man-the-social-animal.
In him spirit and social-being are one.

Meredith stresses the plain meaning. Shibli is recalled from backsliding
by the Pride of the Barber. Amid trials, 'the yearning of the Barber
seized Shibli Bagarag, and desire to shear Shagpat was a mighty overwhelming wave in his bosom, and he shouted, "The Sword of Aklis!
naught save the Sword!"' He, the outcast in a world where his redemptory
rôle is denied, is fated to be Master of the Event, controlling history. He
comes up into the revolutionary moment which grasps entire the frame
of things, breaks and rebuilds it. When he sees the Sword's power, he
exults. 'Praise be to the science of them that forecast events and the haps
of life.' The shaving of the power-monster is the breaking of the State-
power on which the parasite and the cheat depend. It means the end of
the illusions, the idealogical system, which the oppressive State begets and
on which it rests. Shibli is 'upon the track of great things, one chosen to
bring about imminent changes.' Rabesquarat, exposed in her vileness,
cries, 'If he [Shagpat] is shaved, what changes will follow.' Noorna, as the
great day comes, muses, ' 'Tis the messenger of the morning, the blush.
Oh, what changes will date from this day!' Shibli's uncle shouts to the
Flea, 'O thou flea, wilt thou, thou vile thing! hinder me from mastering
the Event, and releasing this people from enchantment and bondage?'
The day of the Event brings about the reversal of existing values. 'How
unfortunate is the race of barbers, once honourable and in esteem! surely
it will not be otherwise till Shagpat is shaved.'

The Event's full significance is given in the motive of the Identical.
Here, as elsewhere in the tale, Meredith draws on levels of myth and
ritual that go far deeper than the ordinary narratives of the Arabian
Nights. The Identical, I have already noted, is a soul-object or external-
soul, and thus derives from a tale-type with roots in the totemic tribe.
In such a tribe every clan-member has actually a soul-object (generally a
piece of wood or stone) with which his life is thought bound up. And the
contests with Karaz which Noorna and Shibli carry on are exactly
analogous with contests common in the tales and rituals of shamanist
cultures, where, as the tribal system decays, witch-doctors become of key
importance. Shamans often engage in spirit-conflicts, thought to go
through various metamorphoses in their effort to steal or rescue a

soul-object. In tales derived from these conflicts the soul-object is generally hidden in a complicated way, inside something inside something else, and so on.

The Identical is thus a typical soul-object of shamanist conflict. Why is this significant for Meredith's purpose? The soul-object, representing the most primitive form of spiritual division, stands at the head of the series that ends in the full-grown religious or metaphysical abstraction—body cut from soul, earth from heaven, man from nature. The process of inner division, to which we may give the generic term of self-alienation, was reaching its climax in Meredith's epoch with the growth of a political and economic system, capitalism, that sought above all to reduce all relations to the cash-nexus and to treat men as things. So in making the Event hinge on the destruction of the supreme soul-object, the Identical, he states that the revolution he foresees and works for will end the process of self-alienation. The Identical is the egoist basis of personality, the false notion of Identity that rests on power and privilege, on a world organised in hierarchical exploitations. It stands for the idea that men have of themselves in a self-divided society of competitive fears and greeds. This notion of Identity is the Illusion overthrown in the successful movement into reason and brotherhood.

Meredith of course could not have analysed his material as I have here done; the anthropological basis for such an analysis was lacking in his day. But his deep poetic insight makes him select exactly the right themes and motives from folklore to convey his vision of history.

In making the fight for the soul-object the crux of the allegory, Meredith defines Shibli's struggle as the effort to end the situation based in self-alienation, in abstract notions of Identity. The eradication of the psychology of the soul-object, the self cut off and transposed into a thing (a capitalist commodity and a metaphysical entity), is also the overthrow of the self-divided society of the cash-nexus. It means the discovery of the true relation of men to nature and to society, the reality of process and the unity of all living.*

Now a glance at more particular meanings. Shibli gains his start by

---

* It seems clear that the source of this folk-element was *Welsh*: the *Mabinogion*. In the tale of Culhwch and Olwen one of the tasks set the lover is to get comb and scissors from between the ears of the terrible boar, so that he may dress the rank head of Olwen's father. Here is the burlesque touch linked with the barber motive in the heroic task derived from ritual myth. From the *Mabinogion* too he could have got the theme of shamanistic conflicts. (*The Head of Bran the Blest* in the 1862 Poems comes straight from the *Mabinogion*.)

Bhanavar may have links with the medieval tale *Melusyne*; and the rejuvenating kiss with the *fier baiser* of *Bel Inconnu*. But note that it is used also in his Gauwain poem, *The Song of Courtesy* (1859).

What we can say is that *Shagpat* is more essentially Welsh than Arabic.

accepting the transformative powers of love: a faith in the future. 'Thou
art that thou art. Not so, but that I shall be.' As a contrast we get the tale
of fatal love, the kind of relationship that must be outgrown.

The evil genie is harnessed to the tasks; for man does not change the
world and himself by an abstract rejection of evil, an absolute concept of
good means and ends. He moves forward by a complex struggle in which
evil is transmuted into good. 'It is the sapiency of fools, to shrink from
handling evil tools.' By means of the mastered genie the hero achieves an
active relation to nature, which includes in turn a new relation to men.
When he sprinkles the magic water in a city, he is told that where man
is, he must question men, not nature. He tames the elemental energies to
his purpose, but is almost defeated by his egoist vaunting in his great new
powers. He then stabilises his gains by entering fully into love and its
responsibilities.

Noorna's tale deals with woman's struggle into freedom and wholeness,
and brings out the way in which, until the final liberation, the strengthening of the forces of good goes on side by side with an intensification of
the evil resistances, the twisting of the people under worse oppressions and
deceits. Then comes the worst trial of Shibli. His enhanced powers trip
him up into a submission to greed, indulgence, vanity, pleasure-cruelty.
He falls and true love is crucified. But his persisting hunger for the truth
saves him; it becomes a realisation of the suffering sources of life. Yet,
having seen through egoist pleasure, he succumbs to egoist power. Here,
as in Noorna's tale, the resolving laugh, which sees both the reality and
the lie, stands for the liberating flash of discovery when the bonds of a
fettering idealogy are broken.

Shibli defeats 'the lures of vanity, the blinding of ambition, and tasting
the gall of the Roc' (the turning-away from life, from fellowship, into
egoist 'disillusion', cynicism or sense of original-sin). And then, at last
getting rid of his crown, he gains the Sword—only to meet his final
temptation, the desire to stare into the void, to turn from reality and
action into the otherworldly obsessions of religion and idealism, into the
death-fantasy. Not till this temptation has been overcome can he fight
successfully against the Identical, against the society of the cash-nexus and
self-alienation.

His success is in turn bound up with his acceptance of the love and
comradeship of woman. Noorna has to aid him at each decisive moment.
Her warm body, her enfolding love, alone save him from the horror of
the void.

A stoical creed of effort, stressing fellowship and faith in the future,
is underlined by the poems, which also give a mass-effect—the

generalisation of Shibli's tale in terms of the distilled wisdom of the
centuries of suffering and struggling men.

> *Thou that dreamest an Event,*
> *While Circumstance is but a waste of sand,*
> *Arise, take up thy fortunes in thy hand,*
> *And daily forward pitch thy tent.*

> *Sun and moon with their bright fingers*
> *Point the hero's path;*
> *If in his great work he lingers,*
> *Well may they be wrath.*

> *Fear nought so much as Fear itself;*
> *For arm'd with Fear the Foe*
> *Finds passage to the vital part,*
> *And strikes a double blow.*

The prose style is fresh and vivid, drawing something from Arabian
idiom, but resting mainly on Meredith's own poetic method—that of the
New Poetry with its emphasis on the dynamic word. Typical of the New
Poets are such epithets as *lengthening* or *sharpening*: words that are both
adjectives and verbs. And especially such pictorial terms as *slanting* or
sloping, in which an effect of light-movement can be uttered.

> The shadow of a mountain was over it, and the slant of the rising sun, down
> a glade of the mountain, touched the green tent of the Emir.
> All was as the snow of the mountains on her round limbs sloping in the
> curves of harmony, and the faint rose of the dawn on slants of snow was their
> hue.
> Her countenance wholly bare even to the neck and to the beginning slope
> of her bosom.
> Slanting up the night-air like fire, till he was seen high up even as an angry
> star reddening the seas beneath.
> The wonder of the light, and its increasing, and quivering, and lengthening;
> and the light was as an arrow of beams and as a globe of radiance.
> Warm as new milk from the full udders were the waters of that sea, and
> figures of fair women stretched lengthwise with the current, and lifted a head
> as they rushed rolling by.
> The whole blade sheening, like an arrested lightning.
> I observed the shadow of his head lengthened out along the grass-plot to-
> wards the mossed walls, darkening it—then drawing back and lessening, then
> darting forth like a beast of darkness irritable for prey.

For extended passages in the same style take the accounts of Bhanavar and
her snakes, of the lovers in their shell on the waters, of the entry into the
vast coppery landscape of Aklis.

To grasp the basis of style here is of importance; for the experiments
are forming the method which for good and bad, with varying tensions

and concentrations, he went on developing throughout his work. The roots are in the rebel soil of the New Poetry, with its desire to define with free intensities the new relation of man to nature, the hero girding himself to face great tasks as he moves into the future. A desire also to deny the balances and symmetries, the stale idioms, on which the expressions pleasing to the middle-class audience reposed.

We can clarify our view of the work further by looking at some of its sources. Meredith was aware of Beckford's *Vathek*, a tale based on the romantic doom-concept, the satanic death-fantasy. Vathek, dominated by his evil mother, moves relentlessly towards the hell of Eblis where the damned gyrate with eternally-burning hearts. The theme is self-damnation, the inescapable pattern of torment in self-consciousness; and the idyllic element appears only to stress the omnipresent triumph of evil.

Shagpat is an anti-Vathek. Diabolism comes into the tale of Bhanavar, only that it may be rejected. The future is freedom and brotherhood, not a surrender to the repetitive pleasure-hell.

A halfway-house between Shagpat and Vathek is Southey's poem *Thalaba the Destroyer*, 1801. Here the hero is chosen by destiny to destroy the spirits of evil in underworld caverns, night's kingdom. Magicians there have killed his father and kept the Sword fated to destroy them. They try vainly to kill Thalaba as a child; and he sets out for Bagdad where he defeats an infidel, encounters a sensual paradise, breaks its charm, and weds a maid who dies on the bridal night. After a fit of madness he is saved by a converted magician; and guided by a green bird (the gentle Leila) he reaches a Valley where the Bird of the Ages tells him the way. He is washed of sins in a spring, gains the Sword, overthrows the Idol, forgives his father's murderer, and is rapt to heaven where his lost bride awaits him as houri.

Here as in *Shagpat* a young man is picked out for a great action, passes through many trials, and wins a Sword in the underworld. Also, Meredith borrowed some of the poem's properties, a speaking falcon and a voyage over an enchanted sea. But his moral tone is utterly different from Southey's. Shibli is a man, liberating men on earth; Thalaba is a saint carrying out the will of providence and finding his goal off the earth.

Meredith's response to Southey appears in an early quatrain:

> Keen as an eagle whose flight towards the dim empyrean
> Fearless of toil or fatigue ever royally wends!
> Vast in the cloud-coloured robes of the balm-breathing Orient
> Lo! the grand Epic advances, unfolding the humanest truth.

But that truth was unfolded, not by Southey, but by himself.

The influence of Sartor I have noted above. Clearly the idea of the destruction of Rags to symbolise apocalyptic change has helped into being that of the shaving of matted hair to symbolise revolutionary action. But Carlyle's grotesquerie aims at showing the absolute incompatibility of man's spiritual life and his everyday necessities, while Meredith's seeks to do the exact opposite—to give a rough realism to the poetic concept, to bring home with a buffet of laughter the basis of the imaginative flight in common life. In Carlyle the method takes apart; in Meredith it brings together.

7a.

Carlyle and Mazzini

BUT Carlyle's influence goes deeper still; and we must grasp the positive elements which Meredith, like Dickens, drew from Carlyle's thought if we are to understand his consciousness of the political struggle and the way in which he expressed that struggle in artistic terms.

Carlyle knew the French Revolution was no passing convulsion. He knew it ushered in an enduring crisis by extending capitalist relations all over Europe. He saw Chartism as a phase of the resulting struggle:

> The 'chimera' of Chartism, not the reality, has been put down. The matter of Chartism is weighty, deep-rooted, far-extending; did not begin yesterday; will not end this day or tomorrow.

He saw Capitalism as substituting the *cash-nexus* for human relationship and striving to turn *people into things*. He saw that it would advance productivity but could not solve the problem of distribution: that the more shirts produced, the less for the shirtless. He saw it powerless in itself to solve this and similar contradictions.

He saw its forms of *cant and humbug* as the signature, the necessary veil of the horrible reduction of men to things. To strip the veil was to advance the victory of truth and help towards the ending of an intolerable situation. A key-part in this struggle was played by the liberating laugh. Stupidity, humbug, egoism were the forms under which the evil forces extended their kingdom over men's souls.*

So far his virtues, which he could not sustain. They came from his early strenuous Radicalism bitter against the State that carried out the massacre of Peterloo and the Corn Laws; and in their light he saw the

---

* He here expresses the highest level of revolutionary consciousness in the 1830's and 1840's (short of Marx's level of stable development). Thus Lamartine in one of his moments of insight declares, 'The code of Egoism: a war to the death between those who work and those who give work: those who sell and those who buy: those who revel in abundance and those who starve.' And Heine of the English, 'I often regard them not at all as my fellow-men, but as miserable automata—machines, whose motive-power is egoism. In these moods, it seems to me as if I heard the whizzing wheelwork by which they think, feel, reckon, digest, and pray,' and their speech is a 'hiss of egoism.' (The English are the supreme egoists of the day because they are the most permeated by the capitalist cash-nexus.)

Cf. Gissing in *Denzil Quarrier* (1892). 'It is the first duty of a Radical to set his face against humbug.' (Throughout, I use the terms *egoism* and *sentimentalism* with the special reference to self-alienation that they had in Meredith's thinking.)

French Revolution at least as a mighty work of Nemesis on oppressors. But by the time of his *Chartism* he was receding from action; he calls himself 'one of the deepest though perhaps the quietest of radicals.' He acclaimed the religious and revolutionary Hero in the 1840's (Cromwell); after the Crimean War he exalted the military victor (Frederick the Great). He had no trust in the common man, and looked back to medieval society for the clue to an organic society, attributing the anarchy of capitalist society to the failure of the ruling class to rule. He could not grasp that the anarchy was the form by which the new ruling-class imposed its political and cultural values, and that in consequence the strong control he wanted could only work out as the matured form, based on monopoly-concentrations, of the thing he began by hating. Hence his opposition shaded off into a demand for the worst possible form of the cash-nexus State; he moved into an imperial creed of white-superiority and Britain's right to exploit the colonial peoples. His practical suggestions for lessening the social crisis were on a crude empirical level—e.g. his support of mass-emigration.

Worse, he dissolved his notion of the cash-nexus into absolute abstractions till nothing was left but puny men lost against the sky of eternity. Hence his need of grotesque humour and wild picturesqueness, to bring out what he felt as an absolute contradiction between human aims and their death-background. Such a method enabled him to feel himself boring realistically into the tragic dilemma of everyday life; to break history down into existentialist oppositions with no solution, no ultimate choice but lonely stoicism before the sense of death.

Hence the entangled virtues and vices of his thought. He drove men towards a recognition of the truth of their society and its conflicts; but he also sought to divert them by shifting his focus from historical reality to furious absolute dichotomies and vicious demands for dictatorship.

Meredith, like Dickens, drew powerfully on the positive side of his work, while resisting his regressive pull. His considered views keep on bringing out this duality in his responses. In 1865 he defended that aspect of Carlyle's humour which did deepen awareness of the contradictions in capitalist society and its defenders in political economy:

> In reading Carlyle, bear in mind that he is a humorist. The insolence offensive to you, is part of his humour. He means what he says, but only so far as a humorist can mean what he says. See the difference between him and Emerson, who is on the contrary a philosopher. The humorist, notwithstanding, has much truth to back him. Swim on his pages, take his poetry and fine grisly laughter, his manliness, together with some splendid teaching. It is a good set-off to the doctrines of what is called the 'Empyrical school.' I don't agree with Carlyle a bit, but I do enjoy him. [To Maxse.]

In December 1869 he commented on Mill, Carlyle, and Ruskin:

[Mill] really does not touch the soul and springs of the Universe as Carlyle does. Only when the latter attempts practical dealings he is irritable as a woman, impetuous as a tyrant. He seeks the short road to his ends; and the short road is, we know, a bloody one. He is not wise; Mill is; but Carlyle has most light when he burns calmly. Much of Ruskin's Political Economy will, I suspect, be stamped as good by posterity. He brings humanity into it. This therefore is not the Political Economy of our day. [To Maxse.]

Next month he repeated: 'Philosophy, while rendering its dues to a man like Carlyle and acknowledging itself inferior in activity, despises his hideous blustering impatience in the presence of progressive facts.' In 1875, in a poem for Carlyle's 80th birthday, he praises him for having 'bared the roots of life with sight piercing,' and in *Beauchamp's Career* he set out the debt that the revolutionary owed to Carlyle. In May 1882 he wrote that Carlyle was 'Titanic, not Olympian; a heaver of rocks, not a shaper. But if he did no perfect work, he had lightning's power to strike out marvellous pictures and reach to the inmost of men with a phrase.'

Thus, he continued to admire Carlyle for his power to break through the thick falsities of their world with a sharp phrase, a momentary depth of realisation; but he more and more despised his reactionary rage, his inability to relate his deep insights to the forward-movement of society through democratic struggle.

And so against Carlyle as an early influence we must set Mazzini, who passionately believed in progress and collective action. He saw history as the evolution of God's thought and humanity as achieved by co-operation with God in successive stages. He distrusted the casual-minded who feared entire partisanship. Action was essential. Let the artist have no dread of plunging into the midmost of struggle, to find there his inspiration. The era of individualism, when outstanding men changed the world, was over; now came the era of association, collective effort, in which difference of sex had no meaning. The unity of Italy would be won as prelude to universal brotherhood when men and women would be perfectly equal and a federation of democracies be formed, a world-parliament at Rome.

This creed was full of callow idealism; there was a naive attempt to harmonise the idea of world-democracy with that of Roman superiority; and there was no grasp whatever of the capitalist contradictions that would have to be overcome before the dream of human unity could be realised. But while Meredith never accepted Mazzini's account of the rôle of God in politics, he respected his deep faith in the future, his preaching of sex-equality, his ceaseless struggles to free Italy as a Republic, and his call for a vitally political art in which the artist boldly tackled the key issues of his time and expressed the fullness of the struggle towards world-brotherhood. (The term Republic, in Mazzinian and radical idioms, always implied a social programme against privilege in all its forms.)

Meredith may thus be said to have taken from Carlyle what was subtly realistic in his penetration into the condition of men under capitalism, but rejected his reactionary pessimism—while he took from Mazzini his blithe optimism, his belief that the era of individualism (egoism) was over, but rejected his implication of God as a (somewhat sleepy) partner in human affairs.

In *Shagpat* he has already integrated these influences in a large-scale definition of the struggles and aspirations of his world.

8

Farina

SHAGPAT WAS a failure, though George Eliot praised it enthusiastically as a:

work of genius, and of poetical genius . . . (with) exuberance of imagery, picturesque wildness of incident, significant humour, and aphoristic wisdom . . . constant alternations of passion and wild imaginativeness with humour and pithy, practical sense.

But she does not say what the humour is significant of; and though she declares there is 'plenty of deep meaning,' she gives no indication of what the meaning is.*

In July 1855 Meredith wrote to Parker with a project of British Songs. 'It is very improbable you will entertain my proposal when I add, that I must sell the book, having spent on it, latterly, valuable time.' Parker did not entertain the proposal, and Meredith destroyed the manuscript. He must indeed have been hard-up. As far as we can add the figures, he earned before *Shagpat* only £31 12s. from *Household Words*, though there were certainly other small sums from periodicals. And he had lost £50 to £60 on *Poems*. Horne had gone off to Australia.

In 1856-7 the Merediths were mostly at Seaforth, a shabby muddy watering-place with grass-grown streets and the nearest railway-station at Newhaven, but with the downs at its back. Here they were friendly with Maurice Fitzgerald, who owned some property in the place: son of an eccentric fanatic of Boulge Hall, Suffolk, and nephew of the translator of *Omar Khayyám*. He had just come of age, known to Cambridge friends

---

* 'No patchwork of borrowed incidents,' in *The Leader*. She also reviewed it in *The Westminster Gazette*, where she thought it laboured towards its end. *The Examiner* praised it as charming, with lively fancy and bright invention. *The Saturday Review* saw it as the work of 'one who can *create*,' and made some small criticisms (e.g. words such as 'to bosom'). *The Sun* found it 'at once exquisitely humorous and splendidly imaginative.' *The New Quarterly* said it was 'destined to be classical,' though 'remote from those facts that usually occupy the mind of man,' with verse inferior to the prose.

The Critic, putting it last in a list of eight books, called it a mistake, though of some use 'as a mere brochure for Christmas.' *The Athenaeum* dismissed it with a few lines, as did *The Idler*. *The Spectator* briefly accused it of lacking 'rapidity and purpose in its action,' or 'power to carry the reader along.'

Meredith considered he was 'abused' for it (referring, it seems, to the public reception), but R. Garnet in 1864 said it 'produced something like a sensation.'

as a good scholar, a gentle sybarite, and a skilled gourmet. He disliked sports and long walks, but approved of literature, whist, good food. Meredith, who called him the Young Mauritius, pilloried him as the ineffably selfish Wise Youth of *Feverel*. A drawing by Samuel Lawrence shows as elegantly handsome as a neo-classic image of a Greek god.

Other Seaforth characters were the Ockendens, the carpenter-wheelwright and voluble wife with a knack of good cooking—Mrs Berry of *Feverel*. The Merediths lodged at the Ockenden house in Marine Terrace.

They entertained many friends here, including one of George's aunts and her son—the last bit of intercourse, it seems, with Portsmouth relations. A dialogue letter reproduces the excited arguments with Fitz over food, and an invitation to Eyre Crowe depicts the amenities:

> Come here and stay a week. The weather is lovely. The heat quite sweltering. Mrs Meredith joins in kind regards. She says you must come under pain of her displeasure. Come, O Crowe! Here is fishing, bathing, rowing, sailing, lounging, running, pic-nicing, and a cook who builds a basis of strength to make us equal to all these superhuman efforts.

Strain was increasing between George and Mary, and Fitz used his sardonic flippancies to ease things. The marriage was not one to weather the hardships of poverty. Mary had done her best to push George into a job of the same sort as her father's. One day (presumably at Lower Halliford) she fixed a promising appointment and sent George off for the London train. On the way to the station, he 'forgot,' wandered off, and came home jobless in the evening. He was determined not to take a position which he felt would break down his resistances to an oppressive world; and this attitude infuriated Mary. We can read his own sufferings in the counsel to a friend:

> Can you bear poverty for her? Will she for you? Can you, even if she would? Think whether you are risking it, and remember that very few women bear it and retain their delicacy and charm. See whether you feel, not what we call love, but tenderness for her. [To Maxse, 1857.]

Christmas 1856 found him ominously alone by the sea, where he wrote *Farina* and part of *Feverel*. The place was so dull, he said, that he worked well there. Now he was writing *Feverel*—he called it *The Fair Frankincense* at this stage, referring to the sacrifice of Lucy and showing that the ordeal of woman was to have been more important than Richard's. He asks for books with dialect and balladry of Hants—no doubt wanting to ensure the right ring for the speech of the country-characters.

In the spring of 1857 he was still at Seaforth; and in the autumn *Farina* came out. The book, set in medieval Germany, told the tale of Farina of Cologne, who is brave like the other town-lads but without their barbarous ways of showing it. By truth and courage he wins the hand of Margarita, daughter of the richest burgess. Baron Werner tries to carry her off but is prevented by Farina and Guy, a jovial Englishman; he manages, however, to separate the lovers, shut Farina into jail, and get Margarita into his own hold. A monk Gregory delivers Farina, to have him as witness of his victory over the Devil on storm-ridden Drakenfels. But Satan, defeated, gets his own back by returning to hell in monkish guise via Cologne, which is empested by the infernal stink. Farina as a chemist controls the situation by inventing Eau de Cologne, and marries Margarita, the heroine who refuses to be afraid of nature. The warehouses of false Farinas promptly display imitations of the purifying water; but the happy lover can laugh at the back-blows of Satan. 'The shadow of Monk Gregory was seen no more in Cologne. He entered the Calendar, and ranks next to St Anthony.'

The story lacks the broad and complex sweep of *Shagpat*. The faith in love and progress is as keen, but the scope is minor. The main theme is the overthrow of the idealist division of body and soul, though the terms are medieval. *Farina* attacks both the thesis of the organic society of feudalism and the Victorian ethical creed of 'spirituality' opposed to bodily function. The monk's contest with Satan is at root a sham fight. By the ascetic defeat of the Devil the intensified empesting and befouling of life are brought about. In fact the Monk and the Devil are accomplices in the perpetuation of a vile system of division which blackguards nature. Whatever the Monk may think he is doing, his creed works out as an alliance with Satan, the great master of the lie, the illusion. Satan is thus the Shagpat of *Farina*, and the Monk is his tool.

Meredith uses ballads, like the apologues and verses of *Shagpat*, to give a wider perspective, a sense of popular forces at play around his characters. Grotesque humour, though more diluted, still merges with the dynamic use of words in the key of the New Poetry, to stress the realism of the allegory and bring out the contradictory pressures in the experience of a hero who strives to grasp and transform a lie-deluded world.

Farina, lacking the intensity and breath of *Shagpat*, has a more specific point of reference. Into it Meredith puts the sense of history stirred by the German scene with its multiple remnants of feudalism; but also, in attacking the creed of anti-nature, he attacks his own society with its illusions bred from fear and division.

In *Harry Richmond* he later defined the grotesque element that he found in Germanic legend, in a modern society loaded with feudal oddments:

> Suddenly one of us exclaimed, 'We're in a German forest'; and we remembered grim tales of those forests, their awful castles, barons, knights, ladies, long-bearded drawfs, gnomes and thin people. I commenced a legend off-hand.
> 'No, no,' said Temple, as if curdling. 'Let's call this place the mouth of Hades. Greek things don't make you feel funny. . . . Those German tales— they only upset you. You don't see the reason of the thing. Why is a man to be haunted half his life? Well, suppose he did commit a murder. But if he didn't, can't we walk through an old castle without meeting ghosts? or a forest?'
> The dusky scenery of a strange land was influencing Temple. It affected me, so I made the worst of it for a cure.

Farina was thus a cure for his remaining attachments to romantic illusion: a parody of the Gothic Novel (and, in this sense, Peacockian) but also a deepening of the emotions of revolt developed inside Romanticism. The hero, after the self-defeating thrills of a stormy romantic experience, turns to the scientific exploration of the facts, the compounding of an antidote for fantasies that recoil into pollution. And so, the rational achievement is fused with the secure happiness of love, fellowship. The last lines tell us how to distinguish the true Farina from the false. He is the one whose act has been ruled by love, which defeats the old divisions and owns the realised Earth:

> Would you know the true Farina? Look for him who walks under the seal of bliss: whose darling is for ever his young sweet bride, leading him from snares, priming his soul with celestial freshness.

Though less highly wrought in style than *Shagpat*, the tale has many fine passages of poetic realism, such as the following in which spatial recession is linked with light-movement and a glittering centralisation of action:

> The sun had risen through interminable distances of receding mounds and thinner veils, realm beyond realms, till he showed fireless, like a phantom king in a phantom land. The lark was in the breast of morning. The field-mouse ran along the furrows. Dews hung red and grey on the weedy banks and wayside trees.

The picture of the undine with her motion of undulating water, who guides and saves the lover, helps us to see why he always took a swimming grace as characteristic of feminine charm.

> Her visage had the lustrous white of moonlight, and all her shape undulated in a dress of flashing silver-white, wonderful to see. The lady of the water smiled on him, and ran over with ripples and dimples of limpid beauty. Then,

as he retreated on the meadow grass, she swam towards him, and taking his hand, pressed it to her. After her touch the youth no longer feared. She curved her finger, and beckoned him on. All that she had done was done flowingly. The youth was a shadow in her silver track. Her own shadow was but a fainter effluence of her form, and moved pale as she passed like a harmless wave over the closed crocuses. . . . Farina was a man working the days intent in a dream. Translucent, he could see the heart in her hanging like a cold dingy ruby.

And here is another passage which Rossetti might well have said to own the virginity of whiteness, which anticipates the later much-used image of the marriage of heaven and earth:

I look on the white sea of the saints. . . . Oh, my beloved! So walkest thou for my soul on the white sea ever at night, clad in the straight fall of thy spotless virgin linen; bearing in thy hand the lily, and leaning thy cheek to it, where the human rose is softened to a milky bloom of red, the espousals of heaven and earth; over them, moving with thee, a wreath of sapphire stars, and the solitude of purity around.*

---

* George Eliot reviewed in *The Westminster*: she said the book would be read with pleasure by all who preferred a lively spirited story to those dull analyses of dull experiences in which the present fiction-school abounded. But she added that M. sacrificed euphony, and almost sense, to the wish for novelty and force of expression. *The Critic* said *Shagpat* had 'obtained a good deal of popularity,' and *Farina* 'cannot fail to amuse.' *The Morning Post* found a 'spirited and captivating style . . . full of the wild dreamy romance of the German school'; *The Athenaeum*, a 'full-blooded specimen of the nonsense of genius.'

The *Examiner* said it was 'German to the core; the plot tended to ramble; the whole was a pleasant work of fancy.' *The Leader* said it was 'wild, quaint, surprising,' wrought with 'excessive elaboration . . . an heraldic artist in the use of colours in bright contrast,' but occasionally wearisome. *The Spectator* liked it better than *Shagpat*, but complained of forced quaintness. The disappointed *Saturday Review* said the theme was not worth handling; the comedy more grotesque than piquant; there was an art in the narrative, but the total effect was flat and dull. *The Eclectic Review* (ecclesiastical) deplored coarse language, admitted cleverness in conception and good tale-telling, but wanted more elevated subjects.

9

Modern Love

THE STRAIN between Mary and George grew worse. She found him fretful and despotic, called him a dictator, and resented their lack of money, his refusal to take a job. Edith Nicolls said, 'They sharpened their wits on one another,' and the son of his second marriage summed up:

> Two highly-strung temperaments—man and wife—each imaginative, emotional, quick to anger, cuttingly satirical in dispute, each an incomparable wielder of the rapier of ridicule, could not find content within the narrow bounds of poverty and lodgings.

Meredith said later, 'No sun warmed my roof-tree; the marriage was a blunder; she was nine years my senior,' and 'Peacock's wife became mad, and there was a family-taint.' He was not the man to say such an ugly thing unless Mary had shown strong traces of melancholia.

They were friendly with Henry Wallis, painter, who painted Mary in his *Fireside Reverie* and who then used Meredith for his *Death of Chatterton*. He also painted a head of Peacock. The Chatterton picture was done in the Gray's Inn Chambers of Austin Daniel of *The Monthly Observer*. One day, perhaps at Seaforth, he had found Mary in one of her melancholic fits and consoled her. In the summer of 1857 she was in North Wales and he seems to have been with her. Then she moved to a cottage at Clifton, near Bristol, attended by her foster-sister, and bore a son in April 1858. The child was Wallis's, though legally registered as Meredith's In the autumn she went off to Capri with Wallis, leaving George to cope with debts, loneliness, and young Arthur.

But her moodiness, her sense of guilt, ensured the rapid failure of the new love. In 1859 she was back in London with the baby, in Twickenham, anxious to see her son Arthur. Life had closed in darkly around her. She paced her room inconsolably with a lock of her son's hair against her breast, tormented, haunted by the conviction of nearing death, repeating the lines:

> Come not, when I am dead,
> To drop thy foolish tears upon my grave,
> To trample round my fallen head,
> And vex the unhappy dust thou wouldst not save.

There let the wind sweep and the plover cry;
But thou go by. . . .
I am sick of Time,
And I desire to rest.
Pass on, weak heart, and leave me where I lie:
Go by, go by.

The poet was Tennyson; and considering the extent to which Meredith was the anti-Tennyson, it seems fitting that the semi-maniac Mary should turn to the poet of false sentiment in falling away from her husband. She wanted the verses on her tombstone. We are told that she attempted a reconciliation, but George stood firm. He had warned her that if she went off with Wallis it would be the end of everything; and he seems never to have seen her again. She went wandering in the trail of lost happiness, or what now seemed to have been happiness. To Seaforth and Hastings, Richmond Hill, then a cottage at Weybridge. In October 1861, aged 41, she died, and no tombstone was raised over her body.

Though George did not write *Modern Love* till after her death, we can best consider its subject-matter here; for, though making no direct transcription of what had happened, he set out to define the essential pattern in his marriage's breakdown. Also, a summary of the poem's narrative may help readers to tackle it as a whole, the only way in which it can be appreciated. Meredith in a letter called it a set of sonnets, and Swinburne in defending it used the same term; but the description has been unfortunate, suggesting a series of separable units that can be tasted one at a time. *Modern Love* is in fact a narrative poem in units made of four quatrains rhyming *a b b a*, and its subtleties can only be grasped by a reader who realises the complex interactions of its analysis. There is a steady sequence of events, though the tale is told in a glancing way in which the account of what happened shifts quickly into a definition of the changing emotional states in the lover.

The married couple lie awake one embittered night in bed, aching for the separation they cannot bring themselves to precipitate. The man feels only the murderous darkness under his wife's beauty: but in remorse he tries to break down his own hard resistances, till the full awareness of the situation's anguish recoils on him. When in the day he notes her glance's irradiating power, he is fascinated against his will, curses her power, yet wants to surrender and take the sweetness she can give. What harm in a kiss on her cool brow? But no, it's useless, he has been deceived; the thing he loved no longer exists; the break must come.

He turns to other interests, in vain. The illusion of distraction is soon gone, and the after-pain is worse. A discipline looking to death is no solution for life's problems. Her household cares seem an hypocrisy, a form of contempt for him, as she is turned elsewhere for her inner experience; and yet the poignant memory of what has been awakes and makes him burn to possess her again. Then a chance caress forces him to feel that her whole being, with all her potentialities of joy and love, is averted from him. Remembering her midnight tears, he hurts himself with thoughts of her wantonness, and this bitter sensual rage rends him as they sit by the hearth and she laughs at some joke. And, as she dresses herself with care, he sees her with the eyes of the man for whom she makes the toilet, and feels her guile of heart worse than bodily infidelity. Her smile is a steel mirror, and yet under it, he knows, she suffers and struggles. He can't make out how they have broken apart, and is ready at a sign to start all over again; yet the beast in him wants to take and break her. He does nothing, torn with her recollected tenderness for the other.

What is his crime? That he dreamed of loyalty and worth beyond her conceptions, and refused to accept the prevailing falsities, to find a place in the world. Now nature's warm beauty only intensifies his sense of loss. What he resents is not so much that she blackens the future as that she turns the past into a thing of mockery. He looks again to nature and wonders why he can't live simply in the present without memory or hope, accepting equally joy or loss, life and death. But the thought is pointless: the whole meaning of human love lies in its yearning for the future, its need of renewal in joy.

So he turns to a woman friend, and feels scorn when his wife shifts jealously into a show of affection. He rouses her from sleep to show her two letters, both passionate: one addressed to him in the past, the other to her present lover. Yet all the while they pretend before the world to be happy and normal. She is an excellent hostess, and he feels a certain zest in the game of lying. They admire each other's skill. He envies the simple joys of the countryfolk, but reflects that beer is what releases them into the 'secret of the bull and lamb.' Torn by conflicting emotions, he decides there's no escape by his own infidelity: that road takes love to the marketplace. And he sinks so low as to feel the village-idiot has the best of the world. Then he is shocked into thinking of his responsibility for the marriage's failure by finding in a drawer an earlier mistress's tress.

One evening, on the lawn, a friend, once a scoffer, tells how he too now loves, and asks the happily-married pair's blessing. Their eyes meet in horror; they do as he asks, and then she faints. The husband wonders if the other sees the situation's irony; and realises that his wife is on the brink of a confession, irresolute, weeping, yet unable to speak. But he won't help her out, and the gulf seems impassable.

At Christmas, in a crowded country-house, they have to share a room. The enforced intimacies stresses the deep mortification dividing them; and he sleeps on the floor, dreaming of a return to love. He feels her pleading and suffering, and yet a guileful cheat. O, for a sign. He'll die rather than show his desire for her.

He questions her ironically on her distaste for a French novel she's reading, with a heroine compelled to choose between husband and lover, and choosing as a woman should. Unromantic but true. He loses any sense of a share in the breakdown, and sees only his own wrong; yet he feels it's still possible to forgive if his wife will throw off all cowardice and frankly confess. But he still won't help her. He decides to take his doctor's advice and find distraction where it's offered. So he plays about with his woman friend (the Lady) in a cynical mood. But once he felt strongly about her, and his emotion now grows stronger, sincerer, than he has meant. To justify himself, he generalises about love, but his fine words end in the old apology for accepting the fleeting moment. The Lady, however, has intelligence as well as charm; his spirit revives in their intercourse. He tries to convince himself that his relationship with his wife (Madam) is superseded, yet is forced to see the episode as marginal, incapable of healing the pang of his broken marriage. He suspects the cure does not lie with any woman, but clings to the Lady, feeling with pleasure how bewildered his wife would be if she read the letter he's writing.

His wife determines to have things out. But his flirtation has left him coldly bitter, and he freezes her with commonplaces and courtesies, though uneasy at the silence created by himself. He feels the thrust when, as they play cards, his wife remarks the game is hardly worth the cost.

He sticks to the conventional level. Lady and Madam are introduced and probe for each other's weaknesses. During a terrace-stroll before dinner all violence seems remote, meaningless. Does the problem really exist? But the conflict springs sharply back as the Lady urges him to return to his wife. He begs her to hold him fast, it's his only hope, the pity she counsels is out of place. His wife, he says, is a child who values a toy only when broken, irreplaceable; to return to her is to return to evil. The Lady yields, and he enjoys a golden hour of moon and song. Surely he has regained a full harmony with the earth. They stand in half dream by a stream; in the shadow a couple are seen—his wife and her lover, with touching hands. All his old anguish and confusion rush back, and he is once more lost in a frenzy of divided impulses.

To return to his wife is no solution, yet her spell wrecks any hope of stable relations with the Lady. He sees his wife's desirability by seeing her through her lover's eyes. Some understanding must be reached. So far, no further, he can see. He tries embracing her; the kisses drive them further apart. Next morning in the harsh east wind he roams the seashore, seeing the clashing wind and water as the tomb that engulfs defiled love. Whose fault the failure is, he can't tell, but the dreaded evil thing is come upon him. He loses bitterness, and though love can't be brought back, he is united after all with his wife by pity. He tries to hide his feelings. She sees through him, though she can't penetrate to the full truth of their failure and falls back on blame of the Lady. He tries vainly to convince her otherwise. And at last an unexpected incident brings things to a head. He looks for her, half-unconsciously, in the glade of their wooing, and finds her there with the lover. Ignoring the man, he offers her his arm, and, without embarrassment, she goes away with him. The lover fades out into the shadows.

Once again she is on the edge of explanations; but before she can speak, he expresses an entire confidence in her. The storm and stress of their alienation seem over; an afterglow of passion suffuses their lives a moment. They stand in the gentle peace of the swallow-eve. At last he can speak openly, and they say all that can be said. But she still fails to understand; her judgment is twisted. When he mentions the Lady, she is deaf to all else and breaks from him, fixed in the idea that she must free him to win happiness with her rival. He finds her by the sea. She takes his hand and seems amenable to control, happy in his solicitude, though without her usual vitality. Some change has come over her. At midnight she calls and asks him to embrace her. She has taken poison.

Clearly the poem is no replica of his experience. Mary went off, she did not commit suicide. But, writing after her death, he probably recalled suicide-threats made in periods of resentful melancholia, and felt that he could best round off his narrative on the poem's lines. The part played here by the Lady, and in *Feverel* by Mrs Mount, makes fairly certain that he did not hold himself free from guilt in the marriage's failure.

Biographically, unit *x* is important; for there he sets out his explanation of the irreconcilable conflict with Mary:

> *In Love's deep woods,*
> *I dreamt of loyal Life:—the offence is there!*
> *Love's jealous woods about the sun are curled;*
> *At least, the sun far brighter there did beam.—*
> *My crime is, that the puppet of a dream,*
> *I plotted to be worthy of the world.*
> *Oh, had I with my darling helped to mince*
> *The facts of life, you still had seen me go*
> *With hindward feather and with forward toe;*
> *Her much-adored delightful Fairy Prince!*

The meaning is plain. Mary wanted a snug warmth of love, a sly refuge, with the world barred out by an acceptance of its terms. But to George those terms were foully false; the murder of the loyalty which alone made life worth living. They denied his dream of brotherhood, his need to struggle for the changing of the world. The clash was between two ways of life; and this it is that makes *Modern Love* more than a subtle psychological document. 'She treated him as something that was tame,' he writes. That is, she denied the rebel in him. Despite all his palterings and falterings, he remains stubbornly true to his larger loyalty; in Mary he resists and fights the lie of his society. By fighting her, he grasps with a new fullness what love is, what truth is.

10

The Ordeal

After Mary's departure he took Arthur to London, and for six years he lavished on his son all the affection that the loss of Mary had dammed up in him. For about a year he lived at Hobury Street, Chelsea, in a drab house, where he completed *Feverel*. Lady Nicolls, Edith's grandmother, looked after the child during 1858; then early next year Meredith moved to Esher. There in a pleasant old house, once a coaching-inn, father and son were reunited. About this time they visited Lynmouth, where a man who enjoyed Meredith's conversation in the evenings records that he liked a lad to wash and dress the child, rather than a woman. In June Chapman and Hall published *The Ordeal of Richard Feverel*.

The subtitle stated the theme of the relation of Father and Son; and Meredith's pondering over the best way to educate a son without distorting his character must have played a part in the novel's working-out. And we may suppose he had read Herbert Spencer's essay on Education in *The British Quarterly Review*, April 1858, which caused much reconsideration of the matter. But at root he was grappling with the whole problem of the conditioning forces in his world; the way they sought to mechanise and dehumanise man. His novel is still in many ways an allegory, but he extends his grasp of everyday event and contemporary types.

Sir Austin Feverel loses his wife, who runs off with a poet. In revulsion from the world of women he brings up his son under his own strict system. The Feverels, he feels, are under a curse, and love is their ordeal; he wants to train his son to meet this test with full self-control and to break the curse. His ideas he sets out in a book, *The Pilgrim's Scrip*. The first rebellion of his son Richard comes in the revengeful burning of a rick because a farmer prevents him poaching. Then he meets Lucy, who is related to the farmer, and falls in love. Sir Austin tries to spoil things, but the lovers are secretly married. In horror Sir Austin separates them, and Richard is seduced by Mrs Mount. She has been put up to the job by a lord who wants to get hold of Lucy. Richard in shame goes off to Germany; but Austin Wentworth takes Lucy to his uncle Sir Austin, who accepts her. Richard learns that he is a father, and rushes into a forest-storm, from which he emerges purged and transfigured. However, on his way home, he learns of the lord's trick, sees Lucy for a few desperate moments, and hurries off to France to fight the lord. He is badly wounded. Lucy is brought to see him, but dies of brain-fever under the long strain. He is left agonised with vain regret.

The book, in its published form, was composed in the tormented period after the loss of Mary, and bears the imprint of changing intentions and divergent aims. It is a Peacockian satire on rigid systems applied to human life; but its political focus involves all the realisation already apparent in *Shagpat* and *Farina*. In witty and detached style it tries to make of the Feverel Scheme a critique of the deep trend in contemporary class-society to impose a sense of sin on men, to maim and divide them, to set them at war with their impulses and make them puppets jerking at the master's manipulation. But into the ironic detachment creeps a fierce anger that disturbs the wit-method; and Meredith's need to show positive forces as well as destructive introduces a lyric verve into the pictures of young love, and into the storm-scene, that shatters the assumption of detachment. As a result of the varying modes of definition the people round Sir Austin tend to belong to the sphere of critical wit, with its playful objectivity, which makes them seem sharply-drawn but bloodless figments of a deadly world, while Richard and his group (the country-folk, Lucy) tend to own more particularised contours and human warmth. The demarcation is not precise, but the two trends are obvious. In them we see something of George's torn and disturbed condition as he writes, and also the strain he feels at the effort to move from definitions determined by a poetic transfiguration of the world into a realistic control of everyday material—while preserving a lyric faith in love and brotherhood, and a clear political critique.

Sir Austin is a study in Egoism, in the complex sense that we have seen attached to the term by Carlyle. Because throughout his work Meredith keeps intact in his mind this understanding of Egoism as the supreme expression of the dominant class-values of his world, he remains always *a political writer* in the deepest significance of that phrase. The point must be made unmistakably at the outset, so that the reader may grasp the social, political, and psychological implications of the term *Egoism* whenever it is hereafter used. Egoism is for Meredith the process of inner division, of self-alienation,* that is the spiritual reflection of class-cleavages;

---

* The term *self-alienation* is mine and not Meredith's; I use it because I believe it enables us to grasp the enriched focus merging personal and social aspects, which M. always struggles to build. What matters, however, are the concrete *images* which M. builds in his work, and these I analyse at some length in his own terms as well as mine, so that the reader can check if I am

and everyone who fights against Egoism is fighting both for personal integration and for world-brotherhood. Egoism reveals the inner discord and split which find cultural expression in a whole complex of abstractions, in the denial of Earth and the separation of body and mind. In self-alienation man is cut off from nature and his fellows, and therefore from his own essence, which he can realise only by union with his fellows and nature in constructive socially-significant work.

So, in this book, Meredith links Egoism with the creed of original sin, which provides an excuse for the Egoist to tamper with the true springs of human motivation. Sir Austin declares that he only wants to make his son a Christian.

The conflict of Father and Son is for the same reason shown as an expression of the division of Mind and Heart, which Meredith sees always as an outcome of social division. It is mutually destructive and can only work by extending the alienating process. Here it wrecks Sir Austin's hopes, brings Richard down in a pit of blind regret, destroys Lucy. Thrice Richard has a chance to grasp the snares besetting his life; when he burns the rick and discovers the depths of brotherly loyalty in the common-folk, the workers; when he breaks through his father's distorting system into a vision of what a happy life on earth entails; and when he passes through the transfiguring storm back into that vision, with the extra-strength gained from suffering. But each time he fails the offered chance, and thus ends by destroying both Lucy and himself. He is too contamin-ated by the system and its pressures of self-alienation. In his first burst of love he had felt the identity of the system and the world it pretends to combat—'Away with Systems: away with a corrupt World!'—but he cannot continue to live in the values of the golden earth that love redeems.

Yet in the three chances he is given we see the way out of the Feverel impasse: unity with common life, acceptance of love and earth, move-ment through stormy struggle into a new life. The lessons are reinforced by the contrast between the commonfolk such as Tom Bakewell or Mrs Berry and the upper-class with the rot at their hearts. And again by the opposition of the two nephews of Sir Austin, Adrian Harley and Austin

---

truly assessing the direction and intention of that work. Part of the tension inside M's work lies in the fact that he to a considerable extent uses the terms of the Carlylese critique (to which he adds those of the romantics rebels generally) while driving forward to levels *where these terms begin to prove inadequate*. The point I here make will only become clear after we have analysed the concrete content of *Vittoria, Beauchamp, The Tragic Comedians* and *One of our Conquerors*.

He is a political writer, not simply because he holds fast to the early Carlyle's concept of Egoism as central in bourgeois ideology, but because also he sees that the critique of the idea is also a critique of the class—and that the angle of attack must be, not from feudal standpoints, but from those of mass-based democracy. He realises the class–We in the egoist I.

Wentworth. Adrian stands for Egoism in its aspect of unadulterated self-indulgence and parasitism; Austin is the man of the upper class who has overcome his egoism. He seduced a housemaid and married her, and is humanised. He has 'the reputation of the poor man's friend: a title he earned more largely ere he went to the reward God alone can give to that supreme virtue'—a statement which seeks to stress the further development of his struggle for the poor and which mentions God's reward only to bring out the lack of any honour for such acts in Austin's society. (The use of the name *Austin* for both the arch-egoist and the anti-egoist can only mean that Meredith wants to underline the importance of their opposition for the novel's theme.) Austin holds 'republican sentiments,' and Adrian calls him a radical and a materialist.

An interesting revelation of the perversion of the middle-class mind of the period was made in the selection of Adrian as the book's hero by some readers—just as Lewes took Akinetes, intended by Horne as the most repellent type of reactionary, to be the hero of *Orion*.

Already the theme of *Sentimentalism* as a basic form of Egoism, of the bourgeois lie or illusion, is to be found. 'Sentimentalists are they who seek to enjoy without incurring the immense debtorship for a thing done.' Lady Blandish is a sentimentalist, who begins to awake to reality; and her awakening is an important aspect of the shattering of Sir Austin. In Germany Richard is being entangled with a sentimentalist when the news of his son swings him towards a fresh chance of regeneration.

In the pictures of the commonfolk, especially Mrs Berry, there is a strong Dickensian influence; and the comparison of Sir Austin with Dombey has a fraction of truth. Both men signify the dehumanising process of their society, the cash-nexus and its thingifying of people; and both are in conflict with their children's effort to become human.

In showing Sir Austin perverted by embitterment over his wife's infidelity Meredith could but be strongly drawing on his own experience. Indeed he gives Lady Feverel the name of Mary and makes her lover write, 'For I am not the first who found the name of Mary fatal.' The novel is in a way a warning to himself, not to lose his balance and fall into accord with the society of self-righteous dehumanisation, not to be deceived by his love for Arthur into becoming the monster he most detested. In the first edition the motive of wifely infidelity was very much more stressed than in the revised version of 1878. The many cuts mainly concern Sir Austin, his lady admirers, his ancestors, and his deterioration under the shock of his wife's running-off. The revised Sir Austin is thus less plausible. No doubt Meredith felt he had drawn too much on his personal suffering in the original *Feverel*, and decided to throw all emphasis on the results of the perverted mind rather than to give too particular an account of the perversion's origins. Thus he made a more generalised application of the theme.

The generalised perspective he had sought from the outset to strengthen by the citing of verses by Mary's seducer, a Tory poet, and Sir Austin's aphorisms, *The Pilgrim's Scrip*. This sort of device, which we noted in *Shagpat* and *Farina*, persists in his work, seeking to give the effect of life moving into art and art moving back into life.

The lyric motive of man's active union with nature is richly developed in the love-scenes, prose-counterparts of *Love in the Valley*. Mary, we must not forget, stirred both that poem and *Modern Love*, and in the novel she is the original of both Lucy and Mrs Mount, the harmoniously joyous mate and the bold ruthless wanton with her individualistic ethic of behaviour. Lucy's death by brain-fever, the suicide-by-poison of Clare (a tormented character who loves Richard) and the suicide-by-poison in *Modern Love*, are aspects of a single motive, linked in fact with the morbid decline of Mary.

A pattern has already evolved in *Feverel* which persists to the end of Meredith's work: the theme that those in the position of power and privilege in Britain have taken the wrong turning, have surrendered to the dehumanising forces of capitalism, which is now their form of dominance and which they cannot deny without committing class-suicide. Individuals may revolt and seek to live a decent life of work in which a true sense of man's earthly existence fuses with a resolve to play a responsible part in social struggle. But they will fail, they will be destroyed by the relentless class-force against which they turn—unless they break decisively from their old relationships and align themselves with the common people's needs and struggles.

This theme Meredith examines from all angles, but never leaves. He strives always to show the positive forces at work, making for the human future, for enlarged democracy and freedom; but he also shows with obstinate realism the defeat of the individuals whose revolt is partial and who attempt to be both in and outside the ruling class—whether at the high levels of landed or financial power, or at the middle levels where the share of power may be less but the acceptance of the values of the cash-nexus, the ethic of egoism, is as great.

Hence the series of portraits, beginning with Richard Feverel and ending with Lord Fleetwood, of young men of the ruling class who seek to break through into love, but are twisted one way or another by the class-forces they cannot fully confront, so that their virtuous decisions are always taken too late. In the end they are left with a sense of intolerable failure, of having done an irreparable wrong; they see the right course and the happiness it would have given them, only after their actions have made it impossible for them. They live in a mirror-world of reflected disarticulated self-images, and cannot see directly the slanted reality beyond.

The last words of *Feverel* express powerfully this class-dilemma in which consciousness seems to arise only as a function of frustration and loss.

> Have you noticed the expression in the eyes of blind men? That is just how Richard looks, as he lies there silent in his bed—striving to image her on his brain.

The critics gave very varied opinions, though inclining to the censorious. *The Critic* disliked the 'minuteness' of the seduction-scene, and found 'great merits and great defects . . . very evenly balanced . . . meat for strong men. . . . There are many passages that lead us to believe that his mind is none of the purest.' *The Spectator* saw in the book enough thought, imagination, wit, humour, pathos, 'to make the fortune of a score of average novels.' *The Westminster Review* (perhaps George Eliot) remarked without much insight:

> The characters are numerous and well-defined; among them will be found representatives of almost every prevailing conception of life; but true to its time, the book offers no solution of any of the difficulties it lays open to us; the XIXth century struggles through it with but faint glimpses of its goal.

The Leader called it 'wild, fantastic, and in some degree enervating,' though 'not without its moral or its purpose.' At first 'through the mist of morbidity and gloom' we seem to see 'a good time coming,' but we are 'unnecessarily and woefully disappointed. G. Meredith can write well and conceive grandly, but he has yet to learn to correct, or at any rate to conceal his eccentricities.' *The Saturday Review* said, 'If this is all that Mr Meredith can do, it is a failure.' *The Athenaeum* found it 'almost as painful a book as any reader ever felt himself inexorably compelled to read through.' Clever, vigorous in style, but

> it is *not* true to real life or human nature; only true to an abstract and entirely arbitrary idea. None of the characters are real, live human beings; but then they are all so like life, their conversation is so bright and spirited, that it affects the reader like a painful reality to see such cruelty and blindness, and blundering, such child's play with the most sacred mysteries of life.

His only consolation is to say, on closing the book, that it isn't true.

The Times attempted a serious evaluation. Here Lucas, four months after publication, declared at length that the book was powerful, penetrative in its deep insight, and rich in its variety of experience:

> But it is also very oracular and obscure in parts, and, as we conceive, extremely weak in the development of its main purpose. On the other hand, it is so crystalline and brilliant in its principal passages, there is such purity mingled with its laxness, such sound and firm truth in the midst of its fantastic subtleties, that we hesitate whether to approve or condemn; and we have a difficulty even in forming a judgment on such strange contrarieties.

The critic seeks to resolve the contradictions by seeing Meredith as a *humorist*, shaping his own world with people 'more entirely symbols and shadows of his thought than ordinary denizens of the world about him.' Then he argues that Meredith does not effectively arraign the System, and ends by defending him against the charges of impurity and corrupt tendency.

It is important to consider these comments; for they reveal the characteristic inability to get inside Meredith's purpose which went on till the end of his days, and which drove him back on himself. *Feverel* has its rigidities, its abstractions, its unresolved contradictions; but the element which baffles alike the friendly *Times* and the unfriendly *Athenaeum* is the deep truth, the grasp of the contradictions in existing society. The critics, and the public, retire bewildered because they dare not follow Meredith into his exploration of the bourgeois illusion, its 'cruelty and blindness, and blundering.' They accuse Meredith of distorting reality at the point where he enters most deeply into it, and want the exposed conflicts to remain 'sacred mysteries.'

The matter did not, however, stay at bewilderment. The book roused instant and strong denunciation by the middle-class reading public. Many parsons seem to have banned it from the parish book-clubs, and Mudie, the nonconformist head of the main lending-library, declared

> that he had advertised it [*Feverel*] as much and as long as he could, but that, in consequence of the urgent remonstrances of several respectable families who objected to it as dangerous and wicked and damnable, he was compelled to withdraw it. Such is the case. There are grossly prurient, and morbidly timid people, who might haply be hurt, and with them the world is well stocked. [Meredith to Lucas from Piccadilly, Oct. 1859.]

Another letter to Lucas shows his depression at the reception:

> I think the 'maidens' may pass. As to the novel: alas and woe me! I find I have offended Mudie and the British Matron. He will not, or haply, dare not put me in his advertised catalogue. Because of the immoralities I depict! O canting Age! I predict a Deluge. Mudie is Metternich: and after him—Meantime I am tabooed from all drawing-room tables.

On re-reading portions I can't but say there is dulness in the book here and there, dulness and weakness. My fingers start to tear out these passages, nevertheless the main design and moral purposes I hold to. I have certainly made it too subtle, for none have perceived it. . . . The moral is that no system of the sort succeeds with human nature, unless the originator has conceived it primarily independent of personal passion. That was Sir Austin's way of wreaking his revenge. However, it requires twice reading to see this, and my fault has been that I have made the book so dull that it does not attract a second reading. At least not among newspaper critics—to whom all honour and glory.

And in December 1861 he wrote to Jessop about the British Matron and 'the snuffling moralist so powerful among us,' and mentioned that his literary reputation was 'tabooed as worse than libertine in certain virtuous societies.' *Paterfamilias* had given Mudie 'a very large bit of his petticoated mind concerning' him, but 'in the matter of Art I never stop to consider what is admissible to the narrow minds of the drawing-room.' And more than thirty years later he tells how *Feverel*

was, I heard, denounced over the country by clergymen, at book-clubs, and it fell dead. They have since had their drenching of the abominable—as all do, who stand against the plea for the painting of what is natural to us. It may be shown recurring through literary history. [Nov. 1889.]

He means that the middle-class hypocrisy has begotten the retort of excessive naturalism, a drenching of the abominable, which he does not himself like, but which he sees as the Nemesis of too much prudery.

After this treatment of his book, its effective boycotting and censoring, he had to face a crisis in his own development. How was he going to carry on, not surrendering to the enemy, yet at the same time managing to maintain his clear purpose? He was too sound and stable in his social sense to contemplate writing for some sectarian group, moral or artistic; and therefore he felt that he had to go on, somehow or other, writing for the only available public. Under the circumstances that meant simultaneously writing for that public and attacking it.

The form of his decision was ultimately determined by the failure of the mass-movement of struggle after 1850. That movement had given its rich dynamic to the work of the Brontës, Dickens, George Eliot; but Meredith was much younger than these writers, he was only now moving towards his first level of maturity. And he thus came into head-on collision with the stabilised middle-class public of the post-1850 epoch. The regrouping and re-expansion of the mass-forces on the new (proletarian) level were only in their embryonic stages; and for a novelist they did not yet provide an alternative audience.

So, in his bitter brooding after the attacks on *Feverel*, he collected his moral and artistic forces afresh, to continue with his exploration of the bourgeois lie, the spiritual processes that he gathered under the term Egoism; and yet had to formulate his method so as to keep at least a minimal point of contact with the audience he abhorred. And while carrying thus on with his task, he slowly set himself to define the counter-types of rebellion and true spiritual integration..

Out of this difficult situation emerged all his virtues and vices as a writer, his ceaseless penetration into egoist self-alienation and his brave effort to construct the positive hero in relations of significant social struggle, but also his angry tensions and complex convolutions of contempt. His style at moments gets free and swings forward richly in a tide of happiness, of liberated love, of passionately engaged struggle; then it is forced back on itself, in furious over-concentrations of bile, in wit-lacerations—as of a man standing lonely at bay and making of his wounds a bitter mockery-song, stricken but undaunted amid the smugly bestial faces of the good philistines.

The same close entanglement of warm concrete apprehension and sharp angry judgment runs throughout his method of characterisation. The result is that he cannot attain the highest level of creative definition; and yet when we realise what he is fighting and what he keeps steadily trying to construct, we cannot but recognise an integrity and driving-force which belongs only to the highest level. A strange contradiction, as the critic of *The Times* saw for a moment, though without the power to grasp what it implied.

As we go on, all that was involved in such a development will become clearer, and we shall look more closely into the social basis and links of Meredith's position. But the points made above will serve to state the nature of the crisis of choice that Meredith faced in 1859. The lines of his decision had in fact already been determined by the critique of the bourgeois made in *Feverel*; but after the attacks on the book he had to grow yet more aware of what he was doing, or decline into a demoralised novelist approved by Mudie's subscribers.

The three volume novels of the day cost thirty shillings, and the main sales came from circulating libraries. A Mudie embargo thus killed a book.

10a.

Carlyle and Richter

ONE PLEASANT result of *Feverel* was a personal acquaintance with Carlyle. Living in Chelsea, he had often encountered the latter, but had no excuse for addressing him. Now Mrs Carlyle read his novel and interested her husband in it. Carlyle wrote to the publishers and Meredith called at 3 Cheyne Row. Carlyle told him that his wife had been at first repelled and had flung the book down, then felt forced to take it up again and read to the end. She read it aloud to Carlyle, who said the author was no fool.

He now advised Meredith to turn to the writing of history. Meredith said there was so much fiction in history he preferred to write his history in the form of novels. Carlyle stressed the importance of Facts:

> I said to him, with all deference, I thought there were greater things in the world than facts. He turned to me and said, 'But facts are truth, and truth is facts.' I said, 'No, pardon me; if I may say so, truth I take to be the broad heaven above the petty doings of mankind which we call facts.' He gave me a smile of pity for my youth, as I suppose, and then said, 'Ah weel, if ye like to talk in that poetic way, ye may; but ye'll find it in your best interests, young man, to stick to Fahcts.'

Meredith himself always insisted on the need of realism, but he wanted it on a philosophic basis, with a power to grasp the typical and define the general movement of society. As he said later, 'To demand of us truth to nature, excluding Philosophy, is really to bid a pumpkin caper.'

As Carlyle was so important in providing Meredith with many of the starting-point of his central ideas, it would be as well to give here some typical passages from Carlyle of the sort that strongly affected Meredith. First here is a picture of Revolution as the ending of the Lie, of Falsity. Carlyle is writing of 1848:

> It is probably the hugest disclosure of *falsity* [C.'s italics] in human things that was ever at one time made. These reverend Dignitaries that sat amid their far-shining symbols and long-sounding long-admitted professions, were mere Imposters, then? Not a true thing they were doing, but a false thing. The story they told men was a cunning-devised fable; the gospels they preached to them were *not* an account of man's real position in this world, but an incoherent fabrication, of dead ghosts and unborn shadows, of traditions, cants, indolences, cowardices—a falsity of falsities, which at last ceases to stick together. . . . *A Universal Bankruptcy of Impostures* . . . (*Latter-day Pamphlets*).

4

Thus he denounces the cash-nexus and in his own terms declares it to be the source of what I have described as the alienating process: all the tumults of the 1840's he says may be regarded:

> as a voice from the dumb bosom of Nature, saying to us: 'Behold! Supply-and-demand is not the one Law of Nature; Cash-payment is not the sole nexus of man with man—how far from it! Deep, far deeper than Supply-and-Demand, are Laws, Obligations, sacred as Man's Life itself: these also, if you continue to do work, you shall now learn and obey. He that will learn them, behold Nature is on his side, he shall yet work and prosper with noble rewards. He that will not learn them, Nature is against him, he shall not be able to do work in Nature's empire—not in hers. Perpetual mutiny, contention, hatred, isolation, execration shall wait on his footsteps, till all men discern that the thing which he attains, however golden it look or be, is not success but the want of success.'

Thus he attacks Egoism as the spiritual core of the cash-nexus world and its inhabitants:

> He thinks that 'enlightened Egoism,' never so luminous, is not the rule by which man's life can be led. That 'Laisser-faire,' 'Supply-and-demand,' 'Cash-payment for the sole nexus,' and so forth, were not, are not and never will be, a practicable Law of Union for a Society of Men. . . . He thinks that said soul will have to be rescued from asphyxia. . . . The resuscitating of a soul that has gone to asphyxia is no momentary or pleasant process, but a long and terrible one. (*Past and Present.*)

And he defines Sentimentalism as the form of irresponsibility indulged in by those who fear the truth of things, a turning away from 'our field and inheritance' which is ours 'to make or mar':

> . . . a race of Sentimentalists, who have raged and wailed in every part of the world; till better light dawned on them, or at worst, exhausted Nature laid herself to sleep, and it was discovered that lamenting was an unproductive labour. (*Goethe.*)

One of the German Romantics whom Carlyle had much praised and discussed, and who certainly had considerable effect on Meredith, was Jean-Paul Richter. Richter's impact on Meredith had somehow entwined with the latter's response to Neuwied Brotherhood; it stimulated his use of a metaphorical style as a form of protest against the dehumanising philistine world of the bourgeoisie.

The son of a poor village pastor, Richter had a heavily loaded style, a discontinuous and allusive way of narrative, as if he wanted at all costs to bring out the veiled interconnection of things:

> Hidden ideas creep out of all the corners of the brain, and every simile becomes the mother of a whole family of metaphors; she gathers her diverse

children around her, and each hangs a picture on the tail of another, like a wandering family of mice.

Meredith may even have been directly recalling those words when he wrote in *Diana*, 'a little mouse of a thought which scampered out of one of the chambers of Redworth's head and darted along the passages.' But certainly he associated through Richter this kind of allusive style with a penetration into the reality under the bourgeois lie, a sympathy for the suffering sources of life, the downtrodden, 'the mean, the poor, the oppressed, the wretched and the suffering, those who rejoice in their constraints and are exceeding wise in their lack of wisdom.' 'In my Historical Lectures,' says Richter, 'the business of Hungering will in truth more and more make its appearance—with the hero it rises to a great height.' But what was passive in Richter becomes rebellious in Meredith. The beginning of wisdom may lie in the realisation that one's position in the oppressed classes gives one the chance of joy and humanity, because it cuts one off from a share in guilty power; but such a wisdom perishes unless it in turn begets a struggle to change the world. And yet, though Meredith's concept of struggle thus denies Richter's acceptances, he gained much from Richter's sense of union with the oppressed people, his poetic power to make the particular event or moment of union into a symbol of universal brotherhood and paradisiac harmony with nature, his way of linking grotesque humour with a conviction of abounding life and with imaginative overtones that evoked the movement into freedom. The profound difference between the two writers lay in the fact that what was passive, at best sadly hopeful fantasy, in Richter, became in Meredith dynamic, feeding always the central concept of transformative struggle.*

---

* Carlyle, in his exaggerating way, says, 'Probably there is not in any modern language so intricate a writer . . . perplexed into endless entanglements and dislocations, parenthesis within parenthesis; not forgetting elisions, sudden whirls, quips, conceits and all manner of inexplicable crochets; the whole moving on in the gayest manner, yet nowise in what seem military lines, but rather in huge parti-coloured mob-masses,' *J.-P. Richter Again*. The image of mass-movement shows real insight into the style, and gives us a key in turn to much of Meredith's method. His style is often an attempt to evoke a feeling of the mass-movement which he knows is lacking in political reality. It seeks to build up a sense of overbrimming life, of keen energy-thews: precisely because he is so aware of thinned and slackening forces.
Hardy in his notes, under 'Cures for despair' lists Wordsworth's *Resolution and Liberty*, a section of Mill's *Liberty*, and Carlyle's *Jean Paul Richter*.

11

Coming Through

DESPITE SETBACKS he was making new friends and widening the scope of his knowledge of affairs. In 1858 he met Frederick Augustus Maxse, then about 25, who had won fame by carrying Raglan's despatches through the enemy's lines in the Crimean War, but who turned his back on a successful career, roused to fierce revolt by the revelation of incompetence and corruption in the carrying-out of the War. Maxse came of a rich merchant-family of Dutch origin, his father married Lady Caroline Berkeley, whom Meredith came to know well; a hard rider at hounds, he is to be seen in the pictures of the Quorn Hunt. The Berkeleys were famous gamblers, hard livers, wild and obdurate; and Maxse, once having set himself against his class, stuck bitterly to his defiance. His mingled literary interests and passion for social reform made him congenial to Meredith who, however, criticised him for streaks of conventionality running through his rebellions and for one-track obsessions that hindered his capacity to work out an effective strategy of protest and pressure.

Maxse's home with his mother was in Surrey, and at least in part to be near him Meredith took his Esher lodgings. Soon he had a cottage of his own at Molesey, from which the pair set out in long tramps over heath and hill. In 1858 George went with Maxse in his cutter-yacht *The Grebe* to Cherbourg; and in 1862 he dedicated *Modern Love* to him 'affectionately,' thirty years later rededicating the poem 'in constant friendship.'

Fitz too was often at Esher, and introduced F. C. Burnand, a jolly fellow who had been thrown out by his father for turning Catholic, and who gives us a breezy picture of his first meeting with Meredith:

> George Meredith never merely walked, never lounged; he strode, he took giant strides. He had on a soft shapeless wide-awake, a sad-coloured flannel shirt, with low open collar turned over a brilliant scarlet neckerchief tied in loose sailor's knot; no waistcoat; knickerbockers, grey stockings, and the most serviceable laced boots, which evidently meant business in pedestrianism; crisp, curly, brownish hair, ignorant of parting; a fine brow, quick observant eyes, greyish—if I remember rightly;—beard and moustache, a trifle lighter than the hair. A splendid head, a memorable personality.
>
> Then . . . his absolutely boyish enjoyment of mere fun, of any pure and

simple absurdity. His laugh was something to hear; it was of short duration, but it was a roar; it set you off—nay, he himself, when much tickled, would laugh till he cried (it didn't take long to get to the crying), and then he would struggle with himself, hand to open mouth, to prevent another outburst.

Meredith was now well in with Bradbury and Evans, proprietors of *Punch* (then a journal with many radical touches), who issued *Once a Week*, with Samuel Lucas as an editor and with illustrations by the best artists of the day. Meredith's poems in it were illustrated by Tenniel, Phiz, Millais, Keene, Sandys; and he extended his acquaintance among the younger artists, especially with Sandys and Rossetti.

Bradbury and Evans had founded *Once a Week* after their break with Dickens, who dropped *Household Words* and went off to start *All the Year Round*. Meredith had not contributed to *Household Words* for some three years, so Lucas from the outset tried to draw him over. Meredith in his depression was afraid that he would be expected to write in a rollicking style, and said that he could not 'properly do facts on the broad grin, and the tricky style Dickens encouraged.' The first issue of *Once a Week* however had his poem *The Song of Courtesy*, and the staff of *All the Year Round*, scornfully watching the new periodical, seem to have made up special jokes about it, for Dickens wrote to his sub-editor, 'I have got your letter this morning, and Wilkie [Collins] and I have been much delighted by your account of Meredith's poem.'

Meredith himself was not very pleased with the issue and wrote a candid letter of criticism to Lucas, saying the items were too short and inconsequential. However, he contributed five more poems during the year.

But his literary earnings were slight; he had to turn to journalism in 1859. Next year he accepted a regular job with the Tory *Ipswich Journal*, writing a weekly letter; and became reader for Chapman and Hall. But even so he had to eke out his income by reading a couple of days a week to a strong-minded old woman at Eltham Lodge, who had translated Lucian but who found both his opinions and his way of stating them too unconventional; she was the sister of Kitty O'Shea, from whose bedroom Parnell's escape down a drainpipe later precipitated a political crisis.

George had also met the Duff-Gordons again. One day as Janet rode to the station, a small boy stumbled in front of her horse. She dismounted, and he told her his papa said little men shouldn't cry. When she took him to the house he pointed out, Meredith answered the door. 'Aren't you Lady Duff-Gordon's daughter?' He clasped her in his arms, 'O, my Janet, don't you know me? I'm your Poet.' That night he dined at Belvidere House, known as the Gordon Arms from its extensive hospitality.

Janet was now a lively handsome girl, with whom George fell in love, over-estimating the tolerance of the Duff-Gordons for a hard-up suitor. But for a while he was happy, going long walks with her or striding beside her cob and brandishing his stick to stress his points. 'The Black Pool in the firwoods was one of our favourite haunts. My Poet would recite poetry or talk about his novels. I made him write down some of the verses he improvised as we sat among the heather.' And she looked after Arthur and taught him German while George was in London.

She had been much flattered as a child. Thackeray drew pictures for her; Dickens told her the Seven Champions of Christendom was the world's most delightful book; Lord Lansdowne sent her a ticket for Macready's last performance, as Wolsey in *Henry VIII*, and offered her a fine Erard; she breakfasted with the banker-poet Rogers; she listened to young Joachim play the violin in his studio, and Watts was there to draw her head; she climbed on Macaulay's knee and said, 'Now talk'; she asked the Master of Trinity to stop her father talking because she couldn't get in a word; she told Carlyle not to be rude to her mama and she rode with him in Rotten Row when his wideawake was blown off and picked up by a worker who got in return, not sixpence, but the words, 'Thank ye, my man; ye can just say ye've picked up the hat of Thomas Carlyle.' To her fifth birthday came Thackeray, Doyle the artist, Tom Taylor, Mrs Norton; Thackeray gave her an oyster and she asked for two more. Heine at Boulogne told her tales of mermaids, watersprites, and a French fiddler and a poodle. Now she hunted rabbits with the Bourbon princes in exile at Claremont.

Once Meredith told her to do up his dusty shoe, and she bade him do it himself: papa said men ought to attend on women, not women on men. Then, sorry, she did up her Poet's shoelace. But he deceived himself if he thought he had tamed her; he was rather in the rôle of her dog that she had trained to pick up her whip or handkerchief.

Later she described the Esher days:

> The Austins had taken a long, low, rambling old house at Weybridge in Surrey, where we used to spend the summer months; but the house was too small for two families, and in the spring of 1851, my father took a house at Esher . . . nothing remarkable in itself, having been, I believe, an inn, with a small cottage near. The space between the two had been built over and made the dining-room and drawing-room, L shaped. But the house was full of quaint old furniture and china, and the pretty garden sloped upwards from the back of the house to Claremont Park palings. The view from the front windows was beautiful; the 'sluggish Mole' and Wolsey's tower in the foreground and Windsor Castle in the far distance. Many a merry boating party did we have on the Mole, with picnics in the wood, varied by now and then knocking a hole

in the bottom of the boat, on one of the many snags and hidden stumps of trees on which the river abounds. Once we lost all our wine, which was hung overboard to cool, and my father and Henry Phillips had to dive for it in very deep water. . . . The rides were most beautiful.

In the autumn of 1859, on the way to Oxshott, they found an old cottage all alone except for a near farm with no barrier between it and the common, with gorse and heather, pine and larch all round, and blue misty tracks converging on a little tree-fringed lake. Nearby was a mossy mound from which to view the stately forestland of Claremont. Meredith rented the cottage and wrote there *Evan Harrington, Modern Love, Sandra Belloni, Poems of the Roadside.*

At Copsham Cottage he thus matured his novel-method and his poetry. The common was the resort of beggars, gypsies, tramps, with whom he liked chatting and from whom he drew a feeling of independent common life:

> The result of hard education since the publication of my boy's book in '51 (those poems were written before I was twenty) has been that I rarely write save from the suggestion of something actually observed. I mean, that I rarely write verse. Thus my Jugglers, Beggars, etc., I have met on the road, and have idealized but slightly. I desire to strike the poetic spark out of absolute human clay. And in doing so I have a fancy that I do solid work—better than a carol in mid air. Note the Old Chartist, and the Patriot Engineer, that will also appear in *Once a Week.* They may not please you, but I think you will admit that they have a truth condensed in them. They are flints, perhaps, and not flowers. . . .
> It may be, that in a year or two I shall find time for a full sustained song. Of course I do not think of binding down the Muse to the study of facts. That is but a part of her work. The worst is, that having taken to those delineations of character and life, one's affections are divided. I have now a prose damsel crying out to me [Sandra], to have her history completed; and the creatures of a novel are bubbling up; and in truth, being a servant of the public, I must wait till my master commands before I take seriously to singing.

A new realistic grasp is being confidently achieved. He wrote to Kate Vulliamy in October 1863, 'As to my walking back at night: I am an associate with owls and nightjars, tramps and tinkers who teach me nature and talk human nature to me.' The first Copsham autumn saw the composition of *Ode to the Spirit of Earth in Autumn* and *Autumn Evensong.* Between his talks with the commonfolk in lane and wood, and Janet's restoration of his self-respect, he felt his earth-roots once more firm, sap-tingling; and though it was a blow when he realised Janet would never be his, he was by then over the worst of his break with Mary.

Janet, late in life, re-read his letters and cried, 'Good God! my poet must have been in love with me.' But that was just part of playing the

conventional game. She wasn't such a fool as all that. Among her papers
were things like the following poem of early Copsham days:

> *We sat beneath the humming pines:*
> *We knew that we must part.*
> *I might not even speak by signs*
> *The motions of my heart.*
>
> *And as I took your hand, and gazed*
> *Subdued into your eyes,*
> *I saw the arm of Fate upraised,—*
> *And stilled the inward cries.*
>
> *I saw that this could never be*
> *Which I had dared to pray:*
> *And in the tear that fell from me,*
> *There fell my life that day.*

Not to mention the lyric, 'Sing aloud that she is mine,' or quatrains with
lines like, 'The chambers of my heart are many, dear, you must not know
in which you sit enthroned,' or such tender murmurings as:

> *Night walks the earth with silver feet,*
> *The upper sky shines cold as steel.*
> *I would I were with you, my sweet,*
> *To tell you what I feel.*

Or the *Addio* on the loss of the beloved, for music by Schubert.

In the tear in which he says his life fell, what actually fell was the
remnant of his social illusions.

Janet of course married a rich man, a banker of Alexandria, twenty
years her senior, who had charmed her with stories of pig-sticking, with
'his admirable wit, his pleasant conversation, and his kindly ways.' And
Meredith of course wrote to her, 'He's a lucky fellow to get you,' but
could not help adding, 'Not that you're romantic, and I don't suppose
you flutter vastly just when you are caught, but still, dear Orange
Blossom, you're a bit of a bird, like the rest.' His true opinion of Henry
Ross is presumably to be read in his picture of Laxley in *Evan*, a well-
bred lout who certainly had a pig among his ancestors. And he could
not have been very sorry when Ross lost his money and Janet had to
keep him.

But at the moment he was hard-hit. When the marriage came off in
October 1860, he lay stricken in bed:

> On the Earth I lie, and imagination will picture the idea that I am going
> under it. Here is a cheerful theme to address to a sweet young bride! But if I
> am not better by Saturday I shall not witness the wreath on my Janet's head,
> nor see the fixing of the ring on her hand.

And when, married, she sent her photo, he replied:

> It admirably represents the occasion. Looking on it, I see the corpse of the
> Maiden Janet. Just what she may henceforth give of herself, and no more. It
> isn't bad, it's pleasant to have, but it's Janet washed out and decorated with
> soot. Behind it lies her free youth. She looks darkly forward on the children
> of Egypt. It's Janet half Copt already.

Into *Evan Harrington* he put all the revulsions and hopes of his relations
with the Maiden Janet. He summoned up his Portsmouth past and savagely
criticised it; and though, to end the novel, he used the romantic formula
of love triumphant with a bag of gold, in the process he had bitterly
criticised the illusion that there was anything morally good in the effort
to rise in the class-world by accepting that world's values.

Janet helped him to gain assurance, reading chapters and pointing out
social errors (though she missed several, e.g. a Duke addressed as My
Lord). She was the heroine Rose; and when she felt Rose was getting out
of character, she commented, 'I should never have said it like this.'

The novel was first published as a book in the U.S.A. in 1860, where
Meredith hoped its anti-aristocratic tone would recommend it; but it
failed and was remaindered. Serialised in *Once a Week* from February to
October 1859, it was written under the pressure of monthly instalments,
to fill a gap caused by Reade withdrawing his *Good Fight* (revised as *The
Cloister and the Hearth*); perhaps for this reason Meredith's closest approxi-
mation to Dickensian gusto and broad characterisation. But he felt the
strain. 'Try to spur me on without giving me the sense that I am absolutely
due,' he wrote to the editor; 'for then I shall feel hunted, and may take
strange leaps.' Lucas asked him to simplify the narrative, and he answered,
'This cursed desire I have haunting me to show the reason for things is a
perpetual obstruction to movement. I do want the dash of Smollett and
know it.' He felt he was disappointing the readers; the novel was accused
of dullness and may have lowered the magazine's circulation, though
Dickens admired it. 'It is finished,' wrote Meredith, 'as an actor finishes
under hisses.' In January 1851 the novel came out in book form in
London. *The Spectator* thought the author's humour was fining down as
he grew older; *The Athenaeum* thought the novel not worth reviewing;
The Examiner in a few casual words mentioned shrewd sketches of
character. *The Saturday Review*, taking the theme to be Tailordom in the
Clouds, of which there was too much, summed the work up as deserving
'a front place in the literature that is ranked as avowedly not destined to
endure.' And so this book of brilliant and flowing narrative, with its
clear social satire, was shrugged aside in criticisms that heaped up praise

on trivial and false works.* Only John Morley, a youth of twenty-two, writing in an unimportant periodical, saw it as an important novel.

The titles considered bring out plainly enough what was in Meredith's mind: The Substantial and the Essential, Shams and Realities, All but a Gentleman, The Taylor's Family, Gentle and Genteel, The Gentleman-Tailor's Family, Gentility and a Gentleman. He finally selected *Evan Harrington; or, He would be a Gentleman*.

The new middle-class were much concerned with the question of what constituted gentility. The argument indeed goes back to medieval days: 'Who was then the gentleman?' There we get the stark rebellion against privilege-by-birth; but already in the seventeenth century come moralisations that seek to extend the notion of Gentleman, e.g. when Decker calls Christ a Gentleman. Such moralisations proliferated after 1850, finding their typical form in Miss Mullock's very popular *John Halifax Gentleman* of 1856, which tries to take over the term for the rising members of the thrifty industrialist class. Ruskin moralised at length on the subject in the fifth volume of *Modern Painters*, calling sensitiveness, sympathy, self-command gentlemanly, while rating callousness, meanness, suspicion, indifference to the interests of others as vulgarity. He denied that Gentlemanliness had anything to do with birth or blood, but sternly attributed vulgarity to those of 'inferior stations' who aped ways and clothes 'unsuited' to them. That is, at this stage of his development, he defended the right of the middle class to share in feudal privilege, but wanted to keep out the workers.

Newman in his *Idea of a University* maundered in the same way at considerable length, defining good-breeding as a refusal to inflict pain—but the gentleman remembers what is due to himself as well as to others! The climax of blinkered class-smugness was, however, attained by T. H. Green who ended his address at the opening of the Oxford High School:

> As it was the aspiration of Moses that all the Lord's people should be prophets, so with all seriousness and reverence we may hope and pray for a condition of English society in which all honest citizens will recognise themselves and be recognised by others as gentlemen.

---

* The memory of the attacks on *Feverel* appears in his remarks to the publishers, 'Perhaps, should it be needful, you may say that we are going to be guilty of no impropriety in this tale, and will never again offend young maids.' And in the novel itself, when the Countess begins seducing her brother-in-law, 'The small beginnings' of forbidden sexual behaviour 'are so easily slid over. But what is the use of telling this to a pure generation? My constant error is in supposing that I write for the wicked people who begat us.' (Compare Dickens' complaints, expressed in his remarks on Mrs Marshall and Podsnap.)

The frankness of the servant-girls is contrasted with the hypocrisy of their masters (at whom, it is known, they look with the licence of cats towards kings); and Dorothy's fresh careless mouth had told how one observant maid, amorously inclined, proclaimed of Evan, to a companion of her sex, that 'he was the only gentleman who gave you an idea of how he would look when he was kissing you.'

This is the background of *Evan Harrington*.

Meredith mercilessly draws on his Portsmouth past for the material. Evan, son of the Great Mel, has visited his sister the Countess de Saldar in Portugal, where he meets the Jocelyns. Taken for a Gentleman, he is invited to their home, Beckley House; but on landing in England he learns of his father's death and returns to Lymport (Portsmouth). He proudly takes responsibility for the family-debts and gives in to his mother's insistence that he must become a tailor. The Countess, however, keeps scheming to marry him off well, and he succumbs to her snares, visits the Jocelyns and woos Rose Jocelyn. The Countess involves her sisters (one married to a brewer, one to an officer of Marines) and sets off a complicated set of intrigues to advance the family. She meets continual threats of exposure with skill and determination, but is finally beaten. Evan meanwhile decides to tell Rose the truth; but though she is now enough in love to overlook his tailordom (his fortunes have been supported by the rich eccentric brother of the brewer), he takes on himself the responsibility for one of the Countess's treacherous acts and breaks away. In the end he is left Beckley House, which has been inherited by a crippled girl who adores him. He magnanimously returns it to the Jocelyns, and he and Rose come together after all.

A summary cannot suggest the magnificently sustained comedy of the Countess's intrigues and struggles. Absolutely unscrupulous, an abysmal liar ready to use her physical charms for social ends and almost admirable in her buoyant determination, she embodies supremely the maniacal snobbery of the Victorian bourgeoisie, the subordination of all human realities to class-aims. She it is who stands out throughout the book, overlife-size, a rich comedic type. The landed aristocrats, the Jocelyns and their friends, dwindle before her gigantic pettiness into trivial or coarse parasites; and she looms up as the emblem of the class-force from which they draw their minor meanings. The way in which the Jocelyns' opposition to Evan crumbles when they learn of his cash-prospects is the final touch sealing them as animalcules in a bourgeois universe ruled by the Countess. Indeed, in her exposure of the class-principles she champions, she becomes the involuntary avenging-angel of democracy:

> Accept in the Countess the heroine who is combating class-prejudice, and surely she is pre-eminently noteworthy. True, she fights only for her family, and is virtually the champion of the opposing institution misplaced. That does not matter: the Fates may have done it purposely: by conquering she establishes a principle. [xxx.]

After suffering the final humiliation of being caught in the act of seducing her brewer brother-in-law, whom she scorns for his democratic

spirit, she retires to Rome and Catholicism. The importance laid by
Meredith on this conclusion is shown by his making her letter on the
subject the last chapter, rounding off his theme. Baffled, she goes to what
Meredith considers the worst reactionary forces in the world. The bourgeoisie, cornered, make an alliance with the feudal enemy to preserve a
class-world:

> We shall yet have an ambassadress at Rome—mark your Louisa's words.
> Yes, dearest: I am here, body and spirit. . . . I *know* it is impossible for the
> Protestant heresy to offer a shade of consolation. . . . It is the sweet sovereign
> Pontiff alone who gathers all in his arms, not excepting tailors. . . . It is
> utterly impossible for a man to be a true gentleman who is not of the true
> Church.

It is amusing that Meredith here forecasts even the correct factual details: for the real Louisa's daughter, as we noted, became the first Portuguese Ambassadress at the Vatican, while other countries still had only
legations, some ten years later than *Evan Harrington*.

His aunt Harriet is treated as unkindly as Louisa, depicted as being as
snobbish, though lacking her sister's demoniac energy. Catherine, however, is shown loving and good-natured, but too weak to resist Louisa
and martyred by a vicious husband. Her grandson protested against
Meredith's picture of the Ellis household (here the Strikes); for Strike
(S. B. Ellis) is not only a snob, a martinet, a brutal domineering man, but
also a scoundrel who accepts his wife's ducal liaison while it is financially
profitable, and who becomes an outraged husband only when the Duke
finds out his business-malpractices. Meredith is here recalling S. B. Ellis's
rôle as director of a company running the Direct Exeter and Plymouth
Railway, which failed in 1852 and sapped his income for several years as
well as carrying off his savings. Meredith himself may have had his
inherited money drawn into the investment; for he tells of a trustee who
'by fraud or folly squandered the little estate' he held. In any event he
shows the most utter contempt of the gallant officer of Marines who
fought the Chinese and became Knight Commander of the Bath.

His father Augustus felt heavily aggrieved. In 1860 a friend found him
depressed; and Augustus, generally uncommunicative, blurted out his
grief over the serial. 'I am pained beyond expression, as I consider it
aimed at myself, and I am sorry to say the writer is my own son.'

Lady Jocelyn is given something of Lady Duff-Gordon's readiness
(within certain definite class-limits) to take people on their merits; but
Meredith cannot help getting in a blow at Duff-Gordon superiorities
through the Countess, who accuses Lady Jocelyn of radicalism and suggests that she must have some low origin. For the Taylors, Lady D.-C.'s

maternal family, had been Norwich millers—and were they then so much better than Portsmouth tailors?

Rose (Janet) is a sort of dream-sketch of what was to be later the full portrait of the New Woman, who, retaining all her femininity, fights uncompromisingly for equality, comradeship, human dignity. She says to Evan on their arrival in England, unsentimentally, refusing to be sad:

> Won't you promise me to come and stop with us for weeks? Haven't you said we would ride and hunt and fish together and read books and do all sorts of things? . . . You can't suppose we could ever see each other every day for ever?

And she refuses to lose her sense of worth as a social being when she does fall in love. 'With Rose love will be fullgrown when it is once avowed, and will know where to go to be nourished'; she 'would not abandon her friends, because she accepted a lover.' (Later, however, Meredith recognised that he had given Rose a simple frankness and honesty which was incompatible with her class-position, and he drew Janet Ilchester, closer to the facts of Janet Ross. And when he came to show how a well-off girl achieved frankness and honesty, as in the case of Nesta Radnor, he defined with subtle fullness the complex struggle through which she had to go in throwing off her inbred illusions and misconceptions.)

The other inhabitants of the upper levels of society are shown as superficial, loutish, useless; and against them are set the two brewer-brothers, who have the sturdy directness of the early industrialist entrepreneur, thinking in man-to-man terms and seeing productive activity as something distinct from, and even opposed to, the finance-system, the cash-nexus. The unmarried brother is depicted as a rough-and-ready anti-aristocratic radical of the 1830 days.

Raikes is a sort of parody of Evan's snob-elements:

> Though he worshipped a coronet and would gladly have recalled the feudal times to a corrupt land, [he] could not help thinking that his cravat now had beaten the Duke's and was better. He would rather not have thought so, for it upset his preconceptions and threatened a revolution in his ideas.

But it is in Evan that the full struggle is fought out; and in his growing abhorrence of all his sister Louisa stands for, he represents the spirit of honesty, the world of honest work opposed to the world of parasitism and exploitation. Gradually he confronts the truth of things. First, with a turmoil of confusions, self-deceptions, compromises. His father's death strikes coldly through his fantasy-world and compels his first stand. But he still oscillates between an acceptance of the common world and the desire to be a gentleman. The account of the drive from London to the funeral excellently brings out his conflict: he meditates on Love and Death, sets a halo round his father's Tailordom, looks down on the scornful world; then, finding he lacks money to pay the driver, is dominated by false pride. Similarly, he attitudinises before Rose, then recoils into self-criticism. 'From a vague sense of being an imposter he awoke to the fact that he was likewise a fool.' He takes on his father's debts through a sense of *noblesse oblige*, then finds his lordly pose has involved him in everything least aristocratic. Yet with all his failings and fallings he keeps on learning; and when at last he stubbornly takes on himself the Countess's actions in order to right a wrongly-accused person (who is all the same a despicable well-born lout), his pride and bitterness have totally changed their orientation. Now they are sharply set against the world of power and privilege into which he had sought to enter; they lock him solidly in with the world of work which he previously despised. They express fundamentally a class-antagonism; for though his proud sense of honour uses the gentlemanly idiom, in practice it sets him against the world of actual gentlemen and sends him back to his origins in the world of work. His rejection of the Beckley estate is the correct expression of his new position.

But Meredith still feels unable to work out the direct political consequences of such a position. Besides, the dream-picture of Rose forbids it, based in the delusion that such girls as Janet have a genuine spirit of independence (the delusion slaughtered in *The Tragic Comedians*). So he falls back on the reconciliation-formula and blurs out the conflicts he has defined, under the romantic solution which seeks dishonestly to make the best of both class-worlds.

Still, the whole bias of the book, with its ruthless picture of Louisa and its honest analysis of Evan's struggles, runs counter to the concluding evasion. (He already sets out his notion of Time as a living dialectical principle of growth, which men must grasp in its wholeness, so that they may purposively inhabit the present while re-concentrating the past and projecting the future.)

11a.

The Political Situation

WHEN I CALL Meredith a political novelist, I do not mean that he habitually deals with the externals of politics, parliamentary elections and the like. I mean that the central focus of each of his works implies a considered judgment, based in political economy, of the fundamental forces determining the general movement of society. The personal struggles of his characters are always seen within this general movement.

We must therefore grasp the main lines of the political-economy situation in post-1850 Britain, when the mass-struggles of Chartism had collapsed and the bourgeoisie were triumphantly expanding into world-supremacy in trade and industry.

Not only did the workers turn to 'practical' problems, but the very rejection of the higher aims [of Chartist days] were extolled as the sublimest wisdom. All the Lovetts, Holyoakes, Coopers and others, who even before had not felt quite at home in the revolutionary movement, now became the advocates of small deeds and humble virtues, and their voices met with a lively response among the wide masses of the proletariat, tired and weary, bleeding from a thousand wounds. This, we say, is the usual corollary of post-revolutionary periods: between the defeat and the rallying of new forces for the resumption of the struggle there lies a period of moral and even physical depression.

But in England this period was protracted for a whole half-century. . . . As against the position of the working class of other countries in similar circumstances, the English proletariat did not find itself isolated, but became the centre of the attention of bourgeois reformers who quite correctly realised their mission: when the workers grew disappointed with the revolutionary struggle, these reformers showered their 'love' on them, built a moral bridge between them and the capitalist class, enabled them to reorganise upon a new platform, compelled the capitalist class to yield a little to the workers' demands in regard to wages, working hours and working conditions in general, and since that period happened to coincide with a spell of great industrial prosperity, from which some crumbs would in any case have accrued to the workers, the ideas preached by the reformers struck deep roots among the masses and became an integral part of the mental outlook of the English proletariat.

The distinguishing feature of this mental outlook was acceptance of capitalist society, which acceptance found its expression in the rejection of political action, and in the recognition of the teachings of vulgar political economy of the harmony of interests as between the employing and the working class. [T. Rothstein.]

The 1850's saw an expansion in all branches of British industry and trade. Take Lancashire cotton-goods. There had been a steady decline in wages after 1810 on to 1840; then things were stationary for ten years; then after 1855 wages rose and by 1874 reached a level held till 1886. This pattern is fairly typical. The first half of the century saw a continual fall in wages; then came a gradual rise up to the mid-1870's. Even when the rise only meant a rise back to the levels prevailing in the earlier century, it was felt as an advance.

At first there came a burst of hopes in a *laissez-faire* world-utopia of peace and plenty, expressed by the middle-class but penetrating the working-class. The first event which on a large scale exposed the falsity of any hopes of peace and brotherhood through capitalist expansion was the Crimean War, 1855. This war came up as a prompt and violent retort to the fantasies born of the Great Exhibition of 1851; and the utopians had to surrender their fantasies or blame the aristocracy, as if the latter were still the dominant force in the State.

Dickens expressed the reaction of those with true insight. 'I feel as if the world had been pushed back five hundred years.' The people, tricked and cheated again into war-passions, were to be lured to sing 'their own deathsong in Rule Britannia and allow their own wrongs and sufferings to be obscured by cannon-smoke and blood-mists!'*

Meredith does not seem to have reacted at once with such a comprehension. 1855–6 was the period of his broken marriage and the wrestlings with *Feverel*. But the war left its mark on him, and his work reveals his steady movement into realisation of the distorting and brutalising factors in the expansion of trade and industry which he had hailed in 1851–2.

The problem was to carry on the ideas of 1848, of Chartism and the National Liberation movements, in the difficult situation in which 1851 and 1855 were landmarks. But to carry on those ideas meant to develop them in terms of the new situation, and this Meredith did, with many confusions and meanderings, but without ever losing the main trail. I have cited above a passage which stresses the passivity of the British people, the workers, after 1850; but it gives only half the picture. In the depths,

---

* Note the transformation of Muscular and 'Socialist' Christianity into Imperial Brutality in 1855. Kingsley shows in *Two Years Ago* the 'regeneration' of middle-class Britain by the War—with the New Poet (Elsley Vavasour, alias Briggs) out of it. Hughes in *Tom Brown's Schooldays*, 1856, wrote, 'I am dead against your peace, when there is no peace, and isn't meant to be' (the usual transfer of emotions of social struggle to war-effort). and G. A. Lawrence took up the job directly and unashamedly in a series of novels starting with *Guy Livingstone*, 1857. (Lawrence tried to get off to fight for the slave-South in the Civil War but was caught by the Northerners.) His hero Guy was finely burlesqued by Bret Harte's *Guy Heavystone*. Lawrence depicts barbarous fighting heroes, and defended the duel. Wilkie Collins in *Man and Wife*, 1870, tried to show the link between the sports-passion and the inhumanity to women.

new consolidations of resistance were going on, most directly manifested in the steady and stable growth of trade-unionism, leading to the T.U.C. and its Parliamentary Committee. We may note too the strong and clear concern of the workers about international events such as the American Civil War, their welcome to Mazzini, their unabated interest in struggles of the Polish and Hungarian people, their widening share in the fight for democracy (e.g. in the Hyde Park demonstration of 1866). Meredith's interests and attitudes will be found throughout the years to be closely linked with those of the advanced sections of the working-class. And in his poem *The Old Chartist* he shows clearly his grasp of the changes and new kinds of consolidation going on among the workers.

He called himself a *Radical*, and we must grasp clearly what the term implied. The Radicals were at first the left wing of the Whigs; Charles Fox seems to have originated the term, in 1797 declaring for a Radical Reform. Radical came to mean a fighter for thorough Parliamentary reform, whether middle-class like Sir Francis Burdett or working-class like the rebel Carlile. After the Reform Bill of 1832 the radical basis narrowed; the radicals were men like F. Place and J. Parkes who wanted the franchise extended to the workers and who after 1835 played an active part in the reformed administration of the towns. They carried out a campaign against waste and corruption, but split off from the workers by their support of the savage Poor Law of 1834. They were afraid of the mass-revolutionary element in Chartism. But when Chartism collapsed, they gained a new lease of life; for they were now the only organised groups through whom anything like an effective political struggle against the worst aspects of the cash-nexus triumph could be carried on. They combined such sections of small-producers, industrialists, traders, artisans, as were opposed to the growth of big-business and its State, with various proletarian sections still in part merged with the petty-bourgeois but also moving towards their own specific forms of class-consciousness and struggle.*

---

* This formulation is not exact. For Chartism itself was *a form of Radicalism*, all its aims being radical; what constituted the difference between Chartism and Radicalism as here treated was rather a variation in method and temper—though ultimately behind the variations lay different class-elements. This variation expressed itself inside Chartism in the debates of the moral-force and the physical-force sections; and the government rightly feared the mass-element in Chartism as revolutionary, since, having gained its radical points of parliamentary reform, it would clearly have used political power to bring about widespread social changes leading to a definite clash with the State and the new ruling-class of capitalists. After 1848 the revolutionary pressure subsided; and Radicalism minus any such pressure became the only form in which proletarian and middle-class progressive elements could express themselves. For decades the regathering mass-forces fitted within the radical mould; but with the new militant unionism that arose from the 1880's and the first bases of the Labour Party, that mould was ruptured.

The National Reform League, led by Edmond Beesly, Marx's friend, fought for extensions of the franchise, which were won for the towns in 1867 and for the country in 1884. Men like F. Harrison, J. S. Mill, Beesley played important parts in the new radicalism, and through the group of officials called the Junta the radicals had complete political control of the Trade Unions. Between 1874 and 1892 every trade-unionist gaining a parliamentary seat fought as a radical. *Reynolds Illustrated News* was the popular radical journal, with a programme of vehement Republicanism, repudiation of revealed or institutional religion, and championship in general of *laissez-faire* and free-trade. Towards the end of the century the London Radical Clubs were probably the most powerful of organised political groupings in Britain. Under Bradlaugh's pressure they then dissolved into the National Liberal Federation, but not before they had played a key-part in the founding of the new Labour Party.

The Radicals in the half-century after the fall of Chartism were thus the only effective group in whom remnants of the revolutionary policies of the 1840's were carried on, and in whom the working-class could regather its shattered energies of resistance. Riddled with liberal ideas, they yet provided a school for the primary consolidation of a socialist outlook.

The variety of trends in this radicalism must then be stressed. The republicanism and the defiant rationalism were directly inherited from the most vigorous sections of working-class thought in the 1800-50 period; while the *laissez-faire* reformism brought the movement into conformity with the bourgeois State. Take for instance this picture of the middle-class Radicals by Gissing in *Born in Exile* (published 1893 but in the cited passage referring to 1874):

> The robust employers of labour (in a Midlands town) . . . were for the most part avowed Radicals, in theory scornful of privileges, practically supporters of that mode of freedom which regards life as a remorseless conflict. . . . The note of the assembly was something other than refinement; rather, its high standard of health, spirit and comfort—the characteristic of Capitalism. Decent reverence for learning, keen appreciation of scientific power, warm liberality of thought and sentiment within appreciable limits, enthusiasm for economic, civil, national ideals—such attributes were abundantly discoverable in each serried row. From the expanse of countenances beamed a boundless self-satisfaction.

In speaking of the characteristics of the capitalism of his day, he means the gifts of capitalists to themselves; nobody depicted with more naturalistic horror what were the characteristics developed among the exploited. Gissing here tries to give the Devil his due, to state such solid virtues as existed among the progressive middle-class. His manufacturers were the right-wing of radicalism, which was soon to lose its virtues and to sink flatly into a vacillating liberalism or a moribund conservatism.

Now for the left wing. Here are some definitions given by Andrieu in *The Fortnightly* of 1871 (and thus generally accepted by its editor Morley). The statement is all the more interesting in that it is made during the attempt to reassess radical principles precipitated by the Paris Commune.

> Radical is not and cannot be any mind, however well-intentioned, that holds it possible to conduct the social state to perfection without a shock, by means of a slow and progressive modification. Radical is he that holds, on the contrary, the firm conviction that the present political and social systems are false, and that gradual reforms and ameliorations therein can at best be like local remedies which in the long run aggravate the disease.

The radical, however, is not 'a professional revolutionist, instinctive conspirator, born demolisher.' He takes 'his starting-point from the conditions of the present.' He 'demolishes, but he replaces.' He conspires only when repression has broken the right of association.

Here we see the persistent though unstable revolutionary element in radicalism, which moves unsteadily towards socialism. Though the efficacy of gradualism is denied, the lack of any precise concept of means and ends ensures that in practice there will be a tendency to confused compromise, and that finally, as conflict sharpens, even left-wing radicalism will swing to defence of the established positions rather than maintain a demand for radical change—unless a definite shift to socialist aims and strategy is made.

As a left-wing Radical Meredith was thus affirming his loyalty to the principles of 1848 and his adherence to the only groupings in his world that carried on something of those principles and enabled the first regrouping of the mass-forces. There was no question of a formal acceptance of radical ideas (their fluid condition made such an acceptance in any event meaningless): in particular no acceptance of the liberal dogmas that ruled in the right-wing. Throughout his work there is no word in favour of free trade and *laissez-faire*; on the contrary he always stresses the inner contradictions of such slogans. Radicalism meant for him the stand for as many of the revolutionary ideas of 1848 as the situation made practicable, the continual criticism of the existing State in terms of those ideas, and the struggle towards a future in which freedom and brotherhood could be wholly realised.

Inevitably there were confusions, compromises; but so keen and concrete was his grasp of the relations between the immediate limited objective and the ultimate goal that he never went far wrong, and always regained his central balance after moments of distraction and weakening.

The worst and the best in him may be exemplified thus. In 1861 the Northerners of the U.S.A. seized from a British ship some Southern envoys on their way to Europe. A wave of indignation rose in the middle and upper-classes in Britain, with even a demand for war against the Northern States. Meredith wrote stupidly in a letter about the resolute calm, the unanimity, with which the crisis was being faced. But he soon realised that it wasn't the 'nation' at all which had been provoked; it was only a ruling-class who took on themselves to speak for the people they morally and physically gagged.

In 1867 in *Lines to a Friend* (Morley) *Visiting America*, he sets out this realisation. The U.S.A., he says, are at a dangerous moment of development, they 'may bless or curse mankind: they have the right.' The British have 'let the blunderers and the wave divide us, and the Devil had sport.' Can a true friendship and fellowship be built up between the two peoples? The Americans have done many magnificent and adventurous things, but the English don't know them, and as for the Americans:

> *Themselves they know not, save that strong*
> *For good and evil still they grow.*

Neither do the Americans know the English people. The England that they hear speak in the Press is not the real Britain.

> *It is not England that they hear,*
> *But mighty Mammon's pipers, trained*
> *To trumpet out his moods, and stir*
> *His sluggish soul: her voice is chained.*

England may indeed in such a mirror seem moribund, torn by the panics of capitalist crisis—

> *That haunting spectre of success*
> *Which shows a hearth sunk low in the girths.*

It is not the true England, the people, who act so vilely:

> *Not she, when struggling manhood tries*
> *For freedom, air, a hopefuller fate,*
> *Points out the planet, Compromise,*
> *And shakes a mild reproving pate:*

> *Says never: 'I am well at ease,*
> *My sneers upon the weak I shed:*
> *The strong have my cajoleries:*
> *And those beneath my feet I tread.'*

It is not the true England that hypocritically talks of peace and wants everyone else to sheathe the sword, 'herself not yielding what it won.'

It is not the true England that at cock-crow preaches her sermon 'on sweet Prosperity—or greed.'

> '*Lo! as the beasts feed, each for each,*
> *God's blessings let us take, and feed.*'

> *Ungrateful creatures crave a part—*
> *She tells them firmly she is full;*
> *Lest sheared sheep hurt her tender heart*
> *With bleating, stop her ears with wool:—*

> *Seized sometimes by prodigious qualms*
> *(Nightmares of bankruptcy and death),—*
> *Showers down in lumps a load of alms,*
> *Then pants as one who has lost a breath.*

It was not the true England who watched sidelong, sneering, the war against slavery in the States and tried to perpetuate the division. No, a monstrous semblance mocks the soul of the true nation:

> *A false majority, by stealth,*
> *Have got her fast, and sway the rod:*
> *A headless tyrant built of wealth,*
> *The hypocrite, the belly-God.*

> *To him the daily hymns they raise:*
> *His tastes are sought: his will is done:*
> *He sniffs the putrid steam of praise,*
> *Place for true England here is none!*

How can the people of the States, from their distance, tell the difference between the true England of the masses and the false England of the capitalist? Certainly not by listening to the ravings of Carlyle who has recently 'called for power.'

> *I love him; but his mountain prose—*
> *His Alp and valley and wild flower—*
> *Proclaimed our weakness, not its source.*
> *What medicine for disease had he?*
> *Whom summoned for a show of force?*
> *Our titular aristocracy!*

> *Why, these are great as City feasts;*
> *From City riches mainly rise:*
> *'Tis well to hear them, when the beasts*
> *That die for us they eulogise!*

These aristocrats are, in fact, the merest puppets of the capitalist's power:

> *Of all the liveried crew*
> *Obeisant in Mammon's walk,*
> *Most deferent ply the facial screw,*
> *The spinal bend, submissive talk.*

He admits that he too once had illusions and thought that the aristocrats might give a magnanimous lead. But now he knows better. They are not a separate class-force; they are sold out to the capitalists, who alone wield power.

> *When fainting heroes beg for bread*
> *They groan: where they are driven they go.*

(Meredith refers to Carlyle's essay, *Shooting Niagara, and After*, recently published, in which sympathy was expressed for the slave-owners of the Southern States and for the landed aristocracy of Britain. The slave-owners and the nobles, it said, are the natural leaders who had been villainously displaced.)

And so Meredith ends his poem with good wishes to his friend, and the hope of fellowship between the British and American peoples for the overthrow of the 'heartless tyrant built of wealth, the hypocrite.'

> *Adieu! bring back a braver dawn*
> *To England, and to me your friend.*

The contrast between the confusion of 1861 and the fierce clarity of the 1867 poem is typical of Meredith's development. Because of the bad period through which he struggles, which isolates him and prevents his idea of mass-action from owning any basis in mass-struggle, he cannot wholly stabilise the realisation that burns in the poem; and yet he never forgets it, he keeps on bringing it forward as the touchstone of reality.*

---

* Meredith in remaining true to the deep going elements of criticism in the early Carlyle continued to express the people's developing consciousness born of struggle; Carlyle, unable to believe in the working class, provided the basis for the New Toryism, the positions developed by Disraeli into full-blown imperialism. The creation of anti-democratic systems out of what began as a critique of capitalism is in one aspect a specially English matter. It deserves more attention than I can give it here, though throughout I am in one sense dealing with it— since I attempt to show how Meredith's development is a ceaseless fight against the reactionary positions elaborated out of the backward-looking elements in Romanticism, and a ceaseless fight to clarify and extend the soundly-based elements of the romantic revolt and its critique.

12

Italy and More Poems

In the 1860's he was in his forties, maturely expanding his philosophic conclusions with an increased realistic grip. He set himself the task of rejecting the romantic formula and defining the types who refuse compromise, the revolutionaries of his world, Beauchamp in England and Sandra-Vittoria in Italy. This step is what marks him as a great writer, realising what lines of development literature needs if it is to break through the fettering bonds of the society of the cash-nexus. He reaches consciously ahead to the lines that were to emerge with full coherence and force in Gorky; and he alone of European writers does so.

Augustus Jessop, headmaster of Norwich Grammar School, wrote praising his poems. 'He says the "Enchantress" scene in Rd. Feverel made him ill for 24 hours: and that he and his friends (Cambridge men) rank me next to Tennyson in poetic power: and so forth.' He'd always wanted to meet three men, Bunsen, Humboldt, Meredith. Meredith replied that he had failed to realise his early ambitions through lack of encouragement, through disordered health and nerves, but hoped to do better with improved health and more independence. And asked Jessop to visit his humble cottage where the cooking at least was good. (His housekeeper was Miss Grange, from whose father he rented his rooms: an invaluable and sensible person, he said, with excellent tongue, tireless energy, and no sex.)

> *Pale the rain-rutted roadways shine*
> *In the green light*
> *Behind the cedar and the pine:*
> *Come thundering night!*
> *Blacken broad earth with hoards of storm:*
> *For me yon valley-cottage beckons warm.*

'My cottage has very much the appearance of a natural product of the common on which it stands.'

Jessop came in December 1861: a kindly man, a keen antiquarian, and, for a parson-schoolmaster of the time, tolerantly unconventional. Meredith liked him and thanked him for the bouncing quality of his praise, but often could not resist mild digs at his religious beliefs.

Fred Chapman the publisher had a cottage by the Mole near Esher Palace; and there was always Maxse. But Meredith had now gained many new friends, Bonaparte Wyse, William Hardman, James Cotter Morison, Lionel Robinson, John Morley, all of whom contributed to his intellectual development.

Wyse, born in 1826, was a grand-nephew of Napoleon I; his father had married Letitia, daughter of Prince Lucien Bonaparte. He was a poet, who chancing on the work of the Provençal school, took to composing in Provençal himself, became friendly with Mistral, and earned a fraternal hail from Hugo. He met Meredith early in 1861 and became one of his walking companions, expected to rush over from Guildford at any tidings of nightingales and getting reproachful doggerel when he failed to turn up.

> I laughed at jests profane to quote,
> I and my Bonaparte Wyse.
> We cracked our jokes improper to quote,
> I and my Bonaparte Wyse.

In high spirits, Meredith read the end of Keats' *Endymion* at the place of its penning, the Vale of Mickleham. 'A new man. I am now bathed anew in the Pierian Fount. I cannot prose.' He summons Wyse:

> The cuckoo has been heard. And through the gates of his twin notes we enter the heart of spring. We will have rare poetizing, no laughter, no base cynical scorn, but all honest uplifting of the body and soul of us to the calm-flowing central Fire of things. Even so, my friend.

His doctor forbade work and tobacco and advised two months' holiday, preferably with glacier-air; and he decided to join Wyse who had gone on a tour of France and Italy in May. He solved the problem of Arthur by taking him along. They landed in Ostend, where they watched peasants picking periwinkles, and then went down the Rhine. In July they were at Zürich, moved on to Munich and Innsbruck, stopped at Meran in the Tyrol. Arthur, tended by Mrs Wyse, collected beetles and butterflies, while Meredith walked thirty miles a day. Wyse, ready for Surrey rambles, blenched at continual long-distances; he found excuses in rain or the chance of it, the heat, the coming-on of night. And he didn't like early rising. 'And he's rather excitable. But still thoroughly kindly and good.'

Wyse's backslidings, however, couldn't spoil Meredith's delight in the Alps, which henceforth haunted his writings. His glad tidings to Maxse will serve to show how they affected him:

> Nothing can be grander than the colossal mountains of porphyry and dolomite shining purple and rosy, snow-capped here and there, with some tumultuous river noising below, and that eternal stillness overhead, save when some

great peak gathers the thunders and bellows for a time. Then to see the white sulphurous masks curl and cover round it, and drip moisture on the hanging meadows, would task your powers of description! . . .

My first sight of the Alps has raised odd feelings. Here at last seems something more than earth, and visible, if not tangible. They have the whiteness, the silence, the beauty and mystery of thoughts seldom unveiled within us, but which conquer Earth when once they are. In fact they have made my creed tremble.—Only for a time. They have merely dazzled me with a group of symbols. Our great error has been (the error of all religion, as I fancy) to raise a spiritual system in antagonism to Nature. What though yonder Alp does touch the Heavens? Is it a rebuke to us below? In you and me there may be lofty virgin points, pure from what we call fleshiness. And so forth.—Wyse is lost in astonishment at me because I don't look out for a woman. . . .

(The image of the lofty virgin point swings him to the theme of Wyse's simple sensuality and his own void.) The Alps now stand to Meredith as the emblems of efforts, ascent; the rarefied heights are the moments of intense spiritual concentration that are essential in the full dialectics of change, rebirth. They are not cut off from earth any more than the moment of sharp withdrawal-into-self, if it is to be fruitful, is cut off from the social movement out of which it comes and into which it returns.

He went on alone to Verona and Venice with Arthur, perhaps to escape the sight of Wyse's connubial bliss. He and Arthur bathed in the Lido's tepid water under huge straw-hats every morning, and floated through the streets of night in gondolas. George felt much better in health and yearned for a pause when he could simply partake of life. 'Could I but afford to rest and look on man for one year.' He followed in the steps of Byron and Shelley:

> Do you remember in *Julian and Maddalo*, where the two, looking towards the Eugenean hills, see the great hell of the Insane Asylum swing in the sunset? I found the exact spot. I have seldom felt melancholy so strongly as when standing there. You know I despise melancholy, but the feeling came. I love both these poets; and with my heart given to them I felt as if I stood in a dead and useless time.

Thus he felt the deep desire for worthy comradeship, the sense of how empty in the last resort were the friendships he enjoyed, which had no basis in active struggle against the evil of the world. All the same, he had mild moments of seduction:

> [I have] received charming salutes from barred windows: from one notably where a very pretty damsel, lost in languor, hung with her loose-robed bosom against the iron, and pressed amorously to see me pass, till she could no further: I meantime issued order to Lorenzo, my gondolier, to return, and lo, as I came slowly into view she as slowly arranged her sweet shape to be seen decently, and so stood, but half a pace in the recess, with one dear hand on

one shoulder, her head slightly lying on her neck, her drooped eyelids mourn-
fully seeming to say: 'No, no; never, tho' I am dying to be wedded to that
wish of yours and would stake my soul I have divined it!'—wasn't it charming?
This too, so intensely human from a figure vaporous, but half discernible!

At Verona and in Venetia he felt strongly the subjection of Italy:

> Yes! those bleeding, tortured images by the wayside were painful and be-
> came exasperating—almost as much as the sight of the crowds of white coats
> through the whole of the Venetian territory. In Verona they have a garrison
> of 45,000 men. The population numbers 60,000. The soldiers have to keep to
> themselves, the officers are cut, and nothing so miserable and menacing can be
> fancied. Even the girls won't be spoken to.
>
> I saw an amusing scene of a couple of officers after two, who led them a
> terrible round and finally drew up at a melon-seller's. There they began
> chattering, wouldn't let Mr Over-lieutenant get in a word; suddenly they
> turned round, fired a volley of contempt and virtuous indignation and retired
> into the applauding crowd.

From Venice he went to Milan, and then on to Como to see Wyse, who
was staying with his mother. He enjoyed immensely the comedy of the
pretentious aristocratic household.

> She has a handsome daughter, fair as a highborn English girl, engaged then,
> and since married, to General T——. Madame la Princesse will be Mdme la
> Princesse, and desires that she should hear it too, as I quickly discovered. I
> grew in favour. She has no difficulty in swallowing a compliment. Quantity
> is all she asks for. This is *entre nous*, for she entertained me, and indeed I was
> vastly entertained. Look for it all in a future chapter.
>
> A good gross compliment, fluently delivered, I find to be best adapted to a
> Frenchwoman's taste. If you hesitate, the flavour evaporates for them. Be glib,
> and you may say what you please. Should you in addition, be neat, and ready,
> they will fall in love with you.
>
> Mademoiselle the fiancée perceived that I was taken with her before I had
> felt it. Hence she distinguished me, till the General came. It's a real love match.
> She wouldn't sing then—couldn't. Nor did I press it: for Oh!—She sings on
> the rapid French style: all from the throat: and such a hard metallic Giordi-
> gianic rang out over Como's water as sure our dear old Muddy Mole never
> knew of! Young General G——, T——'s aide-de-camp, and I, then fell upon
> the Princess. . . .
>
> Before dinner we all bathed in Como, ladies and gentlemen ensemble.
> Really pleasant and pastoral! Mdlle swims capitally, rides and drives well; and
> will make a good hero's wife. She scorns the English for their bad manners,
> she told me. The Emperor allows her £1000 a year: her mother gets £2000.

'Look for it all in a future chapter'—of *Vittoria*.

George and Arthur next went over Mont Cenis to Paris; and then back
to Copsham. 'I am much stronger, and am beginning to be able to work
much better, but have to be careful.' But he was disturbed by the news

of his wife's mortal illness (renal dropsy) this summer. She had managed in the last two years to snatch some stolen interviews with Arthur while George was absent, and clung to relics of him. Life was a *froide plaisanterie* she told Hogg. She begged George now to visit her. He refused; but Emilia Hornby, who was in touch with both Merediths, impulsively drove one evening to Cophsam Cottage and demanded that Arthur be allowed to see his mother. Meredith refused, but must have soon changed his mind; for late in September, Arthur was 'seeing his mother daily.' In October she died.

> [After a week in Suffolk, 'in a dumpling state'] When I entered the world again I found that one had quitted it who bore my name: and this filled my mind with melancholy recollections which I rarely give way to. My dear boy, fortunately, will not feel the blow. . . .

In the same letter he mentions, 'I am engaged in getting ready a volume of poems.' His disturbed state since Janet's marriage had made him turn to verse rather than prose; and now Mary's death came to stir him deeply. By the end of November we find him at work on *Modern Love* (which he first calls *A Love-Match*). By January he had proofs, with thirteen sections yet to be written. And in April 1862 was published *Modern Love and Poems of the English Roadside, with Poems and Ballads*.

The reception was bad, and for many years a large number of copies were not bound up:

> The Notices of my book are scarce worth sending. *The Spectator* abuses me. The *Athenaeum* mildly pats me on the back; the *Parthenon* blows a trumpet about me; the *Saturday Review* makes no sign.

Maxse tried to help with a weak notice in *The Morning Post*; and Browning told Meredith that he was 'astounded at the originality, delighted with the naturalness and beauty.' But Mudie 'my old enemy, who quashed R. Feverel, has hoisted the banner of British Matrondom and ejected me. If novels and poems are to be written for young women only, I must learn the art afresh.'

The Spectator was vicious (and to grasp the class-basis of its hatred of Meredith it is as well to recall that in June 1870 it wrote of starvation as 'the divinely appointed penalty of idleness and unthrift.' Hutton, its editor, 'goes to the ant and is happy: with deans, and bishops, and archbishops, and cardinals he is ready to play their own game,' says Saintsbury, but if Literature makes any advances 'he leaves his garment in her hands and flees for his life'):

> Mr George Meredith is a clever man without literary genius, taste, or judgment, and apparently aims at that sort of unison of point, passion and pictorial audacity which Byron attained in *Don Juan*. There is, however, no kind of

harmonious concord between his ideas and his expressions. . . . The effect of the book on us is that of clever, meretricious, turbid pictures by a man of some vigour, jaunty manners, quick observation, and some putonal (putrid) skill, who likes writing about naked human passions, but does not bring either original imaginative power or true sentiment to the task. . . . Meddling causelessly, and somewhat pruriently, with a deep and painful subject on which he has no convictions to express, he sometimes treats serious themes with a flippant levity that is exceedingly vulgar and unpleasant.

The critic declared that the work was a mere versification of the main idea of Goethe's *Elective Affinities* and should properly be entitled *Modern Lust.**

Swinburne wrote a reply, declaring *Modern Love* a work of subtle strength, depth of delicate power, passionate and various beauty, and Meredith himself 'one of the three or four poets now alive whose work, perfect or imperfect, is always as noble in design as it is often faultless in result.' And he made a counter-attack on the prevailing values in poetry, the sentimental, the nambypamby, the false:

As to subject, it is too much to expect that all schools of poetry are to be for ever subordinate to the one just now so much in request with us, whose scope of sight is bounded by the nursery walls; that all Muses are to bow low down before her who babbles, with lips yet warm from their pristine pap, after the dangling delights of a child's carol, and jingles with flaccid finger one knows not whether a jester's or a baby's bells.

Modern Love had been prefixed, 'This is not meat for little people or for fools.' By little people Meredith meant sentimentalists, egoists, who, tall in their own esteem, were in fact shrunken from full human stature by their falsification of the relation of individual and society. He uses the term in this sense in *Sandra*.

I have dealt with the theme of *Modern Love*. The form on the whole carries out the aim with a fine precision. Diction and rhyme at times flag and become inert, stale; but generally the emotional intensity is linked

---

* He accused the Rosanna poem of noisy vulgarity. Meredith shows 'wretched jocularity as pointless as it is coarse,' and intersperses 'sardonic grins that have all the effect of an unintentional affectation of cynicism.' (M. struck the issue with the attack at Guildford while on a walk with Hardman and thought it by a woman; H. thought the writer some personal enemy.) *The Critic* briefly saw humour and graphic painting; the *Parthenon* (owned by Morison's brother-in-law) saw original genius—the critic was Morison himself with the aid of Hamilton of the B.M.

The Athenaeum found 'spasmodic indistinctness' but occasional 'real force and imagination,' the style was abrupt and obscure, the theme morbid; some of the poems were both prosaic and coarse, outrages on tastes. Meredith must gain 'a healthier purpose, a purer taste and a clearer style.' *The Westminster* found freshness and vigour as well as roughness and obscurity, but deplored the themes 'of guilt and sin.'

'I found to my annoyance,' wrote Meredith, 'that I am susceptible to remarks on my poems, and criticisms from whipsters or women absolutely make me wince and flush.' (*The Saturday Review* at last 'gently whipped me. . . . I am none the worse.')

with pictorial clarity and effectively concentrated statement. Meredith
moves powerfully from the personal to the universal, and back again.

> They from head to feet
> Were moveless, looking through their dead black years,
> By vain regret scrawled over the blank wall.
> Like sculptured effigies they might be seen
> Upon the marriage-tomb, the sword between;
> Each wishing for the sword that severs all. . . .
>
> But in the largeness of the evening earth
> Our spirits grew as we went side by side.
> The hour became her husband and my bride.
> Love, that had robbed us so, thus blessed our dearth. . .
> Love, that had robbed us of immortal things,
> This little moment mercifully gave,
> Where I have seen across the twilight wave
> The swan sail with her young beneath her wings.

The book had also a set of character-poems, drawing to some extent
on Browning's method in his dramatic lyrics, but achieving their own
valid form. *The Patriot Engineer*, with an outburst against the enslavement
of Hungary, attacks the pseudo-romanticism which exalts Alpine scenery
as a kind of abstract beauty, and declares for the greater charm of a donkey
on a green outside an English pub. Beauty cannot be cut away from the
struggle for Freedom and its irradiations. *Juggling Jerry*, a poem of
Copsham Common, gives the last indomitable moments of an old
wandering juggler. *The Old Chartist* tells of a Chartist on his way home
from transportation, who halts by a brook running out of a lord's lands
and watches a rat washing itself. He broods on the old ways of struggle
and his resolve not to give in. 'Again I'll rouse the people up to strike.'
And the hope of a fraternal earth when 'every pot will boil harmonious
in one great Tea-garden,' against which his wife and his respectable
relations will bring every pressure. (But Meredith subtly indicates the way
in which the wife's personal devotion has its link with the ultimate
achievement of a happy earth, by developing the Tea-garden image out
of the picture of her tending the jailed husband of whose politics she dis-
approves.) As the Chartist shoemaker watches the rat, he realises the new
kind of strategy required in the post-1850 world. At first he considers the
creature an emblem of the ridiculous and parasitical dandy, then sees him
as the worker, the democrat, doing his best in a difficult world, cleaning
himself 'thanks to hard labour.' In the same way, he decides himself to
have more patience, to get down to work with a new thoroughness and
bring about 'the setting of the Dandy's day' by means of the new powers
that will thus be generated in the working-class. (The new position he

defines may in fact be illustrated by that of the Amalgamated Society of Engineers of 1850, which, while providing sick, superannuation, accident, funeral, and donation, as well as strike pay, emphasised the need of its members to become first-rate craftsmen.)*

But not all the poems are on this level. *Grandfather Bridgeman*, telling a tale of self-sacrifice, does so in a way that seems to glorify the Crimean War.

In *Ode to the Spirit of Earth in Autumn*, however, Meredith makes one of his finest affirmations of the active relation of man to nature. The Ode describes an autumn sunset and night of storm, and, at the height of the stormburst, moves into a paean of Earth and her powers of sustenance and renewal:

> *Great Mother Nature! teach me, like thee,*
> *To kiss the seasons and to shun regrets. . . .*
> *Great Mother! me inspire*
> *With faith that forward sets. . . .*
> *In life, O keep me warm. . . .*
> *Teach me to feel myself the tree,*
> *And not the withered leaf.*
> *Fixed am I and await the dark to-be.*
> *And O, green bounteous Earth!*
> *Bacchante Mother! stern to those*
> *Who live not in thy heart of mirth;*
> *Death shall I shrink from, loving thee?*
> *Into the breast that gives the rose,*
> *Shall I with shuddering fall? . . .*
>
> *She knows not loss:*
> *She feels but her need,*
> *Who the winged seed*
> *With the leaf doth toss.*
> *And may not men to this attain? . . .*
> *Earth knows no desolation.*
> *She smells regeneration*
> *In the moist breath of decay.*

---

* The poem must be read beside the advice to Maxse in 1865 (cited in the notes to Ch. 11 here) in which he argues against individualistic spasms of revolt. He wants first educational work. 'Let Philosophy sap the structure and work its way . . . till in self-defence they (the reactionaries) will attempt to wield the Dogma and knock us down with a club. In about twenty years' time we may expect a conflict to come.' He is speaking of religion, but the formulation covers also his general political attitude. He expected a heavy attack by reaction in the not-distant future and wanted the forces of progress to be built up with this fact in view, ready 'to take ranks under colours' and fight back with open force as soon as 'open rupture' came.

III

The Positive Hero

13

More Friends and Second Marriage

An 1861 photo shows Meredith with his son. His firm head with its steady glance shows struggle-in-repose, but Arthur has a vague sadness, the precocious seriousness of a motherless boy; a weak version of his father.

Among the new friends was William Hardman, big, square-shouldered, running to fat, with square brow and high colour, a thick beard on his strong chin. A sturdy Lancashire Tory, of a rich family in the mining area of Blackburn, he studied for the bar and acted as Chairman of the Surrey Quarter Sessions from 1865 till his death in 1890. In 1872 he became editor of *The Morning Post*, and was knighted in 1885. A cheerful humorous man, a keen photographer and a tireless walker, he attracted Meredith by his high-spirits, and was nicknamed Friar Tuck—to Meredith's Robin. They disagreed all the while, Hardman opposing his legalistic logic and philistine commonsense to Meredith's enthusiasms. His wife was 'one of those rare women who don't find it necessary to flutter their sex under your nose eternally.'

Hardman has left rollicking accounts of the gay jaunts across the meadowgreen and gorse-gold of Surrey; and Meredith's letters of the time are loud with the urgent desire to hurry into the lanes of birdsong and argumentative laughter. He upbraided or encouraged Hardman in doggerel like the song *Since Tuck is faithless found*, for which Hardman composed madrigal music in setting for three voices. The tone of their relations is hearty:

> Oh, what a glorious day! I have done lots of *Emilia*, and am now off to Ripley, carolling. I snap my fingers at you. And yet, dear Tuck, what would I give to have you here. The gorse is all ablaze, the meadows are glorious— green, humming all day. Heaven, blessed amorous Heaven, is hard at work upon our fair, wanton, darling old naughty Mother Earth. Come, dear Tuck, and quickly, or I must love a woman, and be ruined. Answer me, grievous man! In thine ear! Asparagus is ripe at Ripley.

Hardman introduced Lionel Robinson, Poco, another faithful walker. He stimulated a bawdiness in Meredith, who liked to make up merry verses in defiance of middle-class repressions. On a yacht-cruise Meredith 'was in wild spirits when he was not [seasickly] squeamish, and he

5

composed numerous extempore verses,' including a limerick on Swinburne. The improvised poems were on the lines of this sample:

> Tomorrow I am going,
> I cannot tell you where;
> The wind is stoutly blowing
> The ladies—bare.

In other fragments the mockery of Curates plays a part.*

The bawdy and respectable Hardman set himself to expunge from
Meredith's writing passages likely to offend the middle-class drawing-
room, and seems to have succeeded:

> Meredith . . . is to sleep here, in order to fight with me about my criticisms
> and suggestions anent the second volume of *Emelia*, the proofs of which have
> just passed through my hands. These criticisms mainly relate to an absorbing
> tendency which possesses him for indecent double-entendre. I am determined
> he shall not offend the public taste, if I can help it.

Meredith, it is noteworthy, is the Victorian novelist with the greatest
gusto and delighting in sports and exercises that bring men into contact
with nature. From the cricket-match in *Evan* to the boxing in *The Amazing
Marriage* he keeps a warm pleasure in all such matters of group-play and
is at one with the common folk in his responses. In fact, his stress on the
need for sports is a conscious aspect of his protest against the darkening
and crippling forces that hemmed the people in from nature and healthy
exercise.†

John Morley was another friend of the early 1860's, who often visited
Copsham. Fresh from Oxford, he said that Meredith 'lived at every hour
of the day and night with all the sounds and shades of Nature open to his
sensitive perception.' James Cotter Morison, also more intellectually congenial than Hardman, had been at Lincoln College with Morley. A quiet
versatile man, a positivist interested in the critique of religion, he wrote a
Life of St Bernard and became himself St Bernard for Meredith, whose
epitaph called him 'a fountain of our sweetest, quick to spring in fellowship abounding.' His father, a Scottish West-Indian merchant, had

---

* Hardman called his book on William Cobbett his *W.C.* Meredith said of Maupassant,
'I could be funny if I neglected the proprieties as he did!' One of the poems given to Janet
Duff-Gordon tells of his wishing at midnight to lie at her side, hear her breath and 'mark
your dream—how deep.' But 'what is this? Ah, thought of dread! Ah! thought of rage and
shame! That—lower when I lean my head—I hear—the CURATE'S NAME!'

† Keen on cricket, he preferred hard hitting and quick scoring; despised a drawn game.
He was an excellent swimmer and diver, and till late in life took his daily athletic cold-tub.
'A man should sweat once a day—then he will have a clear brain.' In November 1904 he
wrote in support of sport in *Fry's Magazine*, 'Sport will lead of necessity to observation of
nature. Let us be in the open air as much as possible, engaged in healthy rivalry with our
fellows, or with the instructive, elusive game we are after.'

concocted at the age of 52 a vegetable pill, mainly composed of gamboge, which made his fortune. Morison, thus provided with a life of leisure by Victorian constipation, 'talked well and wrote flatly,' a dilettante enjoying history (especially of the Papacy and Louis XIV), painting, music, architecture, boxing, yachting, riding.

Meredith was now intimate with D. G. Rossetti and Swinburne. Rossetti, after seeing part of *Modern Love*, showed Meredith his own unpublished poems (buried in his wife's grave some three months later). Meredith wrote to Maxse, 'He would please you more than I do, or can, for he deals with essential poetry, and is not wild, and bluff, and coarse; but rich, refined, royal-robed.' This is, however, somewhat backhanded praise, as Meredith had a low opinion of Maxse's taste in poetry and already felt the royal-robing of a singer to induce falsity. His mature opinion of Rossetti appears in the sonnet *A Later Alexandrian*; 'an inspiration caught from dubious hues . . . mystic wryness . . . and Beauty where she walked bloodshot the dews.' He feels the tormented element residing in the creed of Beauty for its own sake, the sickness behind the mysticism, the twist that puts 'essential poetry' (in the abstracted sense) at the service of the forces that wound and maim life.

In the letter to Maxse he acutely said of Swinburne:

> He is not subtle; and I don't see any internal centre from which springs anything that he does. He will make a great name, but whether he is to distinguish himself solidly as an Artist, I would not willingly prognosticate.

Though admiring much in Swinburne's work, he reacted against the infantile lack of any spiritually-organising centre from which a stable development could proceed.

And we must not forget Maxse as a friend. Though aspects of his hasty character irritated Meredith, he remained the closest in his political outlook because he chafed furiously against injustice and oppression. In 1861 Maxse married Cecilia, daughter of Colonel Steel, who lived till 1918.

In the spring of 1862 Meredith was busy at his poems and had begun a verse comedy, *The Sentimentalists*. For some time he had been working on *Emilia in England* (later called *Sandra Belloni*: which name I shall use here):

> I have three works on hand. The most advanced is *Emilia Belloni*, of which I have read some chapters to your mother, and gained her strong approval. Emilia is a feminine musical genius. I gave you once, sitting on the mount over Copsham, an outline of the real story [of Emilia Macirone] it is taken from. Of course one does not follow out real stories; and this has simply suggested Emilia to me. [To Janet, May 1861.]

Late in July he was anxious to finish the novel, yet in November he had left it 'untouched for months.' In June 1862 he was still at it, having largely rewritten the whole thing, 'making the background more agreeable and richer comedy.' In August he admits a 'dreadful hitch.'

In July Swinburne had stayed with him. He came up waving what seemed a pamphlet, and greeted his host 'with a triumphant shout of a stanza new to my ears,' that of Fitzgerald's *Omar Khayyám*. The pair lay on the heathery copse, reading stanzas in turn, till the dinner-bell broke the spell. After dinner they started again. 'Suddenly Swinburne ran upstairs and I had my anticipations. He returned with a feather pen, blue folio-sheet, and a dwarf bottle of red ink. In an hour he had finished thirteen stanzas of *Laus Veneris*' with the same metrical basis as *Omar Khayyám*.

In August Meredith was in the Channel on Morison's yacht *Irene*, in very high spirits; then in September he stayed with a bullion-broker acquaintance at an inn at Marlow, and at Hoddesdon. His housekeeper's niece had smallpox at Copsham; and he decided to send Arthur, now nine, to school, and naturally fixed on Jessop's establishment, which took a couple of dozen boarders. After a few days with Chapman at Tonbridge Wells, he conveyed Arthur to Norwich, stayed at St John's College, for a couple of days at the British Association then in progress at Cambridge, and then returned to Norwich, where Arthur fell 17 feet from a gymnasium ladder in the crypt, but was only badly shaken.

Back in Copsham in early November, he wrote in rhyme an apologetic letter about Arthur's outfit. He meant to revisit Norwich at the end of term, but was held up; so he wrote exhorting Arthur against larks in trains, and awaited him in London. They spent Christmas Day with the Hardmans in Gordon Street; and though Meredith would have preferred the Strand Theatre (with Marie Wilton, puns and burlesque), they gave Arthur what he wanted, Drury Lane Pantomime, where the new management was spending £10,000 on the performance:

> Such pandemonium I have rarely witnessed. The first piece was acted in dumb show, not a word could we hear. The fights in pit and gallery were frequent. The shower of orange peel from the gods into the pit was quite astounding. The occupants of the latter place made feeble efforts to throw it back again, but, of course, never got it any further than the first tier of boxes. I was glad to see the thing once. . . . [Hardman.]

This year, 1862, in the summer, Rossetti had leased a house in Cheyne Walk, to be shared with his brother William, Swinburne and Meredith. 'A strange, quaint, grand old place, with an immense garden, magnificent panelled staircase and rooms,—a palace,' wrote Meredith. 'I am to have a bedroom for my once-a-week visits' for work at Chapman and Hall's, with the use of a sitting-room. The tenancy began in October.

It wasn't a success. Swinburne was drinking much brandy. 'Algernon,' said Rossetti, 'used to drive me crazy by dancing all over the studio like a wild cat.' And Rossetti himself had irregular habits. Meredith declared in 1868 to Hardman:

> Eleven a.m. plates of small-shop ham, thick cut, grisly with brine: four smashed eggs on it: work till dusk: dead tired on sofa till 10 p.m. Then dines off raw meat and stout. So on for years. Can Nature endure these things? The poor fellow never sleeps at night. His nervous system is knocked to pieces.

William Rossetti tactfully summed up as follows: his brother, he said,

> was not at all a mere recluse, incapable of taking very good care of himself in the current transactions of life. . . . He understood character, and (though too often indulgent to its shadier side) he knew how to deal with it, and had indeed rather a marked distaste for that inexpert class of persons who waver on the edge of life without ever throwing themselves boldly into it, and gripping at the facts. But Mr Meredith was incomparably more a man of the world and man of society, scrutinising all sorts of things, and using them as his material in the commerce of life and in the field of intellect.*

Meredith said later, 'The household was too disorderly for him and his work.' He was still paying rent in June 1863, but must have soon given up his room.

There was no bad break. In January 1864 Meredith took Arthur to be painted by Rossetti. With Swinburne, however, there was a slow alienation. When in 1866 *Poems and Ballads* were violently attacked, Meredith wrote to him:

> As for the hubbub, it will do you no harm, and you have partly deserved it; and it has done the critical world good by making men look boldly at the restrictions imposed upon art by our dominating damnable bourgeoisie.

The heyday of their relations was over.

Meanwhile, January 1863 was spent in work and in amusing Arthur, who, finally, after being shown the Bank and the Tower, was given cake and oysters. 'Never mind, papa,' he said on Shoreditch Station, 'it's no use minding it. I shall soon be back to you.' Meredith rushed off to the yacht

---

* M.'s difficulties in work may be gauged from his remarks about method to Clodd. He 'lived day and night with his characters' before he wrote a word; and his main problem had 'always been in the jointing'—the points of movement, change, dynamic interrelation. His intense strain shows in his stomachic disorders, his high-tuned reactions.

Irene, which met rough weather in the Channel. Then in April Arthur on his holidays caught measles and stayed on at Copsham for a while; late in July he was thrown from a horse and dragged by the boot, but, though head-bruised, he soon recovered. Meredith was very upset.

In July they spent ten days at Seaforth with Fitz and his brother, amid much revelry. Burnand the punster, Samuel Lawrence the artist, and H. M. Hyndman, then an undergraduate of Trinity, Cambridge, were there. A Champagne-Loo Party, said Meredith, who lost £5 at Goodwood Races 'in a flower-garden of countesses.' One day as they sat tossing stones into the sea, he was talking with even more than his usual charm and force; and Burnand cried, 'Damn you, George, why don't you write as you talk?'

Arthur was back at school in August, and Meredith rushed to Paris to meet Hardman, stopping at Rouen to see an author who'd sent work to Chapman and Hall. He and Hardman strolled in the Champs Élysées, and next day visited the Louvre and Versailles. 'Could not get Meredith past the more modern French pictures of battles.' That evening they left to meet Robinson at Grenoble. Then they passed through the Grand Chatreuse, strode across Dauphine at twelve to thirteen miles a day, and reached Italy via Mont Genene. Pausing at Turin, they went by Maggiore and Piedmont into Switzerland. At Dijon they parted, and Meredith returned to Paris for four days. On 16 September he was back at Copsham.

Sandra had been lagging. In March he had written, 'I am overwhelmed with disgust at "Emilia." Am hurrying her on like Ye Deuce. She will do. But, ahem!—she must pay.' In July he had the 'last chapter of Emilia to retouch and the proofs.' Now he worked afresh at the book, longing to see Arthur. 'I have never so cut about a created thing. There's good work in her: but the work?'

A letter of this year to Jessop shows how firmly he insisted on stating, even to that amiable person, his earth-based attitude. He is attacking asceticism:

> I turn aching in all my flesh to adore the Pagan, in preference [to the Christian anchorite]. He smites kind nature in the face, to please his God!—St Sim. may be a very strong man. Granting it, I shall think more of Milo. He tears up the groaning oak, which I hold better than to pluck with fanatic fingers at the roots of humanity.—Don't you see that it is not adoration moves the stinking Saint, but, basest of all prostrations, Terror, mighty to knit a man for endurance when allied to a cringing creed for a fair celestial seat.
>
> The Truth is, you sniff the sublime in this creature. Your secret passion is for sublimity. Beauty you love; but, by the way, under protest; and with the sense of being a sinner. Clerical training is to blame.
>
> But, change the system. Beauty is to be sought—let sublimity come. Both

are rare: but the former is our portion—belongs to us. To deface it, is not sublime—villainous, rather! To outrage reason as well as beauty, shows the organisation of a ruffian. Be not misled by this dirty piece of picturesque Religiosity, animated: my gorge rises! I hold my nostrils. I cry for a South-west wind to arise. Plunge them into the pit, O Lord: these worshippers of the pillar.

Already in *Feverel* he has aphoristically set out this position, remarking that the saint who saw nature in the pig then saw the pig in nature.

May 1864 found him for a fortnight at Cambridge with Hyndman, where his wit baffled the undergraduates, 'clever fellows as some of them were.' He never seemed to be conversing 'on the same plane.' Hyndman put this down to the artificiality in 'his incisive modes of expression and the strange way in which he would of a sudden turn into ridicule about half what he had said seriously just before.' Hyndman, of course, considered that he understood Meredith's meaning. The likelihood is that he understood no more than his friends, and that the reason lay in the different 'plane' of Meredith's discourse—that is, a plane which implied a fundamental rejection of their accepted way of life. Hyndman, who was a member of the Sussex County Eleven, adds:

> Though no judge of games, he took pleasure in looking on at rowing, cricket, racquets, and sport of all kinds, being himself always in training and very much stronger muscularly than he looked. In fact he was all wire and whipcord without a spare ounce of flesh in him, and his endurance, as I found out in more than one long walk and vigorous playful tussles, was unwearying.

He threw Hyndman in a wrestling bout.

Sandra was at last done. In January it worried him 'beyond measure,' but he wanted to get on with the sequel set in Italy. 'As to character, I think you will have no doubt of her flesh and blood. How you will like the soul of the damsel, I can't guess,' he told Jessop. In April the book appeared, published wholly at his own risk. 'I give no more to crossing-sweepers, and drink small beer, if Emilia fail to hit the mark.'

He had met in the autumn of 1863 Justin Theodore Vulliamy, a retired wool-manufacturer of Normandy. Of Huguenot descent, the Vulliamys had settled in 1857 in an old red-brick gabled house in Mickleham Vale, with wooded hills at the back. Vulliamy, a recent widower, had three unmarried girls; and with the youngest, Marie, aged 24, Meredith fell in love.

When he visited the Jessops in April she was in Norwich; and they 'cathedralised' together, strolling in the Close and the meadows by the Wensum and the Yare. They travelled back to London in the same train, and he proposed to her.

She had no strong or vital character, and was not particularly intellectual or beautiful. ('I am told by a lady that she would not be considered
handsome though she is perfectly charming in manner and in face. I tell
you this with a rueful drop of the chin and a yearning strain of the eye.
You are not to suppose that I have not called her handsome.') But he felt
'compensated by so very much sweetness.' His comments to his friends
show a touch of apology, but he was genuinely happy.

> She is intensely emotional, but without expression for it, save in music. I
> call her my dumb poet. But when she is at the piano, she is not dumb. She has
> a divine touch on the notes. She is very fond of the boy. Not at all in a gushing
> way, but fond of him as a good little fellow, whom she trusts to make her
> friend. [To Maxse.]

Ominous words for Arthur. Meredith had had some trouble in breaking
down Vulliamy's resistance and had to go through the whole story of his
first marriage. But now, 'when her hand rests in mine, the world seems
to hold its breath, and the sun is moveless, I take hold of Eternity.'

> I never touched so pure and so conscience-clear a heart. My own is almost
> abashed to think itself beloved by such a creature. The day when she is to be
> mine blinds me. Will it come? It flickers like lightning in my brain. It will not
> burn steadily. I can't grasp it. [To Hardman.]

> . . . a very handsome person, fair, with a noble pose, and full figure, and
> a naturally high-bred style and manner such as one meets but rarely. I trust I
> may have strength, as I have honest will, to make her happy. [To Wyse.]

> I write with my beloved beside me; my thrice darling—of my body, my
> soul, my song! I have never loved a woman and felt love grow in me. This
> clear and lovely nature doubles mine. And she has humour, my friend. She is
> a charming companion, as well as the staunchest heart and fairest mistress. [To
> Maxse again.]

Kitty, the sister next in age to Marie, taught the parish children; while
Betty held a service every Sunday evening in a barn. 'Do you smile? . . .
I saw last Sunday a man rescued by Betty from inveterate drunkenness,
and happy. They—indeed all of them, are thoroughly loved by the poor
throughout the district.' They were hated, however, by the parson, who
declared Betty's behaviour a scandal and announced a boycott of the
Vulliamys in the matter of burials, marriages, and blessings. Marie thought
Betty should be milder and bring in the willing curate.

> I have written of love and never felt it till now. . . . She tries to make me
> understand her faults. I spell at them like a small boy with his fingers upon
> words of one syllable. Of course some faults exist. But she has a growing
> mind and a developing nature. Love is doing wonders with her. . . . The best
> specimen of the middle-class that I have ever seen.

No doubt after the experience of Mary Nicolls, which had hit him so hard, a woman like Marie Vulliamy, with her passive femininity, her Huguenot integrity, was best calculated to fill his life harmoniously and give him the aid he needed. The marriage worked out happily, however much his friends might look down on Marie as a mere woman.

They were married in September at Mickleham by Jessop. Janet Ross attended, but does not mention the fact in her memoirs; she apparently didn't want to say what she thought. After a fortnight at Southampton the newly-married spent a month with Maxse at Bursledon.

> The whole business now presents itself to me as if I had been blown through a tube and landed in Matrimony by Pneumatic Despatch.
> We sit on a humorous Olympus, and rule over the follies of mortals. . . . I rise, bathe, run, and come blooming to breakfast. . . . Fancy a salt river, crystal clear, winding under full-bosomed woods, to a Clovelly-like village, house upon house, with ships, and trawlers, and yachts moored under the windows, and away the flat stream, shining to the Southern sun till it reaches Southampton Water, with the New Forest over it, shadowy. . . .

Copsham was too small, so near the end of October they returned to Mickleham where they stayed over Christmas. Then they went to the Cedars, Esher, looking round for a house to settle in.

14

Sandra, the First Stage of the Revolutionary Type

SANDRA GAVE Meredith much trouble and took three years to write. Why these prolonged pains? First, he was breaking into a new dimension of fiction, attempting to show the movement of character on a higher level of truth and humanity through political struggle. And this attempt involved the whole question of audience. How treat such themes truthfully and yet get the book read or even published? From an inner analysis of his novels I incline to think that his writing pangs centred round the problem of breaking down romantic concepts by means of a more realistic grasp of characterisation, a fuller relation of the conflicts of his people with the total pattern of movement in their society. He seems to begin with a romantic or elemental notion which he develops up to a certain point: then he feels a hollowness, a falsity, and proceeds to tear the system to pieces, get inside it, bring out the yet-unrealised discords and contradictions. He next rewrites or rethinks the whole or part of the work in the new focus, but certain aspects of the original system persist in the turmoils of the re-shaped work, or evade his control. Hence what seems, and at times is, an uncertainty of approach: at first he appears to take his characters on their own evaluation, then suddenly turns them inside out. To some extent this method is intentional, admirably suited to stir the reader with a sharp consciousness of the hidden truth in people and society; to some extent it is involuntary, the result of his difficulty in establishing the desired relation between his characters' consciousness, based in prevailing modes of thought, and his own deeper understanding of where they and their society are going. Because he is determined to define positive characters who are steadily more conscious of all that is implied in their struggle to change society, he cannot halt at the methods previously used in the novel.

As in *Sandra* he sets out to define the new positive hero, dynamically integrated in struggle, the inner strain shows plainly for the first time in method. *Feverel* had its own complex set of stresses, linked with the same problem, but not so directly: and *Evan*, using a more Dickensian system of narrative exposition, achieved a new orientation, but without breaking the old moulds. With *Sandra* the new method matures. Though at times the control slips and forms blur, on the whole Meredith achieves the difficult goal he has set himself. To show the development of character through conscious political struggle.

Feverel had already adumbrated the theme of the Italian struggle for liberty:

> They spoke of Italy in low voices. 'The time will come,' she said. 'And I shall be ready,' said he. What rank was he to take in the liberating army? Captain, colonel, general-in-chief, or simple private? Here, as became him, he was much more positive and specific than she was. Simple private, he said. Yet he saw himself caracoling on horseback. Private in the cavalry overriding wrecks of empires. She looked forth from under her brows with mournful indistinctness at that object in the distance. They read Petrarch to get up the necessary fires. *Italia mia!* Vain indeed was this speaking to those thick and mortal wounds in her fair body, but their sighs went with the Tiber, the Arno, and the Po, and their hands joined. Who has not wept for Italy? I see the aspirations of a world arise for her, thick and frequent as the puffs of smoke from cigars of Pannonian sentries!

The novel opens with the Pole family of three socially-aspiring girls, their vulgar merchant father, their gallant officer brother Wilfrid. In their country-house they yearn for gentility and try to get hold of the million-aire Greek Pericles, who worships good music. They lure him out to find a woman who has been heard singing in the woods, and meet Sandra. A young Italian girl (with Welsh mother), she has fled from her drunken father who has plotted to sell her and from whom she inherits a passion for Italian liberty. Following the road of her luck, she is staying at a near farm with a kindly farmer.

The Pole girls take charge of her for their own purposes; and Wilfrid reluctantly slips from flirtation into love. She believes he has saved her from a drunken village-brawl and credits him with her own sincerity. Mr Pole is snared in money-troubles unknown to his children, who are obsessed with getting rid of Mrs Chump, a vulgar Irishwoman, whose money he is embezzling. They succeed as he has a breakdown partly in-duced by Sandra's telling him about herself and Wilfrid when he is scheming to marry the latter off to a Lady. They thus have the humiliation of having to woo Mrs Chump back to relieve the invalid. Wilfrid is exposed in a scene where he makes love to the Lady, overheard by Sandra. Sandra suffers badly, wanders off and is lost in London. She goes to Pericles, but finds her voice lost, and he brutally suggests that she become his mistress.

Finally, through the ministrations of a Welshman, Merthyr Powys, a devotee of Italian liberty, she regains self-confidence and voice. Wilfrid is again exposed in a scene where he makes loves to Sandra, overheard by

the Lady. He goes off to join the Austrian Army, and Sandra, accepting
Pericles' offer to have her voice trained, leaves for three years at Milan.
Pericles has saved the Poles from bankruptcy at her request.

The theme, Meredith states, is the contrast between the passion and
honesty of the child-of-nature Sandra, with her whole-hearted devotion
to the Italian cause, and the sentimentalism and dishonest pretences of the
Poles. But to grasp the full implications we must remember that Meredith
takes Sentimentalism as a typical form of the Egoism or self-alienation
pervasive in Victorian society. Sandra with her political self-dedication,
her refusal to accept class-values, stands for the counter-process which
looks to the day of Brotherhood and strives to bring that day about.

Meredith underlines his meaning by bringing in a philosopher to state
his main points. This intrusion of the author has been much blamed; but
his effort to define a new clarity of social consciousness, he feels, requires
the direct statement. Any illusion broken is the illusion closing men inside
accepted values and meanings. 'We are in a sort of partnership,' he says
of novelist and philosopher, 'and it is useless for me to tell him he is not
popular.'

He has been thinking much about method. He feels it is no use writing
unless the novelist grasps the deep truths of individual behaviour and
social movement, and forces his readers to grasp them as well. Realism
is essential; but it must be philosophic realism defining types as well as
particularised individuals and always making the story definitive of the
general movement of society. By that general movement he meant the
conflict between the forces concretely struggling towards the brotherhood
of man and an earth of peace and plenty, and those resisting. Here lies the
criterion by which the development of character, its integration or disintegration, can be judged.

In a letter of 1864 he seeks to get his terms clear:

> Between realism and idealism there is no natural conflict. This completes
> that. Realism is the basis of good composition: it implies study, observation,
> artistic power, and (in those who can do more) humility. Little writers should
> be realistic. They would then at least do solid work. They afflict the world
> because they will attempt that is given to none but noble workmen to achieve.
> A great genius must necessarily employ ideal means, for a vast conception
> cannot be placed bodily before the eye, and remains to be suggested. Idealism
> is an atmosphere whose effects of grandeur are wrought out through a series
> of illusions, that are illusions to the sense within us only when divorced from
> the groundwork of the real. Need there be exclusion, the one of the other?
> The artist is incomplete who does this.
> Men to whom I bow my head (Shakespeare, Goethe; and in their way,
> Molière, Cervantes) are Realists au fond. But they have the broad arms of
> Idealism at command. They give us Earth; but it is earth with an atmosphere.

One may find as much amusement in a Kaleidoscope as in a merely idealistic writer: and, just as sound prose is of more worth than pretentious poetry, I hold the man who gives a plain wall of fact higher in esteem than one who is constantly shuffling the clouds and dealing with airy, delicate sentimentalities, headless and tailless imaginings, despising our good, plain strength.

Does not all science (the mammoth balloon, to wit) tell us that when we forsake earth, we reach up to a frosty, inimical Inane? For my part I love and cling to earth. . . . [To Jessop.]

By *Realism* he means an expression that stays true to fact, to life as it is lived, and that bites into human experiences. The lesser aspects of this form of expression, nowadays called *naturalistic*, are superficial and limited; but even so, he says, they're better than airy nothings which falsify life at the core and in the end are deathly. By *Idealism* he means here simply the embracing perspective ('atmosphere') which generalises and gives depth in the creative act. In that act philosophy sloughs its metaphysical vices and becomes the universalising element in expression, while realism penetrates to the heart of human process. In separation realism thins to naturalism and philosophy grows abstract, distorting and destructive.

A letter written as he worked at *Vittoria* is also important. Here he discusses the way in which preoccupation with inner conflict becomes morbid, introspective, deadening, when it fails to merge with a full realism and with the philosophic element that looks to the future and sees the point where individual growth grows one with the struggle to become human, to achieve freedom and brotherhood. He is dealing with Hawthorn:

> His deliberate analysis, his undramatic representations, the sentience rather than the drawings which he gives of his characters, and the luscious, morbid tone, are all effective. But I think his delineations untrue: their power lies in the intensity of his egotistical perceptions, and are not the perfect view of men and women. . . .
>
> I strive by study of humanity to represent it: not its morbid action. I have a tendency to do that, which I repress: for, in delineating it, there is no gain. In all my, truly, very faulty works, there is this aim. Much of my strength lies in painting morbid emotion and exceptional positions; but my conscience will not let me so waste my time. Hitherto consequently I have done nothing of mark. But I shall, and *Vittoria* will be the first indication (if not fruit) of it. My love is for epical subjects—not for cobwebs in a putrid corner; though I know the fascination of unravelling them.

If one had to take a single passage making clear the great contribution of Meredith to the Novel, it is this. Here he anticipates the whole trend of culture in the post-1850 expansions, and realises that in such a situation the writers with most penetration into the egoist process will be the ones tempted to halt fascinated at the analysis of that process and thereby to become its tools. Already he rejects the development that stretches from Flaubert and Dostoevsky to Joyce and the Existentialists, whose work is effective in that it reveals what capitalism is doing to men, the hell of the egoist process, but which cannot achieve final greatness and universality since its focus lacks 'the perfect view of men and women.' That is, it lacks the power to fuse the 'egotistical perceptions,' the insight into the self-alienating process, with the vision of the future, with the definition of the struggle against the egoist hell that more and more encloses men. 'The perfect view' is an essential element in the great work of art, since without it there is no criterion for judging the 'egotistical perceptions,' no ability to realise the full relation of character to the pattern of history.

Meredith thus announces that something which has previously been inherent in true works of art, but only partially brought into consciousness, must now become a direct part of artistic aim and method, a conscious part. In the past the good or noble characters have generally tended to be colourless, abstract, utopian; the self-divided characters like Oedipous or Hamlet, Faust or Lear, or the monsters like Trimalchio or Pecksniff, have been the supreme embodiment of human energy in art. Only in folklore has the positive hero, nobly abounding in energy for the good of his fellows, been successfully created. But now, Meredith implies, as the struggle for freedom and brotherhood enters on a new phase, in which the utopian concept can be brought down to the plain earth of political conflict, the artist must boldly and consciously confront all that is implied in the problem of building up the positive hero. The hero who is changing history and knows how and why he is doing so; and who, if he does personally go down in defeat, goes down clear-eyed *without tragic irony and pathos.* For he knows that others are fighting along the same lines and that success may be delayed but not denied.

With *Sandra* Meredith opens this new epoch in culture, which is reaching its first full extension and stabilisation in our own day. He sets out to paint a revolutionary type, a woman who commands our entire sympathy and whose ideals look to the full liberation of man; and yet at the same time he escapes utopianism by showing the limitations forced on her by historical circumstance. We feel in her both the real tensions and conflicts of her world, and 'the perfect view of men and women' which is the pervasive criterion of her actions and thoughts.

He therefore here moves beyond his previous basis in Dickens and the New Poetry. He breaks into a new world and has to build up a new realism, simultaneously psychological and social in its apprehensions, seeing men and women as they concretely are, and yet consciously judging them in terms of a higher level of social development.

Two passages of general comment in the novel deserve a word. First, that in which he defends his style as anti-bourgeois, as essentially popular in basis *because of* its poetic origins. A character asks if 'fiction demands a perfectly smooth surface' like a scientific or philosophic treatise. It's no use saying the English aren't imaginative; what's wrong is the paralysis of their imaginative powers brought about by puritanism (religion set at the service of the money-power). But 'a writer who is not servile and has insight, must coin from his own mint'—refuse to accept the forms controlled by the cash-nexus. Our poets have always done so, in the teeth of the critics; the novelists must have the same courage. Otherwise English literature will go down before American.

> You see, when a piece of Transatlantic slang happens to be tellingly true—something coined from an absolute experience: from a fight with the elements—we cannot resist it. In the same way poetic rashness of the right quality enriches our language.

He thus states his conviction that language must gain freshness from sources closed to the bourgeoisie, the absolute (fundamentally human) experience of common life, the fight with the elements in labour-process.

Secondly, he carefully and ironically links the 'disinterested' delicacy of the Poles with their insistence on Fine Shades and Nuances, their flat refusal to consider the source of their privileged position, their 'innate' superiority, with the violent unscrupulousness of empire-looting and the divided consciousness or false-face thereby produced:

> Hillford had nothing to do with consequences: no more than our England is responsible when she sails out among the empires and hemispheres, saying, 'buy' and 'sell,' and they clamour to be eaten up entire. Foreigners pertinaciously misunderstand us. They have the barbarous habit of judging by results. Let us know ourselves better. It is melancholy to contemplate the intrigues and vile designs, and vengeances of other nations; and still more so, after we have written so many pages of intelligible history, to see them attributed to us. Will it never be perceived that we do not sow the thing that happens? The source of the flooding stream which drinks up those rich acres of low flat land is not more innocent than we. If, as seems possible, we are in a sort of alliance with Destiny, we have signed no compact, and accomplish our world as solidly and merrily as a wood-hatchet in the hands of the woodman.

Sandra tells of the growth of a simple warm-hearted girl into a woman who has sounded the world's duplicity, who has been deeply shaken but has come through with her integrity as vital as ever. She is so intensely honest and direct, so uncompromising in an evasive world, that she seems self-centred. But her self-centre is one of devotion to the Italian cause, to music, to love; and so she emerges as the diametric opposite of the egoists with whom she clashes. Her tenacity, till the point of breakdown and renewal, is extreme; and Meredith brings out the mingled naivety and clarity, childishness and sensitivity, which inevitably make up her personality.

Against her are set the Pole sisters and Wilfrid, who stand for the whole of English middle- and upper-class society. The Poles are subtly drawn, with the vast network of sentimental subtleties that they have imposed on life—a network deriving from their need to falsify reality, above all to escape from the nature and existence of money. The story's comedy derives from the way in which their effort to discard the vulgarities of their origin (the truth about money), represented by Mrs Chump, in fact crashes down their pretences and drives them up against the facts they wish to evade. Their inhumanity is given its sharp highlight by the suicide of Purcell, sacrificed by Cornelia on the altar of respectability (money, a good price in the marriage-market).

But the relations of Sandra and Wilfrid provide the crucial exposure. Wilfrid is merely philandering to enhance his own feeling of worth; but he becomes tangled in the snares of his own conceit. Sandra's absolute candour provides the furnace of his testing; by her simple acceptance of his truthfulness she forces him into a series of actions and attitudes, in which he alternates between the attempt to live up to her idea of him and the cynical pursuit of his career. In the process his egoism, his inner conflict and division, are brought out, and only an extreme effort of self-deception maintains his complacence. Meredith calls this the Riding of the Hippogriff: the lie of the sentimentalist who cannot face the hopeless duality of his emotions and who keeps on hoping that somehow he can evade choice and responsibility, have his cake and eat it. (He is shown as intensely romantic in the worst sense, wanting his woman to be infinitely refined and spiritual. The Hippogriff no doubt comes from Wieland, who opens his *Oberon* with a call to the Muses to saddle the Hippogriff 'to ride into the country of Romance.')

Chapter XXX is entitled, 'Of the double-man in us, and the great fight when these are full-grown.' Subtly Meredith shows that in every personal crisis integration as well as deepening-of-the-split is possible. Wilfrid is young; the very shame that drives him into acting the lover and really wanting Sandra *could* develop from egoism into love—if he had the courage to face his sentimentalism, if he repudiated the class-values that distort his consciousness. But each crisis worsens him. Though he wants Sandra, in a confused mixture of egoist desire and partial insights into her rare quality of spirit, he turns always back into the class-world that denies her, denies the way of life she represents. And yet, because of his glimpses of the truth, the better way, he is tormented as well as smug. As with Richard Feverel, his awareness always lags behind the reality of the situation in which he finds himself; he is increasingly dogged with a sense of failure, of unavailing regret; each step towards losing Sandra begets a step to regain her, but he can never deny his class-conditioning in time; and because he is losing her, he must cling ever more strongly to the class-values which destroy him and which yet become his only source of strength, of egoist stiffening. The climax comes when after his double humiliation he enters the Austrian service, to fight on the side of tyranny against Sandra's beloved Italy.

Her tenacity can become infuriating, but it is a necessary part of her resistances against the egoist world. It both limits her development and saves her from surrender. When Wilfrid's duplicities shatter her self-confidence by breaking her trust in others, her belief in her own intuitions, she has to undergo a painful period before she can return into the world of action, of song, of political struggle.

> The one Emilia, so unquestioning, so sure, lay dead; and a dozen new spirits, with but a dim likeness to her, were fighting for possession of her frame, now occupying it alone, now in couples; and each casting grim reflections on the other, which is only a way of telling you that the great result of mortal suffering —consciousness—had fully set in; to ripen; perhaps to debase; at any rate to prove her.

But whereas Wilfrid succumbs to the ordeal, she comes through substantially intact, stronger than ever in her devotion to freedom and music.

She does not fight alone. Merthyr, the Welsh enthusiast with a personally devoted sister, stands for the element in Britain which looks to the same liberated future. But he is an idealised character, without the complex reality of Sandra and Wilfrid, or even of the Pole sisters and Pericles, Mr Pole and Mrs Chump. And this vague limning no doubt reflects the failure of Meredith to grasp concretely what are the contemporary forces in Britain that own affinities with the mass-forces of revolt so easily discernible in Italy.

He again shows his powers of evoking nature, not so much by direct description as by the dynamic linking of the elements with his people. Round Sandra he builds lyrically a moving nimbus of elemental forces which help to convince us of her entire revolutionary fervour. Thus the implications of man's active relation to nature are being politically worked out.

The commonfolk still depend on a Dickensian method for their portrayal, whether like Mrs Chump they define a vulgar form of middle-class appetite, or like the landlady of Chapter IV they are simply and soundly earth-based. (Mrs Chump is both the Nemesis of the lie of the Pole girls, and the crude truth of what underlies their sentimentalism.) The march of the rival village-clubs and the hearty goings-on at Ipley show how vigorously Meredith can handle common life when he turns to it.

The long broodings and revisions of *Sandra* had brought the characters very close to his daily life. 'To him they are evidently living beings,' said Hardman. 'In fact I know he has felt them such for the past twelve months.' And the result is a work that comprehensively grasps English society in a way that reaches far beyond *Feverel* and *Evan*. The total effect is of a world given up hopelessly to falsehoods and self-deceptions which are accumulative, reposing on the alienating process of capitalist exploitation and expropriation. Wilfrid with his driven inability to achieve the happiness he sees, his worsening surrender to a split between ideals and practices, is the person concentrating the forces of doom; but against him stand Sandra and Merthyr, struggling for a totally different way of life:

> The criticism of English society increases in force and keenness; that which had made up the Countess of Saldar might not be taken seriously, but here the heroine is the absolute opposite of a snob. More than half-Italian, her passion, her simplicity are offered as examples to a hypocritical generation that worships the poverties and lies of sentimentality; the passion for music—who feels it so intensely as the Greek Pericles; and the cause of Italian freedom—only the reflective enthusiasm of a Welshman is allowed to experience its grandeur. Passion, refused to the English, seems to be the privilege of races that they oppress or despise. [Galland.]

Swinburne appears as Tracy Runningbrooke with hair red as blown flame. It has been generally considered that only in a letter about reviewers do we meet the authentic Swinburnian vehemence; but in fact in Tracy's lovely accounts of the new Sandra awakening out of her ordeal (effectively contrasted with the impressions of Merthyr's hostile sister) we read prose akin to Swinburne's own.* No doubt Meredith felt that so constant a singer of the national-liberation movements of Europe as Swinburne deserved a place in such a novel.

The book sold somewhat better than the previous ones; but the critics did not take much notice of it. *The Athenaeum* briefly found it charming but fatiguing, 'the succession of sharp blows eliciting sparks.' Mrs Hardman wrote stupidly in *The Saturday Review*: 'The whole set of people seem to live in a kind of cloudland, and to behave as no English family

---

* See comments on *Lesbia Brandon* in the Notes.

ever behaved or thought of behaving.' She doubted 'the great value of all this profound analysis of the characters of young women.' *The Examiner* noted Richter's influence and praised the 'clear, accurate English, individual, yet unaffected.' *The Westminster Review* gave what was the most perspicacious notice he had so far had for any work. The critic asked why he had such a 'strangely restricted circle of readers.' The reasons were:

> his originality; a subtlety of expression and a delicate indication of modes of thought and feeling, which demand an amount of attention not willingly given; the essentially dramatic nature of his talent, and the artistic manner in which he makes his very numerous actors grow under the reader's eye. In his pages you find no ready-made type whose conduct can beforehand be predicted. . . .
> Again, the peculiar tone in which Mr Meredith criticises the features of modern Society is at first calculated to ingratiate him with no conceivable section of that Society.

An unusually honest statement. Two signed comments have some interest. Richard Garnett in *The Leader* saw 'intellectual pyrotechnics' and a revival of 'genteel comedy,' an 'artificial aspect' and a principle of intelligent selection:

> The story is carefully chosen for the sake of some favourite idea snugly bedded in the centre of it, a Psyche-germ swathed in a rich cocoon of illustration. The personages are all selected with a similar view and their sayings and doings meted out with the nicest accuracy. The style again is highly *recherché*, spiced with epigram, and elaborated even to obscurity.

And Justin McCarthy in *Novels with a Purpose* in *The Westminster Review* dealt with *Feverel*, *Sandra*, and Mrs Norton's *Lost and Saved*. *Feverel* he thought gave 'no solution to that great social question about the sowing of wild oats' (which *isn't* the theme); *Sandra* had 'fewer eccentricities' of style, and Sandra herself was original and perfectly drawn. Lesser characters:

> are walking types, embodied aphorisms; conceits, or fancies, or crochets of the author put into human shape. . . . Their conversation is often unintelligible; a mere interchange of verbal subtleties and quiddities. . . . Rarely reaches, still more rarely commands, the feelings of the reader, although he almost always engages the intellect. . . . [Yet] he has much of a poet's nature, and only needs the courage to trust it more fully. . . . He can therefore describe the growth of young and passionate love as few in our day can or will do. . . .

so his heroes and heroines have passions unlike those of crinoline-fiction:

> Women have especial need, as the world goes, to be shrewd, self-reliant and strong; and we do all we can in our literature to render them helpless, imbecile and idiotic. We are therefore disposed to give a friendly reception to George

Meredith and Mrs Norton, were it for nothing but the mere fact that conventionality might be inclined to shriek out against them. . . . In each of these books the philosophical critic of humanity, the social reformer or social accuser stands behind the story-teller and inspires and guides his utterance.

These notices are remarkable in that they do state the degree to which Meredith's unpopularity derived from his fiercely critical attitude to Victorian society. Hereafter that admission was dropped out, and he was attacked as obscure and too-clever.

Some of the points are stupid, as when McCarthy sees nothing of the theme of *Feverel*; and it is of interest to contrast *The Examiner's* praise of the clear style with Garnett's description of its elaboration, and to note that the smug Mrs Hardman and the friendly McCarthy both fail to understand the rich satire of the Poles. Newman later asked if the sentimental ladies were any worse than the idealistic Merthyr and his sister, and Garnett's realisation of the organic unity of all the variations of the comedic theme is inverted in the view of the American Lathrop:

> It must be confessed that they (Sandra and Vittoria) present a substance almost impossible to analyse. How anyone ever came to conceive these tales, to what purpose they were directed to his own mind, why he should be at the pains to gather in one group so heterogeneous a lot of characters, and how he commanded the patience to pursue the threads of their actions and emotions, I am at a loss to guess.

He supposes the point of the vast panorama is to show that women taken up with politics make bad wives!

It is important to stress the way in which at first we get the direct moral attack on Meredith, and then an inkling of his social and political aims—followed by a blank refusal to notice the latter and a concentration of attack on his form.

Meredith didn't enjoy it. In April he wrote, 'I foresee I shall get knocks on the head from reviewers, and should like to be out of hearing for three months, but Courage!' Then next month, 'I get slaps for having written "Emilia." I am "eminently" this or that, unpleasant, in Review style. . . .'

15

Rhoda Fleming

Arthur was displaced now from his central position in Meredith's affections. Only three months after the marriage, 'we mourn and howl over him.' Things got worse when Marie bore a son in 1865, and it was decided to send him abroad, to a school near Berne based on the Pestalozzi system, and later to Stuttgart. Meredith did not encourage him to come home, but wrote long letters of moral counsel till 1872. The rift then widened, and for nine years there was little or no intercourse. Arthur complained of being kept short of money, though his father was fairly generous, till a great-aunt's legacy made him more or less independent.

A post was found him in a firm near Lille. But soon his health failed. In 1881 Meredith wrote to say that he had heard of Arthur's illness, offered him money, and asked him to visit Box Hill where he could work in a new-built chalet. (Arthur had contributed some meek travel-sketches to a magazine.) He referred uneasily to his impression at their last meeting that Arthur had ceased to love him.

Arthur preferred Switzerland or Italy to Box Hill; and at last settled by Lake Garda. But early in 1889 his health worsened and he sailed for Australia. Meredith wrote to his step-daughter Edith, now Mrs Clarke, to ask her to use her influence in getting Arthur to accept a small sum for expenses; but Arthur refused. On the voyage-out he had a mad drunkard as his cabin-mate; but in Sydney he felt better. On his return, however, he grew more ill and died in September 1890 at Woking in a house taken by Edith, who tended him to the last.

So Arthur ended, still bewildered, weakly proud, dimly handsome, in-effectually talented. I have told his end here, since after 1865 his existence impacted on Meredith only in a few brief moments of regret and bad conscience. In many ways Meredith had blindly repeated with him his own experience with Augustus, and in effect destroyed the boy with too much affection while shutting him out when it suited him.

His marriage coincided with a rise in income, not through any luck but as the result of hard and tiring work. He said he had laid traps for money everywhere; and joined the Garrick Club. No doubt he was determined not to fail a second time in marriage and had in the back of his mind the long interview in which he had to break down Vulliamy's Huguenot fears of such a son-in-law.

After the Cedars, he and Marie went to Kingston and in the spring took a three-years lease of Kingston Lodge, a pseudo-Gothic house with a good garden and ivied tower, the folly of some previous owner. It stood opposite Norbiton Hall, where the Hardmans had lived since 1864. George decided to use the lease-period for a thorough search for a house where he could definitely settle. At the Lodge his son, William Maxse, was born in July 1865. 'What he weighed I know not,' wrote Hardman, 'for Meredith is very superstitious, and would not do anything that ancient crones regard as unlucky.'

Sandys the artist was now a good friend. Born and educated in Norwich, with a shoemaker for grandfather and dyer for father, he came to know Rossetti from 1857 on. Rossetti called him the greatest living draughtsman, and he was indeed a very capable artist, with a fine sense of strong design. Worth two Academicians rolled into one, said Millais. And Meredith, 'He is one of the remarkable "brushes" of our day, with the quaintest stolid Briton way of looking at general things . . . a romantic turn that lets me feed on him.' He made a crayon drawing of Marie in 1864, which bears out the statement that she was no beauty; and he painted at Copsham 'Gentle Spring,' exhibited 1865. A thriftless pugnacious fellow, tall and lean like Don Quixote, he always managed to wear white waistcoats with gold buttons and patent-leather boots. When his *Medes* was crowded out of the Academy in 1868, a strong protest was made, with Swinburne among the signatories; and next year the canvas was hung on the line, while a bailiff occupied his lodgings in Leicester Square. A friend of Beardsley in the 1890's, he drifted along till his death in 1904.

When in the 1890's he tried to get Meredith to sit, the latter lamented, 'When you were young, my dear Sandys, the winged words of wisdom I poured into your ears would have penetrated the skull of a bullock, but you would not listen. Ah, Sandys, Sandys, if you had but listened, what a different Sandys it would have been.'

In July 1861 Meredith mentioned a story *Dyke Farm*, that later became *Rhoda Fleming*. About 1863 he told Maxse that the work was hurrying to its end. 'I don't know at all what to think' of it. He went on collecting materials for the battle-scenes of *Vittoria*, 'but, I have an English novel, of the real story-telling order, that must roll off soon and precede it.' Fifteen months later, 'I really trust to have a one-volume novel for January,' *Rhoda Fleming, a Plain Story*. 'If I compress it into one volume, I shall bring it back complete. But in the same month he calls it a two-volume matter. Then three months later he dropped *Vittoria* to finish

Rhoda off. 'And oh, will it be three? But this is my Dd. Dd. Dd. uncertain workmanship.' Three months more, and only the last two chapters lacked. Now it was definitely three volumes. Speedily written, it lacked revisions and knottiness of style.

Chapman and Hall wanted to delay things, so he sold the work to Tinsley, a new firm aiming at popular library-sales, for £400. It came out in October 1865 and did very badly. Not till Stevenson and Henley took it up did anyone consider it of importance.*

Farmer Fleming in Kent has been left with two girls, Rhoda and Dahlia, for whom 'the mysterious metropolis [London] flew with fiery fringes through dark spaces, in their dream.' Rhoda is a strong character with a touch of sternness; Dahlia, soft and dreamy. Dahlia goes to look after her maternal uncle, Anthony, who has a job in a bank—only a kind of doorman job, which, however, means that he carries a large sum of money out to a deposit daily; and he likes to dazzle his brother-in-law with the delusion that he's a rich miser. In London Dahlia falls in love with Edward Blancove, the banker's son, who seduces her and takes her off to the Continent. On their return he refuses to marry her, and she is too ashamed to see Rhoda or her father. But they glimpse her in a box at the theatre. She evades them, and they think Algernon, Edward's cousin, is the seducer.

At the farm, Robert, who has been in the army and who has given up his reckless hard-drinking ways in love of Rhoda, alienates the latter by not believing implicitly in Dahlia's innocence. He sets out to find Algernon and wring the truth from him. Coming to the country-house where Algernon, Edward and others are staying, he behaves violently, but is checked by Mrs Lovell, a bold corrupt woman, and then by a friend of his, a major whom he once saved from drowning. A scoundrel Sedgett almost murders him at Edward's instigation.

Edward goes off to Paris, leaving Algernon and Mrs Lovell to get rid of Dahlia. They arrange for Sedgett to marry her for money. Robert

---

* *The Westminster Review* found it too clever, and the 'cleverness only makes his weakness more apparent,' a sort of dim imitation of George Eliot. *The Athenaeum* agreed it was interesting because neither in style nor manner did it conform to any current pattern; liked its humour and pictures of rustic life, its occasional manifestations of genuine poetic insight into human nature; but considered it lacked 'the romance-writer's peculiar art.' (And objected to such terms as a crucible-woman.) *The Saturday Review* found it much better than 'the over-subtle and unfruitful speculations upon character and society' in the 'ill-chosen theme' of *Sandra*. It liked the country-sketches, but thought him very weak in construction, but occasionally obscure and inconsiderately arguing 'in seven-league boots.' His art was microscopic, yet 'vigorous and impressive' in the main characters. *The Morning Post* called his way of telling a story difficult, but found the book fresh and invigorating, 'a careful study of human nature.'—But to get these criticisms in focus we must read them beside the higher praises of trivial books.

finds her; and Rhoda, dominating her broken mind, pushes her into the marriage, though Edward, belatedly repenting, comes back to offer amends. In the end it turns out that Sedgett is already married, so he is forced to drop his claims on Dahlia—but not before she has tried to poison herself. Rhoda and Robert at length marry, but Dahlia refuses Edward.

The theme is a variant of the Feverel-Wilfrid drama. Edward is the upper-class youth who commits a grave wrong, is driven to realise his act, and is too late in seeking to make amends. Life has passed him by, and he is left in a hell of unavailing regrets. His worst fall occurs after his 'honeymoon' with Dahlia when he returns into 'society' and succumbs to the dehumanising values and pressures of his class. In his recoil he becomes desperately vicious, ready to connive at murder, as he feels cornered by Dahlia's emotional demands; he is determined at all costs to carry on with his career and own all the enjoyments of his class. Then, alone in Paris, he is driven back on himself, forced to realise something of the evil thing in his spirit; he breaks through, but too late.

Mrs Lovell typifies the corrupt class-values that bring him down. She is one of the Mary Nicoll characters, hard and egoistic, yet intelligent and charming; her moments of better impulse cannot overcome her essential self-division, her corrosion with false pride. She has her own system of values, or rather she holds the values of her class in a specially individualistic way, which seems to her a form of independence and originality.* She has a cult of courage, of showing a fissureless front to the injurious world, of striking remorselessly back, she itches to push men into the test of death, the duel, on her behalf. She and Edward are half-entangled, the protagonists of egoism. He sees through her and fears the ceaseless pressure of her need to try a man, then is afraid she thinks him a coward and almost falls into the trap after all. They come together; but while he is in Paris, she breaks away again, considering his flight a cowardice. He swings towards repentance and is out of her clutches. Her moment of choice comes when she half-subdues, half surrenders to, the major (Robert's friend), who had exposed and humiliated her after she got her first husband killed in a duel in India. She now draws him into an offer of marriage and turns him down as too poor. Also, he sees her too clearly. 'She is all things to everybody, and cannot help it.' That is

---

* Even Stevenson failed to grasp the subtle and stark definition in Mrs Lovell. She rouses 'resentment in the reader; her motives are too flimsy, her ways are too equivocal, for the weight and strength of her surroundings.' She is in fact the key to those 'surroundings,' the world of the bourgeois cash-nexus. (Stevenson and Henley have glimpses of Meredith's anti-bourgeois position, but they tend to abstract it into an individualistic focus that accords in the long run with imperialist needs. Stevenson, however, does wrestle long and hard with *The Egoist*.)

the truth hidden by her mask of bold independence. She marries the rich banker, Edward's father.

Edward and Mrs Lovell are the key-figures who show the distortion of the human essence by the egoism of the cash-nexus. Algernon is the crude example of such egoism:

> Not only had Algernon never failed to dine every day of his life; he had no recollection of having ever dined without drinking wine. His conception did not embrace the dinner lacking wine. Possibly he had some embodied understanding that wine did not fall to the lot of every fellow upon earth; he had heard of gullets unrefreshed even by beer. . . .

He represents in blank form his class's unconsciousness of reality; but he has glimmerings of doom and responds with fancies of escape into the wilds with a country-wench—without the least capacity to do anything about it. The account of his slow embezzlement of the money he is given to bribe Sedgett is first-rate comedy, and one of the ways in which the force of the enveloping cash-nexus is brought out.

Against these corrupted people are set the commonfolk who, with all their limitations and backwardnesses, have the struggling spirit of life in them. Farmer Fleming, by reason of his submission to the world of his betters, has an ingrained hardness, an inability to comprehend or forgive any transgressions of the accepted code, especially by a woman. Such transgressions tear him from the soil and end his conviction of security. In his unrelenting cruelty to Dahlia when he thinks her a sinner, his effort to force her into going with a brute as long as he can regain his own sense of respectability, he gives the effect of a blind elemental force.*

Rhoda shares something of his harshness, but in her it is transmuted by passionate love for her sister. This love, however, because of its aspect of harsh blindness, as surely presses for the destruction of Dahlia as does the almost-mad dependence on the code of her father.

The class-basis of this hardness, this hatred, in Rhoda and her father is underlined. Rhoda cries to Edward when he is agonised by his desire to make reparation. 'You will have to kill me first, if you get near her. Never! you never shall. You have lied to her—brought disgrace on her

---

* Meredith had been strongly affected by George Eliot's essay, 'The Natural History of German Life' (*Westminster Review*, 1856), which, discussing Riehl, says of the peasant, 'Custom with him holds the place of sentiment, of theory, and in many cases of affection. . . . The peasant never questions the obligation of family ties—he questions no custom—but tender affection, as it exists among the refined part of mankind, is almost as foreign to him as white hands and filbert-shaped nails.' This one-sided account helped him to the picture of Farmer Fleming and Rhoda, which is, however, more soundly based than Riehl's generalisations.—Compare also 'The only realm of fancy and imagination for the English clown exists at the bottom of the third quart-pot' with *Modern Love*, xviii. (*Adam Bede*, 1859, also affected M.'s novel.)

poor head. We poor people read our Bibles, and find nothing that excuses you.' He recognises her class-hatred. She goes on, 'I would cut my tongue out, if it did you a service,' and he thinks, 'Citoyenne Corday,' meaning by that a recognition of her revolutionary class-passion.

Robert argues that the commonfolk can take the right course, but the gentry live in a world that justifies cruelty. 'Well, he *says* so; and it's true that gentlemen are situated—they can't always, or think they can't, behave quite like honest men.'

Rhoda then steels herself to drive Dahlia from Edward into the other man's marriage-bed. 'Rhoda departed in another direction, firm, since she had seen Sedgett pass. . . . She endowed him with fair moral qualities, which she contrasted against Edward Blancove's evil ones, and it was with a democratic fervour of contempt that she dismissed the superior outward attractions of the gentleman.'

And when she finds that the poor housekeeper and the old worker Gammon have given their sad little savings to Dahlia, she bursts out:

> 'Dear good humble friends! The poor are God's own people. Christ has said so. This is good, this is blessed money!' Rhoda's cheeks flushed to their orange-rounded swarthy red, and her dark eyes had the fervour of an exalted earnestness. 'They are my friends for ever. They save me from impiety. They help me, as if God had answered my prayer. Poor pennies! and the old man not knowing where his days may end. He gives all. . . . Old man, old man, I love you—how I love you! You drag me out of deep ditches. . . . Everybody in the world is not wicked.'

With less intensity her father takes the same class-position. He accepts Sedgett as 'a farmer like myself.'

This hard deep-rooted passion, with its unrelenting antagonism to the gentry, doggedly blind and battered-down in the Farmer and struggling towards consciousness in Rhoda, is raised to a higher level in Robert's father, where it is directed towards work:

> 'Walloping men is poor work, if you come to compare it with walloping Nature,' he said, and explained that, according to his opinion, 'To best a man at buying and selling was as wholesome an occupation as frowzlin' along the gutters for parings and strays.' He himself preferred to go to the heart of things: 'Nature makes you rich, if your object is to do the same for her. Yorkshire fellows never think except of making themselves rich by fattening on your blood, like sheep-ticks. . . .'
>
> Percy asked him what he thought of his country. 'I'll tell you,' said Jonathan; 'Englishmen's business is to go to war with the elements, and so long as we fight them, we're in the right academy for learnin' how the game goes. Our vulnerability commences when we think we'll sit down and eat the fruits, and if I don't see signs o' that, set me mole-tunnelling. Self-indulgence is the ruin of our time.'

He has his intolerances, his simple puritan objection to his son's wild living; but the root of the matter is in him.

We see then the pressures of a divided society operating in these people, stupefying Farmer Fleming, almost breaking Rhoda but in the end giving her new strength, tearing Dahlia to pieces—though she too gains out of her miseries a deep calm and understanding. 'Help poor girls,' her last words and the last words of the book, sum up Meredith's moral, his effort to show the terrible dilemma of women in a society that enslaves them, sets them rigid rules and yet pushes them towards destruction if they lift their heads out of submission.

If the plain goodness of the commonfolk is shown in the magnificently drawn Mrs Sumfit and old Gammon, the conflict driven in on these people appears in Robert, who is opposed to the doomed Edward as a positive character breaking through his fate and finding his place in the world of work and love. His revolt has taken the blind form of drink and recklessness; but he saves his self-respect and stands out as a hero of the working people. 'What a pride it is, when it's a man,' Mrs Boulby thinks, when he staggers back after the murderous attack on him.

> When a hero can be got from the common popular stock, he is doubly dear. . . . Only death can remove the peculiar distinctions and distances which the people feel to exist between themselves and the gentlemen-class, and which, not to credit them with preternatural discernment, they are carefully taught to feel. Dead Britons are all Britons, but live Britons are not quite all brothers.
>
> It was as the son of a yeoman, showing comprehensible accomplishments, that Robert took the lead. He was a very brave, a sweet-hearted, and a handsome young man, and he had very chivalrous views of life, that were understood by a sufficient number under the influence of ale or brandy, and by a few in default of that material aid; and they had a family pride in him. The pride was mixed with fear, which threw over it a tender light, like a mother's dream of her child.

And he shows his mettle in the scene with the Squire:

> Now mark me, Mr Blancove, you've insulted an old man in his misery: you shall suffer for it, and so shall your son, whom I know to be a rascal worthy of transportation. You think Mr Fleming came to you for money. Look at this old man, whose only fault is that he's too full of kindness; he came to you just for help to find his daughter, with whom your rascal of a son was last seen, and you swear he's come to rob you of money. Don't you know yourself a fattened cur, squire though you be, and called gentleman? England's a good place, but you make England a hell to men of spirit. Sit in your chair, and don't ever you, or any of you cross my path.

Again the confrontations of Robert and the gentry at Fairly Park are shown as class confrontations, in which the gentry cannot behave decently and Robert is drawn from his violent resolution to have things out only by the egoistic deceits of Mrs Lovell and a cowardly attempt at murder. (The scoundrel Sedgett is explicitly made a Tory.)

Old Anthony is a commoner corrupted by the cash-nexus: not into the subtly evil egoisms of Mrs Lovell or the infantile self-indulgences of Algernon, but into a wild fantasy of gold—the result of his thrifty submission to the demoralising values of his masters. His theft from the bank is nothing calculated; it can only bring disaster; it is the spontaneous expression of a long-nursed fantasy of power. It breaks him, and he returns to the Farm, the Earth, Rhoda, in a bewildered effort of escape and self-renewal. There is no way-out for the worker except work and the loyalties born of the work-bond.

Religion is shown as the moral support of the commoners who cannot rise to the concept of struggle; also their evasion and stupefying burden. This idea is most powerfully expressed in Farmer Fleming's character; but is elaborated in a person like Robert's aunt, of whom the kindly Mrs Boulby says, 'Oh, you *good* people! how you make us long in our hearts for trouble with you.' And Mrs Sumfit remarks, 'It ain't good—no, not the best pious ones—I shall, and will say it! as is al'ays ready to smack your face with the Bible.' Of Fleming, Anthony says, 'Th'old farmer attends Methody meetin's, and quotes Scriptur' as if he was fixed like a pump to the book.' That is the old man's preparation for his final stoniness of heart. And Dahlia, broken, but endowed with a new wild penetration into people, says of him:

> 'Yes, poor old man! I have no pity for him. If I am dragged away, I'm afraid I shall curse him. He seems a stony old man. I don't understand fathers. He would make me go away. He talks the Scriptures when he is excited. I'm afraid he would shut my Bible for me.'

The moral of the book is the need for courage, honesty, and, above all, the strength to face facts. When Dahlia in her brokenness realises that Rhoda has deceived and destroyed her, she says only, 'Mind you never lie again,' and rebukes her gently for trying to fight 'sin' with lies. Robert sums things up: 'What miseries happen from our not looking straight at facts.' Rhoda agrees, 'It's ignorance that leads to the unhappiness of girls.' The truth gives pain often, but it is the only road to happiness and love.

Henley was thus only half-right when he said the book's unpopularity derived from its fierce 'attack upon the superstitions of respectability' and from the Victorian middle-class's dislike of problems 'capable of none but a tragic solution.' For what enforces the tragic situation is not a dilemma abstracted from a precise historical setting; it is middle-class respectability that causes all the trouble. Meredith's whole aim was to show that the egoisms of Mrs Lovell and Edward, and the hard-hearted terror of Farmer Fleming, were aspects of the same self-alienating process which sends old Anthony delirious and which is expertly controlled by the banker Blancove. Behind the distortions we feel the judgment-value of 'the perfect view of men and women.' The Roberts and the Rhodas in due time, through struggle, will beget a world where the Edwards do not destroy themselves by a time-lag of consciousness and where the Mrs Lovells can overcome their desperate contradictions.

Rhoda Fleming underlies the work of Thomas Hardy, on whom it had a decisive effect. A comparison between it and *Tess* or *Jude the Obscure* will serve to bring out clearly the point made above. Meredith sees a cruel problem that men can meet by changing society; Hardy sees problems 'capable of none but a tragic solution.' Developing as the alienating grip had tightened, Hardy lacks roots in Chartism and in left Radicalism, lacks any faith in mass-movements of regeneration; he can only lament over what is being done to his people. So they are enclosed in a doom. Meredith's people on the contrary are enclosed in no doom, but in the class-struggle which can liberate them if they stay true to the cause of brotherhood and the clean battle with the elements.*

---

* It might well be argued that after all the last word in Hardy is not with the doom-sense and the angelic pities, and that there is a depth of truth and love in his people which is *truly tragic*—i.e. implies the *renewal* of life in the midst of doom. But the broad statement of a weakening in Hardy, after Meredith, can stand.

16

Work and Talk and War

FOR EIGHT YEARS after 1860 he worked for the Ipswich *Journal*, an old Tory newspaper, founded in 1720. He contributed a weekly leading article and a column of news from London and abroad. Every Thursday he transacted business with the London agent and completed copy at the office in New Square, Lincoln's Inn. Foakes, a barrister, was supposed to be conducting the paper, and Meredith dates Thursday letters Foakes Day, from Foakes Den. When on holiday, a friend (such as Hardman in August 1862) did the work.

Nothing is signed; but much of his contributions can be identified with fair certainty from its style. There seems no doubt that he wrote at times against his own principles, though at times he tried to palliate his conscience or lighten his boredom by an ironical tone. He possibly wrote the article attacking Gladstone's cession of the Ionian Islands to Greece, which annoyed the Ipswich radicals. How did he justify such work? No doubt he argued that it was a purely technical matter, and that somebody else would do it if he didn't, so that it was better for him to get the money and be able to carry on his advocacy of Radicalism in his own signed writing. (Morley, also far from Toryism, took his place when he was abroad.)

He must, however, have felt himself to some extent degraded; and it was no doubt this emotion which both stimulated and inhibited his novel on Journalism which was never completed. And made him so fierce against any attempt to dig up his Ipswich writings.

We must therefore condemn Meredith's work for the Ipswich *Journal* as the one serious moral dereliction of his life; though at the same time we must admit the deep truth of what Frederick Harrison wrote in 1911:

> Few realised what passionate senses of right and wrong, what a high heart, he could keep in all his early struggles to be recognised for what he was, what determination burned within him never to yield one jot of his own ideas and methods to any public demand, to any pecuniary effort.

By 'public demand' there we must understand 'bourgeois demand.'

Meredith explicitly states in, say, the poem *Foresight and Patience* (1894) his wish to set his work unreservedly at the service of the masses struggling to be free and to develop a new stably-based culture.

He also did some work for the Conservative *Morning Post* from 1862. It was this paper he represented as a War Correspondent in Italy. He hoped at one time to represent *The Times* abroad, in vain. And in October 1868 mentions that he is writing almost weekly for the evening-paper, *The Pall Mall Gazette* (edited by the Tory Frederick Greenwood till 1880). Though he differed from Greenwood in politics, he respected him and wanted to build the novel *The Journalist* largely around his personality.

Often dull, yet more congenial, was the job he took on from the autumn of 1860, as literary adviser and reader for Chapman and Hall, where he succeeded John Forster. He held this job till 1894, and its £250 per annum was for some 35 years his main settled source of income. He took it very seriously and read a large amount of work, good, bad, and indifferent with extreme scrupulosity. By setting his face against all debasement of the public taste he lost his firm several best-sellers; but as he advised on settled principles he did not regret such acts.

The most famous of his rejections was the mawkish and sentimental *East Lynn*, which, he declared, stimulated bad taste and made no effort to relate character and incident. 'Opinion emphatically against it. In the worst style of the present time.' It had previously appeared in *The New Monthly Magazine* (1860–1) owned and edited by Harrison Ainsworth, who called twice on Chapman and Hall to urge its acceptance. Meredith was asked to reconsider his judgment; he repeated it. Published by Bentley, the novel sold a million copies. But Edward Chapman, senior partner of the firm, agreed with Meredith's decision: 'the tone of the book,' he thought, 'was not good for the general public.'

Among other rejections were Samuel Butler's *Erewhon*, one of Ouida's early novels, Mrs Lynn Lynton's *Isola* (he disliked her for her anti-feminist positions), Whyte Melville's *Market Harborough* ('of the order of Soapy Sponge's Hunting Tour'), Shaw's *Immaturity*. The weariness of reading strange scripts in pre-typewriter days is reflected in some of his comments, 'Weak wild stuff—MS. looking as a survival of a dozen ship-wrecks,' 'Vile script,' 'bedevilled with erasures, change of hands, pale with pencil, tattered pages.' And his boredom yawns in many of his phrases:

> A provincial maiden aunt of the old time had about the same notions of humour and horror. A similar manner of narrating.
> The dullness of vapid liveliness marks the style of this work.

But when he felt that a writer had talents capable of development, he was ready to spare much time and trouble, both in written counsel and in interviews. The clerk at the desk called him the Reader and his anonymity was so well preserved that even a knowledgeable person such as Ainsworth thought he was Owen Meredith—an error which also suggests the comparative obscurity of Meredith's reputation as yet.

Among the writers whom he helped and decisively influenced were Gissing and Hardy. In 1869 Hardy made his first visit at the office, 193 Piccadilly, and saw Carlyle, in Inverness cape and slouched hat, leaning with his elbow on the clerk's desk. Next time he had an interview with Meredith in a back room, dusty and littered with books and papers. Some sixty years later he remembered Meredith as 'a handsome man with hair and beard not at all grey, and wearing a frock coat buttoned at the waist and loose above, his somewhat dramatic manner lending him a striking appearance.' Hardy had written a satirical novel *The Poor Man and the Lady;* and Meredith in the interview stressed the need of Plot and said, 'Don't nail your colours to the mast just yet.' The novel was crudely violent in its social criticism, and Meredith was right enough in finding it immature. Hardy took the plot-advice to heart and wrote the melodramatic *Desperate Remedies*, not exactly what Meredith had been meaning him to do. 'He gave me no end of good advice, much of which, I am bound to say, he did not follow himself.'

No one who reads *Rhoda Fleming* can doubt how central was Meredith's influence on Hardy; and in general Meredith's power of landscape-evocation, of linking nature and man, strongly affected Hardy's whole outlook and method. Hardy omitted Meredith's positive and optimistic view, and took the class-forces of oppression and alienation as the human condition; and nature in his work, still lyrically realised, tends to be a hostile power. But he works on the ground cleared by Meredith, using his psychological realism and much of his social sense without his faith in man's power to break through obstructions and master his destiny.

Meredith recognised the element of greatness in Hardy, his deep feeling for people and his understanding of the terrible ordeal through which they were historically passing, his insight into nature. In 1892 he wrote, 'Hardy is one of the few men whose works I can read. I had always great hopes of him.' He admired *Tess*, but felt that it flagged.

> The work is open to criticism, but excellent and very interesting. All of the Dairy Farm held me fast. But from the moment of the meeting again of Tess and Alec, I grew cold, and should say there is a depression of power, up to the end, save for the short scene on the plain of Stonehenge. If the author's minute method had been sustained, we should have had a finer book. It is marred by

the sudden hurry to round the story. And Tess, out of the arms of Alec, into (I suppose) those of lily necked Clare, and on to the Black Flag waving over her poor body, is a smudge in vapour—she at one time so real to me.

But he was flatly opposed to the idea of Life's Ironies and tried to argue Hardy out of it, vainly. 'Hardy was here some days back. I am always glad to see him, and have regrets at his going; for the double reason that I like him, and am afflicted by his twilight view of life' (1905).

Hardy has left a fine tribute in the poem written after Meredith's death:

> Forty years back, when much had place
> That since has perished out of mind,
> I heard that voice and saw that face.
>
> He spoke as one afoot will wind
> A morning horn ere men awake;
> His note was trenchant, turning kind.
>
> He was of those whose wit can shake
> And riddle to the very core
> The counterfeits that Time will break.
>
> Of late, when we two met once more,
> The luminous countenance and rare
> Shone just as forty years before.
>
> So that, when now all tongues declare
> His shape unseen by his green hill,
> I scarce believe he sits not there.
>
> No matter. Further and further still
> Through the world's vaporous vitiate air
> His words wing on—as live words will.

A poem that eloquently states what he felt as Meredith's achievement: the ability to see through 'the counterfeits that Time will break,' to criticise the present in terms of the future, to bring the freshness of truth into a vitiated atmosphere. And in that judgment we can see also what Hardy took from Meredith as his ideal for himself; for Meredith defined 'counterfeits that *Man* will break,' and felt his work as one of the instruments of the breaking. Hardy's passivity appears in the idea of leaving to Time the job of fighting the evil thing.

Gissing was also influenced by Meredith's power to break down the counterfeit and get to the truth of men and women in their living relationships—though he, like Hardy, lacked the master's sturdy faith. Meredith pointed out the faults and merits of a manuscript of his, and suggested improvements; the revised work was published in 1884 as *The Unclassed*, Gissing's second book. In his next work, *Isabel Clarendon*, he had even more aid from Meredith who criticised the manuscript in detail

6

two or three times. Olive Shreiner too revised her *Story of an African Farm* after some interviews, and the work was accepted in 1882.*

We have already had glimpses of Meredith as an insatiable talker, gay and easy with one or two intimates, dominating and epigrammatic in company. Some listeners, like the conceited Hyndman, stress the strain, the determined brilliancy. Henry Sidgwick too was rather disappointed.

> He was not affected or conceited and talked fluently, but not exactly at ease.
> . . . Once or twice there was an amusing stroke of humorous fancy, as when he talked of an unhappy singer's voice being 'like the soul of a lemon in purgatory'; but these things did not come often. [1886.]

Blunt in 1894 found his discourse 'like one dictating to a secretary, a constant search for epigrams.'

Others found a fuller satisfaction in his talk. Sidney Colvin tells of his comments beginning quietly and plausibly, till his inventiveness gripped him; he went up in spirals to a burlesque empyrean where he stayed without effort, at the same time bringing in touches that pierced the essential character of the person parodied or analysed. Comyns Carr admits that he sometimes ventured into fields which he had only half-conquered, but

> he loved to submit his creations to the instant pressure of their time, and with this purpose it was his business, no less than his pleasure, to equip himself intellectually with garnered store of knowledge in fields into which the ordinary writers of fiction rarely enter.

Thus an assistant of *The Fortnightly* (W. Burnett Tracy) depicted the talkers in the office:

> Trollope was the loud but sound-hearted John Bull of the trinity; he would sit probably on the table with a big cigar. Lewes, the smallest and most frail in appearance, would sit with his thin legs crossed, his big white bulldog at his feet, and murmur with captivating fluency a running commentary. Meredith would stand and gently swing a cane pendulum fashion, always with the philosophic air which had no taint of assumption, but fitted him as neatly and becomingly as did his clothes, and he was a born artist even in these details. Thus he would take his turn in the talk, and his expression would frequently sound uncommonly like blank verse, uttered with an occasional hesitation that was the faintest suggestion of a meditative drawl.

---

* The stress of writing for a Tory paper and of reading large numbers of bad or conventional novels undoubtedly contributed to the contorted and enigmatic elements in his style; to his feeling that one could not speak out to such a generation of fools and liars, the post-1850 middle-class public. To this extent the jobs were harmful. They gave him independence, but at the cost of inner qualms and intellectual discomfort. Things grew worse when in 1863 he also took on reading for another firm (Saunders and Otley) which had been bought by a friend of Lady Duff-Gordon. He had to keep this job secret as it was morally dubious to read for two publishers. 'I never refuse work,' he told Hardman, in ineffective self-defence. Thus he was trapped in the network of money-making after all.

At moments the gossipers succeed in conjuring him up in the moment of felicitous outburst—crying in the summer-eve, in the moonlight, 'Listen, do you hear the hounds—the hounds of Tanhurst chasing the ancient Briton?' or telling Alice Brandreth 'when you were in London, your face was like a sheet of white paper; and *now* it looks as if I had written a sonnet upon it.' Elaborating a comic image, 'She's a woman who's never had the first tadpole wriggle of an idea . . . but she's a mind as clean and white and flat as my plate—there are no eminences in it.' Or rising to a great imaginative height, as when he said of the actress who as Lady Macbeth in the sleepwalking scene pushed her hands from nose to ear, 'I assure you she came through her hands like a corpse stricken with mania in the act of resurrection.'

He disliked banal quotations and countered with a fantastic pseudo-quotation; satirised the duets and piano-practices of his wife and Alice with farmyard-imitations; made up comic dialogues on his walks and devised romances about the neighbours in peculiarly unsuited rôles; im-provised ribald rhymes on Women's Suffrage while championing it; in-vented odd things about the people in newspaper-advertisements. In such matters we see his vivid mind playing round every detail of everyday life. He in particular liked improvising ideas for novels and suggesting that one of his hearers should write the outlined work.*

In April 1865 he visited Milnes, Lord Houghton, at Fryston; and though Swinburne was there, he described the place as the dullest house with the driest company in the dismallest country he knew. The dry company included the Bishop of St Davids and a positivist philosopher J. H. Bridges. Milnes, Swinburne's Baron Tattle of Scandal, must have been controlling his tongue and keeping his extensive library of erotic and murder items quiet. On the 20th Meredith spent the afternoon with Mrs Carlyle, and was upset to hear that next day she died suddenly while driving in Hyde Park.

Vittoria was nearing conclusion. He had been working on it since 1863,

---

* His son Will was given to conventional remarks, which M. mocked at: 'Behold the Sagamore, mark that lofty brow, stand in awe with me before the wisdom that sits there enthroned. . . .' Once when his daughter came in her best clothes to dinner he waited for a hush to say, 'The blessed dearie come down wearing a wreath of roses to fascinate the military captain.' Of his wife he smilingly complained, 'She's a mud fort! You fire broadsides into her, nothing happens.' Alice says, 'his words never really hurt,' but that seems hardly true.
   He liked puzzling the servants with magniloquent outbursts. Cole the gardener would interpret, 'He means put less pepper in the soup.' Clodd details a speech of religious mockery made when the girl asked if the 'puddin wanted saving.' Murray cites his account of a water-drinking student in Germany, who died in agony, asking M. to perform the autopsy. 'When I made the first incision, the glitter of the stalactites in the poor fellow's gastric cavities positively blinded me—I had to wear blue glasses for months after.'

interrupted by *Rhoda Fleming* and his marriage. In May 1864 he wrote of the need to visit Italy for some local colour, and was hoping to sell serial rights to the *Cornhill*. In June Emilia was 'running very fast in Italy' and he hoped to see 'the damsel of the fiery South (no longer tripped and dogged by Philosopher or analyst) by late Autumn.' In July the heroine was going 'swimmingly,' then she lagged. By January 1865 a third was done. By the end of the year he had completed the job. We have already seen how he rejoiced in epical achievement, which he contrasted with the cobwebs of introspection. In a similar mood he wrote to Maxse.

> I am very hot upon *Vittoria*. Lewes says it must be a success; and it has my best writing. . . . Perhaps I have given it too historical a character to please the brooding mind of Fred [Maxse himself]. But, we shall see. I think one must almost love Italy to care for it and the heroine. There are scenes that will hold you; much adventure to entertain you; delicate bits and fiery handlings. But there is no tender dissection, and the softer emotions are not kept at half gasp upon slowly-moving telescopic objects, with their hearts seen beating in their frames.

Lewes agreed to serialise the novel in *The Fortnightly*, which had begun in May 1865, with Trollope chairman of the proprietory Board (subscribing £1,200 of the £9,000 capital); the first of our periodicals to take as its rule the signing of contributions. (Meredith had possibly been suggested as sub-editor; and he acted as editor when Morley was in the U.S.A. late in 1867—Morley having taken over from Lewes at the end of 1866.) *Vittoria* ran from January to December 1866, earning £40.

When war broke out between the Austrian Empire and the Italian insurgents, Meredith was fired with enthusiasm and wanted to be on the spot. He persuaded *The Morning Post* to send him out, and sent his first despatch from Ferrara where the Italians were gathered ready to force the Po, on 22 June. Early in July he was at Bozzolo, the H.Q. of the Italian Eleventh Division; went on to Torre Malimberti; and accompanied the troops to the new H.Q. at Piadena. He then moved to Gonzaga where he saw a good deal of camp-life. Via Teviso and Venice he left Italy for Marseilles, where he arrived on 24 July. He returned, however, through Austria to Italy in August; and passed through Venice, Padua, Vicenzo. He did not see much fighting in these months, but spent some weeks moving about with the Italian troops; and in Venice saw the triumphal entry of Victor Emmanuel and met Janet Ross by chance 'One whole day we spent at Torcello.'

In Vienna he met Leslie Stephen for the first time; and at Milan, Hyndman. In Venice, in the group of war-correspondents—Henty of *The Standard*, Hyndman of *The Pall Mall Gazette*, Sala of *The Daily*

Telegraph—he had a quarrel with the bumptious and bounding Sala, that man of bombastic anecdotes. The cause of the dispute seems to have been the wine to be drunk. Meredith, not so well off, choosing a wine of the country and Sala roaring for champagne.

> Meredith, though just in his dealings and hospitable in his way, was by no means liberal, while Sala, though extremely liberal, and hospitable as well, was by no means always just. Anyway, there arose a tremendous storm on Sala's part, and he insulted Meredith grossly at the hotel table (on the Pizza San Marco). Meredith could easily have killed Sala in any personal encounter, but he kept a strong restraint on himself and simply went away. [Hyndman.]

An episode very like something from one of Meredith's novels.

By Christmas he was back in Mickleham, keen to use his experiences to add reality to *Vittoria*. He was just in time to revise the book, which appeared in December.

Again the critics jeered, and the book had no success. In two letters to Swinburne he remarked:

> *Vittoria*, as I am told by Chapman and others, is not liked; so you may guess what pleasure your letter has given me. For I have the feeling that if I get your praise, I hit the mark. It seems that I am never to touch the public's purse. . . .
>
> *Vittoria* passes on to the limbo where the rest of my works repose. . . . I see the illustrious Hutton of the *Spectator* laughs insanely at my futile effort to produce an impression on his public. I suppose I shall have to give up and take to journalism, as I am now partly doing.—Yes. If you could get a place to say something of *Vittoria*!

Hutton of *The Spectator* said it was 'written in such a falsetto key, that apart from the crowd of uninteresting and dim figures on the canvas, no one would wish to read it again. . . . The greater number of characters, including the heroine . . . are ambitiously conceived Shadows, which seem to be striving vainly after a personality which they never attain. . . . The literary egotism in the foreground dims or eclipses all the subjects on which he exercises his art.' The dialogue is 'spasmodic and enigmatic.' All is 'effort, mannerism, affectation.'

The shrewdness of these blows have a true malignity. The exposure of bourgeois egoism is obscured by the accusation of Meredith himself as an egoist; the definition of people in the pangs of revolutionary growth is described as the search for an unattained personality.*

---

* *The Pall Mall* found obscurity, carelessness, unaccountable comings and goings, yet 'the incidents are full of interest, the dialogue exceedingly spirited.' *The Saturday Review* saw 'a wide disproportion between the expenditure of ability and the result obtained . . . very clever, though often unreadable, performance.' *Athenaeum* found 'a piece of good and honest hard work,' but 'how are human beings with limited faculties to understand all the distracting threads of this unmerciful novel?'

17

Vittoria

VITTORIA CARRIES on many characters from *Sandra*: Sandra-Vittoria herself, Merthyr and his sister, Pericles, Wilfrid and his sister Adela (now Mrs Sedley), Major Gambier, General Pierson, but it also introduces a number of new characters, Italian and Austrian. Its theme is the 1848–9 rising under Mazzini; and it opens with a conspiratorial meeting in the mountains, where several Milanese patriots, Vittoria among them, come to hear Mazzini's decisions. They resolve that the revolt will break out in Milan, the signal being given by a revolutionary song that Vittoria is to sing at the Opera House. She is thus to have the honour of inaugurating the uprising. As the conspirators go, she encounters an English group that includes Adela and Wilfrid, and she leaves a note warning them not to go to Milan. This warning, which she repeats in a note to Wilfrid, is discovered by a worker-patriot Barto, a sort of Marat of the Risorgimento, who decides she is a traitor. Thus the night of insurrection-song is approached in considerable confusion. Vittoria knows that she has been denounced, but refuses to withdraw from the plan without direct instructions from the Chief, Mazzini.

She sings, and there is an uprising which is suppressed. She manages to escape from Milan, thanks to Wilfrid and Carlo (a young aristocratic Republican, with whom she is in love). With her is Angelo, a cousin of Carlo, with a price on his head. A daredevil Austrian, Captain Weisspriess, pursues them but is badly wounded by Angelo in a duel in a defile. Vittoria gets to the Lenkenstein castle of Sonnenberg, whither her friend Laura has come. Wilfrid and Merthyr are also there. Wilfrid is engaged to Lena von Lenkenstein (Anna to Weisspriess). To save Angelo, Vittoria forces herself to lure Wilfrid back to her spell. Then she goes with Laura to Turin.

Here she sees King Victor and is convinced that he is the one to save Italy. She thus falls away from her faith in Mazzini, from her agreement with Carlo. Carlo, however, doesn't try to reason with her, he merely commands her to go to his mother. She ignores him and follows the King's army as a nurse, but is carried off by Pericles and the Austrians. When the King fails the revolution, she weakens and yearns for marriage with Carlo, for peace, for an end of the long strain; she obeys Carlo in going to his mother, but leaves her to stay in Milan, nursing Merthyr. Carlo in turn has partially lost his balance; he has come under the influence of a woman whom he early loved, the Countess Violetta, now an Austrian agent. She tries to break him from Vittoria; and then, when Merthyr has got the lovers married, she persists in setting him on the wrong track. He won't listen to Vittoria, who now wants him to go to Mazzini in Rome. Violetta feeds his ambition, his impulses of separatism; and then, having involved his followers in a hopeless uprising, he feels that he cannot desert them in honour. Violetta has betrayed everything. With his followers he joins the Brescian revolt, to die. But he escapes into the hills with partisans after the bombardment of the city. There he is captured by the Austrians and shot. Vittoria, who has come to find him, is too late.

The story is much more complex than this summary suggests. The vendetta of the Guidascarpis and the Lenkensteins, the various intrigues of the latter, above all the unhappy and lost trajectory of Wilfrid across the events, help to give an effect of multiple human fates wrapped up in the single great moment of history. But everything centres on the action, the development, of Vittoria, which in turn is entwined with the inner struggle in the forces of the Italian patriots.

Generally critics have seen her action in warning Wilfrid and Adela as out of character, a deed that neither the young impulsive Sandra nor the more matured Vittoria could perpetrate so stupidly. But such a view ignores her element of blinkered tenacity, her blind trust in her own intuition (which later twists her even worse askew in turning to the king). Meredith, with all his lyrical verve, does not idealise his heroes. He shows them carried so far by their first burst of passionate resistance to the oppressive world, their first vision of a different way of life; and then he reveals the emergence of an unresolved contradiction, a confusion that must be clarified if they are to lift their resistance, their vision, on to new levels of spiritual and political organisation. Vittoria's blind act in warning her old friends defines the element in her that fails to grasp fully the nature of the struggle in which she is involved; the element that still accepts the class-values she has otherwise broken through. She still thinks she can harmonise her devotion to Italian freedom and her attachment to that freedom's enemies. The illusion is not accidental; it exposes a deep flaw, a point of blindness, which in the end destroys her personal life and renders her ineffective as a rebel. It is based in a self-idealisation which insists that all her actions must be good and right because she carries them out through her private morality of honour. Her concept of integrity thus ends by inverting itself and betraying her, so that she involuntarily betrays others, even her lover Carlo.

The opening scene thus sets the key of her problem, which is also the problem of the liberation-movement. She is sure that she faces Mazzini with entire self-dedication, and yet she promptly commits what amounts to an act of treachery. The rest of the book is the consistent working out of this contradiction.

She is still in part the romantic rebel with a cult of spontaneity and absolute virtue; one corner of her personality thus touches the distorted development of persons like Mrs Lovell. In the last resort it is an un-realised class-bond that brings her down. She belongs to the working-class, and is clear in her feeling for the people. She wants to take her art to the labourers; but at the same time she aspires to music's grand levels, which in her world are based in the patronage of the rich and the leisured. In accepting the aid of the millionaire Pericles, she ties herself to a class, when she thinks she is simply giving herself to the people, the cause of freedom. For she never squarely confronts the problem, she accepts her place in the world of the wealthy and noble, and marries a noble, Carlo. She makes no attempt to assess the class-basis of the men competing to hold or possess her, the middle-class Wilfrid with his hopeless split, the ruthless financier Pericles with his creed of art-for-art's-sake, the idealist landowner Merthyr, the noble seeking to achieve political responsibility, Carlo. She judges them as 'individuals'; and that means in the last resort she judges them egoistically as aids or obstructions to her own advance (with which she naively identifies music and freedom). So she ends in a politically impotent state. The vital concrete element in her, with its effort to break through all conventions and grasp only the immediate human reality, inverts itself into a mixture of egoism and helplessness, and she cannot save Carlo when he most deeply needs her.

The proletarian Barto is thus right in his way when he sees her as a traitress to the revolution, even though he oversimplifies things. And when he finally faces her with the charge, she admits it. She does not mean what he means; and yet in the last resort their meanings come together.

But this definition of Vittoria's inner conflict, the real theme of the book, is not treated as an abstracted psychological matter. It has depth and significance only because it is also a definition of the level of develop-ment reached by the liberation-movement in Italy; and this wider relation is brought out partly by her relations with Carlo and the others, partly by the social bases of the various types of rebels who throng the novel's pages.

The first twenty chapters, with the mounting excitement as we near the opera-night, are magnificently sustained. Faced with her denunciation, she undergoes a crisis in her concept of herself:

> Her intense ideal conception of her duty sank and danced within her brain as the pilot-star dances on the bows of a tossing vessel. All were against her, as the tempest is against the ship. Even light above (by which I would image that which she could appeal to pleading in behalf of the wisdom of her obstinate will) was dyed black in the sweeping obscuration; she failed to recollect a sentence that was to be said to vindicate her settled course. Her sole idea was her holding her country by an unseen thread, and of the everlasting welfare of Italy being jeopardised if she relaxed her hold. You mariners batten down the hatchways when the heavens are dark and seas are angry. Vittoria, with the same faith in her instinct, shut the avenues to her senses—would see nothing, hear nothing.

The revolt-song is thus the culmination of the Vittoria with a naive faith in her spontaneous virtue. The old Vittoria dies that night, on the stage and in the spirit. On her flight she talks with the desperate Angelo.

> 'Do you fear death?'
> 'Sometimes; when I am half awake,' she confessed. 'I dislike thinking of it.'
> He asked her curiously: 'Have you never seen it?'
> 'Death?' said she, and changed a shudder to a smile; 'I died last night.'
> Angelo smiled with her. 'I saw you die.'
> 'It seems a hundred years ago.'
> 'Or half-a-dozen minutes. The heart counts everything.'
> 'Was I very much liked by the people, signor Angelo?'
> 'They love you.'
> 'I have done them no good.'
> 'Every possible good.'

Something has broken in her; and after she refuses to confess to the priest at the castle, the sense of failure bears her down:

> She thought of the Chief, whose life was stainless, but who stood proscribed because his aim was too high to be attained within compass of a mortal's years. His error seemed that he had ever aimed at all. He seemed less wise than the old priest of the oratory. She could not disentangle him from her own profound humiliation and sense of fallen power. Her lover's imprisonment accused her of some monstrous culpability, which she felt unrepentingly, not as we feel a truth, but as we submit to a terrible force of pressure.

Thus she loses her blithe faith; and the problem is whether she will understand the elements of blindness and self-idealisation that have brought her to this pass, whether she will give way to despair, or whether she will fall into worse illusions about herself.

The feeling of shame is riveted on her when Laura drives her to play up to Wilfrid and use him to save Angelo from capture.

'Do you fancy that Carlo wishes you to be for ever reading the line of a copy-book and shaping your conduct by it? Our Italian girls do this; he despises them. Listen to me; do not I know what is meant by the truth of love? I pass through fire, and keep constant to it, but you have seen some vile Romance of Chivalry in your head; a modern sculptor's figure, "Meditation"; that is the sort of bride you would give him in the stirring days of Italy. Do you think it is only a statue that can be true? Perceive—will you not—that this Lieutenant Pierson [Wilfrid] is your enemy. He tells you as much; surely the challenge is fair. Defeat him as you best can. Angelo shall not be abandoned.'

'O me! it is unendurable; you are merciless,' said Vittoria, shuddering.

She feels herself polluted, but cannot refuse; and so she brings Wilfrid down again and finally wrecks his life.

And then at Turin she herself goes downhill. She succumbs to the atmosphere of incense and does 'what makes a woman excessively tender and opinionated; she was petting her idea of the misunderstood one; she was thinking that she divined the King's character by mystical intuition; I will dare to say, maternally apprehended it.' She shames Carlo by kissing the King's hand when the betrayed people of Milan are hooting him and the true revolutionary forces are struggling on under Mazzini. As Carlo writes,

> I send you greeting from the Chief. He marched in the ranks from Bergamo. I saw him on the line of march strip off his coat to shelter a young lad from the heavy rain. He is not discouraged; none are who have been near him.

And too late, after having resisted Carlo, she finds out the lack of virtue in the King.

When she does marry Carlo, they cannot achieve true comradeship. Laura says to Merthyr, 'She has two husbands,' Merthyr and Carlo—the expression of her inner division. And so Carlo goes to his doom.

And yet the last word is not with the forces of frustration and alienation. The deep faith and love which has carried Vittoria so far will in time carry others beyond the point that has arrested her. 'Vittoria incarnates indeed a victory,' Galland says well. 'She puts a son into the world, she perpetuates life, she assures continuity, she makes progress possible.' And the deep and pure force of life in her, undefiled in the last resort by her failures, is beautifully uttered in her quest in the hills for Carlo.

> Vittoria read the faces of the mornings as human creatures have tried to gather the sum of their destinies off changing surfaces,—fair not meaning fair, nor black black, but either the mask upon the secret of God's terrible will, and to learn it and submit, was the spiritual burden of her motherhood, that the child leaping with her heart might live. Not to hope blindly, in the exceeding anxiousness of her passionate love, nor blindly to fear; not to let her soul fly out among the twisting chances. . . .
> Rarely has a soul been so subjected by its own force. . . .

The whole of this account of her quest expresses the anguish of a new birth of consciousness as well as the new life stirring in her body. And the last word is with Merthyr:

> 'Tell her?—she will die,' said Laura, shuddering.
> 'Get tears from her,' Merthyr rejoined; 'but hide nothing from her for a single instant; keep her in daylight. For God's sake, keep her in daylight.'

There is thus a profound difference between the end of Vittoria and Carlo, and the end of Richard Feverel and Edward Blancove. With all four the self-alienating process wreaks destruction; but whereas the latter pair are left with a hopeless regret at the apparently insoluble dilemma of human consciousness, the former have broken through that dilemma and there is nothing tragic in their end. Or rather the tragic element is present but is subsumed in a larger whole, that of the unconquerable struggle into human wholeness, into a society that has thrown off the alienations, spiritual and economic, of the class-world.

Meredith's greatness lies in the fact that he, first of the significant novelists of the 19th century, announces this fact. A new art is born, the art of the positive hero who transcends the whole nexus of contradictions that make up the tragic dilemma. Meredith's position has nothing in common with what he calls Abstract Optimism—that is, an optimism which maintains its smile by averting its eyes from the terrible sufferings of men in a society of self-alienation. His optimism relies on a penetration that goes as deep as can be gone into the alienating process and *then* drives beyond.

The quest of life and death, loss and renewal, which ends the book, must be read against the mountain-scene that opened it. The lofty tryst with the Chief is eloquently described to bring out its significance as the deep moment of finally-pledged loyalties, of separation-out from the oppressive world that is to be defeated and transformed. Mazinni, the spirit of the scene, the testing-moment, is defined as the serene revolutionary leader in whom the certainty of the future is embodied:

> If this man was a problem to others, he was none to himself. . . . He saw far, and he grasped ends beyond obstacles; he was nourished by sovereign principles; he despised material present interests. . . . If the title of idealist belonged to him, we will not immediately decide that it was opprobrious. The idealised conception of stern truths played about his head certainly for those who knew and loved it. Such a man, perceiving a devout end to be reached, might prove less scrupulous in his course, possibly, and less remorseful, than revolutionary Generals. His smile was quite unclouded, and came softly as a curve in water. . . . For as he had an orbed mind, so had he an orbed nature.

He vindicates the revolutionary rôle of women. 'Without their aid, and

the fire of a fresh life being kindled in their bosoms, no country that has
lain like ours in the death-trance can revive.'

But if he represents the undeviating leadership needed by the immortal
forces of the people, in the lesser rebels are shown all the shades of social
and political opinion that have to be brought together in the national
movement and that yet keep breeding fissiparous tensions. We see the
frightened nobles who want to keep the popular movement under control,
the veering middle-class, the workers who want a social as well as a
political revolution, brotherhood as well as national autonomy. Meredith
here poses the key-problem of a mass-movement: how is the maximum
union of allies to be gained and held without a betrayal of the movement's
aim?

Thus, Agostino feels uncomfortable between the noble he distrusts and
the worker he fears:

> You will come to Medoles tonight, Carlo. You need not be too sweet to
> him, but beware of explosiveness. I, a republican, am nevertheless a practical
> exponent of the sacrifices necessary to unity. I accept the local leadership of
> Medole—on whom I can never look without thinking of an unfeathered pie;
> and I submit to be assisted by the man Barto Rizzo. Do thou likewise, my son.
> Let your enamoured sensations follow that duty, and with a breezy space
> between. A conspiracy is an epitome of humanity, with a boiling power
> beneath it.

Carlo has the ideal of making himself a democrat, but keeps falling back
on the pride of birth, the inherited right to lead:

> Democrat as he imagined himself to be, he despised with a nobleman's con-
> tempt creatures who were so dead to the character of men of birth as to suppose
> that they were pale and remorseful after dealing a righteous blow, and that
> they trembled! Ammiani looked at his hand: no force of his will could arrest
> its palsy.

Sections of the aristocracy and the petty-bourgeois are scared of the
revolt.

> The count would speak pityingly of the poor depraved intellects which
> admitted the possibility of a coming Kingdom of Italy united; the lunatics who
> preached of it he considered a sort of self-elected targets for appointed files of
> Tyrolese jägers. But he was vindictive against him whom he called the profes-
> sional doctrinaire, and he had vile names for the man. Acknowledging that
> Italy mourned her present woes, he charged this man with the crime of
> originating them:—and why? what was his object? He was, the count declared
> in answer, a born intriguer, a lover of blood, mad for the smell of it, and old
> Man of the Mountain; a sheaf of assassins; and more—the curse of Italy! There
> should be extradition treaties all over the world to bring this arch-conspirator
> to justice. . . .

Count Serabiglione stands for the most extreme separatist tendencies and
an abject fear of social revolution:

> 'Not being for Italy, you must necessarily be against her. . . .
> 'No!' he cried; 'no; there is no question of "for" or "against," as you are
> aware. "Italy, and not Revolution": that is my motto.'
> 'Or, in other words, "The Impossible," ' said Laura. . . . 'Do you really
> imagine that "Italy without Revolution" does not mean Austria?'

Carlo's mother feels similarly, and Carlo himself is tainted with her ideas:

> Her soul shrank at the thought of the revolution being yielded up to theorists
> and men calling themselves men of the people—a class of men to whom Paolo
> her soldier-husband's aversion had always been formidably pronounced. It was
> an old and wearisome task for Carlo to explain to her that times were changed
> and the necessities of the hour different since the day when his father conspired
> and fought for freedom. Yet he could not gainsay her when she urged that the
> nobles should be elected to lead, if they consented to lead; for if they did not
> lead, were they not excluded from the movement?
> 'I fancy you have defined their patriotism,' said Carlo.
> 'Nay, my son; but you are one of them.'
> 'Indeed, my dearest mother, that is not what they will tell you.'
> 'Because you have chosen to throw yourself into the opposite ranks.'
> 'You perceive that you divide our ranks, madame my mother. For me there
> is no natural opposition of ranks. What are we? We are slaves: all are slaves.
> . . . I am content to take my patent of nobility for good conduct in the
> revolution. . . .'

And the inn-keeper in the hills says to Angelo who has called him a cur
and a traitor, 'Ah, signore, one might know you were a noble. You can't
understand our troubles, who carry a house on our heads, and have to
fill mouths agape.' And again, 'The taxes: we have to sell our souls to
pay the taxes.'

When the people of Milan rise, the nobles promptly feel terrified at the
unleashed force. 'The first crack of a division between the patriot force
and the aristocracy commenced this day,' Meredith comments; 'the day
following it was a breach.' And the King's seemingly weak tactics are
dictated by fear of revolution.

> Distrusting the revolution, which was a force behind him, he placed such
> reliance on its efforts in his front as to make it the pivot of his actions.

That is, he wants the people to bear the brunt of the fighting, so that he
will hold his army intact to suppress them after, if need be. And Agostino
remarks of Carlo's last exploit that if he wins, 'he will only have the
King and his army against him then.'

Against all these partial or confused loyalties there stand out on the one

hand Mazzini's abiding faith in the people, and on the other the unshak-
able revolutionary energy of the worker Barto, who owns the concrete
experience of suffering and outrage which Mazzini lacks. Together they
make up an unconquerable force. Barto is acutely aware of the elements
in the Italian cause which are ceaselessly making for a betrayal of the
people; that is why he watches Vittoria so narrowly:

> Never had an Austrian force seemed to him so terrible. He had to yield the
> internal fight, and let his faith sink and be blackened, in order that his mind
> might rest supine, according to his remembered system; for the inspiration
> which points to the right course does not come during mental strife, but after
> it, when faith summons its energies undisturbed—if only men will have the
> faith, and will teach themselves to know that the inspiration must come, and
> will counsel them justly. This was a part of Barto Rizzi's sustaining creed; nor
> did he lose his grasp of it in the torment and darkness of his condition.

Carlo hates and fears him, while aghast at his energy. 'He has Satanic
blood, and the worst is, that the Chief trusts him.' Laura says that then
she too trusts him; and Vittoria, knowing that he is against her, echoes her.

And yet, with all the diverse and eddying attitudes, Meredith gives the
effect of a great wave of popular energy, which is vastly greater than any
of its parts; and repeats his faith in revolutionary activity to regenerate
life. 'The sword reunites.'

> 'Carlo, if three generations of us pour out our blood to fertilise Italian
> ground, it's not too much to pay to chase these drilled curs.' Luciano spoke in
> vehement undertone. . . .
> The heat and whirl of the hour struck his [Carlo's] head, for tomorrow they
> might be wrestling with that living engine which had marched past, and
> surely all the hate he could muster should be turned upon the outer enemy.
> He gained his mother's residence with clearer feelings.

Against this deep ever-stirring force of revolt are set the Austrian oppressors, their army the privileged class of the Empire:

> 'They torture, too, they torture! It's a woman; and insults will be one mode
> of torturing her. They can use rods. . . . Think of the rough hands, and foul
> mouths! She will be seized on the boards——'
> 'They *flog* women, they do not shoot them. They shoot men.'

The Austrians have the superior-race attitudes:

> Vienna counselled measures mildly repressive;—'conciliating,' it was her
> pleasure to call them. . . . One (young officer) had bidden his Herr General
> to 'look here,' while he stretched forth his hand and declared that Italians were
> like women, and wanted—yes, *wanted*—(their instinct called for it) a beating,
> a real beating; as the emphatic would say in our vernacular, a thundering
> thrashing, once a month:—'Or so,' the General added acquiescingly.

And they anticipate Hitler's dictum that a big lie is a truth:

> The General will say, 'Oh! a very big lie's equal to the truth; big brother
> to a fact,' or something; as he always does, you know.

One more important aspect of the book: against Vittoria and her idea
of engaged art, of art at the service of the revolution, is set the millionaire
Pericles with his passion for pure art.

> To his mind it was the vilest treason, the grossest selfishness, to conspire or
> to wink at the sacrifice of a voice like Vittoria's to such a temporal matter as
> this, which they called patriotism. He looked on it as one might look on the
> Hindoo drama of a Suttee. . . . The religious belief of the connoisseur ex-
> tended to the devout conception that her voice was a spiritual endowment,
> the casting of which priceless jewel into the bloody ditch of patriots was far
> more tragic and lamentable than any disastrous concourse of dedicated lives.

This idea of pure art is linked with the fear of the aristocracy that Vittoria
will let loose an uncontrollable tide of popular forces.

> The Italians present, one and all, rose up reverently and murmured the re-
> frain. Many of the aristocracy would, doubtless, have preferred that this public
> declaration of the plain enigma should not have rung forth to carry them on
> the popular current; and some might have sympathised with the insane grin
> which distorted the features of Antonio-Pericles, when he beheld illusion
> wantonly destroyed, and the opera reduced to be a mere vehicle for a fulmina-
> tion of politics.

Thus the song that liberates the forces of rebellion is an emblem of the
new relation that must henceforth rule between art and life, a new
dynamic relation in which the artist is vitally a part of his audience and
its needs. And by his story Meredith brings powerfully out the way in
which theories of pure art, of art-for-art's-sake, are an aspect of the reactionary forces, of high finance and monopoly-power. Considering the
set-up he is here analysing and demolishing only came into existence in
a developed form long after the 1860's, his political penetration is remarkable.

The same episode that opposes the notions of art held by Vittoria and
Pericles brings out Meredith's ideas of the political basis of significant
art-forms. The opera *Camilla* which has been written for Vittoria is a
tale of love and jealousy; but he makes clear his notion of the way in
which such a tale becomes political when its meaning is projected beyond
the mere personal entanglement into a larger focus that *implies and gives
a richer significance to the social pattern behind.*

> While confessing his guilt to Camilla, Leonardo has excused it by an em-
> phatic delineation of Michiella's magic sway over him. (Leonardo, in fact, is
> your small modern Italian Machiavelli, overmatched in cunning, for the reason

that he is always at a last moment the victim of his poor bit of heart or honesty:
he is devoid of the inspiration of great patriotic aims.) If Michiella (Austrian
intrigue) has any love, it is for such a tool. She cannot afford to lose him. She
pleads for him; and, as Camilla is silent on his account, the cynical magnanimity of Camillo is predisposed to spare a fangless snake. Michiella withdraws
him from the naked sword to the back of the stage. The terrible repudiation
scene ensues, in which Camillo casts off his wife.

If it was a puzzle to one Italian half of the audience, the other comprehended
it perfectly, and with rapture. It was thus that Young Italy had too often been
treated by the compromising, merely discontented, dallying aristocracy.
Camilla cries to him, 'Have faith in me! have faith in me! . . .'

And so on, with the Austrians slowly restive, and the audience ever
clearer as to the political message, till the final revelations:

> The multitude break away from Camilla—veiled no more, but radiant;
> fresh as a star that issues through corrupting vapours, and with her voice at a
> starry pitch on its clear ascendency:—

> > *Tear up the insufferable scroll!—*
> > *O thou, my lover and my soul!*
> > *It is the Sword that reunites;*
> > *The Pen that our perdition writes. . . .*

Into the murder of Camilla and her triumphant rising out of death as the
immortal people:

> *There is an end of joy: there is no end*
> *To striving; therefore ever let us strive*
> *In purity that shall the toil befriend,*
> *And keep our poor mortality alive. . . .*
> *Our life is but a little holding lent*
> *To do a mighty labour: we are one*
> *With heaven and the stars when it is spent. . . .*

> *I cannot count the years,*
> *That you will drink, like me,*
> *The cup of blood and tears,*
> *Ere she to you appears:—*
> *Italia, Italia shall be free! . . .*

And we must note that it is the revolutionary moment, the full acceptance
by the artist of the active partisan nature of his art in defence of life, that
restores to the people their penetration into the inner meaning of art—just as it
gives to the artist the power of uniting realism and symbolic depth with
a new dynamic clarity of impact.

Vittoria is then the epical tale of the first stages of the Risorgamento. It
is on the one hand a sweeping tale of action—and in this relation we must
not forget that Meredith named Scott as one of his formative influences—
but on the other it is an intricate presentation of the clash and involvement

GEORGE MEREDITH WITH HIS SON
ARTHUR IN 1861
from a photograph taken by Sir William Hardman

GEORGE MEREDITH CARRIED TO THE POLLING
BOOTH AT LEATHERHEAD, JANUARY 26, 1906

of class-forces in the revolt; and it is here that we see the extraordinary realism of Meredith's vision, in which, while lyrically expressing his whole-hearted absorption in the positive aspects of the historical situation he treats, he defines always the points of obstruction and frustration, the degree of clarity-in-struggle and unclarity which has been reached in the movement towards human brotherhood. In Vittoria and Carlo he defines the forces that ensure both the temporary defeat of Italian freedom and its ultimate triumph.

In one passage he describes the novel as 'a field of action, of battles and conspiracies, nerve and muscle, where life fights for plain issues . . . in the day when Italy reddens the sky with the banners of a land revived.' The critics have called the construction tortuous; but in fact the first half, over which Mazzini presides, has a great single sweep, and it is only the second half, which defines the recoil of the baffled revolutionary forces, the breaking-out of the temporarily-overlaid class-conflict inside those forces, which can be called labyrinthine. If, however, one grasps the political point, the second half is not at all difficult. Most of the exclamations over Meredith's difficulties are merely confessions of political opacity.

'My love is for epical subjects.' We have already discussed that letter. In another, to Swinburne in March 1867, he stated:

> You alone have hit on the episode of the Guidascarpi [Angelo and his brother]. . . . I would have carried it into fulness, but the vast machinery pressed on me. My object was not to write the Epic of the Revolt—for that the time is yet too new: but to represent the revolt itself, with the passions animating both sides, the revival of the fervid Italian blood; and the character of the people: Luigi Suracco, Barto Rizzo, etc. Angostino Balderini is purposely made sententious and humorously conscious of it: Carlo Ammiani is the personification of the youth of Italy of the nobler sort. Laura Piaveni and Violetta d'Isorella are existing contrasts.
>
> I am afraid it must be true the style is stiff; but a less condensed would not have compassed the great amount of matter.

He had, however, written an epic, *a new sort of epic*. Not the one that is shaped from immemorial traditions, but one born from the fire of great events in which the writer whole-heartedly and immediately participates.

The bad reception of the book convinced him that there was not, and could not be, any common ground between him and the middle-class public. In 1883 he told someone who wanted a copy that the effect of the attacks was to make him indifferent to his works after they'd gone through the course of castigation. Now he felt so heavy a burden of hostility and stupidity that he meditated the abandonment of literature. But his feeling for the future was so strong that he had no choice but to go on with novel and poem—for unborn readers.

18

Richmond Roy

LATE IN 1867 he found his home, Flint Cottage on Box Hill, set on the lower slopes against a background of woodland on Juniper Hill and Mickleham. A white gate opened from the rough chalk hillroad on to a garden of grass and flowers with tall yew-hedges. A few steps under a trellised porch led into a small hall with dining-room on right and parlour on left. His bedroom at first looked out on a little ravine and faced the sunrise over Box Hill; but after 1876 he had a chalet, built on the higher ground where he generally slept in the tiny side-room. In front of the house the long green slope moved leftward in a charming line to the hill-top of trees from which there was a fine view over champaign country to the downs, almost indeed to the sea. West and north ran hills and hanging woods. In such a setting he once again returned to poetry.

Before the end of the year he disposed of his Kingston lease and moved on, but Christmased at Mickleham, where he stayed most of January. By month-end he was at his new and lasting home:

> I am every morning at the top of Box Hill—as its flower, its bird, its prophet. I drop down the moon on one side, I draw up the sun on t'other. I breathe fine air. I shout ha ha to the gates of the world. Then I descend and know myself a donkey for doing it.

Alice Brandreth, who became one of his pets, tells how at the age of thirteen she stayed with her relations, the Gordons, nearby, and her Eton cousin took her up the hill to see the sunrise. 'I know a man who lives on Box Hill. He's quite mad, but very amusing; he likes walks and sunrises. Let's go and shout him up.' They shouted him up. Then 'I was weary in mind and body when I returned home, but I knew that I had watched the sun rise beside a Poet and a Thinker, his enthusiasm, his personality, one with Nature, the summer and the morning.'

The anecdote reveals more than Alice meant, the amused contempt of the gentry, the superficial response to 'poetry'—a response that he rather liked when it came from attractive girls or women, but which he generally resented as no true reaction to his meanings.

He was growing surer in his realisation of where his loyalty lay:

I see no desire for it [reform] below. If there were, I would give it (interest); I have no fear of Radicals. Democracy must come, and the sooner it overflows rulers who are cowardly, the better for all. We say—Democracy, as if it were some deadly evil; whereas it is almost synonymous with Change. Democracy never rests. The worst of it is that it can be violent in its motion. [April 1866.]

But he accepted that violent motion when necessary (as his work from *Shagpat* to *The Crisis* of 1905 shows), and realised that, when necessary, it became also the only possible mode of regeneration:

> Fred, it's clear there is no such spirit [of independence] now in this pot-bellied country—none of it. . . . I declare to you, I have watched the changes of mood in the Government, the Journals—say, the people: and I have seen them moved by apprehension and panic, and by nothing else in their foreign relations; by little else in their dealings at home. The aristocracy has long since sold itself to the middle-class; that has done its best to corrupt the class under it. I see no hope but in a big convulsion to bring a worthy people forth. The monied class sees the same, and reads it—will do anything to avoid it. . . .

Thus clearly he realised what is happening, yet kept his faith in the future. 'Democracy must come; democracy never rests: *a great convulsion to bring a worthy people forth.*'

In the 1867 autumn he worked at Southampton in the elections; for Maxse, having this year retired as Rear-Admiral, was standing as Radical. His readiness to do election-work of this sort marks him out from any other important writer of the century; and the experience strengthened both his awareness of the existent corruptive pressures and his faith in an ultimate reversal of things:

> My two months down with Captain Maxse was a dead [financial] loss of time to me. I never regret anything I am able to help him in, as you will believe, but that's another matter. We were badly beaten at Southampton, but I think it will be proved that bribery was done there. We on our side were not guilty of it, I know.
>
> It is a very corrupt place. It has been found by experience of the enlarged franchise that where there are large labouring populations depending upon hire (especially in a corrupt and languishing town like Southampton) they will be thrown into the hands of the unscrupulous rich. At all events, it is one of the evils we have to contend against until the poor fellows know by enlighten-ment where their own interests lie and the necessity for their acting in unison and making sacrifices.
>
> Old Toryism has still a long spell of life in this country where the vitality has need to be strong in the centre of thick decay that won't be shovelled out. —I fancy Captain Maxse had to pay about £2,000 for the attempt. He acted simply in a spirit of duty, that he might enter Parliament to plead the cause of the poor.
>
> —Our commercial failures of two years back still press on us. Artists and authors suffer particularly. But the strain will be over with me very soon. My

novels have been kept back by having had to write on newspapers—the only things that paid. . . . [To Arthur.]

He learned at Southampton how deeply the bourgeois corruption had eaten into the workers, but also he learned the workers' needs 'to act in unison' against the bourgeoisie. He still had no idea of the forms of organisation and struggle thus implied; but the general concept had lodged deep in his mind.

His journalistic work, as he complained, was such a burden as to impede his work on novel and poem. In late 1867 he edited *The Fortnightly* while Morley was in the States, 'and that with incessant composition and potboilers kept my hands tied. But I am training my toes (first and second of right foot) to indite epistles and "Ips. Journal" while I pursue my course complacently above.' A light moment had been provided by Queen Victoria's *Journal of Life in the Highlands*, which he called England's Book. 'It sent me up Box Hill dancing a Tupper-jig' at its abysmal mediocrity of mind.

In the 1869 summer he went abroad with Lionel Robinson to see Arthur. In 1870 his father-in-law died; and in the summer he visited Maxse and yachted. He and Marie stayed with the Cotterills at Tongswood, and took rooms for a while at Eastbourne. The outbreak of the Franco-Prussian War stirred him profoundly, as it did most intellectuals of the day; and its effects, as we shall see, were lasting on his work and outlook.

For some time he had been on a new novel, first called *The Adventures of Richmond Roy, and his friend Contrivance Jack: Being the History of Two Rising Men* (May 1864), 'a spanking bid for popularity.' By January 1870 the course of the book has much changed. The picaresque conception has become *Harry Richmond*, in which 'I fear I am evolving his personality too closely for the public, but a man must work by the light of his conscience if he's to do anything worth reading.'*

Harry Richmond is a long story: 169 characters in it have been listed. It appeared serially in *The Cornhill*, running fifteen months, and then as a

---

* Letters to Jessop give some idea of what he was groping towards, though he only partly achieved the aims in *Harry Richmond*. 'It is to show you the actions of minds as well as of fortunes, and here and there men and women vitally animated by their brains, at different periods of their lives—and of men and women with something of a look-out on the world and its destinies.' Thus he tries to state his method of linking individual action with the total historical movement, and of building the positive hero. He goes on with a rejection of any idealist or mystical element in the 'destinies':—'the mortal ones: the divine I leave to Doctors of D.—I daresay the novel won't be liked, but I know my plan, I do my work, and if I am kept very poor I hope to pay all in time. As for recognition of the stuff in my writing and the system it goes on, I care little for it now, and when I thrust myself into the pillory by publishing, the smack in the face and the pat on the shoulder are things in the day's order.' And his hackwork goes on: 'soon it will be jogging the gibbing cab-horse.'

three-volume novel in the winter of 1871. In it Meredith returns to the autobiographical material already used in *Evan Harrington*, but organises that material with more concentration. Richmond Roy is essentially the Great Mel, blown up in even larger dimensions and given a much more extended field of action and fantasy. Apparently after the epical strain of *Sandra-Vittoria* Meredith felt the need to fall back, to return to origins, to use his own childhood and youth for the explication of the conflicts and illusions in the English scene.

Richmond Roy is the bastard of an actress, who has built up the fantasy that he is the child of a royal duke, and who hopes somehow or other to have his birthright vindicated. He manages to fascinate and marry a daughter of the rich Squire Belsham; but she goes mad through his bad treatment of her (not clearly specified). Their son Harry has been brought up by the Squire. One night, shortly before the wife dies, Roy turns up and demands to see her; the Squire refuses, but lets him carry off the son. Harry has a grand time in London with his father, who is then arrested for debt. After a while Roy (who gets mysterious regular payments which he attributes to the Government trying to buy him off) re-emerges, puts Harry in a school, and disappears. At first Harry is well treated; then as no payments arrive, he is humiliated.

This section of the novel we have considered in relation to Meredith's own youth; and there is no need to cover anew the extremely fresh and perceptive way in which it depicts adolescent growth.

Harry at last runs off, takes up with some gypsies (in particular a comely girl Kiomi), and in the end returns to the Squire. He still longs for his father; and getting an indication that Roy is in the Bench Prison, he slips off to London with his friend Temple. Lost in a fog, they are taken on a ship by a kindly sailor and carried off by the Captain, Welsh, who thinks them deboshed young fellows, brands to be snatched from the burning. They arrive in Germany, and Harry chances on some acquaintances of the days when he travelled with his father. He extorts from them the news that Roy is in a small German principality, and sets off thither.

He arrives just as a statue is being unveiled. This statue turns out to be his father, gilded and made up to save his patron, the Margravine, who has sworn to have a statue ready in an impossibly short time. Roy, in fact, is a sort of jester at the court. Harry falls in love with the young princess Ottilia, who returns his affection. He goes back home to the Squire, who has long determined that he'll marry the daughter of a neighbour, Janet. But he cannot forget his father, and joins him for a while at Bath, where a Welsh heiress has fallen in love with him. Then, at Harry's expense, they go yachting. Roy arranges things so that at

Ostend they find Ottilia, who has been ill, and they all yacht together. Again at the court, Harry fights a duel with a suitor of Ottilia, and is wounded. Roy tells Ottilia that Harry has been wounded to death in an attack, and she comes to him. She despises duels, and, on learning the truth, finds herself in a false position. However, at his advice, she withdraws in time.

The Squire learns that Harry has been financing Roy, and turns very fierce. Roy swears the money will be returned; and sets about snaring Ottilia afresh. Harry has been beaten near death by the gypsies, who mistake him for the seducer of Kiomi (Heriot), his false hero of the schooldays. Roy gets word to Ottilia that Harry is dying, and she rushes to the Isle of Wight where he lies. Once again she finds herself deceived. But now Roy comes out in his full colours. He blackmails the prince, saying that he'll publicly compromise Ottilia, and for a while it seems that he'll triumph. However, suddenly the tables are turned. The Squire reveals that the sums supposed to come from the Government are in fact paid by his second daughter, who is in love with Roy; and a German prince who has turned up at the Margravine's suggestion is accepted by Ottilia as her husband. Roy breaks down under the proof that his life has been based on a fantasy.

Harry has now come close to love of Janet, grown from a pettish and greedy small girl into a strong and fine, though limited, character. She, however, has become engaged to a young aristocrat whom she hopes to reform, and Harry goes off disconsolate to travel. He is summoned by Ottilia to her court where he finds Janet waiting for him. Her bethrothed did not turn up at the church for the wedding—it appears he had been carried off by Captain Welsh, as Harry and Temple were; he had seduced a girl whom the Captain compassionately adopts, and when he comes to claim her on board the ship he is abducted. The ship sinks. Janet and Harry are married.

The theme is that of a father-son relationship; but though Roy tries to model Harry in his own likeness, as Sir Austin does Richard, his ideal is that of the Great Mel swollen to giant size. Many years later Meredith spoke of the tingling reality he had felt in the persons of this book. 'When Harry Richmond's father first met me, when I heard him tell me in his pompous style about the son of a duke of blood royal and an actress of seventeen years of age, I simply roared with laughter.' And the way in which he turns back to his childhood is stressed by the Hants setting, more or less the same as that in *Evan*; the area south of Petersfield— Riversley Grange can be identified as a few miles from Harting.

Roy has Dickensian elements: he is akin to the more grandiloquent

specimens in Dickens's large gallery of spongers. But no Dickensian parasite is on quite such a tremendous scale. Nothing less than a throne will
satisfy his claims; he stands for the idea of class-privilege in its most rabid
form. (Du Maurier's drawings gave him a close likeness to the royal
dukes of the early century.) Into him Meredith distils the essence of his
own family-experience of snobbery, which is also the essence of bourgeois dreams of superiority and power.

Harry is held by his father's image; and his growth into a sense of the
truth of things is slow and difficult. Even when he discovers his father's
lies and shortcomings, he is still spelled. The statue-episode gives the first
big shock to his worship: Roy elevated into golden majesty and exposed
as a masquerading jester-cheat is the perfect emblem of the book's theme.
Yet Roy is no mere cipher of snobbery; he is given fullness by his mixture
of qualities. He has generosity, magnanimity, even capacity for organisation; and at the root of his self-aggrandisment is a genuine love for his
suffering mother, a wish to vindicate her. And when he is defeated in his
infantile effort to overcome all problems by a fantasy-union with the
sources of power in his society, he swings into furious rebellion. He slips
away to a City Banquet and makes a violent speech against those sources
of power.

> He bade his audience to beware of princes, beware of idle princes; and letting
> his florid fancy loose on these eminent persons, they were at one moment silver
> lamps, at another poising hawks, and again sprawling pumpkins; anything
> except useful citizens. How could they be? They had the attraction of the
> lamp, the appetite of the hawk, the occupation of the pumpkin: nothing was
> given them to do but to shine, destroy, and fatten. Their hands were kept
> empty: a trifle in their heads would topple them over; they were monuments
> of the English system of compromise. Happy for mankind if they were monu-
> ments only? Happy for them! But they had the passions of men. . . . They
> were the monuments of a compromise between the past and the terror of the
> future: puppets as princes, mannikins as men, the snares of frail women, stop-
> gaps of the State, feathered nonentities! . . .
> [Then] he gave his audience an outline of the changes he would have effected
> had he but triumphed in his cause; and now came the lashing of arms, a flood
> of eloquence. Princes with brains, princes leaders, princes flowers of the land,
> he had offered them! princes that should sway assemblies, and not stultify the
> precepts of a decent people 'by making you pay in the outrage of your morals
> for what you seem to gain in policy. . . .'
> The remark was current that a great deal was true of what had been said
> of the Fitzs.

This is the anti-feudal wisdom of the early revolutionary bourgeoisie
of which an element survived in the Republicanism general among the
progressive middle-class and politically-minded workers of the period.

Meredith ensures that we will see the relation by making the amiable but respectably dim lawyer Temple anti-monarchical:

> Though a strict Constitutionalist, he had words of disgust for princes, acknowledging, however, that we were not practical in our use of them, and kept them for political purposes often to the perversion of our social laws and their natural dispositions. He spoke of his son's freak in joining the Navy. 'That was the princess's doing,' said Temple [his son]. 'She talked of naval heroes. . . .' [xlii.]

Roy sets out the Carlylean (or for that matter, Disraelian) thesis of the royally-born reassuming leadership, wresting it from the capitalists, and setting up a new kind of feudalism on the bases created by the capitalist forms of production. He has offered this alternative; but it has been rejected. And so the world is lost. Meredith is correct in developing these ideas out of the cracked Roy; but he seems to have written the Banquet speech first as a straight attack on capitalism:

> I was here and there hand-tied, too, by gentlemanly feeling in relation to the reigning Royal House, sweet Tory Tuck! or I should (and did on paper) have launched out. The Speech at the City Banquet would have satisfied a Communist Red originally. And I had planned startling doings for the season of the Grand Parade. [To Hardman, Nov. 1871—shortly after the Commune.]

Roy's speech is important in bringing out the latent political moral of the tale; and it cannot be stressed too much that Meredith's pangs in writing and constructing derive from his resolve to make every detail subserve a central concept, political and psychological, so that the conclusions of his novels in particular bring out into the open what he has been keeping under cover as his organising system.

Roy is opposed to Squire Bentham, a Tory of landed property, who has gone over into alliance with capitalism and proved himself a capable finance-expert. Meredith stresses this point—also that the Squire is a mine-owner—though we see the man only as a landlord.

> He was a curious study to me, of the Tory mind, in its attachment to solidity, fixity, certainty, its unmatched generosity within a limit, its devotion to the family, and its family eye for the country. . . .
>
> He has rarely invested but to double his capital; never speculated but to succeed. He may not understand men quite so well, but then he trusts none entirely; so if there is a chasm in his intelligence, there is a bridge thrown over it. . . .
>
> One of the boasts of Riverseley was, that while the rest of the world ate and drank poison, the Grange lived on its own solid substance, defying malefactory Radical tricksters.

The Squire then represents the successful merging of feudal survivals with the dominant bourgeoisie. Roy stands for the failure of feudal privilege to assert itself as an alternative way of life, of State-power; and his last

outburst expresses his recognition of that failure. What then is the true
alternative in the Squire's way? what is the course of struggle to be
followed by Harry?

Here it is that the book fails. Meredith has meant to show the clash of
Roy's and the Squire's ideas and methods within and without Harry, who
moves from the romantic delusions into a positive view of the world, but
who does not accept the Squire's egoist greed as a solution. But though
the movement from the romantic delusions is shown with a certain
success, the development of constructive ideas in place of the Squire's
tyrannous power-greed is hardly sketched in at all. The book ends with
the shallow formula of reconciliation like *Evan*, but this weakness is here
more disastrous than in *Evan* because the theme attempts a more definitely
political formulation. To be consistent, Meredith should show Harry
awakening to revolt against the class-power of the Squire instead of
smugly accepting it as his birthright.

What ensures the weakness of the book is the princess, Ottilia. She remains a fantasy-figure of subtle sensibilities, with no basis in the real
world: she is one of the Pole sisters as those sisters saw themselves. In so
far as she has any reality, she belongs to the 18th century world—say, that
of the liberal prince under whom the Neuwied schools were founded. In
the Squire's world she has no meaning; she is a relic from the feudal past,
a dream-creature of Roy's madness; her function is only to be swept
away. And her end in the novel is a sort of parody of her pretensions. To
save her feudal dignity and her father's—to save her abstract conception
of herself—she leaves the man she loves, and marries the boisterous Prince
Hermann (a sort of very crude Humboldt) who admires British rule in
India and describes the Indian masses as elephants 'servile till they trample
you, and not so stupid as they look.'

The whole German section miscarries. Meredith needed some episode
like the Neuwied school to bring out the type of debt he wants Harry to
owe to Germany; but what he does is simply to put him into a sort of
exteriorisation of Roy's fantasy. The sole event with the effect at which
Meredith aims is Harry's chat with the professor:

> 'You are one of the main drainpipes of English gold. What is your object?
> To spend it?'
> 'I shall hope to do good with it.'
> 'To do good! There is hardly a prince or millionaire, in history or alive, who
> has not in his young days hugged that notion. Pleasure swarms, he has the pick
> of the market. . . . Your nobles are nothing but rich men inflated with empty
> traditions of insufferable, because unwarrantable pride, and drawing substance
> from alliances with the merchant class. Are they your Leaders? . . . Not even
> in military service! . . .'

'It is widely respected. . . .'
'Widely!' he repeated. 'It is widely respected; and you respect it: and why
do you respect it?'
'We have illustrious names in our aristocracy . . . a race of nobles who
have stood for their country's liberties.'
'So long as it imperilled their own! Any longer?'

But there can be no real relation of the rebellious radical professor and
the tinpot feudal court where he is set. By linking Ottilia and the professor
Meredith commits an anachronism, a falsehood; and the idea that their
influence fuses to push Harry into a socially-valuable and responsible life
carries no conviction. He is in fact remembering Neuwied, his gratitude
towards Goethe and the German philosophers of development, the German historians and free-thinkers; he tries to translate this Germany into
a setting that kills it, a Germany looking towards war-expansion and
imperial State-unity. Prince Hermann indeed puts the case:

> Then he talked of the littleness of Europe and the greatness of Germany.
> . . . India was for the land with the largest sea-board. Mistress of the Baltic,
> of the North sea and the East, as she eventually must be, Germany would
> claim to take India as a matter of course, and find an outlet for the energies
> of the most prolific and toughest of the races of mankind,—the purest, in fact,
> the only true race, properly so called, out of India, to which it would return
> as to its source, and there create an empire magnificent in force and solidity.
> . . .

Thus Meredith states German racialism in terms of the period's Aryan
theory. The Ottilia whom Hermann marries can only be an obedient
supporter of the Bismarckian Empire which was emerging as Meredith
wrote.

Harry's growth blurs as the book goes on. The professor's jeer, 'To do
good!' demolishes his vague aims—the aims that still are as vague when
he inherits the Squire's estates and stocks-and-shares with horse-loving
Janet. We recall Captain Welsh's belief that the idle and lost can sweat
the Devil out only by hard work, by facing the terror-of-death as the
elemental world heaves up against them and only labour-skill can save
them.

> 'If the Archbishop o' Canterbury sailed the sea, and lived in Foul Alley,
> Waterside, when on shore, and so felt what it is to toss on top of the waves
> o' perdition, he'd understand the value of a big, clean, well-manned, well-
> provisioned ship, instead o' your galliots wi' gaudy sails, your barges that can't
> rise to a sea, your yachts that run to port like mother's pets at first pipe o' the
> storm, your trim-built wherries.'
> 'So you'd have only one sort of vessel afloat,' said I. 'There's the difference
> of a man who's a scholar.'

'I'd have,' said the captain, 'every lad like you, my lad, trained in the big ship, and he wouldn't capsize, and be found betrayed by his light timbers as I found you. Serve your apprenticeship in the Lord's three-decker; then to command what you may.'

But even apart from the fine chapters on Harry's childhood and youth, there are many striking passages of description and character; and many penetrating glances at the Victorian world. Meredith sees (and states through a German) that Britain, the industrial pioneer, is already being outstripped by rivals. He gets in shrewd blows at Toryism:

> 'I thought, sir, things were getting better,' said the captain.
> 'The damnedest mistake ever made, William. How about the Fall of Man, then, eh? You talk like a heathen Radical. It's Scripture says we're going from better to worse, and that's Tory doctrine' [says the Squire].

And Harry has his moments of realisation:

> I had been folded in a dream: I had stretched my hands to the highest things of earth, and here now was the retributive material money-question, like a keen scythe-blade!

But he does not ask the final question, why the aspiration in such a world is scythed down by retributive money.

However, when the worst is said, the figure of Roy remains a gigantic creation, typifying in masterly fashion a whole epoch of bourgeois illusions. His crash is also in the last resort the crash of his rival, the Squire, since both men are rooted in a world of power-privilege which needs its illusions if it is to maintain its grip on men's minds. It is a crash which bequeaths to the son the problem of exploring the insecure foundations of that world and of building a different sort of edifice. Harry may not convince us of the rebellious stamina required for such a task; but Meredith himself moved in his next book into defining a character of more valiancy, who faced the crash of the middle-class illusion and what it implied.*

---

* Much of the narrative of *Harry Richmond* flows with great ease and charm: a *Fortnightly* reader took it for a work by Lever. The *Athenaeum* found the book 'a sketch in three volumes in spite of the extraordinary minuteness of description,' 'short staccato sentences,' facts shaped according to the story's exigencies. The *Examiner* found 'the wildest vagaries of plot-making' and a style of 'meaningless sententiousness,' English life not as it is but as it pleases M. to present it, 'unpleasant and unprofitable.' *The Spectator* relented from its usual virulence to find Ottilia a 'beautiful picture,' but, after some praise, found the book 'stuff for half-a-dozen first-rate novels' rather 'than a first-rate itself,' lacking movement, flow, ease, and style affected. *The Westminster* found 'gay fancies and wealth of poetry' but said that after the spell snaps with the closing of the book, one became critical. *Blackwood's* could 'hardly force' its way through the thickets of the latter part. The Dailies (*News, Telegraph, Graphic, Post*) were more friendly, but without understanding.

19

The Radical Revolutionary

HARRY RICHMOND achieved a second edition before the end of the year; but it was more likely the weaknesses of the book than its virtues that created this unusual demand. Clearly Meredith was at a difficult point of growth; he could follow up the weaknesses and become a successful novelist, or move uncompromisingly into the critique of English society. He chose the latter course.

The Franco-Prussian War was a shock, a source of continual strain. 'This war agitates me; gazing on an old tree, or talking with you [Morley] are my febrifuges.' He tried at first abstract assessment of the moral and civic virtues and vices on each side; he wanted to be a good European, standing for civilised values; and he could not rise at once, as Ruskin did in *Fors Clavigera*, to the realisation that the war derived from the conflicts of capitalism. So he vacillated, trying to weigh aspects that could not effectively be weighed for the answer he wanted. But he found his emotions inclining more and more to France as soon as he felt a popular element asserting itself after the fall of the Emperor. And so, late in 1870, he struggled at a long Ode which would embody his conviction of elements from the great French Revolution reviving and bursting out. His Ode has behind it the direct stimulus of Swinburne's Ode on the Republic's Proclamation (in September), and more deeply, the ideas of Hugo's *Les Châtiments*, *La Légende des Siècles*, *Napoléon le Petit*. France has fallen, he says, because of her failure to maintain the revolutionary principles of 1789.

> *We look for her that sunlike stood*
> *Upon the forehead of our day,*
> *An orb of nations, radiating food*
> *For body and for mind alway.*
> *Where is the Shape of glad array;*
> *The nervous hands, the front of steel,*
> *The clarion tongue? Where is the bold proud face?*
> *We see a vacant place;*
> *We hear an iron heel.*

He summons up the memory of the liberations of the Revolution:

> *O she that made the brave appeal*
> *For manhood when our time was dark,*
> *And from our fetters drove the spark*
> *Which was as lightning to reveal*
> *New seasons, with the swifter play*
> *Of pulses, and benigner day;*
> *She that divinely shook the dead*
> *From living man; that stretched ahead*
> *Her resolute forefinger straight,*
> *And marched towards the gloomy gate*
> *Of earth's Untried, gave note, and in*
> *The good name of Humanity*
> *Called forth the daring vision. . . .*

That France succumbed to corruption and division. He details some of the inner contradictions emerging in post-revolutionary France; but expresses his belief that in the turmoil of her present suffering she will reassert her energies for the triumphant progress of man into full rationality and brotherhood:

> *Not whirling in their narrow rings of foam,*
> *But as a river forward. Soaring France!*
> *Now is Humanity on trial in thee:*
> *Now mayst thou gather humankind in fee:*
> *Now prove that Reason is a quenchless scroll;*
> *Make of calamity thine aureole,*
> *And bleeding head us thro' the troubles of the sea.*

The *Ode* appeared in the *Fortnightly* in January 1871. 'Latterly I have felt poetically weakened,' he wrote to Morley, 'but this is going, and a fuller strength comes of it, for I believe I am within the shadow of the Truth, and as it's my nature to sing I may now do well.'

With this conviction of grasping the whole truth of his world, stirred by events in France, he worked at a new novel in which he set out directly his view of the political struggle in England. We have no letters showing his reaction to the Paris Commune during the time of its existence; but we have various indications of what he felt. First, there is the statement that he first made Roy at the Banquet speak out like a Red Communist; and secondly, there is the fact that his revolutionary emotions appear far more powerfully clarified in the work written under the direct stimulus of the French events than in any other of his works. And there is the contributory evidence of the response of other positivist radicals like Harrison and Morley, as we shall see later on.

What is certain is that the French events gave him the strong impulse towards a renewal of the revolt that in many ways had slackened in *Harry*

Richmond. Already on 2 January 1870 he was meditating on the serried forces of reaction in England and on Ruskin's clue to the truth in political-economy: his insistence that the producers, the workers, are the source of wealth and that any system of ethical decencies must base itself on this fact:

> Carlyle preaches work for all. Good. But his method of applying his sermon to his 'nigger' is intolerable.—Spiritual light he has to illuminate a nation. Of practical little or none, and he beats his own brains out with emphasis. . . .
> I am inclined to think the present generation of P. Economists wrong—that they don't see the obligations of Wealth pertain to its sources, and that R[uskin] has some vague truth for a backbone to his preposterous priestly attitudes and inebriate conceit as against adversaries.
> The Parsonry are irritating me fearfully, but a non-celibate clergy are a terrific power. They are interwound with the whole of the Middle class like the poisonous ivy. Oh! for independence, that I might write my mind of these sappers of our strength.

Ruskin's didactic priest-like idiom annoys him; but he admits the truth under his denunciations of capitalist political-economy.

The letter just cited, like most of his serious efforts to grapple with the realities of Victorian society in his letters, is addressed to Maxse. He sympathises strongly with Maxse's rebellious aims, and yet can't help baiting an element of bitter impatience and sectarian rigidity in his friend, which he feels self-frustrating. In July 1871 he moralises on a toy that Maxse had given young Will Meredith:

> Willie is delighted with his toy, and all day long we hear shots and may see men transformed into women in a jiffy—to the mockery of the actual!—Will your poet's dreams ever bring us to the happy state of toys, that one crack in the eye may turn a hairy beast into a lovely beauty? You quote your poets, Fred, and expect them to perform just similar prodigies. Not what we should be, but what we can, as a step thereunto, is the reasonable aim. Nor will any of your pop-guns pelleted with uncompromising decisions affect much the existing state of things, though they will, I often fear, wear you out before your time.
> You do well, and even nobly, but you are one half wrong, for you go against nature, and nature says that to work soundly the creature must be in that state of contentment to which philosophy points you and poetry elevates you. You deny to man the right to be in this state while there is one miserable upon the earth, and you deny to the little ones peace in their infancy because of the existence of error. To put it in one word, the character of your opposition is impatience. Adieu.—I love you. . . .

He is not arguing that human nature can't be transformed; the whole of his work is based on the passionate belief that it can. What he wants is the clear grasp of how things concretely are, and all the conviction of vital fellowship that such a grasp in its fullness implies, the happiness of accepting life on earth and one's place among men—and *then* the ceaseless struggle to change the world. Or rather, out of the acceptance, at its innermost heart, the struggle. What he feels in Maxse is an ultimate lack of love, of stable fellowship, which owns, as one of its facets, an incapacity to realise the present in all its complexity of good and bad elements.

Yet all the while his thoughts revolve round the ardent rebel, probing his strengths and weaknesses, so that he may make of him a type of all that is most valid and vital in the political conditions of their England. When Maxse tells him to write politically, he reacts with ribaldry; for Maxse's inability to see that *all* his writing is political is a revelation of the flaw in Maxse's own political thinking:

> Fred as usual. He declares he knows a lady—a great novel-reader—who finds *Harry Richmond* quite unintelligible in parts. He advises me in these serious times 'to take to political writing.' I reply that it demands special study. He insists that I have only to give my genuine convictions. . . . Morley is quoted as being utterly of his opinion.
>
> I propose to him an Opera libretto to popularise the Democratic movement and bring our chief personages before the eyes of the nobility. O—— in love with the Princess L—— meditates the *enlèvement* of that lady that he may breed Radicals from Royalty: delivers idea in ballad. B——, impressionable to poetry and music, is half won, but checked by religious sentiment:—Ballad —The Waverer.
>
> Fred savagely: 'Good God! How can you spout buffoonery in times like these!'
>
> Pathetic ballad by M. 'In times like these.' [To Morley.]

At the same time he himself hardens in his antagonism to the ecclesiastical forces that justified inequality, division, obscurantism. In 1872 he contrasts Christian morals of brotherhood with the 'ecclesiastical dogma' as an 'instance of the poverty of humanity's mind hitherto,' which has 'often in its hideous fangs and claws shown whence we draw our descent.' He asks Maxse not to call his daughter Millicent, 'a proper parson's wife's name; it overflows with female priggery. You have to lift the nose to enounce it.' In August 1873 he is pleased at a scandal (the Beecher-Tilton):

> There is a sickly stuffiness about the religious fry that makes the tale of their fornications and adulteries absolutely repulsive to read of, and but for the feeding of the reptile sarcasm in our bosoms, it would disgust more than a chronicle of the amours of costermongers.

In the same month, watching a pigeon asleep on his windowsill with head tucked in bosom, he thinks of a Bishop, and recalls one whose leg he pulled about a portrait of the Virgin. 'He was (to make use of one of

their distinctions) High Church. One may be high and not see far.' In
September he is roused by the clergy's attacks on an address of Tyndall's.
'The man or the country that fights priestcraft and priests is to my mind
striking deeper for freedom than can be struck anywhere at present. I
foresee a perilous struggle with them.'

Before we turn to *Beauchamp's Career*, it would be as well to glance at
the ideas of Maxse himself. His many pamphlets, from *The Education of
the Agricultural Poor* (1868) to his collapse into imperialism in *Judas*! (1894),
give us a good picture of his fervid confused mind. For our purposes *The
Causes of Social Revolt*, 1872, will best serve: a lecture given in London,
Portsmouth, Nottingham, Derby, Greenwich, it was published at 1s.

The foreword states that its viewpoint is 'founded upon a recognition
of Class divisions.' It is hypocrisy to ignore the fact that 'society is made
up of classes. Who made classes?' Certainly not the workers, who would
never willingly have entered into bondage.

> It is easy for people whose position secures them abundance to deprecate
> class allusions. They forget that the enormous labour class is condemned,
> generation after generation, to an incessant struggle for mere existence. And
> so long as this struggle continues, a cry must come up, increasing in volume
> as intelligence spreads, for a less hazardous state. *This class has as yet to inherit
> civilisation* [his italics].

Past civilisations have fallen because they were not worth preserving;
they expressed only the 'conflicting articulate interests,' while the working
masses remained inarticulate. The only stable civilisation is that which is
'the property of the many. Nature cares only to preserve the good. The
imperfect and the abortive invariably perish.'

But having made this statement of the class-struggle, he says that he
speaks for every class. He wants to reconcile them all in a common effort
of goodwill—despite his cogent question, 'Who made classes?' which
shows awareness of the basis of the class-state in force.

He goes on to speak sadly of the Paris Commune, a 'terrible instance'
of social revolt, which, however, provides a lesson for class-society. Later
in the lecture he states his position here in more detail. He opposed the
uprising as reckless and even criminal; it could not succeed except for a
moment, and thus, he considered, it must strengthen reaction. (Marx, in
an address of the International, called on the French workers not to fight
the provisional government, but to use the Republic 'to organise their
own class thoroughly'; but when the Commune began, he hailed it as
the work of heaven-storming Titans, a decisive inspiration for the workers
everywhere.) Having declared his opposition, however, Maxse unlooses

all his keen indignation against the murderous violence with which the bourgeoisie crushed the all-too-gentle revolution. He refers to that

> terrible week in May, when an ignorant soldiery entered Paris, on behalf of religion and order, and rioted in the bloodshed of Paris workers and their families, while the clerical journals hounded them on to massacre; and one of them indignantly demanded why only 40,000 Communists had been killed.

And again:

> We may dragoon, sabre, and shoot down democracy by means of deluded peasants, dressed up in uniforms, in the manner they have been doing recently in Paris; we may invent any hideous epithet wherewith to depreciate those who labour for the collective improvement of mankind. . . . Still, while the divine inspiration of human justice, the glorious vivid idea, not the parrot formula, continues to survive, so long will men be found, some madly but others wisely, to devote themselves to an incessant struggle for radical change.

And he declares of the Communards that their leaders 'believed in the Better or Higher.'

The primary cause of Social Revolt, he says, is the ghastly condition under which the mass of the workers live. He mentions the Report on the employment of children, youths and women in agriculture, with its appalling revelations. 'For myself I am overwhelmed with indignation and shame,' and 'despair when I witness the apathy' of the ruling-class.

He attacks the Individual Competitive Theory, discusses the vast pressures to demoralise the poor, and asks, 'Can the ten million labourers all become capitalists?' He attacks the Political Economy of liberal *laissez-faire* as the pretext for unbridled egoism and exploitation. He glances at the pretensions of a 'false' aristocracy, and deplores Carlyle as 'the most powerful calumniator of democracy,' the 'apostle of king-ship, force, oppression, and servility,' who praises the 'heaven-born docility of man.'

Under the heading 'Democratic Aspirations cannot be suppressed by Bayonets or Acts of Parliament,' he discusses the bloody suppression of the Commune and defends the International. Then he makes a forthright assault on the Daily Press, denouncing the idea that the press represents national opinion. The papers are 'organs for the *suppression* of much of the most earnest and vital thought in the country.' They are wholly commercial; their sole concern is to conciliate the propertied or ruling class; and such divergences of opposition as they show reflect only conflicts of interest inside that class.

He discusses the press's antagonism to educational reforms or extensions, its contemptuous indifference to any unanimous working-class demand. (But he doesn't like *Reynolds*, which seems to think that no person of the upper-class can be 'respectable.') And he holds that one dangerous result of the class-basis of the prevailing papers is that the ruling-class have no notion whatever of the thoughts and feelings of the people. The press is solidly intolerant to Thought. And its ignorance results in such things as a sudden scare at discovering that England has a strong Republican movement—a scare which is explained as the consequence of lack of royal pageants! One paper said that the populace loved being spattered with mud from a royal coach.

Another bad tendency of the existing class-system is the growing antagonism between town and country.

He next discusses the use of abusive terms such as Atheist against reformers—for instance against the Communards. In Paris the press shouted Atheists to justify the 'merciless task' of murder.

He declares that there are two rival creeds, one believing in the past, one in the future; and sets out his remedies for the bad state of things in England. He praises the Co-operative movement (and asserts that no Co-operative members joined the Commune) and takes his stand on compulsory free secular education, reform of land-tenure to spread landownership, direct instead of indirect taxation, and electoral reform. Then, after saying that a small rich class controls the State, he tells radicals that they must not be afraid of being dwarfed in numbers. All great movements begin with a small resolute group.

Maxse has little knowledge of socialism. He defines the communards or communists as men who wanted to revive the self-governing commune; and the only socialism he knows is the vague Utopian creed of Robert Owen and Louis Blanc: a substitution of co-operation for antagonism and of association for conflict. Besides this he sees only schemes for a 'forcible sub-division of private property,' which he rightly considers the invention of the reactionary press. (The attitudes of Owen and Blanc vary in details, but they share an inability to grasp the nature of the class-State; and so a radical like Maxse correctly feels their kinship with his own position. There is only argument as to the extent of association and the particular modes of procedure best suited to extend it without the breaking and remodelling of the State-form. Thus it is that pre-scientific socialism and radicalism easily merge at many points.)

And yet it is odd that a man who saw so clearly the ruthless suppression of the Commune and his own class's reaction to the report on cheap agricultural labour, should imagine that an appeal to reason and goodwill could unite the masses and the rulers in a single programme of progress.*

---

* In *Our Political Duty* he cites with assent the report of the Trade Union Commissions (the section signed by Thos. Hughes and F. Harrison): 'It is beyond question that every fresh expansion of industry, is accompanied by a vast train of destitution.'

In the last resort we are driven back to the explanation that the lack of militancy among the British workers in this epoch helped to strengthen such contradictions in all our thinkers and fighters who could not advance into a fully-grounded analysis of the class-State and the part to be played by the organised working-class in breaking down that State. The nature of the Commune was thus a key-point; and Maxse did not understand it at all. He saw it as only one more violent retort of a goaded and oppressed class, not as the first decisive rupture with old forms of protest.

We have an interesting statement of what was in Meredith's mind at this time in *Up to Midnight*, a set of dialogues published in *The Graphic*, December 1872 and January 1873. The talkers include Brighton, an optimist, Finistare, a pessimist, Helion, M.P., who admires Thiers, Sir John Saxon, a Tory, Sir Patrick, M'Nimbus and Dr Anthony. They lightly discuss foxhunting, India, polar exploration, famine-fears, Ireland, spiritualism, the late war, Germany's suppression of gambling resorts, Stanley, international arbitration, and the picturesque.

On India Finistare says, 'I can prove it is a matter of anxiety to those who use foresight.' Brighton demurs. But 'we are roofed with thatch in India. Let but one spark out! one will be quite enough, if there should happen to be a European complication at the same time.' Sir John denounces unrest among his labourers. Helion says that Hodge's 'malady has been the total absence of agitation in his system for I don't know how long.' He wants independence among the labourers. Sir John attacks the dreamers 'who ought to have it proved on 'em they're gabbling incendiaries.' He praises the Tory historian Froude—'with a whip in his hand,' comments Sir P. And then he goes on to abuse Trade Unionism as 'a conspiracy that needs a front to meet it.' Finistare points to the Gas-strikers and fears a dark age of 'total obscuration,' 'the reign of the brutal many.' Sir John replies, 'Not without a fight for it.'*

M'Nimbus (vaguely Ruskin) prefers good boots to bad poems and says the picturesque is good only when 'it harmonises with the actual present truth.'

But the political core of the chat comes when Brighton attacks a reliance on the Army and Navy, on Discipline, as the basis of society:

---

* 1872 was a prosperous year. At Beckton Gasworks in the late summer a Union was formed, and the men asked a wage-increase of 6d. a day—labourers got 3s. 6d. a day; stokers, etc., from 31s. to 38s. 9d. for a 7-day week, often 80 hours. After dismissals and lockings-out, they went on strike. Six men were prosecuted for Conspiracy, and were sentenced in November to a year's jail. The struggle of the farm-labourers, led by Joseph Arch, had begun in 1872, meeting vicious repressions from the landlords.

This is the everlasting cry of the retrogressionists—Trust to Force! namely, the force of the strong arm. . . . You are in a difficulty, and you instantly make your appeal to a system that shall turn men into machines. . . .

He describes the Greek Gods as:

an aristocracy of power opposed to a democracy of mortals—prayed to, feasted, sacrificed to, hymned to, adjured and entreated with blood and incense, but hated, hated! yes . . . hated; and because they were feared, and were supposed to be propitiated by gifts. They were the Lords of the Middle Ages, and the Capitalists of ours.

Finally he tells Finistare:

French Communism has frightened you; French Imperialism, resulting from French Republicanism, has appeared to warn you and advise you; German success, owing to Prussian solidity, has presented itself to you as the solution of your puzzle. So now you are for a king, who is to be a king indeed. You are for a Minister who scoffs at sentimental fallacies, at all systems which he can prove unsound with the strong arm. . . .

And he attacks the repression of workers in Paris.

There we have the clear note of Meredith's own convictions, a succinct statement of the after-effects of 1871.

Further, we can gauge the agitation and the kind of responses among the left radicals and positivists, the group with whom Meredith felt most affinity, by looking through *The Fortnightly*, edited by Morley. When the war broke out, the progressive middle-class tended to be rather anti-French through hatred for Napoleon III and vague notions of German civic virtue; but the proclamation of the Republic had a profound effect, and the fact that reactionaries like Carlyle and Freeman had rallied to the support of Bismarckian Germany swung the radicals even further to the defence of France. The Odes of Swinburne and Meredith are part of this development. After Sedan and Metz, Harrison and Beesly began to advocate intervention to save France from being crushed. Harrison wrote on these lines in *The Pall Mall Gazette* of December and took an active part in a January meeting that urged action to aid the Republic. Maxse also participated in this meeting. The latter's pamphlet shows how strongly he was caught up in the tide.

The Fortnightly of 1871 has two articles by Karl Blind on the war, others by E. Dicey on Paris after the Peace, by Sandwich on Earl Russell, the Commune, and Christianity, by A. Desmoulins on the Paris Workers and the Commune, by J. Andrieu on the Commune, and three by Harrison: *The Effacement of England, The Revolution of the Commune*, and *The Fall of the Commune*. There are also articles based on the problems raised by the war: S. E. Cairns writes on Our Defences, Tollemache on the question whether Military Interventions Promote Peace, and Viscount Amberley on the project of a League of Peace, an international authority.

Though there are criticisms of the Commune as rash or hopeless, there is throughout sympathy with its political aims (which are not always clearly grasped) and a fierce denunciation of its repression. It is a tribute to these writers that they are nowhere stampeded by the propaganda about Red Atrocities (as was, for example, Swinburne—and even Ruskin, who, however, never faltered in seeing the war and the Commune as expressions of capitalist crisis and in declaring that the real war was between the capitalists and the workers of Europe). Desmoulins remarks that for centuries the bourgeoisie have used the workers as allies against feudalism, but now they seek in their triumph to build their own system of rigid privilege and to suppress the workers. Sandwich deals with a meeting at Willis's Rooms where Earl Russell denounced the Communards as Atheists. He himself is against action by force, but he protests vigorously at the description of the Communards in the press as 'the scum of society.' He says that 'it is necessary to notice that orthodox Christians can believe in nothing good that is not backed with wealth,' though their religion was founded on a 'peasant workman, a street preacher,' not even a householder, who was murdered by the Conservatives of his day as 'a revolutionary demagogue.' He refers to a letter in *The Spectator* from an English clergyman who was in Paris during the Commune and who was impressed by the good order and the freedom from vice. Then he points to the way the Conservatives have supported Governor Eyre, guilty though he was of murderous violence in the West Indies, and cites *The Naval and Military Gazette* of 27 May as having seriously suggested that vivisectionists be let cut up the Communards alive. 'We are deliberately of opinion that hanging is too good a death for such villains to die.' He also cites *The Times* as saying that the Paris workers had good wages, but had brooded so long in their workshops about Capitalism that 'their conceptions grew actually monstrous' and

> the one object of their hatred, envy and antagonism was capital, and they resolved to take capital into their own hands. For the future they would lead easy lives, and be the lords instead of the slaves of their old detested enemy.

Finally he notes the international character of the revolution. 'On the outbreak of the struggle in Paris an address of sympathy, signed by many thousands, was sent from Berlin to their brothers in Paris.'

But far the most important essay is that of Harrison in the May issue: a key-document for the understanding of Left Radicalism at this phase. He claims the Commune for Positivism. He sees as a basic aim of the

Communards the protest against over-centralisation, and sets out five main aspects of the revolution. (1) The creation of a Republic. This involves the breaking-down of class-privileges and 'the honest devotion of the whole public purse to the sole end of the public good.' Harrison says that 'alone of modern communities they [the Commune] have preserved from compromise or corruption the principle which is now the life-blood of all human society.' (2) The repudiation of the dogma of universal suffrage. By this he does not mean that he, and the Communards, want to hand voting-power back to the privileged and propertied classes. On the contrary he means that in a corrupt class-society the ruling-class can bribe, confuse, and nullify the voting power of the masses, and that in the name of progress it may be necessary to disenfranchise the reactionaries. (3) Direct instead of indirect government:

> The council is a committee for action. . . . Nothing so completely shows the political sagacity of the working classes or their true estimate of that demoralising nuisance, the unwieldy talking parliament. . . . Government, by the parliamentary system, is government without real responsibility, without efficiency, and without simplicity. . . .

What is needed, as the Commune saw, was 'a responsibility of the governing body, real, direct, and personal, the greatest simplicity of authority, and the utmost supervision of opinion.' He contrasts with the Commune the bourgeoisie in Versailles; their parliamentarianism which was 'flatulent cowardice alternating with impotent ferocity.' (4) The abolition of the standing army. (5) The principle that workers may be called to the functions of active government: this wipes out the lie that there is some mystery in government which restricts it to a traditional ruling-class. 'Man for man, these working shoemakers and printers have shown out well beside the chattering crew at Versailles.'

He records with approval several of the Commune's actions, such as the establishment of free secular education, the separation of Church and State, the change of the police from agents of repression into genuine protectors of society. 'Words cannot describe the insane injustice' with which the British Press has treated every aspect of the Commune. He cites one editor who on being corrected as to points of fact replied that 'it would never do to say anything in favour of the Commune,' and an English officer, who, after seeing the Communard positions, promptly reported their weaknesses to the Versailles Generals.

He denies that the rising was Communist; for following Comte he understands Communism as meaning the equal sharing-out of everything. But his defence of the Communard actions is magnificent:

A society in which generation after generation passes away, consolidating vast and ever-increasing hoards of wealth, opening to the wealthy enchanted realms of idleness, luxury and waste—laying on the labourer, generation after generation, increasing burdens of toil, destitution, and despair; a society in which capital has created a gospel of its own, and claims for the good of society a divine right of selfishness, the right to exert its powers at will indefinitely for the indulgence of its own desires, rebelling against any social control, and offering up 'with a light heart' the misery and degradation of the poor as a sad but inevitable sacrifice in the altar of competition—such a society these workmen of Paris will not for ever tolerate.

The war and the siege had rudely broken the splendid flow of the stablished order of things. For once luxury, pomp, and accumulation had been arrested in mid-career. For six months they had all stood, rich and free, side by side on the rampart. They had seen themselves all brought down to the simple worth of man. They had seen the millionaire unable to buy a loaf with his hoards; they had seen the master of factories as poor and as helpless as Crusoe on his island. They had been called on in turn to serve, and they had served. They had been ill-led, ill-governed, distrusted, and eventually stung by a crushing and unexpected surrender. And now they were told that it was all over.

Their idle season was ended. The workshops in time would reopen; in the meanwhile, they must shift for themselves, and in the first place pay the arrears of rent and debt which had grown up, whilst the war had suspended trade and cut off their earnings. It was hard, but they must submit to the law of competition, and supply, and demand. They must shift for themselves; the great god Competition would, somehow, bring them out at last. In the interval, numbers might starve or rot; but soon trade would revive; capital, if they were quiet, would timidly return, and condescend to send for them; the gaiety and life of the city was even now recovering; luxury, wealth, self-indulgence, and gilded vice were hastening back to their old haunts after their tedious absence in foreign capitals; pleasure would come back to her wild satyr dance, and enterprise to her grand mill, by whose myriad wheels colossal fortunes would be reared, and through whose gates the poor might crowd and crush for their pittance. The old familiar world had been suspended; but was not dead. It was about to restore its wonted triumphs; and whilst the poor scrambled and struggled for bread and life, Competition and Riot should renew the spectacle of selfish and pitiless ostentation.

And this, the workmen of Paris, with arms in their hands, this, they said, should not be for ever.

And he adds the memorable summing-up.

Their great political programme is effectually founded in France: it is sufficiently suggested to Europe; and the bloody vengeance of the monarchists will not blot it out from the memory of the future.

Words that sound in harmony with Meredith's comment to the British middle class, 'French Communism has frightened you. . . .'

In *The Fall of the Commune* (August) Harrison examines the current

atrocity-tales and disproves them, passionately protests against the infinitely vile and lying procedure of the British press, and declares that now
the crisis of capitalism is out in the open. But he still clings to his positivist
theses of reform, while stating that henceforth the choice lies only between
Positivism and Communism.* He believes it is still possible to bring about
a 'moralised capitalism,' in which privilege and monopoly have been
broken and in which property is reasonably well diffused.† It is indeed
remarkable that a man who saw so clearly into the maddened hatred that
the ruling-class in Britain as in France felt for the Commune, who so
admirably defined the decision of the Communards—'the workmen of
Paris, with arms in their hands'—should thus fall back on the petty-bourgeois dream of a world of moderate peace and plenty achieved without
conflict. But the sharp contradictions in his position with its revolutionary
insight and its reconciliation-formula at the end bring out perfectly the
attitude of Radicalism at this phase—which was also the attitude of the
mass of the more advanced workers, it must be remembered. The contradictions reposed on the fact that the lack of militant organisation kept the
workers only half separated out from the petty-bourgeoisie; and into the
radical position there flowed both elements carried-over from the bourgeois revolution of the past and elements moving forward to the new type
of revolution, of which the Commune, though immature, was already
the definite type.

It is of interest to note the articles that accompany those on the Commune in *The Fortnightly*, since they show further how the left radicals did
keep on grappling, however inconclusively, with basic issues. F. Seebohm
points out that things have now come to the pass it is not enough for the
people to regain the land; capital needs spreading out as well; Hoskins
wants the ending of all feudal restrictions; another writer deals with
agrarian troubles in Ireland; a fourth with Taxes on Land; J. S. Mill discusses Maine on the Village Community. Viscountess Amberley wants
equal pay for women, the vote, and the lifting of all the various legal
disabilities. Three papers discuss Italy, one of which is by Mazzini on
Republicanism while another is strongly anti-clerical. Karl Blind discusses
the futility of universal suffrage while the ruling-class can cajole, confuse
and bribe; and says that revolutions have failed because their leaders
trusted too much in the masses at once seeing the beauty of the

---

* Morley wrote to him of this essay, 'I go with you in every word, and cannot say how
grateful I am to you for so humane a deliverance. It will reach the heart of every man young
enough to have a humane fibre left in him!'

† Thus his Positivist ideal is in fact a version of the sharing-out system which he incor-
rectly attributed to the Communists!

'revolutionary aspirations.' (His proposals are, however, dubious: educational tests, and the larger representation of the cities as the centres of intellect and industry against the stagnant rural areas.)

Viscount Amberley proposes a world-league of peace, a federal system for the suppression of war; but in a postscript opposes the plan set out, since he wrote, by the reactionary Seeley, who wants a united Europe in which the States hand over all military powers as well as other executive activities (*Macmillan's Magazine*, March).

And there is an essay by Cairns, *Our Defences: A National or a Standing Army?* This helps us to understand Meredith's attitudes to conscription. It sets out the case for a national or conscripted army as opposed to a standing one, and stresses the 'pacific tendency of the principle of popular armies,' whose object is defence. The standing-army is thus identified with State-oppression and aggression, the national army with the 'people in arms' like the Communards, 'the workers of Paris, with arms in their hands.' (Meredith himself makes this point explicit in a 1908 letter to Hyndman: he considers a conscripted army the armed people who at a pinch will take things in their own hands against the capitalist State. Here, as throughout his political confusions, we find an insufficient grasp of the State's nature, a tendency to think of the imperialist State as owning characteristics of the feudal State in decay, when the free people-in-arms was a feasible proposition.)

Finally Tollemache's essay is worth noting. He concludes that 'if science were fairly let loose on the path of destruction, it would be difficult to say where it would stop.' But he too fails to ask what kind of society, what kind of State-power, would permit and encourage such a course?*

It is a surprise to find, amid all these strenuous efforts to think, a poem by William Morris, *The Dark Wood*, with the pessimistic ending, 'Yet now with barren longing I grow weak, yet now I mourned that I had none to seek.' I cite it so that we may realise why Meredith and Morris never joined forces. At this phase Meredith despised such writing as Morris had fallen into; and when Morris had become an active socialist, Meredith was falling away into his crippled condition that inhibited any effective contacts with the world of struggle.

---

* There are also essays by Bagehot, Huxley, Herbert Spencer. Mazzini sets out his principle: 'The liberty of all through the association of all: such is the republican formula.' He, like these others, thinks of Republicanism as a positive social programme, not merely as an absence of kingship or of feudal privilege. This point should be borne in mind when the term Republican comes up in Meredith's writings. Cairns on Political Economy attacks dogmatic formulations of *laissez-faire* that rouse the workers and produce 'what but this spectre of socialism—that rank growth of economic ignorance.'

From Clodd's notes of the mid-1890's, however, we learn that Meredith had come to love and admire Morris. That they did not meet during Morris's socialist years is unfortunate. An echo of Morris's doings could not have the effect that his robust presence would have done. 'Feels Morris's death very much,' Clodd records, but unfortunately provides no further indication of why Meredith felt the loss.

19a

Rebel's Career

MAXSE'S PAMPHLETS, Meredith's dialogues, the essays in *The Fortnightly*, give us an ample picture of the crisis in Left Radicalism brought about by the Commune: the ferment of ideas out of which came *Beauchamp's Career*. Maxse was the basis, but Beauchamp was in no sense a simple copy of him.

> There was a time when there was no name better known or honoured in England. . . . There was nothing that he was not considered capable of doing, and of reaching. But Admiral Maxse lived and died in something like obscurity, or in a certain notoriety that was almost as killing as death and obscurity. . . .
> I remember still the mild horror with which people spoke of this man who, while wearing the officer's uniform of Her Majesty's Navy, spoke with such merciless disrespect of so many things then held in honour. . . .
> I remember seeing him at Carlsbad, and often, of course, in London—a thin, rather sickly, though distinguished-looking man, with a certain air of detachment and disappointment. [T. P. O'Connor.]

Meredith concentrated on the positive aspects of Maxse. Beauchamp had the heart torn out of his breast by beauty; Maxse was conventional in art-judgments. Beauchamp penetrates the revolutionary elements in Carlyle's thinking; Maxse read more superficially. Beauchamp has his points of confusion, but we cannot imagine him getting into such an intellectual mess as Maxse did in the 1880's.

We have no chance of watching the novel's earlier stages. In April 1873 Meredith was too busy on it to meet Jessop in London, and expected to be working all June.

> And it is already full to bursting—it and I. 'The world is too much with me' when I write. I cannot go on with a story and not feel that to treat of flesh and blood is to touch the sacredest; and so it usually ends in my putting the destinies of the world about it—like an atmosphere, out of which it cannot subsist. So my work fails. I see it. But the pressure is on me with every new work. I fear that Beauchamp is worse than the foregoing in this respect. The centre idea catches hold of the ring of the universe, the dialogues are the delivery of creatures of this world, and the writing goodish. But altogether it will only appeal (so I fear) to them that have a taste for me; it won't catch the gudgeon world.

Thus he states his need to take an historical view, to relate the growth of his people to the full pattern of social development. 'So my work fails.' No, so his work succeeds.

In March 1874 *The Cornhill* turned the novel down, but Morley agreed to serialise a cut version in *The Fortnightly*.

> That, which may be stated to be the personal abnegation coming, in spite of errors here and there (and as it were in spite of the man himself), of a noble devotion to politics from the roots up, I think I can retain uninjured—possibly improved by the exclusion of a host of my own reflections.

In June he summarised his intentions in the novel:

> It is philosophical—political, with no powerful stream of adventure: an attempt to show the forces round a young man of the present day, in England, who would move them, and finds them unutterably solid, though it is seen in the end that he does not altogether fail, has not lived quite in vain. Of course, this is done in the concrete. A certain drama of self-conquest is gone through, for the hero is not perfect.
>
> He is born of the upper class, and is scarcely believed in by any class, except when he vexes his own, and it is then to be hated. At the same time the mild spirit of a prosperous middle class, that is not extremely alarmed, is shown to be above persecuting; so that the unfortunate young man is in danger of being thought dull save by those who can enter his idea of the advancement of Humanity and his passion for it. In this he is a type. And I think his History a picture of the time—taking its mental action, and material ease and indifference, to be a necessary element of the picture.

He was bothered by the desire to re-write, but in November the book appeared.

Nevil Beauchamp is an orphan reared by a rich uncle, Romfrey, and his housekeeper, a widow Rosamund Culling. He begins with a strong naive patriotism, serves in the Crimean War with distinction, and is shocked into the realisation that something is badly wrong somewhere. Convalescing at Venice with the family of a French officer whose life he has saved, he falls in love with the latter's sister, Renée, and almost carries her off. Continuing his naval service, he takes part in clearing up the slave-traffic, grows more definite in revolt, and at last shocks his relations by standing as radical in the elections at Bevisham (Southampton). He is friendly with an old intransigent radical, Dr Shrapnel, at whose house Rosamund calls to see him; in her timid confusion she gives Romfrey the idea that she was insulted there.

Beauchamp's Tory friends try to trick him into a bad mishap, but he is warned by a Colonel's daughter, Cecilia Hackett. Renée, now married to an old profligate, summons him to Normandy. He goes for a few days, only to find that she has merely made a bet on his obedience. On his return he loses the election through the lampoons about his behaviour; but is more ardent than ever on his rebellious ideas and is determined to start a newspaper, *The Dawn*, which can offset the lying press of the cash-nexus. He falls in love with Cecilia; but the glamour of Renée holds him back till it is too late. The Tory Captain Baskelett, an unspeakable character, makes Romfrey think that Shrapnel has maligned Rosamund's character. Romfrey horsewhips Shrapnel, and Beauchamp resolves at all cost to make him apologise to the old man who is lying at death's door. Rosamund, scared, equivocates.

Romfrey becomes Lord Avonley and demands an apology from Beauchamp to Rosamund. Beauchamp refuses and is ordered from the family-house in London. At this moment Renée appears, in flight from her husband. Beauchamp no longer wants her and has to use his utmost tact not to hurt her unduly and to save her reputation. Rosamund helps him, and before Renée goes off, agrees to marry Lord Avonley. Cecilia, finally revolted by what seem fresh proofs of Beauchamp's infatuation for Renée, makes her father take her off to Italy; and on her return she agrees to marry the fat Tory Tuckham. Beauchamp arrives just too late with his proposal. He and Cecilia part in despair, and he falls ill. Rosamund, pregnant and tormented by her conscience, makes her husband apologise to Shrapnel. Beauchamp turns to Jenny, Shrapnel's niece, a rather conventional girl; and after some hesitations they are engaged. They go on a boat-trip, are married, and find themselves surprisingly happy. Shrapnel calls for a return to action. But Beauchamp is drowned, saving the life of a worker's child.

Everything here centres round Beauchamp and his development. The *Career* of the title is ironical: every time Beauchamp could cash in on a situation like other members of his class, he further detaches himself. Morally and politically, he ascends; from the point of view of his class, he goes down. The story opens with the French scare of the early '50's, in which Beauchamp to save the national honour challenges in a boyish letter the whole of the French Guard (modified to the Colonels by Rosamund's advice). He develops ideas of leadership-by-the-aristocrats, but is disillusioned of his class by the Crimean War. He turns towards republicanism and zealously helps in putting down the slave-trade. Then he stands as radical for Bevisham after having paid several visits to the industrial areas and attended mass-meetings there.

In his experiences during the election we get a thorough and vivid picture of the conflict of political ideas in the England of the 1860's, in all shadings and involvements. Beauchamp himself grows in certainty.

> 'Yes,' he [Tomlinson] said, on the question of classes, 'yes, I fear we have classes in this country whose habitual levity sharp experience will have to correct. I very much fear it.'
> 'But if you have classes that are not to face realities—classes that look on them from the box-seats of a theatre,' said Beauchamp, 'how can you expect perfect seriousness or any good service whatever?'
> 'Gently, sir, gently. No; we can, I feel confident, expand within the limits of our most excellent and approved Constitution. I could wish that socially . . . that is all.'
> 'Socially and politically mean one thing in the end,' said Beauchamp. 'If you have a nation politically corrupt, you won't have a good state of morals in it, and the laws that keep society together bear upon the politics of a country.'

In the county-view:

> He seemed to acquiesce in some of the current contemporary despair of our immovable England, though he winced at a satire on his country, and attempted to show that the dull dominant class of money-makers was the ruin of her.

At moments he sees England as doomed by her approaching failure to dominate the world-markets:

> Dr Shrapnel and Captain Beauchamp have recently been speculating on our becoming a nation of artists, and authorities in science and philosophy, by the time our coalfields and material wealth are exhausted. That, and the *cataclysm*, are their themes.

The cataclysm is the Revolution.

But he also has a vision of the socialist future, a brotherly England of peaceful construction, which he outlines to Cecilia.

> 'You are clad in steel; you flash back; you won't answer me out of your heart. I'm convinced it is pure wilfulness that makes you oppose me.'
> 'I fancy you must be convinced because you cannot imagine women to have any share of public spirit, Nevil.'
> A grain of truth in that remark set Nevil reflecting.
> 'I want them to have it. . . . Bevisham looks well from here. We might make a North-weatern Venice of it, if we liked.'
> 'Papa told you it would be money sunk in mud.'
> 'Did I mention it to him?—thoroughly Conservative!—So he would leave the mud as it is. They insist on our not venturing anything—those Tories! exactly as though we had gained the best of human conditions, instead of counting crops of rogues, malefactors, egoists, noxious and lumbersome creatures that deaden the country. Your town down there is one of the ugliest and dirtiest in the kingdom: it might be the fairest.'
> 'I have often thought that of Bevisham, Nevil.'

He drew a visionary sketch of quays, embankments, bridged islands, public buildings, magical emanations of patriotic architecture, with a practical air, an absence of that enthusiasm which struck her with suspicion when it was not applied to landscape or the Arts; and she accepted it, and warmed, and even allowed herself to appear hesitating when he returned to the similarity of the state of mud-begirt Bevisham and our great sluggish England.

It is indeed in his arguments with Cecilia that he develops his ideas best, that we feel him growing as he strives to convince her of the brotherly future before man.

Cecilia is well drawn: intensely English, protestant, with a rich inner life based on the sentiment of personal dignity, of family and national honour. She is slow, modest, reserved; but what she is convinced of becomes a stable part of her nature, her whole outlook.

At first she scorns politics as a trivial or dirty sphere. She is worried at Beauchamp's passion. 'Do you not feel that it is playing traitor to one's class to join those men?' He replies that that is the Tory way of thinking. 'The Tories uphold their Toryism in the place of patriotism.' She argues that the greatness of England has been built by the Tories, and is irritated at being made to talk politics, not a matter to be imposed 'upon the elect ladies of earth.'

He leaves her and watches a graceful yacht among the colliers, trawlers, cargo-ships. It seems a symbol of luxury, of the beauty developed to serve a leisured class. Maybe it helps men in general by stimulating them and by setting a certain standard; but he feels a finer quality in the ships 'who fought the grand, and the grisly, old battle with nature for bread of life.'

> Those grimy sails of the colliers and fishing-smacks, set them in a great sea, would have beauty for eyes and soul beyond that of elegance and refinement. And do but look on them thoughtfully, the poor are everlastingly, unrelievedly, in the abysses of the great sea.

He realises with a new fullness the task he has set himself.

> Beauty plucked the heart from his breast. But he had taken up arms; he had drunk of the *questioning* cup, that which denieth peace to us, and which projects us upon the missionary search of the How, the Wherefore, and the Why not, ever afterward. He questioned his justification, and yours, for gratifying tastes in an ill-regulated world of wrong-doing, suffering, sin, and bounties unrighteously dispensed—not sufficiently dispersed.

He is one who having seen into reality must follow out the consequences, 'not less rapidly and naturally than tremendous Ergo is shot forth from the clash of the syllogism.'

At their next meeting he begins with remarks that express both his clarity, his grasp of the class-struggle, and his surviving illusions about national unity, the nature of the class-State, class-reconciliation.

'I have no pleasure in canvassing,' said he. 'I cannot canvass poor men accustomed to be paid for their votes, and who get nothing from me but what the baron would call a parsonical exhortation. I'm in the thick of the most spiritless crew in the kingdom. Our southern men will not compare with the men of the north. But still, even among these fellows, I see danger for the country if our commerce were to fail, if distress came on them. There's always danger in disunion. That's what the rich won't see. They see simply nothing out of their own circle; and they won't take a thought of the overpowering contrast between their luxury and the way of living, that's half-starving, of the poor. They understand it when fever comes up from back alleys and cottages, and then they join their efforts to sweep the poor out of the district. The poor are to get to their work anyhow, after a long morning's walk over the proscribed space; for we must have poor, you know. The wife of a parson I canvassed yesterday, said to me, "Who is to work for us, if we do away with the poor, Captain Beauchamp?"'

Cecilia quitted her bower and traversed the wood silently. 'So you would blow up my poor Mount Laurels for a peace-offering to the lower classes?'

'I should hope to put it on a stronger foundation, Cecilia.'

'By means of some convulsion?'

'By forestalling one.'

Then, seeing a warship, he pleases her with remarks on the need for defensive readiness against attack. But when she cites her father's ideas about an army being needed to preserve order, he replies, 'So, then, an army to threaten civil war.' She replies, 'To crush revolutionists.' 'Agitators, you mean,' he corrects her. They turn to the question of conscription. He says that he objects to the middle-class being armed while the Colonel fears arms in the hands of the workers. She asks if Shrapnel hates the middle-class.

'Dr Shrapnel cannot hate. He and I are of opinion that as the middle-class are the party in power, they would not, if they knew the use of arms, move an inch farther in Reform, for they would no longer be in fear of the class below them.'

'But what horrible notions of your country have you, Nevil. It is dreadful to hear. Oh! do let us avoid politics for ever. Fear!'

'All concessions to the people have been won from fear.'

'I have not heard so.'

'I will read it to you in the History of England.'

'You paint us in a condition of Revolution.'

'Happily it's not a condition unnatural to us. The danger would be in not letting it be progressive, and there's a little danger too at times in our slowness. We change our blood or we perish. . . .'

She speaks of mobs; he replies:

> 'It's the Tories that mob together and cry down every man who appears to them to threaten our privileges. Can you guess what Dr Shrapnel compares them to?'
> 'Indeed, Nevil, I have not an idea. I only wish your patriotism were large enough to embrace them.'
> 'He compares them to geese claiming possession of the whole common, and hissing at every foot of ground they have to yield. They're always having to retire and always hissing. "Retreat and menace," that's the motto for them.'

The Colonel comes in, and Beauchamp talks about the clergy whom he sees as indispensable agents for preserving bourgeois class-discipline and for holding down the workers:

> The Protestant parson is the policeman set to watch over the respectability of the middle-class. He has sharp eyes for the sins of the poor. As for the rich, they support his church; they listen to his sermon—to set an example: *discipline*, colonel. You discipline the tradesman, who's afraid of losing your custom, and the labourer, who might be deprived of his bread. But the people? It's put down to the wickedness of human nature that the parson has not got hold of the people. The parsons have lost them by senseless Conservatism . . . and . . . call the men that do the work they ought to be doing demagogues. The parsonry are a power absolutely to be counted for waste, as to progress.

He goes; and Cecilia, seeing a Tory lampoon about him and the Marquise (Renée), is disgusted with her own side, her own class.

Next comes the meeting where he talks of a transformed Bevisham, and goes on to attack the legalised theft of the people's land by enclosure. 'A flat robbery.' She is astonished and asks if it's still being done. He mentions a local case which Shrapnel has managed to hold up. 'At present we have no Government,' only a shifting set of exploiting class-interests. He fears, he says, that the ruling-class, to thwart and corrupt the onward march of the people, will contrive a Despotism.

Later, she tells him in 1848 the crowd ('mob') were quieted in an Austrian town by the army-band playing. 'It's a soporific,' says he. She asks, 'You would not rather have had them rise to be slaughtered?' 'Would you have them waltzed into perpetual servitude?' She says hesitantly, 'If one can have them happy in any way?' He tells her sternly, 'Then the day of destruction may almost be dated.'

Thus he gradually breaks down her preconceptions; she is afraid, but drawn on by her conscience for the truth. And his words are given strength by her realisation of the ruthless and unscrupulous tactics of her own class against him. She is moving close to him when the arrival of Renée upsets their relation and throws her back on doubt of his stability. He loses her. In fear, to escape him, she accepts the Tory Tuckham.

Behind Beauchamp stand the two antagonists, Shrapnel and Romfrey. Here we are not dealing with two aspects of the same system, as with Roy and the Squire, but with the defender of the class-world and the prophet of a new dispensation. According to Maxse, Shrapnel was based on Dr Hearne, one of his nominators in the election; and we may therefore take it that Meredith was impressed by a tough old radical at Southampton. But into Dr Hearne were fused elements from Carlyle, Ruskin, Mill, and Meredith himself.

Shrapnel calls himself a fire-worshipper, a sun-lover, and demands a new materialist concept of the unity of the life-process.

> 'It's harder work to travel from this place to this' (he pointed at ear and breast) 'than from here to yonder' (a similar indication traversed the distance between earth and sun). 'Man's aim has hitherto been to keep men from having a soul for this world: he takes it for something infernal. He?—I mean, they that hold power. They shudder to think the conservatism of the earth will be shaken by a change; they dread they won't get men with souls to fetch and carry, dig, root, mine for them. Right!—what then? Digging and mining will be done; so will harping and singing. But *then* we have a natural optimacy! Then, on the one hand, we whip the man-beast and the man-sloth; on the other, we seize that old fatted iniquity—that tyrant! that tempter! that legitimated swindler cursed of Christ! that palpable Satan whose name is Capital! —by the neck, and have him disgorging within three gasps of his life. He is the villain! Let him live, for he too comes of blood and bone. He shall not grind the faces of the poor and helpless—that's all.'

The last remarks are confused by the personification of Capital; but they merely mean that the capitalists, after being expropriated, will be given work that is not a form of exploitation.

Despite an advocacy of prayers, Shrapnel is as materialist as Meredith and attacks the notion of Providence as idol-worship. His views in general are set out in a letter which the Tories thieve from Beauchamp and read aloud with insulting comments—a device which makes Meredith's point of their total lack of decency or honour when once their class-interests are threatened, but which also enables him to detail Shrapnel's philosophy without producing a dull and solid disquisition.

Shrapnel says that so far the masses of men have only had bare life, the minimum necessary to keep them alive. And so far philosophers and leaders have sought to kill truth by their quest for idealist absolutes—'to drive the dagger to the heart of time and put the axe to human growth,' to replace light by darkness. The evil things, the rules of fear and greed, are too deeply entrenched to be ended by mere argument. 'We cannot root them up out of us without blood.' In England the bourgeoisie has absorbed the landed class and keeps royalty as 'a ricketty ornament like

that you see on a confectioner's twelfth-cake.' The loyalty of the bourgeoisie is only fear of 'the so-called rabble, i.e. the people, the unmoneyed
class, which knows not Comfort.' But 'the people are not with them but
against,' they will reverence only true leadership and service; and their
love, when it is given, is the only love worth having, 'because it is disinterested love, and endures, and takes heat in adversity—reflect on it and
wonder at the inversion of things.' So with Christianity, which has life
in the poor, but goes rotten among the bourgeoisie, who make of it
mummy-wraps or political truncheons. 'They call it statesmanship. . . .
Deadmanship, I call it. . . . Parsons and princes are happy with the
homage of this huge passive fleshpot class.'

> The people are the Power to come. Oppressed, unprotected, abandoned;
> left to the ebb and flow of the tides of the market, now taken on to work, now
> cast off to starve, committed to the shifting laws of demand and supply, slaves
> of Capital—the whited name for the old accursed Mammon; and of all the
> ranked and black-uniformed host no pastor to come out of the association of
> shepherds, and proclaim before heaven and man the primary claim of their
> cause.

The papacy and some form of bourgeois dictatorship are the dangers
to be guarded against; and the men who must fight to rouse the people
are so few. 'No extension of the army—no! A thousand times no. Let
India go, then! . . . At present India means utter perversion of the policy
of England. Adrift India! rather than England red-coated!' (Shrapnel is
himself confused here, succumbing to muffled imperialist ideas. 'If India
is to be held for the good of India, throw open India to the civilised
nations. . . .' And he expects Beauchamp to think he goes too far.)

England is ruled by 'a band of dealers in flesh-pottery.' 'The stench of
the trail of the Ego' makes up our history. At each stage—of early king-
ship, of feudalism, of the bourgeoisie, always Ego has ruled. 'It is ego—
ego, the fountain cry, origin, sole source of war! Then death to ego, I
say! . . . Now comes on the workman's era.' (Again he sprawls in confusion. He suggests that the worker's State will make ego 'inter-dependent
and dispersed,' but then goes on to say that maybe the balance will be
unstable; then will return the cycle of despots and revolutions.)

Finally comes a passage of complete inability to apply the lesson of the
preceding argument. He says Society 'is our one tangible gain.' We must
defend it for progress. 'If it be martyrdom, what then? Let the martyrdom
be.' He goes on, 'Rebellion against Society, and advocacy of Humanity,
run counter. Tell me that Society is a whited sepulchre . . . and I say, add
not another disfigurement to it; add the purification of it.' Society protects the weaker, especially women.

Such a statement blankly forgets all that has been said of the class-divisions in society and the way in which progress has been achieved by struggle. It suddenly assumes a unity of interests. What has gained certain protections for women is not Society (one of the idealist absolutes that Shrapnel has earlier denounced), but *the struggle in society*. The only thing that can justly be called a rebellion against Society is the class-egoism that Shrapnel-Meredith has described, which perpetually tries to break down the gains; the struggle against a ruling-class is not rebellion against Society, but an effort to eliminate the egoist forms and forces of exploitation that seek always to throw men back, to reverse history, to intensify alienation, spiritual and economic, and thus to sap the safeguards which Shrapnel wants maintained.*

The comment of the shrewdly cool Tory Austin has some validity:

He perceives a bad adjustment of things: which is correct. He is honest, and takes his honesty for a virtue; and that entitles him to believe in himself: and that belief causes him to see in all opposition to him the wrong he has perceived in existing circumstances: and so in a dream of power he invokes the people: and as they do not stir, he takes to prophecy. This is the round of the politics of impatience. The study of politics should be guided by some light of statesmanship, otherwise it comes to this wild preaching. These men are theory-tailors, not politicians. They are the men who make the 'strait-waistcoat for humanity.'

The basis of this comment is reactionary: it is the alienating forces, not Utopian theories, which jail and contract men. But it is true that a subjective element has intruded to limit the effect of Shrapnel-eloquence; and this element is based, as Austin says, in the prophet's isolation from the masses. The moral is not that which Austin proposes in the vein of Burke, an acceptance of the *status quo* as 'statesmanship'; it is the need of men like Shrapnel or Beauchamp to advance from the theory of fellowship to the full union of theory and practice. Meredith is clear enough to see what is holding Beauchamp (Maxse) back, but he cannot realise what will liberate him into effectiveness. For the political development of the workers in Britain has not yet, in the 1870's, reached the level at which the concept of the organised working-class can reveal to him its full concrete meaning.

He understands that there is greater militancy in the industrial areas of

---

* Compare the Essay on Comedy: 'proper esteem for the society we have wrested from brutishness, and would carry higher.' He is thus not denying the political and cultural struggles that he knows have done the wrestling and will do the carrying-higher. The edge of his argument can lie only against class-egoism or any position that denies the basis of civilisation in common life, in labour-process and its collective activity; but the way in which Shrapnel makes his formulation shows a confusion as to the nature of the State.

the North than at a place like Southampton; and Shrapnel, insisting on the deputation of workers being let in to his sickbed, remarks:

> Trust me, Beauchamp, if we shun to encounter the good warm soul of numbers, our hearts are narrowed to them. The business of our modern world is to open heart and stretch out arms to numbers. In numbers we have our sinews; they are our iron and gold. Scatter them not; teach them the secret of cohesion.

The secret of cohesion is indeed the issue, but Shrapnel does not know what it entails in the formation of a working-class political party.

Ruskin and Carlyle are cited in the book. Ruskin's *Stones of Venice* presides over the lovers in Venice; and Carlyle is Beauchamp's favourite author in youth. Rosamund Culling sees only

> a style resembling either early architecture or utter dilapidation, so loose and rough it seemed; a wind-in-the-orchard style, that tumbled down here and there an appreciable fruit with uncouth bluster; sentences without commencements running to abrupt endings and smoke, like waves against a sea-wall, learned dictionary words giving a hand to street-slang, and accents falling on them haphazard, like slant rays from driving clouds, all the pages in a breeze, the whole book producing a kind of electrical agitation on the mind and the joints.
>
> This was the effect on the lady. To her the incomprehensible was the abominable, for she had our country's high critical feeling; but, while admitting that he could not quite overmaster it, liked it . . . getting nibbles of golden meaning by instalments, as with a solitary pick in a very dark mine, until the illumination of an idea struck him that there was a great deal more in the book than there was in himself.

And later Beauchamp compares Dr Shrapnel's style. 'His own style, not the leading article style or modern pulpit style. He writes to rouse.'

Against him is set Romfrey, who calls himself a Whig, but is the most arrant reactionary. 'He stood for King, Lords, and Commons . . . , harping the triad as vigorously as bard of old Britain,' for to omit Commons from the traditional phrase might suggest that there could be Commons without Lords or King. While the triad stood, he felt safe for his birds, 'to his mind the game-laws were the corner-stone of Law, and of a man's right to hold his own.' His game are pests for his tenant-farmers, 'but no tenants were forced to take his farms. . . . He gave them liberty to go to Australia, Canada, the Americas, if they liked.' With keen irony Meredith sets out Romfrey's attitude to the negroes whom Beauchamp is freeing as a naval commander engaged in putting down the slave-trade:

> Practically humane though he was, and especially towards cattle and all kinds of beasts, Mr Romfrey entertained no profound fellow-feeling for the negro,

and, except as the representative of a certain amount of working power commonly requiring the whip to wind it up, he inclined to despise that black spot
in the creation. . . . Nevil's captures and releases of the grinning freights
amused him for awhile. He compared them to strings of bananas, and presently
put the vision of the whole business aside by talking of Nevil's banana-wreath.
. . . Nevil, in his banana-wreath, was set preaching 'humanitomtity.'

He detests all progressive ideas and hates the industrialists:

> You should see the miserable lank-jawed half-stewed pantaloons they've
> managed to make of Englishmen there. My blood's past boiling. They work
> young children in their factories from morning to night. Their manufactories
> are spreading like the webs of the Devil to suck the blood of the country.

Beauchamp as a lad is impressed; but later he learns that the opposition of
the landed Romfrey and the industrial capitalists is a false one, since
Romfrey and his fellows are now ultimately dependent on the capitalist
forces for the maintenance of the class-State and their privileges.

Traill in his review pointed to the completeness

> with which the author has succeeded in individualising a series of characters
> belonging generically to the same type in respect of social position and politics.
> . . . The feudal Toryism of Everard Romfrey, the martinet unidea-ed Toryism
> of Col. Halkett . . ., the hard-headed Philistine Toryism of Blackburn
> Tuckham, and the sceptical eclectic conservatism of Seymour Austin and
> Stukeley Culbrett, belong to four separate and clearly marked types. . . .
> Nor is there less felicity of discrimination displayed in the Radicalism of
> Nevil, of Dr Shrapnel and of Lydiard. Mr Grancey Lespel represents thoroughly
> well the 'landed variety' of the old Whig. His wife, the middle-aged woman
> of the world, with her decorously regulated taste for scandal, is a living
> portrait. . . .

He thinks only Turbot, the provincial Liberal editor, and Lord Palmet,
are at all caricatures, and even there the line is kept between comedy and
burlesque. He might, however, have added that the Liberals include men
like the spouter Timothy, who is ready to use a radical phrase as spice
but who has an utter contempt of anyone carried away by radical doctrine; or Cougham, 'a chrysalis Tory' pointing to France and washing his
hands of excesses, who obstructs everything with 'Are we practical?' and
who wipes out all enthusiasms with 'Yes, I have gone over all that.'

And then there are the electors, such as the dogmatic Sabbatarian
shoemaker.

But I must keep to only a few more points from this rich book. For
instance, Tuckham and his relations with Beauchamp. It is remarkable to
think that the portrait of the complacent and brutal Tuckham is openly
drawn from Meredith's friend Hardman (even to having his name made
up of the nickname Tuck). In conversation with Cecilia, Tuckham jeers

at the idea of 'fair play' for men who challenge the capitalist system. 'Fair play, I say, is not applicable to a man who deliberately goes about to stir the wild beast.' He holds that no man of sense and education, not certifiable as a lunatic, can be a radical. 'Those views are out of politics, they are matters for the police.'

> 'Dutch dykes are built to shut away the sea from cultivated land, and of course it's a part of the business of the Dutch Government to keep up the dykes, and of ours to guard against the mob. . . .'
> 'They speak,' said Miss Halkett, 'of educating the people to fit them——'
> 'They speak of commanding the winds and tides,' he cut her short, with no clear analogy, 'wait till we have a storm. It's a delusion amounting to dementedness to suppose, that with the people inside our defences, we can be taming them and tricking them. As for sending them to school after giving them power, it's like asking a wild beast to sit down to dinner with us—he wants the whole table and us too.'

Property is 'funded good sense,' the only guarantee of patriotism, and 'men of property should lead the nation.' With Britain's control of world-trade threatened,

> either your Radicals do not know the first conditions of human nature, or they do, and if they do they are traitors, and the Liberals opening the gates to them are fools; and some are knaves. We perish as a Great Power if we cease to look sharp ahead, hold firm together, and make the utmost of what we possess.

Beauchamp, after losing Cecilia to him, remarks that he 'would govern Great Britain as men of that rich middle-class rule their wives—with a strict regard for ostensible humanity and what the law allows them.'

Their clashes on the matter of Beauchamp's paper, *The Dawn*, bring out the irreconcilable hatred of the Tories for every measure of progress. Beauchamp decides that he must have a daily, otherwise it is impossible to challenge in time the ceaseless lies of the capitalist press.

> The covert Toryism, the fits of flunkeyism, the cowardice, of the relapsing middle-class, which is now England before mankind, because it fills the sails of the Press, must be exposed. It supports the Press in its own interests, affecting to speak for the people. It belies the people. And this Press, declaring itself independent, can hardly walk for fear of treading on an interest here, an interest there. It cannot have a conscience. It is a bad guide, a false guardian, its abject claim to be our national and popular interpreter—even that is hollow and a mockery. It is powerful only while subservient. An engine of money, appealing to the sensitiveness of money, it has no connection with the mind of the nation. And that it is not of, but apart from, the people, may be seen when great crises come. Can it stop a war? The people would, and with thunder, had they the medium. But in strong gales the power of the Press collapses; it wheezes like the pricked pigskin of a piper.

At its best Beauchamp regarded our lordly Press as a curiously diapered curtain and delusive mask, behind which the country struggles vainly to show an honest feature; and as a trumpet that deafened and terrorised the people; a mere engine of leaguers banded to keep a smooth face, quite soullessly.

In *The Dawn*, however, things would be different. Turn the sheets, 'and it is the manhood of the land addressing you, no longer that alternately puling and insolent cry of the coffers. The health, wealth, comfort, contentment of the greater numbers are there strived for, in contempt of compromise and "unreasonable times".'

Tuckham says *The Dawn* will be in lawsuits all the year.

'And by the time it has won a reputation, it will be undermined by a radi-caller Radical Journal. That's how we've lowered the country to this level. That's an Inferno of Circles, down to the ultimate mire. And what on earth are you contending for?'
'Freedom of thought, for one thing.'
'We've had quite enough free-thinking.'
'There's not enough if there's not perfect freedom.'
'Dangerous,' quoth Mr Austin.
'But it's that danger which makes men, sir; and it's fear of the danger that makes our modern Englishman.'

Tuckham taunts him that he won't get any good writers; they're bound up with the respectable well-off papers which can pay good prices.

Finally there is an argument in which Beauchamp lays at the feet of the Tories, the capitalist class, the whole responsibility for a corrupting press. (This, like so many other passages of the novel, is more relevant today, in the 1950's, than it was when written, so surely has Meredith put his finger on the essential trends of his day.)

'By the way,' said Colonel Halkett, 'there are lots of horrors in the paper today; wife kickings, and starvations—oh, dear me! and the murder of a woman: two columns to that.'
'That, the Tory reaction is responsible for!' said Tuckham, rather by way of a joke than a challenge.
Beauchamp accepted it as a challenge. . . . He charged the responsibility of every crime committed in the country, and every condition of misery, upon the party which declined to move in advance, and which therefore apologised for the perpetuation of knavery, villainy, brutality, injustice, and foul dealing. 'Stick to your laws and systems and institutions, and so long as you won't stir to amend them, I hold you accountable for that long newspaper list daily. . . .'
Tuckham . . . condensed his indignant rejoinder to: 'Madness can't go further. . . .'
Beauchamp . . . stuck to his charge against the Tory party. And moreover: the Tories—and the old Whigs, now Liberals, ranked under the heading of Tories—those Tories possessing and representing the wealth of the country, yet had not started one respectable journal that a lady could read through without

offence to her, or a gentleman without disgust! If there was not one English newspaper in existence independent of circulation and advertisement, and of the tricks to win them, the Tories were answerable for the vacancy. They, being the rich who, if they chose, could set an example to our Press by subscribing to maintain a Journal superior to the flattering of vile appetites—'all that nauseous matter. . . . Those Tories,' he bowed to the colonel, 'I'm afraid I must say you, sir, are answerable for it.'

'I am very well satisfied with my paper,' said the colonel.

Meredith, partly because he shares the Beauchamp-Maxse weaknesses, but also because he sees the flaws in Maxse, defines Beauchamp as carrying on many Tory elements into his revolt against Toryism. Thus, when the Colonel reads from the paper about an expedition against Indian hill-tribes and trouble in China, Beauchamp supports the Chinese but doesn't agree about the surrender of Gibraltar to the Spaniards. Tuckham has a justified sneer, yet at the same time Beauchamp sees how Britain as a capitalist country is a primary danger to world-peace. 'Dogs with a bone!— instead of living, as Dr Shrapnel prophesies, for and with one another. It's war now, and money's the weapon of war. And we're the worst nation in Europe for that.' Though he adds hopefully, 'But if we fairly recognise it, we shall be the first to alter our ways.' Remnants of his old class-outlook cling. He makes money by cattle-breeding and puts £10,000 into a Club to educate radicals, but Tuckham comments:

> Beauchamp's no Radical. He hasn't forgiven the Countess of Romfrey for marrying above her rank. He may be a bit of a Republican: but really in this country Republicans are fighting with the shadow of an old hat and a cockhorse [Rosamund has married Romfrey now an Earl].

He wants women to play their full parts in life, but he carries on something of the old ideas of their inferiority.

One difficult point he successfully weathers—that of peace and its connection with the Free-trade Industrialists. Tennyson in *Maud* had great play with the link between a peace-policy and the corruptions and horrors of commerce, drawing the moral that war would regenerate the nation. And so it was possible to argue that the whole Utopian dream of the Free-trade capitalist of 1851 was a deliberate cheat, a villainous veil meant to hide the ruthless extension of the profit-system. Ignoring the subjective sincerities or insincerities of any individual industrialist, we may recognise much truth in this contention; but if we leave the matter simply at that, we are ignoring the deep hope of the masses for peace and work, which had buttressed the employers' lie or delusion. And so the thesis of *Maud* works out as the conscious smirching of the idea of peace, it obscures the fact that the movement into war is not the regenerative movement against cash-nexus corruption and discord, but the expression of that corruption and discord at a more advanced stage of the system.

Meredith never got this point fully clear; it is the only serious flaw in his political ideas. That is, he never got fully clear the nature and function of the class-State, though at moments his definition is accurate enough. He remains unstable at this point because he did not move on to find his place in an organised working-class with its party seeking always to unify theory and practice, and always fundamentally opposed to the class-State. Hence he wobbles from a powerful statement of the class-struggle as the sole key to progress into reconciliation-formulas that can only work out as betraying progress—'national unity' in 'defence' of ill-gotten gains.

But he does not fall into the shrewd and vicious trap of *Maud* in this novel. As a midshipman Beauchamp stands up for the positive aspect of the 1851 dream without accepting the exploitations that distorted it.

> And oh! to feel for certain *which* side was the wrong side in our Civil War, so that one should not hesitate in choosing! . . . He hated bloodshed, and was guilty of the 'cotton-spinners' babble', abhorred of Everard [Romfrey]. . . . Somewhere, somehow, he had got hold of Manchester sarcasms concerning glory. . . .
>
> [Romfrey] directed Nevil to look home, and cast an eye on the cotton-spinners, with the remark that they were binding us hand and foot to sell us to the biggest buyer, and were not Englishmen but 'Germans and Jews, and Quakers and hybrids, diligent clerks and speculators, and commercial travellers, who have raised a fortune from foisting drugged goods on an idiot population. . . . So long as Manchester flourishes, we're a country governed and led by the belly.'

Beauchamp accepts the denunciation of capitalism, but not the smirching of the ideal of peace. Thus Meredith bitterly describes the war-hysteria in 1855.

> And now came the war, the purifier and the pestilence.
>
> The cry of the English people for war was pretty general, as far as the criers went. They put on their Sabbath face . . . and told with approval how the Royal hand had trembled in committing itself. . . . If there was money to be paid, there was a bugbear to be slain for it; and a bugbear is as obnoxious to the repose of commercial communities as rivals are to kings.
>
> The cry for war was absolutely unanimous, and a supremely national cry, Everard Romfrey said, for it excluded the cotton-spinners.
>
> He smacked his hands, crowing at the vociferations of disgust of those negro-philes and sweaters of Christians, whose isolated clamour amid the popular uproar sounded of gagged mouths.
>
> One of the half-stifled cotton-spinners, a notorious one [Bright], a spouter of rank sedition and hater of aristocracy, a political poacher, managed to make himself heard. He was tossed to the Press for a morsel, and tossed back again to the people in strips. . . . The world of England discovered that the peace-party which opposed was the actual cause of the war.

So the outbreak is seen through Romfrey's eyes. But Beauchamp does not react as his uncle expects.

> . . . the infamous miauling cotton-spinner. Nevil admired him. He said so bluntly . . . the one heroical Englishman of his day. 'I maintain he speaks wisely—I don't mind saying, like a prophet; and he speaks on behalf of the poor as well as of the country. . . . [The poor] pay for war.'

Later Romfrey tries to blame what is wrong with the war on the fact that it is 'conducted by milky cotton-spinners and their adjuncts,' but still gets no response from Beauchamp, who has begun to see deeper.

Again, Beauchamp admires the efforts of the Quakers to avert the war by their mission to Russia (which found whatever chances of success it owned, deliberately wrecked by warmongering leaders in *The Times*); while Romfrey accuses 'the Quakers of dry-rotting the country.'*

Beauchamp's end needs some words. His early affair with Renée, narrated with extreme charm, shows his youthful Quixotism, still tinctured with romantic ideals of self-sacrifice; but even then, he is fighting to get beyond the romantic inner-split:

> Beauchampism, as one confronting him calls it, may be said to stand for nearly everything which is the obverse of Byronism, and rarely woos your sympathy, shuns the statuesque pathetic, or any kind of posturing. For Beauchamp will not even look at happiness or mourn its absence; melodious lamentations, demoniacal scorn, are quite alien to him. His faith is in working and fighting.

But because in the midst of the election he responds to the call from the Romantic Moment that no longer has meaning to him, he involves himself afresh with Renée and destroys his chances with Cecilia. Cecilia, we feel, could have helped him to a settled and mature basis of struggle; but, having lost her, he turns to the rather conventional Jenny and is weakened. Once more we have the theme of 'too late.' But the errors which catch up Sandra-Vittoria and Beauchamp, and bring them down, are not the same as the errors which destroy a Feverel, an Edward Blancove—or in the later novels, an Alvan, a Radnor, a Lord Fleetwood. Because

---

* In a sense M. had been confusedly working out his own inner conflict, his sense of the 'shadowfight' between Liberal and Tory, in the Ipswich contributions. Thus, a part of him was able sincerely enough to attack the 'money-grubbing creed of Cobden and Bright. 'What has made the thirst for gold a fever throughout the country? What has caused the accumulation of wealth to be followed up with almost the fervour of a religious inspiration?' He answers: 'the rule of Manchester.' But he swung to the Right in sharing the anti-Yankee rage caused by the *Alabama* incident (as did also his friends the radical Maxse and the Tory Hardman. Maxse wanted to postpone his marriage and fight in the navy against the North Americans). M. in fact wrote the first and last chapters for a book based on the log and journal of the *Alabama's* captain. All the contradictions of this period are, however, resolved in the poem to Morley and *Beauchamp's Career.*

Vittoria and Beauchamp are truly rooted in struggle we are left with the entire conviction that their failures lead to a new and stabler basis of purpose in those who carry on where they left off. There is nothing pessimist in their ends.

Beauchamp's marriage with Jenny opens with a compromise, a church-marriage, which outrages all his convictions. He tries to argue with her. The priest is 'against the cause of the people. Very well: I make my protest to the death against him.' He falls to some extent under Jenny's sensuous spell, and Shrapnel has to cry out:

> What! to draw breath day by day, and not to pay for it by striking daily at the rock Iniquity? . . . How far will you push indolent unreason to gain the delusion of happiness? There is no such thing: but there's trance. That talk of happiness is a carrion clamour of the creatures of prey. Take it and you're helping tear some poor wretch to pieces, whom you might be constructing, saving perchance. . . .

But he cannot advance to mass-struggle. He dies in an individual act of heroism, which expresses his anguished desire for union with the common people but which also kills him, returning him to romantic loss. He dies saving a worker's child from drowning. Shrapnel and Romfrey are linked in the thought over his corpse: 'This [the muddy urchin] is what we have in exchange for Beauchamp!' But though Meredith in one sense means this phrase ironically, tragically, he is also pointing simply to the solution that has evaded Beauchamp. There can be no irony in the end of such a man; the saved child is the future for which he has striven; the child is the working-class with whom the next word lies. Beauchampism is the reverse of Byronism; but it still carries on the Romantic split in so far as it can conceive only of individual action, individual heroism and self-sacrifice, and fails to grasp 'the secret of cohesion.' Beauchamp's death expresses both his failure and the overcoming of his failure. In it there is the tragedy of wasted powers, broken aspirations; but there is also the scorn of tragedy and the unfaltering faith in the future which salves and transforms the personal grief, which defeats death.

> The comic wanders and prowls unceasingly round Beauchamp, seeking the chink in his armour, but in vain: Beauchamp is modest, sincere, noble. Indeed, where there is nobility of soul, ardent sincerity, devotion to something that goes beyond us, the comic by its inability to make these traits ridiculous accentuates them. Foes or friends of Nevil can laugh at his youthful extrava-gances: neither his uncle's sarcasms nor Baskelett's caricatures touch his in-tegrity. Rather these efforts bring out the failure of their authors to grasp moral beauty. . . .
> [The book's humour] is a reagent which detaches, frees the latent absurdity, and allows the reader to retain only the heroism, the extraordinary virtue of a man who perfectly forgets himself. [Galland.]

This magnificent novel is the one great novel on an explicitly political theme in its century, the one novel which throughout sees the struggle for personal integrity as a struggle against capitalism and its values *at all levels*.* To grasp its profundity we must keep in mind what was said earlier of the passivity of the masses in the period. Even the New Unionism was in the future, let alone any kind of socialist activity or theory gripping the workers or any significant section of them. That was why Meredith was driven to end the book as he did, despite his wife's protests against Beauchamp's sudden death.

Consider some of Engels' remarks on the English proletariat over these years, even though they do not compass the whole situation:

> The English working class has been gradually more and more deeply demoralised by the period of corruption since 1848 and had at last got to the point where they were nothing more than the tail of the great Liberal Party, i.e. henchmen of the capitalists. [11 February, 1878.]
> The English labour movement has been revolving (now and) for a series of years in a narrow vicious circle of strikes for wages and shorter working hours, and this not merely as an expedient and a means of propaganda and organisation but as an end in itself. . . . The trade unions exclude all political action. . . . The workers are divided politically into Conservatives and Liberal-Radicals. . . . [17 June, 1879.]
> Do not on any account whatever let yourself be deluded into thinking there is a real proletarian movement going on here. . . . A really general workers' movement will only come into existence here when the workers are made to feel the fact that England's world monopoly is broken. [30 August, 1883.]
> Here in England one can see that it is impossible simply to drill a theory in an abstract dogmatic way into a great nation, even if one has the best of theories, developed out of their own conditions of life. . . . The most repulsive thing here is the bourgeois 'respectability' which is grown deep into the bones of the workers. [7 December, 1889.]

And he declared that the English bourgeoisie, not content with being the most highly developed section of that class in the world, had brought about a bourgeoisified proletariat. (The last of his passages, that about drilling a theory abstractly into the people, is specially relevant to Meredith's novel.)

These analyses by Engels help us to appreciate the force of one of Beauchamp's later realisations. 'Elsewhere the Radical' (by whom he

---

* No such statement is ever absolute, of course. There were two forerunners: George Eliot with her *Felix Holt* (1866: more or less contemporary with his Sandra-Vittoria epic) and Disraeli with his *Sybil*, 1845. And we must not forget Chernichevsky's parallel effort with his *What Shall We Do?* in 1862. But Meredith posits the issues with a richness and depth that are all his own; *Beauchamp* shows an incomparably fuller notion of political reality than *Felix Holt* or *Sybil*.

means anyone fighting the capitalist state) 'smites at iron or rotten wood; *in England it is a cushion on springs'*—his italics.

Though H. D. Traill praised the novel in *The Pall Mall Gazette*, sales fell away from the level of *Harry Richmond*.

> It has been stated by one prominent critic that Meredith's reputation was not materially advanced by this story, 'overlaid by political disquisition,' and 'its somewhat monotonous hero.' I understand it was at this date that Mark Pattison warned his readers against opening a volume which bore on its cover the name of George Meredith. [S. M. Ellis.]

Swinburne, though admitting power and beauty and fine truthfulness, saw only a book ruined by 'lust of epigram and habit of trying to tell a story by means of riddles that hardly excite the curiosity they are certain to baffle'—though there are, in fact, no riddles whatever in the book:

> By dint of revulsion from Trollope on this hand and Braddon on the other, he seems to have convinced himself that limpidity of style must mean shallowness, lucidity of narrative must imply triviality, and simplicity of direct interest or positive incident must involve 'sensationalism.' It is a constant irritation to see a man of such rarely strong and subtle genius, such various and splendid forces of mind, do so much to justify the general neglect he provokes. [To Morley.]

(We may contrast this effort to belittle Meredith to his friend Morley with Meredith's efforts to get reviews for Swinburne's books at this time.) Not one word from the poet, once a rebel, about the content of the book. He has joined the chorus who croak about Meredith's demerits as a stylist to evade his plain meanings or who admit his great powers only to lament their ruination.

One review with considerable insight into Meredith's method and the new powers it brought into our literature appeared in the freethinking *Secularist*, signed B.V. (James Thomson the poet). For the first time Meredith was seen as the master he was:

> He loves to suggest by flying touches rather than slowly elaborate. To those who are quick to follow his suggestions he gives in a few winged words the very spirit of a scene, the inmost secret of a mood or passion. . . .
> He has a wonderful eye for form and colour, especially the latter, a masterly perception of character; a most subtle sense for spiritual mysteries. His dialogue is full of life and reality, flexible and rich in the genuine unexpected, marked with the keenest distinctions. . . .
> He has this sure mark of lofty genius, that he always rises with his theme, growing more strenuous, more self-contained, more magistral, as the demands on his thought and imagination increase. His style is very various and flexible, flowing freely in whatever measures the subject and the mood may dictate.

At its best it is so beautiful in simplest Saxon, so majestic in rhythm, so noble with noble imagery, so pregnant with meaning, so vital and intense, that it must be ranked among the supreme achievements of our literature. . . . He is great in the fiery record of fiery action. . . .

Meredith himself, though at times expressing dissatisfaction with the novel, said in his last years to Clodd:

Sometimes *Harry Richmond* is my favourite, but I am inclined to give the palm to *Beauchamp's Career*. There is a breezy, human interest about it, and the plot has a consistent and logical evolution which *Feverel* lacks. Then, a thing that weighs with me, the French critics liked it; they said Renée is true to life.*

And Alice Brandeth found that he spoke of it as his special favourite.†

---

* Again, 'M. thinks *Beauchamp's Career* his best book,' Clodd's Notes (June 1895).

† Traill has no insight into the deeper meaning, but he appreciates the skill with which the various political types are assembled. He praised M. for 'the close objective study of social types,' in *The Novel of Manners* (*The Nineteenth Century*, Oct. 1875), saying that he alone maintained the art.

Generally the critics still lamented M.'s cleverness. *The Athenaeum* thinks he has a fluctuating style, at its best his own; but his anti-sensational tone prevents his popularity. The reader 'is not let all at once into the secrets of the heart of every personage, but is left to discover their character by means of study, every whit as close as is required in real life.' *The Examiner* says he is too terribly in earnest to be a comfort for the ordinary reader. *The Academy* decides that M. will never be a novelist, though he may get somewhere as critic or essayist. *The Saturday Review* follows Traill's lead.

20

Some Short Works

HE LIKED to rise early, stroll into the boxwood grove and the cover where he had seen foxcubs play, leftward to the open valley with fritillaries and early butterflies, noting the little details of growth and movement. He loved the pale spring leaves of the beech, the primrose mountains of Love in the Valley, the sudden cloud of the wild cherry. 'A rapid walker, poetically minded, gathers multitudes of images on his way,' said *The Egoist*. He worked often till late at night, stopping only when the gardener Cole brought his meals to the chalet, or striding a while on the terrace or the woodland-track, with an improvised Rabelaisian song on his lips. He wrote in an armchair with a teak board on his knees, using a quill and blue ink. 'My ideas flow with the ink from the pen.' 'I constantly brood, argue, speculate, and to write relieves me.' To Cole he said, 'I have something of great power and I must use it: I can put a glass in men's chests, and see what is working inside.' Cole ruminated: 'There wasn't a happier master and man in the whole kingdom.'

In the 1874 summer he relaxed, and often his friends came to late breakfast in the garden, with hock. He took to vegetarianism, and Hyndman has a ridiculous story. 'It was well-nigh the death of him. But he had persuaded himself that that was the right sort of food to give the highest development to body and mind. . . . So poor Mrs Meredith had a hard time,' watching him daily more hungry-eyed and thin, till in desperation she got the local baker to include shredded meat in his loaves!

His ardour over wines had slackened with his stomach-trouble, though he kept a small good cellar of burgundy, claret, hock, and even champagne. As late as 1908 he said, 'I drink wine and I smoke.'

Among his friends of the period were Morley and Leslie Stephen, with Maxse, Morison, Greenwood still sharing his talk. And in 1878 R. L. Stevenson was to bring the impact of the Young Men. The one demerit of the house, Meredith felt, was its small size; visitors generally put up at the near inn.

Morley had many of the compromising weaknesses of the liberal; and his development from the days when he welcomed Harrison's defence of the Communards to those when he supported repression in India was one of steady moral decline. But at his best he held to a faith in science and progress, in a movement towards universal justice, in the human power to achieve new forms of adaptation; he disliked sentimentalism and emotional self-indulgence. Lacking wit and humour, he could appreciate them in others, and Meredith called his conversation a mountain air for the soul.

His lapse into acceptance of the increasingly close-meshed imperialist State exemplifies the fate that these left radicals could not escape if they did not break from gradualism and hold firmly to the need of a revolutionary rupture in State-power. Though Meredith shared many of their weaknesses, he was saved from their fall by his concrete realisation of the deepening egoist split in bourgeois man.

Leslie Stephen was another positivist, without Morley's solid weight, but inclining more to a free-thinking combativeness. Born in 1832, he gave up his tutorial fellowship at Cambridge through religious doubt, and came to London to live as a writer. He edited *The Cornhill* from 1871 to 1882, and was the first editor of *The Dictionary of National Biography*. A disciple of Locke and Hume, he distrusted metaphysics and called himself an agnostic, but had no insight into the bourgeois illusion. With his deep-blue eyes under thick straight brows, curling brown hair, dark beard and moustache, he had at first an air of icy reserve. An intrepid alpinist and keen walker, he founded in 1879 the Sunday Tramps, who rambled from October to June in Surrey, Kent, Herts. Meredith, a sort of high honorary member, could not in the 1880's go far with them, but used to meet them, walk part of their itinerary, and feed them at Flint Cottage, which they left for the train at 10 p.m. In 1891 Stephen had to resign his presidency, but went with the Tramps at times till 1895.

Meredith's attitudes to Nature are partly based in his fierce and sometimes tormenting sense of constriction in the stifling world of the cash-nexus, through which he wanted desperately to break. But they are also rooted in his effort to grasp a true concept of development. There is, however, something silly and repellent in the picture of beefy Victorian gentlemen like Hardman and the others trying to feel good and healthy by furious exercise, by a pseudo-cult of Nature and Wordsworthian communions. In a person like Stephen there is a tinct of Meredith's attitudes, but also a retreat of fear from the world's conflicts (other than those that can be stated in terms of an abstract rationalism). The fear-elements, present in Meredith as one aspect of his resistance against the repression forces, tend to dominate in a Stephen and to beget a cult of hearty movement, alpinism, health as things-in-themselves. 'I have fancied myself on such occasions to be a felicitous blend of poet and saint,' says

8

Stephen; but he was neither. He was merely a man running away from the realities of social conflict—though, morally superior to the Hardmans, he did continue with the restricted rationalist fight.*

There was something of the same flight, though more aestheticised, in Stevenson's cult of tramping; and Meredith brings out both the falsity and the element with potentialities of something better, in his picture of Woodseer in *The Amazing Marriage*.

In 1876 he was playing about with Alice, who was keen on theatricals but whose genteel mother wouldn't have young men as stage-lovers. A series of Shakespearean readings were held, with Alice as heroine and Meredith as greying lover. Mrs B. acquiesced, 'as he understands girls so well,' though she regretted his inability to write as well as Charlotte Yonge. Alice, a yachting girl, fond of horses and Old England, pertly criticised his style and quoted a writer who said he hadn't time to learn shorthand and read his novels. Meredith replied, 'Yes, I know what you'd like me to say: "She went upstairs, her heart was heavy as lead. . . ." ' And went on stringing out that sort of trite phrase.

Edward Bannreuther, who incidentally played music for the readings, gave chamber-music concerts at his Bayswater house, and there the Merediths met Wagner. They were also now accepting invitations to the rich country-houses around, where Meredith gained useful copy but was certainly looked on as an oddity more than he realised. Alice comments on his resentment of anything that seemed like patronage, and the fact that no one dared to try it on twice.† 'Well, have you been to many gabble-gobble dinner parties?' he'd ask, and so on. One day at a garden-fête a footman spilled strawberries and cream on a new Paris gown of Mrs Meredith's. She laughed and said there were plenty more gowns where that one had come from; Meredith whispered, 'I can hear her give a fifty guinea sigh.' We hear too of Soapbubble Parties (the bubbles being waved up by Japanese fans) and charades on abstract qualities, in which he always refused to act. At one dinner-party Alice sat between Fitz-James Stephen (later a Justice) and Meredith. Fitz-J., a hard reactionary,

---

* Indeed Meredith admits the fear in the account of Vernon (Stephen) in *The Egoist*. 'He walked heroically, his pedestrian vigour being famous, but that means one who walks away from the sex, not excelling in the recreations where men and women join hands.'

† 'He was by nature very proud, and haughtily resented anything like patronage. He had a certain carriage of the head that we grew to recognise whenever he suspected anyone of attempting to patronise him. They did not do it a second time.' The girl whom he had called London-pated at their first meeting did understand a little of him. 'I do not think Mr Meredith liked the company of very rich people, and I remember well as a child how puzzled I was, and what a new idea it appeared to me when I heard him say that in many cases the vision of rich people was limited by their personal possessions, and that their mental horizon was bounded by their own park gates.'

kept saying that he'd read *Paradise Lost* and he did think it the most foolish poem ever written. Meredith expostulated. Fitz-J. agreed there were a few nice things about the Devil, but he did think it was the most foolish poem ever written. 'Afterwards he and Mr Meredith were very rude to each other about bottle-nosed whales.'

August saw him happy in the sun, 'I climb the hills of mint and thyme, and can compare myself only to the Leg of Mutton stewing in herbs.' In January 1877 his first short novel, *The House on the Beach*, appeared in the *New Quarterly Magazine*. In February he gave his one and only lecture *On the Idea of Comedy and the Uses of the Comic Spirit* at the London Institute, and was pleased that no one walked out; Morison said he spoke distinctly. At home he was enjoying the Chalet, working and sleeping there. 'The dark line of my hills runs up to the stars, the valley below is a soundless gulf. There I pace like a shipman before turning in.' He called to Morley in April, 'The nightingale is now in sweet song: there's not the ghost of a harvester to bite you even in fancy.' In June he wrote to Morley in Germany, saying he'd like to be with him to savour the contradictions of the Germans. In August he wrote to Maxse on the difficulty of working. 'I fear I am again condemned to trot round my circle, like an old horse at a well, everlastingly pulling up the same buckets full of a similar fluid.'

In July *The Case of General Ople and Lady Camper* appeared in the same magazine as *The House on the Beach*, and, writing to Hardman after a visit to Aldershot on 25 September, Meredith said that he thought the original of the General would be remembered. He refused an invitation to another lecture. 'It makes me nervous, and I have to give up my inner mind's working to it. But I have the question going on, whether I ought to decline anything, I, unlucky, portionless, ill-paid.'

With the bells for 1878 ringing in his ears he looked up at the night sky:

> To come from a gaze at the stars—Orion and shaking Sirius below him— is to catch a glance at the inscrutable face of him that hurries on, as on a wheel, from dust to dust.—I thought of you and how it might be with you this year: hoped for good: saw beyond good and evil to great stillness, another form of moving for you and me. It seems to me that Spirit is,—how, where, and by what means involving us, none can say. But in this life there is no life save in spirit. The rest of life, and we may know it in love—is an aching and a rotting. It is late. I have been writing all day. With all my heart I wish you well. [To Morley.]

This year he corresponded with the free-thinker Foote who had written to him about obstacles put in the way of the circulation of his books. He thanked Foote; and his words show how hard-hit he was by his inability to gain a public.

> To feel that men like you and 'B.V.' read and have a taste for what I produce is full of encouragement to me to write on with good heart.—We will not speak of our public which is a funny public, pardonable for its humours, and wants rough shaking and persistent teaching before it will have a zest or respect for literature that is not directed to adorn a library or illustrate a draw-ing-room table. *Peut-être que cela lui vient d'un manque de coeur.* At any rate, the English cure one early of a desire for applause, and as well as I could do, I have worked without thought of that and the profit coming from it.—I should not fancy that cheap editions of my writings would sell. Perhaps they will go better in time. . . .

The 'public' is the middle-class public with which he was so ceaselessly at odds. His only hope, he knew, was a different sort of audience, the awakened common-man, but he had no means of getting at that different audience, which lay in the future. An audience which would not lack heart because it was not afraid of life. And indeed in men like Foote and Thomson, strong freethinkers of the radical mass-stream, he foretastes something of that audience, as he did not taste it in Morley or even in Maxse.

All the same it was pleasant to get the homage of the literary young, as he did when R. L. Stevenson visited him in April. Stevenson was then 28, and had published some essays in *The Cornhill.* He stayed at Burford Bridge Inn, with a letter to the Gordons, but in order to meet Meredith. They soon met and Alice (who had married her cousin, Jim Gordon) tells how they chatted on the Gordon lawn and how she was surprised when Meredith 'prophesied great things for Stevenson.' Stevenson was very thin, with chestnut hair and bold merry eyes, with the air of a Shelley and a Bohemian fiddler. He and Meredith got on well together. Meredith would invent something at the cost of Stevenson, who would then travesty the parody, and so on, till Meredith threw back his head in one of his roars of laughter.

He was working on the *Egoist.* But in October he was feeling ill:

> I have been nowhere but on my weekly hack-cab-horse expeditions [to Chapman and Hall], and it is doubtful that I shall ever go anywhere except on that tramroad, until I proceed in mute accompaniment to my Last March. Life under these conditions is not so seductive as it appeared in youth, though in youth I looked out under a hail of blows. I don't complain, you see, of inconsistency in my career.
>
> If I could quit England, hold off from paper, and simply look on for the remainder of my term—mountains near—I would ask for no better. To be mixed up with them is hard, these English are so astonishing to my ideas of

dignity and valour. Their present hugging of their India, which they are ruining for the sake of giving a lucrative post to younger sons of their middle class, is a picture for mankind.

Here he makes amends for the confused remarks about India in *Beauchamp*; and indeed we continually find him thus correcting errors as he lives and learns.*

In April 1879 he was sick, and in May still 'lank, limp, and cavernchapped' through stomach-catarrh, which has left a bad cough. 'In fact, the hangman has you by the throat each ten or twenty minutes.' Recently he met Browning at a picture-gallery, and through Foote he has come to know James Thomson, who, after a hard life as a sailor's orphan, had carried on certain aspects of the New Poetry in his *City of Dreadful Night* and his London poems. Meredith admired his work, and said of *The City*, 'There is a massive impressiveness in it that goes beyond Durer's Melancholia, and takes it into upper regions.' He wrote to Thomson:

> The Reviewers are not likely to give you satisfaction. But read them, nevertheless, if they come in your way. The humour of a situation that allots the pulpit to them, and (for having presumed to make an appearance) the part of Devil to you, will not fail of consolation. My inclination is that you will find free-thoughted men enough to support you. [1879.]

They met twice. In September Thomson visited Box Hill under a cloudy but rainless sky, and the two poets strolled among the yews and red-berried ash. Meredith tried to help Thomson with an introduction to Morley, but by June the younger poet was dead.

> He was a man of big heart, of such entire sincereness that he wrote directly from the impressions carved in him by his desolate experience of life. Bright achievement was plucked out of the most tragic life in our literature. . . . He had, almost past example in my experience, the thrill of the worth of moral valiancy as well as of sensuous beauty . . . the exhibition of nobility at war with evil conditions.

Thus Thomson was for Meredith in no sense a poet of pessimism, but a poet who struggled through the night of cash-nexus alienation with a true sense of man. 'I am in love,' he had written earlier, 'with the dear London lass who helped you to the idyll of Cockayne.' And he admired Thomson all the more for his free-thinking attitude. The crushing of such a poet by poverty he held an indictment of their society.

---

* The cut and revised version of *Richard Feverel* came out in 1878. Miss A. Shore in *The British Quarterly Review* sees M. as a poetic philosopher of enduring fame who stands 'outside his creations,' and *Beauchamp* as his most mature work. Thomson in *Cope's Tobacco Plant* saw in M. as in Browning 'the intellectual power and the creative energy wrestle as in a war embrace.' His style is as 'vital and plastic as the ever evolving world it depicts, equal to all emergencies,' able to deal with all classes, 'yet rise to all grandeurs of Nature and Destiny and the human soul in fiercest passion and action.' Words that bleed if you touch them.

In July 1879, *The Tale of Chloe* appeared; and Meredith was in West-moreland with Morley, 'battling with rain and mist,' and stiff from hill-tracks. In the late summer he went to France, leaving the family in Normandy, he crossed Touraine and went on to Nimes, Marseilles, Bordighera. But his health was not much bettered. On his return to 'old galley-slave England' he was found to have bradyspepsy, and by the end of 1881 his spine was affected.

Before we pass on to the *Egoist* we had better look at the short novels, the lecture on Comedy, and the poems of the 1870's. First the *House on the Beach*, which, set in Seaforth, had been started in '61 as *Van Dieman Smith*; in the second version Meredith filled out Tinman with elements drawn from one Busby of Kingston, whom Hardman had told him of. (The Crickledons, as mentioned, were based on the Ockendens.) Mere-dith had been reminded of his unfinished tale by a great flood at Seaforth in 1876, which he now used for his climax. (In the actual flood Ockenden's house adjoining Marine Parade had been much damaged, and his timber floated about like battering rams.)

The story is of a mean treacherous tradesman, bailiff of the Cinque Port of Crikswick. The villas all round with their five-feet gardens boast 'titles of royalty and bloody battles,' and Tinman has schemed to present an address to the Queen on the wedding of one of the princesses. He practises in court-dress before a big mirror. The tale opens with Van Dieman Smith, returned from Australia with his daughter, crashing into this mirror, which a man is carrying in the night-street: an episode that sets the theme—the smashing up of Tinman's snob-pretensions and local tyranny by the bluff rough Australian. Van Dieman Smith, under another name, had deserted from the army, and Tinman uses his knowledge of this fact to blackmail Smith into accepting him as son-in-law. Finally a great storm overwhelms Tinman's house and reveals his full villainy.*

Tinman is thus of the kin of the Countess de Saldar and Roy, in a mean nasty way. A marketing mother has launched him from a small shop into a big one, and so he learned to 'start himself as a gentleman.' Like 'the rest of his countrymen,' he is bursting to rise above the others and 'shake them class by class as the dust from his heels.' He clashes with Smith in the municipal allocation of moneys. 'Tinman was ever for devoting them to the patriotic defence of "our shores"; whereas Van Dieman, pointing in detestation of the town sewerage reeking across the common under

---

* The early draft, *Van Dieman Smith*, was written in the same year as Dickens' *Great Expectations*, from which it took the theme of the returned 'Australian' under the threat of the law, who brings about the social 'exposure.'

the beach, loudly called on him to preserve our lives, by way of com-
mencement.' (This theme keeps recurring in the tale, and sets the social
moral. Thus, Smith says that he'll become bailiff and beat Tinman. 'I love
my country, but hang me if I don't purify it!' Tinman moans, 'Always
the poor! the poor! money for the poor. I say doctors have said the drain
on the common is healthy. . . .')

The storm thus becomes a sort of rebellious uprising, an elemental
emblem for the triumph of the Smith forces against the Tinman.

> O you Revolutionists! who would have no state, no ceremonial, and but
> one order of galligaskins! This man must have been wooed away in spirit to
> forgetfulness of the tempest, scourging his mighty neighbour [the Sea] to a
> bigger and a farther leap; he must have obtained from the contemplation of
> himself in his suit that which would be the saving of all men, in especial, of
> his countrymen—imagination, namely. . . .
> [The fishermen think] Heaven be thanked, no fishing boats were out.
> Chiefly well-to-do people would be sufferers—an exceptional case. For it is the
> mysterious and unexplained dispensation that: 'Mostly heaven chastises we.'

Finally there is the motive of the liberating laugh. Smith's daughter
Annette, who has been forcing herself to accept Tinman out of loyalty to
her father, is released to her true-lover by a long laugh.

> It rolled her heart and senses in a headlong surge, shook her to burning tears,
> and seemed to her ideas the most wonderful running together of opposite
> things ever known on earth. The young lady was ashamed of her laughter; but
> she was deeply indebted to it, for never was her mind made so clear by that
> beneficent exercise.

Those are the last words of the tale. The laugh that fuses opposites in a
new unity of understanding, of penetration into reality, follows on the
storm of revolution that unseats the social-climber Tinman.

The tale is slight, but of interest in showing clearly the method by
which Meredith built his political symbolism.

General Ople was based on the case of General Hopkins, retired and
resident at Norbiton, who took an action against the woman next door,
Lady Eleanor Cathcart, who had kept on sending caricatures of him
gardening, etc. Hardman knew the General.

Meredith transferred the tale to Norbiton Hall and Kingston Lodge,
the houses that Hardman and himself had inhabited; and worked out an
ingenious reason for the persecution. The General's daughter is in love
with Lady Camper's nephew, and he is too self-centred to notice. Lady
Camper tries to wake him up, and he thinks she is making advances. She
uses her skill in drawing to shatter his complacency, to compel him in the
end to see himself as he is, and to drive him back into an active life.

The theme is thus the attack on the bourgeois stereotype (amusingly expressed in the story by the General's use of the conventional diction of his class). The stereotype, which standardises men in terms of the cash-nexus, is one (Meredith says) with the lie, the hypocritical egoism, of the ruling class. The General makes his first decisive step when he is driven by Lady Camper's persecution into breaking a convention; he goes to a party without tie or collar. Lady Camper explains her behaviour as determined by her Welsh origin. 'You English have the smallest experience of humanity.'

Again the tale is slight, but pleasantly lets us into Meredith's method.

Chloe (originally called *The Lamentable Tale of Chloe*) is of a different type, set at The Wells in the 18th century. Chloe, who has been deceived and impoverished by Sir Martin Caseldy, is put in charge of a Duchess (a milkmaid before her marriage). Caseldy comes to woo the Duchess under pretence of reuniting himself with Chloe. Chloe gradually deciphers his treachery. At last the lovers plan to elope at three one morning. Chloe hangs herself at the door of the sitting-room, so that the Duchess, slipping out, comes up against her body dangling and is halted by the shock.

This is a delicately lyrical and tender tale of a fine spirit broken and yet wholly unresentful, making a final affirmation by self-sacrifice. Meredith uses his favourite device of ballads to enlarge the social focus. Chloe, needless to say, is Welsh.*

In the lecture on Comedy, Meredith distinguished Comedy from Satire with its direct moral aim, Irony which is the humour of Satire, and Humour which is a pervasive human warmth with 'lights of Tragedy' on its laughter. He also analyses the main comic expressions from Aristophanes onwards. There are suggestive comments throughout, but what concerns us here is the definition of the Comic Spirit.

The meaning and justification of individual experience and suffering lie in each man's possibility of rising to his full human stature, with his qualities as developed as they can be. Comedy shows the points of failure, the division between actuality and potentiality—between men as they are and as they might be; between theory and practice. It thus points the way

---

* The original was Miss Fanny Braddock who, losing at play, hanged herself at Bath in 1731 with a silken girdle; Goldsmith brought in a faithless lover (*The Life of Richard Nash*). Also Christina Rossetti. She (M. told Violet Hunt) had been tempted to run away by the lover whom she rejected for becoming a Catholic and who had married; her devoted elder sister Maria lay across the frontdoor mat every night for a week. (See also the story of the Earl of Exeter and Sarah Hoggins, 1791, behind Tennyson's *Lord of Burleigh*.)

It would seem then that *Goblin Market* by Christina is a symbolic expression of the event that M. uses.

towards the overcoming of the division, to the realisation of the full possibilities of human life, individually and socially—the two aspects are indivisible. Comedy is the guardian of the human process, the guide into the new epoch of community, in which the active development of men and women on a higher level of unified consciousness will begin. It is a test. The Comic Spirit is not the light of the Future, but it makes the Future possible by its keen testing of the concrete and immediate for the full truth, the revelation of division, conflict, forward-movement, potentiality. It brings out the contradictions of existence in order to make possible their overcoming. As *The House on the Beach* told us, it fuses opposites in a new liberating vision of reality.

> If you believe that our civilisation is founded in common sense (and it is the first condition of sanity to believe it), you will, when contemplating men, discern a Spirit overhead; not more heavenly than the light flashed upwards from glassy surfaces, but luminous and watchful; never shooting beyond them nor lagging in the rear; so closely attached to them that it may be taken for a slavish reflex, until its features are studied. It has the sage's brows, and the sunny malice of a faun lurks at the corners of half-closed lips drawn in an idle wariness of half tension.

> That slim feasting smile, shaped like the long-bow, was once a big round satyr's laugh, that flung up the brows like a fortress lifted by gunpowder. The laugh will come again, but it will be of the smile, finely tempered, showing sunlight of the mind, mental richness rather than noisy enormity. Its common aspect is one of unsolicitous observation, as if surveying a full field and having leisure to dart on its chosen morsels, without any fluttering eagerness.

It is earthy, the ceaseless correction of idealist abstraction, but it has nothing of Peacockian detachment or Carlylean contempt-of-earth, for it owns a universalising quality—civilisation being founded on common sense, on rationality—and it thus unites men as well as intensifying their individual apprehensions of the concrete world of experience. It is the 'spirit born of our united social intelligences.' It denies or ignores Utopias; but it essentially opposes all that is reactionary, all that disregards what draws men together in a fuller and more truthful grasp of reality.

> Men's future upon earth does not atract it; their honesty and shapeliness in the present does; and whenever they wax out of proportion, overblown, affected, pretentious, bombastical, hypocritical, pedantic, fantastically delicate; whenever it sees them self-deceived or hoodwinked, given to run riot in idolatries, drifting into vanities, congregating in absurdities, planning short-sightedly, plotting dementedly; whenever they are at variance with their professions, and violate the unwritten but perceptible laws binding them in consideration one to another; whenever they offend sound reason, fair justice; are false in humility or mined with conceit, individually, or in bulk—the Spirit overhead will look humanely malign and cast an oblique light on them, followed by volleys of silvery laughter. That is the Comic Spirit.

There Meredith details some of the opposites or contradictions which Comedy brings together in its revelation of a fuller humanity. Though not itself philosophic, it implies a wealth of philosophic ideas—of justice, reason, human unity (and all that breaks it), unity of theory and practice: otherwise its universalising quality could not function. It is not directly concerned with the future, but its universalising basis means that the critical values which at every point accompany its penetration and grasp of the concrete are concerned with the future, the direction in which men are moving. For the liberating laugh, the vision of opposites fused and transformed into a new unity, implies social and political struggle (other-wise its 'concreteness' becomes a delusive variety of abstraction); and it implies further a perpetual struggle towards the unity of theory and practice. This struggle, Meredith insists, cannot be viewed through some neutral kind of spectacles. Such neutrality halts and undermines the whole movement of civilising forces. The Comic Spirit is not narrowly partisan, enslaved to some particular personal or class-interest; but is profoundly partisan in its enthusiasm for life, for more life and better life. By its very nature it is linked with a humanist view of progress into ever-greater universality and freedom through the mastery over nature and the political extension of equality and brotherhood.

Thus, Meredith stresses, the Comic Spirit demands equality of the sexes or the movement towards such equality. For the suppression of one sex attacks at the root the universalising attitudes of that Spirit.

The lecture was printed in *The New Quarterly Magazine*, 'cursed with misprints,' but did not appear in book form till 1897. Shaw then reviewed it at length, but showed his too-frequent wrong-headedness, a resolve to use the text for his own wise-cracks without any effort to understand. Meredith had remarked that the English with all their existent weaknesses had the basis of the comedic spirit in them, an esteem of common sense. He did not mean that they were ready to respond there and then to the humanist revelations of the Spirit, of which they stood badly in need, but that the basis for the Spirit's struggle could be found. Shaw denied that the Englishman had any common sense apart from the qualities making for 'money and social precedence.' Therefore, 'self-satisfiedly unconscious' of their 'moral and intellectual bluntness,' they made comedy impossible. 'Whereas the function of comedy is to dispel such unconsciousness by turning the search-light of the keenest moral and intellectual analysis right on to it.'

Now, that last sentence states very clearly just what Meredith had said. Why then does Shaw fail to understand? I think the only answer can be that by 'analysis' Shaw means something different from Meredith's concept of penetration into the concrete and its inner conflict. Meredith implies a unity with the audience with which the poet is struggling; Shaw expresses contempt and superiority towards the audience. His 'analysis' is made from outside, 'intellectually' in the narrow sense, whereas Meredith wants the poet *to participate while criticising.*

If Shaw then shows the recoil from Meredith's idea of the need to implicate art vitally in life, the following passage of 1920 shows the total failure to grasp anything of Meredith's meaning.

> The intellectualist method of Meredith was old fashioned enough to assume both the normality and the permanence of this civilisation now fluttering autumnally down, and so to reduce comedy to a quasi-logical repudiation of whatever was inconsistent with this normality, this permanence. Today, from wealth of experience, not of wisdom, we see that assumption as itself stuff for comedy. [*The New Statesman.*]

First, Meredith's thesis is not 'intellectualist,' though Shaw's criticism of it was. Secondly, Meredith never identified capitalism and civilisation as does this critic, who is naively unaware that in 1917 a great new society had been founded, based on a pervasive belief in humanist rationality. Meredith implied that the cash-nexus society was the deadly enemy of the Comic Spirit, for the Spirit had as its business the unmasking of the egoist inner split on which that society depended. Therefore Meredith would certainly have held in 1920 that comedy's job was the 'repudiation' (not quasi-logical, but very logical indeed) 'of whatever was inconsistent with this normality and this permanence.' In short, he would have seen the job of Comedy as the unmasking of the vast deepening of the inner split which the breakdown of capitalism was bringing about, and as the approval of the new society which was carrying on 'this normality and this permanence.' And incidentally he would have seen the critic as a first-rate figure for the smiling malice of his Spirit.

Finally, the poems of this period: not many, but showing the poet re-rooting himself in his earth of poetry. There are some fine wood-poems, *Woodland Peace, Dirge in Woods,* and *In the Woods,* in which he reaffirms his acceptance of natural process. Not passively, but as a part of nature in which change and upward-struggle are integral.

> *My foot on the nodding weed,*
> *My hand on the wrinkled bark,*
> *I have made my choice to proceed*
> *By the light I have within;*
> *And the issue rests with me,*

> *Who might sleep in a chrysalis,*
> *In the fold of a simple prayer,*
> *Between the two twilights.*

He attacks the 'lust' that chillily believes in an after-life, an other-world, and acclaims the love of life that 'sees a flame in our dust and a gift in our breath'—that accepts earthly life and seeks to develop it as such, with a vision that is one with natural process.

A Ballad of Post Meridian defines again his acceptance, as he feels that he has passed the climacteric of his days—with Life and Death, Hope and Memory, merged in the dialectical movement of experience. *The Song of Theodolinda*, using Christian imagery, deals with the moment of deep change as a furnace-transformation. Any theological idiom is rare with Meredith; and he apparently uses the legend of the Queen having the Nail of the Cross laid red-hot on her breast and hammered there into a crown, because he wanted some extremely strong image to express a violent pang and aspiration of change. The poem was published in 1872 when he was struggling with the first shapes of *Beauchamp's Career*.

Finally there is the long *Ballad of Fair Ladies in Revolt*, a debate on woman's rights between a Conservative and several women who 'lean beneath the ever-falling fountain of green leaves.' The narrator-poet listens and in the end takes the side of the women, with whom he goes off. The argument is charmingly set out, and the growth of a new spirit of courage and independence in women, which does not destroy or distort their natures (as the Conservative asserts) but in fact releases that nature on a higher level, that of the epoch of community.

> *Have women nursed some dream since Helen sailed,*
> *Over the sea of blood the blushing star,*
> *That beauty, whom frail man as Goddess hailed,*
> *When not possessing her (for such is he!)*
> *Might in a wondering season seen afar*
> *Be tamed to say not 'I', but 'we'?*

The Nuptials of Attila (1879) expresses his gathering fears of imperial power (German or English). The image of the wild revelling Huns is merged with that of the great river, the Danube, in its varying moods. Against the mad horde is set the silent bride Ildico, in whose bed Attila dies. The war-horde breaks up as the Danube 'with a shout of power loosens his imprisoned tides'; the anarchic dissolution of empire is both fused and contrasted with the spring-movement of the waters.

> *. . . island on ice-island rears;*
> *Dissolution battles fast:*
> *Big the senseless Titans loom,*
> *Through a mist of common doom*

> *Striving which shall die the last:*
> *Till a gentle-breathing morn*
> *Frees the stream from bank to bank.*
> *So the Empire built of scorn*
> *Agonised, dissolved and sank*
> *Of the Queen no more was told*
> *Than of leaf the Danube rolled.*
> *Make the bed for Attila!*

The war-horde are blindly lost in nature; they do not control it as the builders of peace do. But the Danube, with its renewals, flows on; history flows on, and it too has its renewals. The Empire built of scorn (that is, of the ignoring of human right and dignity) goes utterly out. Ildico who represents the oppressed peoples (in the person of the specially oppressed sex) is lost; but her deed—the poem leaves open whether she killed Attila or whether he died of a burst blood-vessel—survives in the new chance given to life, the gentle-breathing morn that obliterates the wrack of winter, the ruins of Empire.

21

The Egoist

In JUNE 1870 he wrote to Stevenson saying how he had enjoyed *An Inland Voyage*, and adding that *The Egoist* was well on its way. Begun in 1877, it was finished in February 1880 and published in October. He had worked on it through bad health, often in long night-hours; and it left his heart worse than ever. But he still went on athletically tossing 'the beetle.'

The new work was a compressed version of the Book of Egoism, the biggest book on earth, he said; and dealt with single-minded concentration on the Egoism which had always been a main theme in his novels— egoism as no mere accidental or incidental aberration of personality, but as the essence of bourgeois life, bringing to a head the whole long process of spiritual and economic alienation.

> It is a comedy, with only half of me in it, unlikely therefore to take either the public or my friends.

That is, the aim was largely destructive, and the tale lacked any strong positive characters to oppose the central Egoist. The Comic Spirit here did its work of revealing the ghastly gap between ideals and realities in Victorian society; and though the light of a consciousness striving beyond the cash-nexus contradictions provided the focus, there were no Bagarags, Sandras, Beauchamps, expressing the achievement of that light.

He sought to clarify his purpose in the Preface, to make clear that his Egoist was no sport-figure, no exaggerated monster, but the normal type of bourgeois man—appearing abnormal only because of the exposing light. Patterne is simply the admired English gentleman, the 'idol' of the bourgeois public. 'Really a superb young English gentleman,' Mrs Mountsteward says, summing up public opinion. His name Sir Willoughby Patterne suggests the Willow Pattern of the favourite china-sets that fill respectable drawing-rooms—a point made in Chapter xxxiv. Meredith used to say of the English, 'They're all of a pattern.' Sir Willoughby is thus the stereotyped man of bourgeois manufacture.

The long concentration on sheer Egoism makes the book hard-going. 'As it comes mainly from the head and has nothing to kindle imagination,

I thirsted to get rid of it soon after conception, and it became a struggle
in which health suffered.'

Almost all the characters are variations of Egoism. Patterne the supreme
egoist is set amid a crowd of lesser specimens, the self-indulgent Dr
Middleton would see his daughter damned before he'd leave some first-
rate port, Dale the valetudinarian egoist, De Craye the treacherous philanderer, Letitia who has idealised the Egoist, Vernon Whitford immersed
in his cut-away scholarship, the great ladies living for scandal and inter-
ference with other people's lives, the crushed aunts of the supreme egoist,
and so on. The lad Crossjay, however, is too young to be malformed like
the others: he still has a capacity for self-sacrifice and loyalty. And Clara
Middleton, though caught at first in the general trend, does awake to
something of the horror of it and begin to struggle.

The story is simple, as befits its concentrated theme. Patterne is engaged
to a lovely girl, who gets a glimpse of his coldly cruel spirit and runs
away. He is then engaged to Clara, who in turn realises what a monster
she is entangled with and tries to escape. But now his fears of becoming
a laughing-stock are so excited that he does his utmost to hold her in the
snare. Feeling lost, he turns to Letitia, whose adoration he has exploited
for years; but she, stirred by Clara, has lost her unquestioning attitude and
refuses him. Clara fights on, and in the end he loses her to Vernon.
Shattered, he returns to Letitia on her terms, not his own.

Brooding on Comedy, Meredith has used something of a Molière-
method; thinking of such characters as Tartuffe. And he returns to some
extent to Peacock, and so to *Feverel*. Sir Austin had his system for per-
verting his son: Patterne is the system incarnate, the son totally-perverted,
a pure reflection of the alienating process. Dr Middleton, indeed, is in
many ways Peacock himself, glossed with a conventional piety; and the
recrudescence of wine-panegyrics, looking back to *Gryll Grange*, is a
Peacock-touch.

In the preface Meredith made clear that he meant to embody in
Patterne the last stage of egoism, of self-alienation: the final disintegrative
form of 'the grand old Egoism that aforetime built the House.' He shrank
only from the plain statement: Here is the ruling-class, about to give up
the ghost—beyond them comes up the day of brotherhood, the 'convulsion' of a new society. He felt like that, but he was inhibited against
stating the issue quite so obviously—though he had practically done it
in *Beauchamp*. To go a step beyond what he had done in that latter novel
in direct statement, would have meant a complete divorce from any
existing audience and would have robbed his work of any action on his
world; would in fact have ended the publication of his work. It was not

fear of any direct conflicts with the middle-class which in the last resort inhibited him; it was the fact of having no alternative audience to that which in his world bought novels. This lack of the desired audience merged with his own confusions to make him feel that the only effective formulations were those that he did in fact make. In 1874 he at first intended a preface to *Beauchamp*, but gave up the idea:

> I am very shy of prefaces, and by introducing my one or two remarks incidentally I hope to escape from a tone that seems to avoid the apology only by some loftiness—or the reverse. I am afraid it would not be I who could put the intermediate touch. Conception rarely fails me, though ability does, and I can barely conceive of its being done in the proper tone. . . . For a piece of fiction having a serious aim, and before a public that scorns the serious in fiction, and whose wits are chiefly trained to detect pretension, it is more than commonly difficult.

He fell back on the feeling that the definition after all was *there*, concretely, in the novel. If the reader couldn't grasp the living truth, would a plain signpost do more than deter him before he began?

The thought-processes of Patterne are all self-alienating:

> to produce division of himself from himself, a concentration of his thoughts upon another object, still himself, but in another breast, which had to be looked at and into for the discovery of him. By the gaping jaw-chasm of his greed we may gather comprehension of his insatiate force of jealousy.

Thus Meredith analyses what we now call the existentialist concept of being, the maddened dialectic of the self and its divisions abstracted from concrete resolution in act, in history, in social movement. But where an existentialist sees only the *huis clos*, the vicious-circle of the self closed in on itself, the image trapped in an infinitely-recessive pupil of its own eye, Meredith analyses this condition of mind in order to reject it as the last disintegrative stage of capitalist egoism.

'Possession without obligation to the object possessed approaches felicity.' This is the egoist dream of love. But it is also the capitalist relation to production.

Patterne is shown to detest and fear poetry (as Sir Austin did); for what he fears in poetry is the revealing light that Meredith has defined as Comedy. And he is thus related to the anti-poetry of the Tennysons, which acts as blinding the true eye of vision and soothing the sentimental ego. Whether or not Meredith was aware of it, he has made this relation by his emphasis throughout Chapter II on Patterne's Leg, which revives the image of the Restoration when 'the leg was ribbanded with love-knots and reigned.' This is the image he uses for Tennyson's egoist verse, 'a mannered trickster airing a leg with love-knots.'

The one person who stands up against Patterne is Clara. She begins her revolt from something of his own level, merely shocked at finding that he means to make her will a reflection of his own. But her growing critical understanding of his outlook and method deepens her revolt and begins to affect others. It shakes the enslaved Letitia and gives her a grain of self-respect, and it shakes the inturned Vernon with a spasm of love. And so Clara makes the book tolerable: otherwise the stale sickly air of the egoist labyrinth would be impossible to breathe. She is charmingly alive; and though she begins as her father's daughter, wayward, selfish, vacillating, ready to lie, she takes on a new worthiness as she struggles for independence. Meredith is saying: Yes, she is all-too-female, but that is what our society has made of girls, you can't blame her for using the only available weapons as she strives to grow into an individual. Thus it is true that

> Clara is the prototype of all the independent and emancipated young girls who appear in vulgarised form in the novels of many an English writer in the early years of the 20th century—compare *Ann Veronica* by H. G. Wells. [Galland.]

Because she fights Patterne, she discovers sympathy with the other victims, Crossjay, Letitia, Flitch (whom Patterne cannot forgive for having left his employ). And she awakens Vernon from his lethargic submission to the Patterne world.*

The critics, though harping still on Meredith's difficulties, began now grudgingly to admit his power. Thus *The Spectator* tried to minimise his achievement:

> We have been amused, impressed, bored, and filled with admiration and disappointment . . . [he] regards the world as a foolish piece of protoplasm, chiefly valuable as stuff out of which to cut epigrams and apt similes. . . . He is a sort of modern hermetic philosopher of drawing-rooms; there is often more novelty in his way of saying a thing than in the thing he says. . . . He describes his characters admirably, piecemeal; when it comes to the putting of them together, he does it coldly . . . a picture-puzzle . . . clever.

But what was of more interest was the reaction by the young writers such as Henley and Stevenson. Henley, deeply infected by imperialist ideas like Kipling, had a cult of 'strong life' in the abstract—a compensation for his own crippled condition (though Kipling, in his own way, had much the same attitude, which made him feel at home among brutalities). These young men have a taste for realism, incisive psychology, clear-cut

---

* Her father brings out the ultimate political consequences of her small revolt, 'This maenad shriek for freedom would happily entitle her to the Republican cap—the Phrygian —in a revolutionary Parisian procession.'

art-ordonnance, as part of their sense of being members of a nation (in fact, class) holding the world down, masterfully manipulating and directing events, battering down opposition. That is, their realism, insight, clarity have very definite limitations; they are blinkered sharply by their fear of the deeper meanings of their world, while enjoying a sense of being braced to look a crude reality in its vicious eye. In Meredith they are ready to see things that their smugly bludgeoning fathers dared not see; but his meaning they can read no better. Henley reviewed *The Egoist* three times:

> (*Athenaeum*) His stories are not often good stories, and are seldom well told. . . . There is infinitely too much of statement and reflection, of aphorism and analysis, of epigram and fantasy, of humours germane and yet not called for; so that in the end the impression produced is not the impersonal impression that was to be desired, and the literary egoism of the author of Sir Willoughby Patterne appears to overshadow the amorous egoism of Sir Willoughby himself . . . [yet] one of the strongest and most individual productions of modern literature.
>
> (*Pall Mall Gazette*) He fails of acknowledged pre-eminence in his art. And the reason appears to be that he writes for himself alone. . . . He fatigues and bewilders. . . . You cannot see what he would do for the sparks he beats out in the doing.
>
> (*The Academy*) Its personages are not human beings, but compendiums of humanity. . . . Like Shakespeare, he is a man of genius, who is a clever man as well; and he seems to prefer his cleverness to his genius . . . so diabolically ingenious and sympathetic and well-informed and intellectual. . . . It is odds that the multitude will decline to listen. Nor, so far as I can see, is the multitude alone to blame.

No word about the inner meaning of the theme and no attempt to grasp why Meredith feels cut from his audience. What is based in Meredith's historically-conditioned sincerity is treated as a wilfulness.*

Stevenson, who soon broke from Henley, and who was never so closely grappled to imperialist trends, was specially affected by *The Egoist*. When

---

* Henley also noticed the book in *The Teacher*. *The Examiner* complained, 'All the people in the book are given to enigmatic and elliptical utterances,' yet the book is not dull and Patterne 'often moves our pity, almost our sympathy.' *The Saturday* asks why M. is not popular, and says that he lets the reader know no more about the characters than he can see for himself. 'The only author who has adopted this method is Mr Flaubert, in *l'Éducation Sentimentale*, which always reads as if it had been constructed by the process of writing it in feuilletons, and then suppressing each alternate one.' *The New Quarterly* said that M. was his only enemy as far as popularity went. *The New Quarterly* said his style was 'a cross between Carlyle's and Browning's.' *The Westminster*, giving it some twenty lines as against thirty to Lynn Linton's *Unto which Lord*, says he is over-fastidious and not popular at Mudie's. 'If he were more simple, he would be far more effective.' *Blackwood's* found 'the first volume fine, the second tedious, the third beyond all expression wearisome.'

Yet the general effect was more respectful than before. Thomson wrote in his Diary, 'At length! Encouragement! A man of wonderful genius and a splendid writer may hope to obtain something like recognition after working hard for thirty years, dating from his majority.'

Meredith read him some chapters, in 1879 or during his second visit after wintering in California, he protested that Patterne was based on himself. Meredith replied, 'No, no, my dear fellow, I've taken him from all of us, but principally from myself.'

Stevenson's tributes are worth citing; for they show how Meredith's new socio-psychological realism, his penetration into the nature of bourgeois man and the struggle to break through into a different way of life, affected the sensitive young who yet missed the political clue. Writing on books that had influenced him in *The Art of Writing*, he said:

> I should never forgive myself if I forgot *The Egoist*. It is art, if you like, but it belongs purely to didactic art, and from all the novels I have read (and I have read thousands) stands in a place by itself. Here is a Nathan for the modern David; here is a book to send the blood into men's faces. . . . [Unlike satire that merely attacks others] it is yourself that is hunted down; these are your faults that are dragged into the day and numbered with lingering relish, with cruel cunning and precision.

Thus he sees the book's universality; but sets the moral and psychological method in a political vacuum. In April 1882 he wrote to Henley:

> I have just read for the third or fourth time *The Egoist*. When I shall have read it the sixth or seventh, I begin to see I shall know about it. . . . I had no idea of the matter—human red matter—he has contrived to plug and pack into that strange and admirable book. Willoughby is of course a pure discovery; a complete set of nerves, not heretofore examined, and yet running all over the human body—a suit of nerves. Clara is the best girl I ever saw anywhere. Vernon is almost as good. The manner and faults of the book greatly justify themselves on further study. Only Mr Middleton does not hang together; and Ladies Busshe and Culmer *sont des monstruosités* . . . I see more and more that Meredith is built for immortality.

Thomson also reviewed in the obscure *Cope's Tobacco Plant*. He, like Stevenson—though more surprisingly—does not grasp the political content of Meredith's work; but again he makes what is the first and best tribute yet made to the positive aspects of Meredith's style:

> The speeches do not follow one another mechanically adjusted like a smooth pavement for easy walking: they leap and break, resilient and resurgent, like running foam-crested waves, impelled and repelled and crossed by undercurrents and great tides and brief breezes; in their restless agitations you must divine the immense life abounding beneath and around and above them, and the Mudie novice accustomed to saunter the level pavement finds that the heaving and falling are sea-sickness to a queasy stomach. . . .
>
> Discriminating countless shades where the common eye sees but one gloom or glare, pursuing countless distinct movements where the common eye sees only a whirling perplexity. . . .

It is of interest that where there is deep fellow-feeling as with Thomson, the rich positive aspects of the style are first seen; where there is a deep political dissension as with *The Spectator*, the stylistic difficulties or un-familiarities are stressed to the total ignoring of what the work is about. Stevenson's words are worth recalling when the brittle convolutions which are too often repellent aspects of Meredith's style become irritating: 'The manner and faults of the book greatly justify themselves on further study.'

The Tragic Comedians

THE YEAR 1879 saw both *Atilla* and *The Egoist*: a poem on the collapse of an Empire built of Scorn, with Ildico as the agent, and a novel on the crashing of the House of Egoism, with Clara as the agent.

In 1880 Meredith wrote *The Tragic Comedians* in some six months, a short work for him; and after a condensed version ran in *The Fortnightly*, the book came out in December. His mood is shown in a March letter to Maxse. 'Radicalism should be avowed, and the sham medium done away with. But then there would be no prospects of Office for a long term.' The country is still Tory, and the anti-Tory party, Liberalism, is not a genuine party at all, since Tories and Liberals have the same views on property. Liberalism represents only a grouping brought about by some particular pressure of self-interest; when the pressure goes, the grouping breaks up. 'There is no soul of Liberalism, and its leaders have put back the cause of progress twenty years at least.' (He is thus demanding a party that will be a true alternative to the two capitalist parties; and though he is not at all clear how such a party would operate, his mood of disillusion about compromise persists and underlies the new novel.)

As usual, he was doubtful about the reception. To Hardman, now editor of *The Morning Post*, he gave a copy, 'not to be reviewed: only to be read at your entire leisure. I fear you will not care for it. But it is history, and a curious chapter of human nature.' He apologised for not having seen much of Hardman. 'An unpopular author has to work hard.'

The story is that of the German Social-Democratic leader, Lassalle, and Hélène von Dönniges: Alvan in the book, and Clotilde. The brilliant Jewish lawyer falls in love with the young aristocratic girl, dominates her, tries to get her to elope. When, however, she does come to his rooms, he hands her back to her parents, so that they may marry with all propriety. The infuriated anti-semitic parents refuse to let him see her, and his conviction that he can dominate anyone is broken. The girl's fears and prides are worked on till he in rage challenges her father. The prince to whom she had been betrothed fights in place of the old man, and kills Alvan. Clotilde then marries the prince.

The novel follows the story as told by Hélène, and there is little effort to correct that story by other evidences or to fill in the background with precise historical details. But for Meredith's purposes Hélène's story, true or not in its account, suffices. Though the novel is in no way a sifted-out statement of the facts and conflicts surrounding Lassalle's death, the essential truth is grasped. What Meredith is concerned to show is the failure, *the betrayal of revolutionary responsibility.* He depicts with remarkable insight the dilemma of the Social-Democrat who will go so far in his separation-out from bourgeois society and who then feels the need to return back into that society's bosom. Beyond the point in question lies the total rupture with bourgeois relations, the new society to be based on the organised working-class; but the Social-Democrat loses his nerve there, retreats, and finds all sorts of excuses for the retreat from the crucial moment of revolutionary change. He seeks to regain his status among the bourgeoisie, to compel them to admit his virtues, to prove that at their level too he is a good fellow. Thus he confesses, in the need to justify himself in the eyes of those he has declared the enemy, a collapse and betrayal of the revolutionary impulse and understanding in himself, which is in turn a betrayal of the proletarian masses trusting him.

The opening chapters are written in an excited style which makes us think that the author is accepting Alvan and Clotilde at their own valuations, that he is romantically carried away by their inflated views of their own personalities. But this is only Meredith's device for making us feel what the pair might have been, if they had been true to the genuine lyrical impulse that brings them together.

Alvan is presented in full self-intoxication. He calls for action. 'The war with evil in every form must be incessant; we cannot have peace. Let then our joy be in war: in uncompromising Action. . . . Action energises men's brains . . . and is the guarantee of positive conquest for the benefit of our species.' But it must be directed action. 'No life without brain! The brainless in Art and Statecraft are nothing but a little more obstructive than the dead. It is less easy to cut a way through them. But it must be done, or the Philistine will be as the locust in his increase, and devour the green blades of the earth.' But under such talk lies the weakness that drives him to surrender to the enemy.

Similarly we first see Clotilde as a girl striving towards independence of spirit and refusing to be bound by dead conventions. But as the story goes on, we realise that she is largely the creature of a fashionable pose and that she has mistaken flattery of her intelligence for proof of strength of character.

And yet, such is Meredith's skill in these subtleties, we feel both that the breakdown of the relationship was rendered inevitable by the flaws of vanity, the unrealised hold of class-values on the two actors, and also that the dream of a great love linked with the struggle for brotherhood was not a mere illusion. What these lovers failed to achieve, others will achieve, just as the working-class movement will achieve the aims from which Alvan-Lassalle falls away.

The flaw in Alvan shows up clearly first in his attitude to women:

> Among Alvan's gifts the understanding of women did not rank high. He was too robust, he had been too successful. Your very successful hero regards them as nine-pins destined to fall, the whole tuneful nine, at a peculiar poetical twist of the bowler's wrist. . . . His tastes had led him into the avenues of success, and he had not encountered grand resistances, he entertained his opinion of the sex. The particular maxim he cherished was, to stake everything on his making a favourable first impression. . . .
>
> He would have stared like any Philistine at the tale of their capacity to advance to a likeness unto men in their fight with the world. . . .

Then he drives Clotilde back to her family. 'I, your lover, cannot fail, for it is impossible for me to waver.'

> She seemed a dead thing; but the sense of his having done gloriously in mastering himself to give these worldly people of hers a lesson and proof that he could within due measure how to their laws and customs, dispelled the brief vision of her unfitness to be left. The compressed energy of the man under his conscious display of a great-minded deference to the claims of family ties and duties, intoxicated him. . . . He had to lead forth a daughter for Alvan's wife. . . .

As he develops this mood in himself he retreats further:

> Ceasing to be a social rebel, he conceived himself as a recognised dignitary, and he passed under the bondage of that position.

The bourgeois bonds grow stronger:

> Alvan was a revolutionist in imagination, the workmen's friend in rational sympathy, their leader upon mathematical calculation, but a lawyer, a reasoner in law, and therefore of necessity a cousin germane, leaning to become an ally, of the Philistines—the founders and main supporters of his book of the Law. And so, between the nature of his blood, and the inclination of his mind, Alvan set his heart on a damsel of the Philistines, endowed with their trained elegances and governed by some of their precepts, but suitable to his wildness in her reputation for originality, suiting him in her cultivated liveliness and her turn for luxury.

Thus his future with her is doomed to political compromise:

> The Republican will be in danger of playing prematurely for power to seat her beside him high: while at the same time, children, perchance, and his hardening lawyer's head are secretly Philistinising the demagogue, blunting the fine edge of his Radicalism, turning him into a slow-stepping Liberal, otherwise your half-Conservative in his convictions.

Note how Meredith uses Radicalism here for revolutionary principle; the Baroness in the novel, intended as a revolutionary, is called a Radical.

At the same time Meredith makes us feel that there is something admirable in the desire for a good life on earth, for the fullness of experience. Alvan is brought down by his hunger for happiness, because he lets it get in the way of his political course instead of seeking to find the true link between his vital outreaching into life and his self-dedication to the revolution.

His failure has the effect of destroying whatever capacities Clotilde had for development into freedom and self-respect. He breaks her will, to grapple her to himself; and in her brokenness she becomes the victim of her parents. So she ends in complete demoralisation, and he shows his failure even more clearly by blaming her as woman. 'She became that ancient poisonous thing, the woman; his fury would not distinguish her as Clotilde.'

The ageing Baroness, once his lover, sees starkly what is happening. She realises that in Clotilde Alvan is succumbing to the bourgeoisie:

> A peasant girl, a workman's daughter, a tradesman's, a professional singer, actress, artist I would have given my hand to one of those in good faith. . . . She will drag him down, down. . . . She will set him aiming at power to trick her out in the decorations. She will not keep him to his labours to consolidate the power. She will pervert the aesthetic in him, through her hold on his material nature, his vanity, his luxuriousness. She is one of the young women who begin timidly, and when they see that they enjoy comparative impunity, grow intrepid in dissipation, and that palling, they are ravenously ambitious.

She understands that Alvan now 'aimed at standing well with the world,' catching 'at the thread of an alliance with the decorous world.'

His fall is brought out in his turning to Horace as his poet. The Baroness upbraids him without effect.

> Friend Sigismund, you have no philosophy, you never had any; and the small crow and croon of Horace would be the last you could take up. It is the chanted philosophy of comfortable stipendiaries, retired merchants, gouty patients . . ., old men who have given over thinking, and young men who never had feeling—the philosophy of swine grunting their carmen as they turn to fat in the sun. . . . He is the versifier of the cushioned enemy, not of us who march along flinty ways: the piper of the bourgeois in soul, poet of the conforming unbelievers!'

Finally, in the last chapter, Meredith explains his title. There is a tragic quality in the story because of the noble aims which have stirred his unhappy pair; but the pattern is not tragic in any absolute sense of doom. The pair fail through errors that could have been obviated. So they are comic in Meredith's sense of the term. They reveal the gap between theory and practice, the self-deceptions, characteristic of their class-society, which others will overcome.

Otherwise, in the reflection of their history, life will seem a thing demoniac-ally inclined by fits to antic and dive into gulfs. The characters of the hosts of men are of the simple order of the comic; not many are of a stature and a complexity calling for the junction of the two Muses to name them.

Now for some of the passages in which Meredith makes even more explicit the political significance of his story. Alvan at the outset mingles his love-intoxications with his dreams of political triumph. 'I win that seat by service, by the dedication of this brain to the people's interests. They have been ground to the dust, and I lift them. . . . I am the soldier of justice against the army of the unjust. But I claim my reward. If I live to fight, I live also to enjoy. . . . I am soldier and prophet.'

And his hopes are throughout entangled with his sense of the rising proletarian power. Take for instance the fine passage in Chapter XV, where, in the morning by the lake, he feels happiness in the nearness of the workers passing, in the sound of their marching feet.

He listened to the workmen's footfalls. The solitary sound and steady motion of their feet were eloquent of early morning in a city, not less than the changes of light in heaven above the roofs. With the golden light came numbers, workmen still. Their tread on the stones roused some of his working thoughts, like an old tune in his head, and he watched the scattered files passing on, disciplined by their daily necessities, easily manageable if their necessities are but justly considered.

Those numbers are the brute force of earth, which must have the earth in time, as they had it in the dawn of our world, and then they entered into bondage for not knowing how to use it. They will have it again: they have it, partially, at times, in the despot, who is only the reflex of their brute, and can give them only a shadow of their claim. They will have it all, when they have illumination to see and trust to the leadership of a greater force than they— in force of brain, in the spiritual force of ideas; ideas founded on justice; and not the justice of these days of the governing few whose wits are bent to steady our column of civilised humanity by a combination of props and jugglers' arts, but a justice coming of the recognised needs of majorities, which will base the column on a broad plinth for safety—broad as the base of yonder mountain's towering white immensity—and will be the guarantee for the solid uplifting of our civilisation at last.

Here Meredith comes his closest to a concept of revolution by the action of the organised working-class. A tinct of paternalist ideas persists in the term 'easily manageable,' and there is no tackling of the problem of the ways in which the ideas based on justice are to become the motive force of the proletariat. There is still a vagueness, born of fear and lack of direct contact, which wants some educational controls from above over the masses—though what is said is profoundly true if it is understood as meaning that the masses must develop *their own theory*, their own party, their own education, their own regeneration of the ideas of justice. But take it as it stands, with all its blurred points, the passage is a noble recognition of the way in which the future belongs to the workers and the just State which they alone can build.

We may note further the fine sense of class-virtues: 'disciplined by their daily necessities.' That goes to the root of the matter and proves that Meredith had in him to grasp realistically what the future belonging to the workers would be like, and to accept it. Also, we may note that he is speaking, not of 'workers' in a Carlylese generalisation, but of the industrial working-class in their specific situation of work and struggle.

It defines the highest moment of Meredith's political consciousness, to which his work has been moving ever since he wandered in the night-streets of London and watched the outcasts, ever since he thrilled with the brotherly calls of 1848, ever since he set Shibli Bagarag on his wanderings for the liberating Sword. It thus provides us with the ultimate criterion by which to judge all his definitions, fables and ideas. In it, with a wrench, he moves beyond all positions attached to the middle-class and shows how the vital elements in Radicalism move into the first definite stages of Socialist theory and practice.

The same confusion, noted above, as to what is meant by educating the workers, appears in various statements by Alvan. On the one hand he is clear that the State is Power, and the political struggle is a struggle for power.

> Politically also we know that strength is the one reality: the rest is shadow. Behind the veil of our human conventions power is constant as ever, and to perceive the fact is to have the divining rod—to walk clear of shams. He is the teacher who shows where power exists: he is the leader who wakens and forms it.

But later he conjures the 'young Republicans' not to surrender to the embrace of 'dead materialism, because, as they fancy, they have to depend on material weapons for carving their way, and have no help from other quarters! The spiritual weapon has done most, and always does. They are sons of an idea. They deny their parentage when they scoff at idealism. . . . It leads back to the old order of things, if we do not trim our light.' If by this he means that the power of ideas must not be ignored, and by 'idealism' merely means organised ideas (he tends to such a loose use of abstract terms), then the comment is correct enough. But by opposing ideas to materialism (in the question-begging form of 'dead'), he is perpetuating the very split that the proletarian movement must overcome. If the statement is meant to show the confusion of Alvan, one cannot complain; but one feels that it is one of the passages where Alvan and Meredith speak together.

Had Meredith ever read Karl Marx? From a close scrutiny of his work, I feel assured that he never had, though it is possible he saw odd sections of Marx's writings. It is more than probable that all he knew of Marx came through the muddy channel of Hyndman.

In February 1887 he wrote to George Stevenson:

> Perhaps if I am not driven to the novel, I shall be at a Poem treating of all the Explosives in the modern mind and manufactories: the Anarchiad. What do you say?—The hero, Karl Onyx, has as many adventures as Odysseus. I am at times moved strongly by the theme. On the other hand I have a Knight of Perfectibility in prose, who is very seductive to my pen.

Karl Onyx can be no one but Karl Marx, and Meredith's taking him as the poem's hero proves a thorough feeling of goodwill. But the poem's title shows that he can have had little precise knowledge of Marx's doctrines, though *Anarchiad* no doubt meant for him only Epic-of-Revolutionary-Explosiveness.

Alvan is not at all close to Lassalle in details—later Meredith complained that he could not get even a portrait of Lassalle. But though a genuine historical novel on Lassalle would have had to deal with his character and ideas in a much more complex way, and go much further back to show the flaws and conflicts in them, Meredith has put his finger on the key-thing. Essentially he is right all along the line in the way he shows the stubborn re-emergence of bourgeois characteristics to break revolutionary integrity.*

When Meredith was writing, Bismarck had introduced, with the aid of the National Liberals and the Conservatives, his Socialist Act (October, 1878), which declared illegal all associations, meetings, and printed matter directed to the overthrow of the existing State; and which empowered the Government to suppress socialist 'agitators' and, in certain cases, to proclaim a state of siege in whole districts. This Act remained in force, with small modifications, till 1890. (At the same time Bismarck carried out his system of workers' insurances.) It is therefore of much interest that in this novel Meredith writes of the Marxist Party that Bismarck had

---

* It is of interest to note that though Meredith was not setting out to draw an historical picture of Lassalle, his judgment of Alvan coincides in many points with Marx's of Lassalle. 'Lassalle wanted to play the Marquis Posa [of Schiller's play] of the proletariat with Philip II of Uckermark, Bismarck acting as intermediary between him and the Prussian kingdom. . . . For a theatrically vain nature like Lassalle (who was not, however, to be bribed by paltry trash like office, a mayoralty, etc.), it was a tempting thought: an act directly on behalf of the pro-letariat, and executed by Ferdinand Lassalle! He was in fact too ignorant of the real economic conditions attending such an act to be critically true to himself,' (To Kugelmann, 23 Feb. 1865). Thus Marx, dealing with the purely political aspects, comes to the same conclusions about an inner split of vanity and self-dramatisation as Meredith dealing with the love-relations.

legislated against, as 'a growing party, and [which] is not yet a collapsed, nor will be, though the foot on it is iron.'

Though of course we must not attribute to Meredith the prophetic vision that could see in Alvan's breakdown the later corruptions and backslidings of Social-Democracy—the failure to keep the pledge against imperialist war in 1914, the attraction of Royal Garden Parties for so many English Labour leaders, the surrender of Attlee and Bevin to U.S.A. Imperialism in the post-1945 years, etc., etc.—yet he has written in *The Tragic Comedians* the perfect fable which in its root-meaning and moral covers all those corruptions and backslidings. This remarkable achievement derives from his deep interest in the character of the revolutionary, and his unfailing insight into the class-survivals which held the revolutionary back and which (if not understood) inverted him into the defender of the system he had once fought.

The novel's reception was bad. Henley couldn't understand it in the least and called it tedious, its protagonists creatures of gossamer and rainbow, phantasms of spiritual romance, abstractions of remote dispiriting points in sexual philosophy. W. L. Courtney was even less friendly in *The Fortnightly*. Burnand made more than one attempt and couldn't read the work. *The Athenaeum* hostilely found the book 'congested . . . overwrought,' a study in oblique narration, 'condensing epigrams into adverbs and allegories into adjectives.' George Moore later called it pretentious and blatant, 'it struts and screams, stupid,' absurd as a cockatoo; he couldn't read more than fifty pages. (He also thought *Rhoda* a commonplace story, its people lacking subtlety like a Drury-Lane melodrama.) And to come nearer today, Siegfried Sassoon in 1948 finds it 'an assault on the nervous system. . . . I suspect the book of having been a potboiler . . . clenched and overstrung quality.' Not one word about the story's meaning.

It is pleasant amid so much opacity to find how Prof. MacCallum, in a lecture in Sydney, in 1892, remarked that some nine years before he had tried to read the book and found it a wild extravaganza; then he struck an edition with an historical introduction. Armed with this new knowledge, he made another attempt and found to his surprise that the style wasn't tumid or stilted at all, 'but aglow with passion and thought, the action set forth, the characters interpreted, with a grand poetic power,' and so he went on to read all the other novels by Meredith.

MacCallum states the right way to approach Meredith. Once the historical and political basis is grasped, the reader can tolerate compression and knottedness of language, and even find that some aspects of the style against which he reacted have a highly moving and poetic force.

IV

The New Woman

23

Poems Again

WITH INCREASING age and bad health he felt the cramping pressure of money-grubbing at uncongenial work. 'I am really a slave, and not in love with my chances,' he said in 1880: things at the moment being made worse by a cook who had 'whiskified and flared up,' so that there was only a cat's meal. In late March 1881, 'The dreadful curse of verse is on me, and has been for two months.' But this summer his health kept degenerating. In June he says that the nerve-strain followed by whooping-cough after *The Egoist* has left his digestion in a bad way. In July, 'As I am unpopular, I am ill-paid, and therefore bound to work double tides, hardly ever to lay down the pen. This affects my weakened stomach, and so the round of the vicious circle is looped.' In August, 'The Fates have destined me for a cab-horse, and I find myself getting the jogging soul as well as the pace over everlasting sameness.' In November he was pleased to hear from a young Russian, Zaffalovich, who had written on him in the *Journal de St. Petersbourg*, but 'the malady seems to be nervous, affecting the spine.'

Still, in 1882–3 he visited London more than he'd been doing, and went at times to the theatre, though complaining in May of nervous prostration. Stevenson had been staying with wife and father at the inn: 'We speculated on the impression produced by his costume *de Bohème*, which he seems to have adopted for good.' In September, after a visit to Arthur in North Italy, Meredith was with his brother-in-law near Dreux.

In June 1883 came *Poems and Lyrics of the Joy of Earth*, published at his own risk and cost. Why, he asked Maxse, should he go to such labour and loss of money for the third time, 'with a certainty of being yelled at, and haply spat upon, for my pains?' It must be habit, or else 'a remainder of esteem for our public.' 'I scorn myself for my folly. Where he can get no audience, a spouting Homer would merit the Cap and Bells,' so little use had he for self-expression in a void or for art-for-art's-sake. Ten days after publication he was still saying what a fool he had been, to ask to be bellowed at 'from stagnation.'

There were so many misprints that Macmillan reprinted at their own costs. Reviews were on a very low level. Watts-Dunton, in *The*

Athenaeum, admitting vigour and picturesqueness, complained of the rugged, harsh, flinty nature of the writing: Courtney in *The Fortnightly* found the poet too artificial to catch 'the soul of Nature'; Mark Pattison described *Love in the Valley* as diffuse in conception and design on 'the average level of the minor poet.' W. P. Ker in *The Contemporary*, however, noted 'a fire which is dangerous to obstructions and commonplaces.'

The book's title indicated the main idea, a consolidation of Meredith's efforts to define man's place in nature. *Love in the Valley*, rewritten and published in a magazine in October 1878, appeared in its mature form, purged of mere weak implorations and any hint of amorous egoism. It now merged the emotion of comradely equality with the lyrical eagerness while uttering the bright union of the girl with the valley.

In *Melampus*, which like *Admetus* is linked rhythmically with *Love in the Valley*, he used Greek mythology to bring out his notion of man's entry into nature, as a transformed force of nature, to wrest her secrets. Melampus, the physician-seer who 'dwelt among men' and healed them, is the humanist fighter who had passed beyond fear and realised the patterns of natural process as part of his struggle for human wholeness:

> *He knew the Hours: they were round him, laden with seed*
> *Of hours bestrewn upon vapour, and one by one*
> *They winged as ripened in fruit the burden decreed*
> *For each to scatter; they flushed like the buds in sun,*
> *Bequeathing seed to successive similar rings,*
> *Their sisters, bearers to men of what men have earned . . .*
> *Through love exceeding a simple love of the things*
> *That glide in grasses and rubble of woody wreck.*

The *Day of the Daughter of Hades* repeats the lesson of living in the fullness of time, of earth, passing beyond the split self into the truly human condition. Young Callistes goes out at dawn into the vale of Enna and sees Persephone rise to visit her Mother the Earth in the sunlight. He witnesses the embrace of the pair and swoons. When he recovers he sees a maiden, Skiageneia, Shadowborn, who has slipped from her mother's care, longing to stay in the light. She roams with him through the Day, till her father Pluto hears her song of thanksgiving at evening, rises and reclaims her for the under-earth. Callistes is left to sing of her Day-in-Light for the good and the use of men.

This poem is over-long; but it gives in its hurrying metre and its earth-imagery a sense of the poignancy of Time, the unutterable sweetness of life on earth, the need to make the most of our days in work and song, in truth and love.

> *The song did give him to eat:*
> *Gave the first rapt vision of Good,*
> *And the fresh young sense of Sweet:*
> *The grace of the battle for food,*
> *With the issue Earth cannot refuse*
> *When men to their labour are sworn.*

Phoebus with Admetus might be called the *Melampus*-theme applied to farmwork, and has many lovely glinting lines, a vision of earth fulfilled in fertility. Yet it is odd to note that here we have the last, though transfigured, note of the old snob-theme. In *Evan Harrington* Raikes says, hoping that a rich old man will adopt him: 'He wouldn't have judged me by my attire. Admetus' flocks I guard, yet am a God!' But now the allegory has changed: Phoebus obscured is the creative force in man, expressed in labour-process, which transforms life and achieves new levels of civilisation.

The Woods of Westermain is another of the extended attempts to define the harmonious and active relation to Nature. He who fears Nature will be destroyed; only when man stands his full stature and tackles Nature with love and courage can he dare the Woods. The throwing-out of fear is bound up with the overcoming of the split-self and the achievement of an active integration of self through love, brotherhood, struggle. Egoism is imaged as the Dragon that must be slain in the recesses of Nature, so that change may be truly accepted and man may play his full part in the work of transformation. But if you once fall into the egoisms of power and hate, you are lost:

> *Grasp you with the monster's claws;*
> *Govern with his truncheon-saws;*
> *Hate, the shadow of a grain;*
> *You are lost in Westermain:*
> *Earthward swoops a vulture sun.*
> *Nighted upon carrion. . . .*

And once again the overcoming of the split-self is linked with the struggle for equality between the sexes.

The Lark Ascending, with a rapturous delicacy and strength defines the larksong, making the lark the emblem of the poet who ascends into a higher view yet remains the singer of earth. The spirals of ascent, the very trembling sweetness of the crystal drops of song, the widening sphere of vision, and the persisting union with earth in wild bud and sown crop, are rendered by the masterly movement of the couplets:

> *For singing till his heaven fills*
> *'Tis love of earth that he instils,*
> *And ever winging up and up,*

> Our valley is his golden cup,
> And he the wine which overflows
> To lift us with him as he goes:
> The woods and brooks, the sheep and kine,
> He is, the hills, the human line,
> The meadows green, the fallows brown,
> The dream of labour in the town;
> He sings the sap, the quickened veins;
> The wedding song of sun and rains
> He is, the dance of children, thanks
> Of sowers, shout of primrose-banks. . . .

till the final ecstatic expansion and union:

> With showerings drawn from human stores,
> As he to silence nearer soars,
> Extends the world at wings and dome,
> More spacious making more our home,
> Till lost on his aerial rings
> In light, and then the fancy rings.

In saying that he is 'seraphically free from taint of human personality,' Meredith does not mean that the poet loses warm touch with common human life or ceases to be himself. He refers to the new dynamic unity of poet and people, of art and life, which transcends all the old egoisms, as he carefully explains:

> So pure that it salutes the suns,
> The voice of one for millions,
> In whom the millions rejoice
> For giving their one spirit voice.

One feels that he is in this poem consciously rejecting the Shelleian Skylark, a blithe spirit who never was a bird. True, Shelley wants to speak to men through the bird, with the bird's voice; but Meredith feels that it is no longer valid to *express the wish*, the poet must bring it true. He speaks through the bird, he humanises Nature and fuses Nature with man in a new way, because he sees the wedding song of Sun and rain as one with the labour of man that fertilises and transforms the earth.

Earth and Man is a full-length set-piece in which he attempts to state explicitly his philosophy of man in Nature, the opposition-and-unity of Nature and man, the way in which the labour-process is the key to the dialectics of this relation, and the need to achieve a deepened consciousness of the dialectics so that men may build world-brotherhood and overcome self-alienation. 'As yet he will.' He will 'burst the chrysalis of the blind,' and throw out 'his distempered devil of Self . . . the coveter of life in soul and shell, the fratricide, the thief, the infidel,' the thief of other men's labour, the man who lacks faith in earth. Then all fantasies of an other-world will go.

Meredith is clear in this poem that it is the labour-process which under-lies and creates the active relation to Nature. Man's entering into Nature is the use of natural process and forms on a higher level, 'his gains by work achieved.'

> He builds the soaring spires,
> That sing his soul in stone: of her he draws,
> Though blind to her, by spelling at her laws,
> Her purest fires.

These poems go far beyond the position of any of the Romantics, though in one stanza of *Earth and Man* Meredith spoils his thesis by a vague reference to 'him' (God—he shies off the overt term). He feels the need of some term to express the purpose of universality and freedom which emerges from the active relation of man and Nature; but his falling-back on a formulation that revives, in however ghostly a form, the reprobated idealist split, shows the point of instability in his thought.*

It may well be asked how far he owed a debt to Darwin and the other evolutionists, to the critics who had undermined the old attitude to the Bible. Oddly, he makes no reference to Darwin anywhere, and only some slight references to the Biblical controversies. We can only surmise that already by the time he read Darwin, Huxley, Spencer, he was so prepared in his revolt, based in his own working-out of the inner conflict of the Romantic poets and in his admiration of the Enlightenment, that he ac-cepted Darwin's thesis without question, finding in it the scientific con-firmation of his own moral and poetic convictions. But his poetic working-out and his faithfulness to the principles of 1848 prevented him from falling into the pseudo-Darwinism of Spencer and Huxley justifying exploitation as 'the survival of the fittest.'

In June 1883 he was hopeful about the nearness of Revolution. 'Saw H [Harrison?]. He sees Revolution, fears the forces are not sufficiently hot to make it quite close on.' (The official collection of letters here breaks off and prints dots. Why?). In March, Engels had written in London, 'The

---

* The gap between his materialist concept of Earth and his strong but unstable realisation that labour-process plays the key-part in man's development appears this vague intrusion of an immanent He on to the all-sufficient Mother, e.g. *Feverel*, xxxiii, or the end of *A Faith on Trial*. All the same, this He is so wraithlike that a critic in *The Fortnightly*, Dec. 1907, apolo-gised for M.'s disuse of God, and argued that he had substituted Earth because of the need of language to refresh itself. (We might say that the He intrudes to the extent that the concept of Earth is mystic and not materialist—i.e. rooted in unrealised family-relationships and reconciliation-concepts rather than in a clear grasp of social process.)

final victory is certain, but circuitous paths, temporary and local errors—
things which even now are so unavoidable—will become more common
than ever. Well, we must see it through. What else are we here for?'

In July he writes about going to Wagner's *Flying Dutchman* and dining
with Browning; and in September, Foote had been put into jail for
blasphemy, and Meredith wanted to send him his book of poems, 'but
fancy it would not be handed.' In September he wrote to Maxse on a
death:

> You know my feelings about sentimentalists. If I did not take them for
> subjects of study, they would enrage me past any tolerance; and as it is, I find
> the promptings to fling too heavy a word at them hard to restrain. The
> Tempter of mankind has never such a grin as when he sees them mix the true
> and the false.

In 1883 he was finding it hard to walk much and by February 1884 he
calls himself a cripple. In November 1883 he wrote to a reader who had
praised his work:

> As to the 'neglect of the public,' I have never felt that I was running a race
> for its favour. . . . The art of writing novels is to present a picture of life, but
> novel-writing embraces only a narrow portion of life. I trust that I keep my
> eyes on the larger outlook, as little as possible on myself.

In March of the next year he wrote to Stevenson praising *Treasure
Island* as 'the best of boys' books, and a book to make one a boy again.'
He again calls himself a cripple. By May of 1885, 'Hope is at an end with
me. . . . I live for the day, trying to work, though the machine has
latterly got crazy.' His wife too was ill, under a nurse at Eastbourne. In
June:

> Speechlessness oppresses her. The malady has now reduced her self-command,
> she cannot help excessive fretfulness. She bore two operations with a noble
> fortitude.

He was struggling to write *Diana* through all this terrible period, and to
compose his mind:

> I should think it a vileness to crave for the happiest of renewed existences.
> The soul's one road is forward. . . . And yet it is quite certain that the best of
> us is in the state of survival. We live in what we have done—in the idea: which
> seems to me the parent fountain of life, as opposed to that of perishable blood.
> I see all round me how much the Idea governs; and therein see the Creator;
> that other life to which we are drawn. . . .
>
> Consciousness excited human felicity to kill it. Past consciousness, there may
> be a felicity eternal. These are not words, they are my excruciated thoughts—
> out of bloody sweat of mind, and now peaceful, imaging life, accepting what-
> ever is there. [August 1884.]

These words show the same strength and weakness as the poem *Earth and Man*; and in the formulation, 'Consciousness excites human felicity to kill it,' he falls away from the key-idea in his work, that such a killing occurs only where the inner split dominates, and that what is needed is always *more* consciousness.

> As it is, I sink at times. I need all my strength to stand the buffets of the harsh facts of existence. I wish it were I to be traveller instead. I have long been ready for the start, can think prospectingly of the lying in earth. She [his wife] has no thought but of this light—and would cry to it like a Greek victim under the knife. [June 1885.]

The same confusion and contradiction appears in comments on politics in 1885. Thus the first of the following passages accepts the imperialist position, the second rejects it, the third turns away in horror:

> Either we surrender our position universally, or we must have men in arms —soldiers as well as sailors. Nothing, I suppose, but war will push the English to this policy. . . . Not less than an addition of 100,000 men to the army was needed when we set foot on Egypt.
>
> All our morning papers write as in a clamour of madness . . . the ravings of the Tory Press for War. I look at the telegrams each morning with apprehension—so insensate has the nation become.
>
> As for Politics, it is a foul wind. I turn my back. Puffs of London dung-dust resemble it.

And even the first passage is followed by a jeer at the Liberal Press for its loyal sycophancy at the coming-of-age of a prince.

Diana of the Crossways had been published in February; and was a success with both reviewers and public. But he was in no mood to get any pleasure from the event. His wife, who had gone to Eastbourne in April, came home in June and died on 17 September after being stricken for close on sixteen months. Their son William was sent off to Normandy, Marie went to the Morleys at Wimbledon, and Meredith was left alone to brood, crippled, and weak in the stomach, at Box Hill. Nothing before him but increasing pain and physical impotence. 'I am utterly alone.'

24

Diana of the Crossways

WHAT THEN of the book written under such stress and achieving the first general success of any of his books?

Diana appears in his letters from early January 1884 as near completion, but at moments 'in the Doldrums.' It was based on Mrs Norton, 'but I have had to endow her with brains and make them evidence to the discerning. I think she lives.'

> I am now writing daily very hard, and though the work flows to its end in full view, my health at present is of a kind hardly to bear the strain. . . . I hope to finish with the delivery of the terrible woman afflicting me (a positive heroine with brains, with real blood, and demanding utterance of the former, tender direction of the latter) by the end of April.
> I could have killed her merrily, with my compliments to the public; and that was my intention. But the marrying of her, sets me traversing geminine laby-rinths, and you know that the why of it can never be accounted for. I shall be free certainly after the first week in June.
> My 'Diana' still holds me; only by the last chapter; but the coupling of such a woman and her man is a delicate business. She has no puppet-pliancy. The truth being, that she is a mother of Experience, and gives that dreadful baby suck to brains. I have therefore a feeble hold of her: none of the novelist's winding-up arts avail; it is she who leads me. But my delay of the conclusion is owing to my inability to write of late.

This last passage comes from a letter of August when seven chapters had already appeared in *The Fortnightly*, now edited by Escott, where it was abruptly closed down after a little over half the chapters had been printed.

First, the story. Diana at a Dublin Ball meets her old friend Lady Dunstane and is introduced to Redworth who loves her but thinks his income is too small for a proposal. On her round of visits she is pestered by attempts at seduction; even at the Dunstane place, Copsley, Sir Lukin has his try. In recoil she gets engaged to Warwick, and Lady D. suspects a rush into a loveless marriage. Redworth is devotedly heaping up cash out of railway-speculations, but too late. The Warwicks visit Copsley, and Warwick is found a humourless gentlemanly official.

Soon rumours of dissension arise, and Diana is coupled in talk with Lord Dannisburgh of the Cabinet. Warwich encourages her for worldly reasons, but is jealous; he ends by taking divorce-proceedings. Diana is so keen to escape him that she is about to leave England and let things take their course, but Lady D. sends Redworth to stop her. Diana wins in the court; and thus has Warwick attached still to her. There are signs that he means to reclaim her by law. She travels. On the Nile she meets Percy Dacier, nephew of her Cabinet friend, a rising young politician. Redworth, now an M.P., joins the party awhile. Later in the year at Rovio on a mountain morning Diana and Percy both feel passion stirring for the first time in their blood.

Back in London she writes novels. The first succeeds: unknown to her, Redworth has pushed it by advertisements. She carries on an extravagant household, with Percy at all her fine parties. The Cabinet Lord dies, and she obeys his wish in waiting by his body all night; Percy joins her and gossip wags afresh. Her second novel, obviously about Percy, makes things worse, also it doesn't do so well—Redworth doesn't corrupt the Press this time. But she continues living wildly, and now heavily speculates. To escape Warwick's solicitors she goes to a small French watering-place. Percy follows. She checks his advances, but is forced to recognise that she wants him. Back in London, she tries to write a third novel and heaps up more debts with witty dinners.

Percy comes to her for advice; she is his political right-hand. He hears that Warwick has won the process for the return of his wife, and asks her to throw in her lot with him. She agrees to go off to France, but as she is about to leave, Redworth turns up to say Lady D. is near death. Percy waits in vain, then follows her to Copsley. Neither refers to the baffled plan to live together. Lady D. recovers and Diana tells her all.

Back in London she continues unpaid-for witty dinners. After one of them Percy returns with a great political secret, which must not be divulged for a month. When he tries to embrace her, she resents it. He tries to get a date for their union, and leaves with a sense of damaged dignity. She promptly sells the secret to Tonans (Editor of *The Times*). Next day Percy finds himself betrayed. When she admits her act, he goes off at once and betroths the rich Miss Asper, his constant admirer. Two days before the wedding Warwick dies. Diana falls badly ill, nursed by Lady D. Then Redworth, who believes in her soul, gets her with his bank-balance of railway-shares.

The summary shows at once that something has gone wrong with the novel. Though there are superficial political elements—the Parliamentary background and so on—there is a comparative lack of the deep Meredithian political focus. So the public applauded. There is something of the old positions, it is true, in the whole concept of the woman struggling against a world of unjust man-made laws, but the struggle is not fully related to the deeper struggle against egoism, self-alienation, the ruling cash-nexus, as in every other work of Meredith's. Here he uses the mechanism developed in his previous works to build a psychological structure in something of a political void—or rather, the political focus is ultimately there, as we shall see when we probe deeply enough, but it can be ignored more than in any other of his novels.

Some critics, who have felt a weakness in the book, have argued that Diana, so far from being a charming and true woman, is the Female Egoist. They point to her loveless marriage contracted merely to escape the persecution of males in the useless aristocratic society where she moves; her inability to live in lodgings, her need to carry on in a self-indulgent way surrounded by flattery; her lack of courage and integrity in desperately juggling debts and credits, which causes all her troubles; her vanity in choosing this way of life; her complacence in accepting an unmarried union with Percy, and then taking a high moral attitude when he expresses love for her—though it was only sheer chance that kept her from his bed; her pretence that she did not know the importance of the secret she sells, though Percy has stressed it and she is shown as a practised politician in the superficial sense. All this is true, but it does not solve the problem. Clara Middleton, at a less intense level, showed the same shifty 'femininity,' yet we feel that her tricky instability expresses a level of development, fostered by a bad society, out of which she can and will grow. That is because The Egoist has its central and pervasive political concept, which Diana lacks. Meredith does not directly relate the fix of the woman to the ubiquitous forces of division and alienation in her society. Or perhaps it would be more true to say that he does so by implication, but, because he fails to set the positive side of struggle against the negative side of corruption, he falls below his usual standard of definition. For there is no question here of the single sharp satiric focus of The Egoist.

Consider what does happen when Diana falls. Meredith has shown her throughout as afraid of sexual contact, a fear that has been accentuated by her moral weakness in marrying to gain social status. She has resolved, under pressure, to go off with Percy, but circumstances have stopped her; and the bad illness of Lady D., which was the cause of her not going-off, has switched her whole being in a different direction, increasing her sense of confusion and guilt. Therefore, when Percy does in a moment of personal triumph take her in his arms, she feels hurt. 'Would Percy have humiliated her so if he had respected her?' This recoil is not ridiculous; it derives from, and further reveals, the deep frustration and fear that dominates her life. And Meredith makes quite clear why she feels this frustration, this fear. It is because she is prevented by her society from feeling Percy's equal. She asks if he takes her for an

> adventuress, who was a denounced wife, a wretched author, and on the verge of bankruptcy? . . . And she had a secret worth thousands! . . . She began to tremble as a lightning-flash made visible her fortunes recovered, disgrace averted, hours of peace for composition stretching before her.

And so she acts blindly, controlled wholly by her desire to reach equality with Percy—*through money*. She says later confusedly, 'I went . . . like a bullet: I cannot describe it; I was mad . . . I went blindly.' Only when confronted with Percy can she understand. 'For the first time since her midnight exhibition she felt a sensation of the full weight of the deed. She heard thunder.' She feels, 'Now I see the folly, the baseness. I was blind.'

This aspect of the situation Meredith some years later put to Ulrica, a young woman with whom he was friendly:

> Ulrica says of herself, that she has imagination. Then she ought to be able to enter the breast of a passionate woman, a wife widowed, in love, much needing to be on her guard against the man, ready to fly with him, hating to intrigue; and while she totters in this juncture, assailed by monetary needs, vain of her touch on political secrets, subject in a crisis to a swoon of the mind —mark that, O imaginative lady! for there are women and noble women who stand unpractised and alone in the world, liable to these attacks, driven for the moment back on their instincts.

It was because he felt that he had really shown something profound of women's dilemma in the world of the 1880's that he continued to like the book himself. And it was precisely the meaning of this definition of Diana's crisis that none of the critics grasped; they saw as a blot, or as one incident among many, what is the whole point of the book.

Diana's crisis-moment then is the test of Percy's love and insight. He fails. How does he fail? At first glance his resentment seems amply justified. Meredith, however, is saying that on one level, the petty and immediate level, it is indeed justified; but on a deeper level it shows his own pettiness and lack of humanity. Diana has been impelled by resentment against him, which in a blind fit of defiant impulse carries her off into the act; but underneath she has wanted the end of the false relationship forced by her society on all men and women who do not rebel. If she is bitterly leaving Percy behind at one level, she is hoping to meet him at the higher level of awakened rebellious consciousness. His failure is that he cannot see the striving as well as the resentful Diana, that he cannot rise above the personal nexus and see her also as Woman, fettered Woman.

If he could make the social correlation, he would be able to recognise the striving and aspiring Diana; and by his turning to her he would release her from her devil of fear, her sense of inferiority which is expressed in her desperate effort to make money. Her effort for independence would be freed from its false element, its wish to beat men in the money-market; her work would become true work; she would have comradeship in the struggle. And so a new consciousness of what the struggle meant would be born.*

The failure of Percy drives her back on accepting the devotion of Redworth, of becoming a wife in the conventional sense of the day. Hence her shrinking in the latter part of the book. She is marrying a fairly decent fellow instead of the worthless creature that has been her first husband, a man who will appreciate much of her; but she has fallen away from the real struggle and become 'dependent' in a subtle yet crushing fashion.

Meredith keeps on almost bringing out his full point, but not quite. At the outset (in Chapter I, which is really a long preface) he announces that he is going to continue his basic feud:

> And how may you know that you have reached to Philosophy? You touch her skirts when you share her hatred of the sham decent, her derision of sentimentalism. . . . Go to her, if in no other way, by the sentimental route:— that very winding path, which again and again brings you round to the point of original impetus, where you have to be unwound for another whirl; your point of original impetus being the grossly material, not at all the spiritual. . . . This is the sentimental route to advancement. Spirituality does not light it; evanescent dreams are its oil-lamps, often with wicks askant in the socket.

He certainly meant to show in Diana's progress the liberation of a woman from the sentimental (i.e. self-divided) world, as he had done with Sandra. But Sandra's development is convincing, because she always lives and grows through her devotion to a great cause, Music and Freedom. Diana is devoted to nothing—except herself, her integrity in an abstract way. In her, 'integrity' has become the ingrown subjective concept, without a secure point of reference in the outer world, which in Meredith's view is the inevitable begetter of sentimentalism and falsity.

---

* Diana lacks even the element of struggle in her original, Mrs Norton, who wrote *English Laws for Women in the Nineteenth Century*, 1854, and a *Letter to the Queen* on the subject; her *Lost and Saved*, 1863, is a society novel setting out a plea for the wronged woman. Her *Old Sir Douglas* depicts a chivalrous old gentleman whose weak good nature is rewarded with ingratitude. Some of her minor characters show a capacity for satire. She died in 1877.

The Married Woman's Property Act, which redressed some of her main grievances, was passed in 1882; it may have brought her back to M.'s mind.

Note how Dacier's retreat to his adorer, Constance, links him with the Egoist in his retreat to Laetitia.

This is not to say that the novel is worthless. There are many finely written passages. What Meredith can do with lyricism and psychology without the full political focus, he does. Diana (who is of course a Celt) is 'a queenly comrade, and a spirit leaping and shining like mountain water'—on a lyrical mountain-top. The fresh air blows all round her, but when she descends, it is to a life cushioned by railway-speculations. When she is out in the open air, Meredith does his best with her; for then the gap between the lyrical image and social struggle is least obvious. At moments he brings her close to consciousness:

> Give us the means of independence, and we will gain it, and have a turn at judging you, my lords! You shall behold a world reversed. Whenever I am distracted by existing circumstances, I lay my finger on the material conditions, and I touch the secret. Individually, it *may* be moral with us; collectively, it is material, and thereof comes the social rebel. I was once a dancing and singing girl.

And Meredith, in the end that caused him so much trouble, makes her say, 'I have sentimentalised up to thin smoke.' She sees, at least with a part of her, that the marriage with Redworth is a dereliction. 'It is all dead flat earth at once. . . . I am going into slavery to make amends for presumption.' Emma replies, 'Your business is to accept life as we have it.' When Redworth clasps her hand, she says, 'It must get used to the shackles,' and she takes him into her cottage. 'I have a growing love for the place. . . . If I had begun life in a cottage.' Then she adds, 'All that I have had to endure! . . . or so it seems to me: it may be my way of excusing myself: —I know my cunning in that peculiar art. I would take my chance of mixing among the highest and the brightest.' And Redworth tells her, 'You pushed for the best society like a fish to its native sea.' She corrects him, 'Pray, say, a salmon to the riverheads.'

Thus Redworth tries to see her as falsely justified. What in Sandra was a drive to the sources of life in art and the struggle for freedom has become in Diana a drive to get among 'the highest and the brightest' (identified with the ruling classes). This indeed is the lie, the division, which Meredith castigated in Wilfrid Pole. For the first and only time he asks us to believe in a development on to a higher level without showing the struggle for it.

> Now Redworth believed in the soul of Diana. With her, or rather with his thought of her soul, he understood the right union of women and men, from the roots to the flowering heights of that rare graft. She gave him comprehension of the meaning of love; a word in many mouths, not often explained. With her, wound in his idea of her, he perceived it to signify a new start in our existence, a finer shoot of the tree stoutly planted in good gross earth; the senses running their live sap, and the minds companioned, and the spirits made

one by the whole-natured conjunction. In sooth, a happy prospect for the sons and daughters of Earth, divinely indicating more than happiness: the speeding of us, compact of what we are, between the ascetic rocks and the sensual whirlpools, to the creation of certain nobler races, now being dimly imagined.

All very well, but a dream, not an aim wrung out of life in the sweat of struggle.

What spoils *Diana* is not the weaknesses and self-deceits of Diana, which make her a real woman of the contemporary world, but the final abandonment of any struggle against the society that has twisted her; she merely succumbs to a conventional marriage, and hopes that 'marriage might be the archway to the road of good service.' A conclusion acceptable to the middle-class public: that is why this novel at once gained such a success in both Britain and the U.S.A. Its many merits are thus outweighed by its sentimentalism; and Shaw was right in saying that it was behind the times, far behind *Our Mutual Friend*—though his malice is shown in picking on this one book to denigrate Meredith and ignoring all the other novels.

The critics all agreed that here at last was a Real Woman. Noble in the *Academy* praised Meredith as a brilliant social essayist using the novel. Cosmo Monkhouse in *The Saturday Review* and Henley in *The Athenaeum* found Diana a supreme picture of vivid womanhood. The public, hearing that the novel dealt with an actual high-society scandal, rushed to buy.*

Meredith remained unconvinced that he was popular. The reason for his failure to achieve his wonted focus in *Diana* must be laid to the charge of the awful strain under which he had written it. And the fact that he thus largely builds the book on the first romantic conception and does not go on adequately to break that conception down by penetrating into the inner conflict and relating the conflict to the environing social pressures, may be taken as a proof of what I suggested earlier. His method was to begin with the romantic view and then to proceed to the antiromantic; and the struggle he had with most of his books derived from the difficulties provided by the clash of the two views, from which he gained his final unifying focus. In *Diana* he was too tired and anguished to complete the process.

---

* *The Spectator* could not resist referring to the 'difficult process of mental decipherment,' and *The Literary World* said, 'We get another insight into women's rights and wrongs,' but the novel fails to move us—the critic preferred the wit and wisdom 'of a happy wife and triumphant mother.' Gissing wrote, 'Right glorious. Shakespeare in modern English.'

From the letter cited early in this chapter it seems he had meant the novel to end with Diana's death, but was diverted uneasily into the marriage.

25

A Reading of Earth

ON THE first day of 1886 he wrote to Morley:

> I am still at my questions with death, and the many pictures of the dear soul's months of anguish. When the time was, and even shortly after, I was in arms, and had at least the practical philosophy given to us face to face with our enemy. Now I have sunk, am haunted. It causes me to write of her, which scorches the brand. I have need of all my powers. The thought often uppermost is in amazement at the importance we attach to our hold of sensation. So much grander, vaster, seems her realm of silence. She is in earth, our mother, and I shall soon follow. And in truth, the doing of good service is the right use of this machine.

But he had twenty-three years of life yet. In March he says that when he wakes up, he feels as if his head has been cut from the spine, 'as if Somnus had served as headsman.' And he tells an admirer who wants a photo:

> The human waves roll like the seas, with a momentary difference in the features, and that small, and not distinctly significant. I like to see the portraits of our greatest, and of beautiful women. Not being one or the other, I fancy it will require accident or the police to subject me to the operation.

The obliterating sense of death is still on him.

He met Clodd, another freethinker, this year; and R.L.S. paid him a last visit, for four days, in the summer. Flora Shaw called while they were there and stayed the night. A keen journalist, she ran the Colonial Department of *The Times* for a while; the daughter of a general, she married Lugard, who did much shrewdly to rivet British rule on West Africa. She picked up in cheap fashion some of Meredith's ideas. ' "By intellectual courage," he said, "we make progress." ' And with such chatty vulgarisations she helped to work up interest in him in the U.S.A., where 'for a long time even the great libraries were without a volume by Meredith, except perhaps, a small, poorly-printed, bowdlerised edition of *Diana*' (E. M. Fullerton). However, Meredith liked bright-eyed girls and women around his loneliness. He wrote in 1889 of Flora that to know her was 'to look through an Eyelet on the Promised Land. . . . She is Irish and French— that's why. Quite as delightful to talk with as to look at; with more of the solid Permanency to carry away with you after it, and no bucks headed by a Porker Prince [the Prince of Wales] to ride you down in competition.' His daughter Marie was now a lively young thing of fifteen, and it eased his lost and crippled state to watch young people, especially girls, springing, up, happily growing and making their first attempts to grasp at reality.

Another girl who pleased was Hilda de Longueuil, cousin of Grant Allen who was living fairly near. She talked intimately, and he fell in love with her in a way.

> Perceive that I embrace your whole existence, all that may or could in the chances have befallen you, and am, with this feeling of mine, barely of our world when I ally myself with your destinies and speculate on them, past and future. I ask to hear nothing that does not lead me to help you on to a healthier viewing and footing of the world. . . .
>
> Feel me in your soul's home. And believe that you have done more for me in so strangely making mine a habitation for you than I can ever repay by services.

They had met late in 1886; and four months later she was still his 'friend and dearest,' but by September 1877 he writes her an ordinary descriptive letter.

The relation was thus fervid but brief. She called herself a 'starved cat with black-currant eyes,' and he criticised her nostrils as not lively, nervous, dilating to air. But when she grew animated, 'I would back her, for true illumination of beauty, against the field of enchantresses.' At the second interview, he took 'a dive into an eye that sparkled pure light and still detains me.' He had been haunted by hearing a friend tell of 'the welcome you give to Sleep and Death.' Soon he was 'your most faithful, Your devoted. I salute you, press and kiss your hand, am at your feet.' 'My thoughts hang over you solicitously, and tend you, body and spirit.' Both in a poem for her, and in his letters, he discusses an affair of hers, in which he feels the lover unworthy. 'It has gone and had to go. It is not lost, be sure. . . . Nothing ceases. Notice in this, how loss and sweat of anguish produce a piece of writing that I tear to strips and there seems not a vestige left, yet it has entered into me. It changes, akins, diverts me in some way.'

> Can love be born from hearts
> That love has left outworn;
> Appearing dead to sweet desire
> For mouths of earth once mounts of fire?

He describes the runaway wife who tosses her cap over windmills for a not-much-of-a-creature, and tells a story about an old lady of Devon saying of her son who went off with someone's wife, 'Why, he only had

her for a fortnight.' 'The old grow sane. And by and by, when possession
ceases to be a masculine noun in man's grammar-book, we shall have
larger ideas of purity and especially clearer as to its place of residence.'

He tries to make her feel what happiness lies in the true sense of nature
and fellowship in struggle. 'A world of nature that we can trim if we
please, that can go on independently and healthfully because joyfully:
always busily; whose death is life; whose rest is nothing but variations.
We perceive also a world of men, certainly bettered by the ages but not
yet in harmony between their desires and their capacities: hence their
wretchedness.' She must not revolve her meditations grievously and shut
her sensations 'from fellowship with the outer world out of nature and
human kind.' He bids her grapple with the political world. 'Consider, if
you denounce political life, and turn from the arts—what is left but a
choice between the priest and the manly sportsman?'

He finds that she likes ballads. 'Your heart is in the woods? we will
enter them together, and I sing to you, for I am of the woods.' He decides
to write for her *Letters to a Lady on the Art of Fiction*.

And so it ends. Whatever he has given her, he says, it is nothing beside
her gift to him.

His mood is of stoical calm, of bitterness subdued to faith in man.

> In origin I am what is called here a nobody, and my pretensions to that rank
> have always received due encouragement by which, added to a turn of my
> mind, I am inclined to Democracy, even in Letters, and tend to think of the
> claims of others when I find myself exalted. This is the advantage I have gained
> from sharp schooling. Good work is the main object. Mine I know to be
> faulty. I can only say generally that I have done my best to make it worthy.
> On the other hand simple appreciation, without comparisons of me with con-
> temporaries, is welcome to my heart.
>
> Someone—is it you?—accuses me of cynicism. Against that I do protest.
> None of my writings can be said to show a want of faith in humanity, or of
> sympathy with the weaker, or that I do not read the right meaning of strength.
> And it is not only women of the flesh, but also women in the soul whom I
> esteem, believe in, and would aid to development. There has been a confound-
> ing of the tone of irony (or satire in despair) with cynicism. [To Fullerton,
> Nov. 1886.]

In February 1887 he wrote on request a letter to *The Pall Mall Gazette*
protesting against the Ambleside Railway as destroying landscape beauty
that was the property of the people. 'Where there is dissention between
rich and poor, I do not commonly side with the former. I am against the
project because it does not promise to be of good use to the people. . . .
We have here one of the few instances of Sentimentalists pleading for the
general interests, Conservatives upholding the cause of Democracy. I

suppose that an Ambleside railway would offer a paying investment to the shareholder. . . .' He had *Ballads and Poems of Tragic Life* in the Press, ready for late March, 'if the Germans do not force on a war.' In April, with digestion and nerves bad, he wrote on the dark reactionary time they were passing through. As in all the years to come, we find him wavering between the imperialist position of the need to 'defend' Britain against rival powers and a perception of Britain's own evil basis in loot and oppression. Again in this letter we see how clear he is when he comes up against facts; generally he admired Gladstone as a Liberal, but when he meets him he sees into his vain, tortuous character, what Marx called his 'oleaginous hypocrisy' and Carlyle his capacity to convince himself that he conscientiously believed whatsoever tended to his political advantage:

> We Liberals, Radicals, practical Christians, are going through a gloomy time. Politics, even when they have us in thorniest thickets, do not obscure me. I see under the edge of the cloudiest. But it is nevertheless distressing to observe one's countrymen bemuddled by their alarms and selfish temporary interests.
> On Tuesday night I was a guest at the Eighty Club, was introduced to Gladstone (who favoured me with the pleased grimace of the amiable public man in the greeting of an unknown), and heard a speech from him enough to make a cock robin droop his head despondently. . . . This valiant prodigiously gifted, in many respects admirable, old man is, I fear me, very much an actor.

Haldane and Dillon were visiting Box Hill; and no doubt the way in which leading Liberals now courted Meredith, something of a celebrity since *Diana*, had an effect in strengthening his confusion on the 'defence' issue. For there was now a strong swing of Liberals and many sections of Radicals into blatant imperialism, led by Joseph Chamberlain. Maxse succumbed and went as far as becoming a Tory. 'I tried a few sentences of serious expostulation,' said Meredith. 'He burst through every one midway. So I retired to an eminence and worried him with shafts, whereat he kicked and roared and lashed his tail.' (In 1888 we find Meredith at the Parnell Dinner with Haldane and Asquith one side, and Balfour and Morley on the other: bad company indeed for a true Radical.)

In May 1887 *Ballads and Poems of Tragic Life* appeared. We have already noted the best of its poems when they came out in periodicals, *France, Attila, Theodolinda*. Many of the ballads deal with violent conflict of man and woman; *A Preaching on a Spanish Ballad* links the conflict with the head-heart division of self-alienation. *Manfred* mocks at the romantic raving on mountain-top: if a man really scaled the heights, the sweat and toil would bring him down to earth and he wouldn't summon 'Nature to her feud with bile and buskin Attitude.' *Solon* records the poet's feelings about 'the gloomy time,' a democratic advance followed by tyrannous reaction, but giving no grounds for despair:

> *Unripe! unripe! The times are overcast.*
> *But still may they who sowed behind the plough*
> *True seed fix in the mind an unborn Now*
> *To make the plagues afflicting us things past.**

In June the rebel spoke out about the Jubilee:

> We are still in the drench of the Jubilee. Our Queen has thanked her subjects, printing her personal pronoun in Capitals. People are beginning to complain of . . . this dry Norse wind. There is a general groan for a change. Another week of it and we shall have the Mitred Cant commanding petitions to his Lord for a change. Ah! if he would but appeal to the purblind Commons to cease blowing politically Norse in compliance with the wishes of their over-peers. . . .
>
> What I am going to do this summer I know not. My last poor volume continues to receive drubbings from reviewers. . . .

In July he sent his good wishes to Foote, now out of jail. 'You carry on a brave battle, for the best of causes, personally profitless.' And he thanked a young American:

> When at the conclusion of your article on my works, you say that a certain change in public taste, should it come about, will be to some extent due to me, you hand me the flowering wreath I covet. For I think that all right use of life, and the one secret of life, is to pave ways for the firmer footing of those who succeed us; as to my works, I know them faulty, think them of worth only when they point and aid to that end.
>
> Close knowledge of our fellows, discernment of the laws of existence, these lead to great civilisation. I have supposed that the novel, exposing and illustrating the natural history of man, may help us to such sustaining roadside gifts. But I have never started on a novel to pursue the theory it developed. The dominant idea in my mind took up the characters and the story midway.

And he returned to the theme of critics.

> In England I am encouraged but by a few enthusiasts. I read in a critical review of some verses of mine the other day that I was 'a harlequin and a performer of antics.' I am accustomed to that kind of writing, as our hustings orator is to the dead cat and the brickbat flung in his face—at which he smiles politely; and I too; but after many years of it my mind looks elsewhere.

This summer the Merediths, with Leslie Stephen close by, took a house

---

* *The Spectator* said that Meredith's low reputation as a poet derived from the fact that his verse was 'inarticulate. It is in no sense meaningless; it is simply unable to say what it desires to say.' Henley in *The Athenaeum* said there was genius but 'no felicity . . . congestion, clottedness, an anxious and determined "dandyism of form and style".' Arthur Symons in *The Westminster* found the theme of M.'s poetry Nature as a source of joy and healing, Life as a tragic tangle; but his art was 'uncertain.' Foote praised the book in *Progress* and pleased Meredith.

at St Ives in North Cornwall. After thirty days of brilliant weather, they went on to Torquay.

In January he was coughing and sneezing. Living so much alone he felt 'at the mercy of the haunting demonry' of the past, and assured an admirer that he was no celebrity and feared all honours. In March he told an American compiler of extracts from his books that he disliked such a gathering of plums, which was indigestible. He defines the spiritual life as the way of man in harmony with nature:

> If a man's work is to be of value, the best of him must be in it. I have written always with the perception that there is no life but of the spirit; that the concrete is really the shadowy; yet that the way to spiritual life lies in the complete unfolding of the creature, not in the nipping of his passions. An outrage to Nature helps to extinguish his light. To the flourishing of the spirit, then, through the healthy exercise of the senses.

In the summer he went with his daughter to Wales where his son was working as an electrical engineer at Llanelly. In seventeen days at Tenby 'we drove to ancient castles and sea-fowl rocks, bathed, surfeited on cream, became green as Neptune, and were alternate days drenched.' At Llanelly he went to the steelworks; and a man who was there wrote in 1908, 'he was intensely interested in what he saw, and his description of the pyrotechnic display from the charging of the steel furnace is still a vivid memory.' At Llandilo they saw more castles and waterfalls, and were drenched. They they went via Llandrindod to Brecon, and at Ferndale he went down the pit and had a long chat there with the colliers. He learned some Welsh, liked Welsh scenery and eyes, but didn't like the hotel cooking. And 'no places of amusement.' He ends a letter on the trip by calling himself Radicalism incarnate. At Merthyr, where the party arrived late at night, he wanted to heckle a parliamentary candidate who was holding a meeting in front of the hotel; and the others had trouble in getting him away.

In December his book of poems, *A Reading of Earth*, was published; and from now on he refused to send out review-copies—that is, he appealed to the reader against the critics.

We find him in his best form as a nature-poet. *Hard Weather* and *The South-Wester* finely give strong pictures of earth in turmoil and fuse the turmoil with the strenuous life of man in shaping himself and the earth to new uses and an enriched consciousness of process:

> *Behold the life at ease; it drifts.*
> *The sharpened life commands its course.*
> *She winnows, winnows roughly; sifts,*
> *To dip her chosen in her source:*

Contention is the vital force,
Whence pluck they brain, her prize of gifts,
Shy of the senses! on which height,
Not disconnected, yet released,
They see how spirit comes to light. . . .

Seed-Time links the earth-cycle of change with the need of renewal in man, the need to drive forward. *The Appeasement of Demeter* nobly links the earth-laugh with the mating-act, with liberation and abundance. *Earth and a Wedded Woman* shows the soldier's wife achieving her discipline of waiting, not by puritanism, but by her deep feeling for fertile earth, her sense of union with the moment of germination. This is one of Meredith's best poems, as is the *Hymn to Colour.* In the *Hymn* he used the great moment of lightburst, light-change, the Dawn, to express the dialectics of human change. Light, Darkness, Colour are paired with Life, Death, Love. The poet walks between Life and Death, when Love appears and the Dawn begins. Under the 'transforming sky' Life and Death fade out, and Love tells the poet that unless he sees Life and Death as the fused opposites of a single system of process, he cannot realise the unity that emerges from their fusion, which is Love. This statement is given force by the lovely picture of Dawn which illustrates it. As the subtle dawn-hues fade, Love, looking on his rosy memories, sings a song of thanksgiving to Colour as the vivifying and transfiguring quality of nature, one with all that stirs and changes men, one with the struggle of men into a free and harmoniously realised earth, their delighting and rich home, 'themselves the attuning chord.' Life and Death return, and the poet looks on them with new eyes, changed by his experience, more fully entering into the unity of process.

A Faith on Trial tells of his anguished ordeal at the death of his wife. He goes out in the shadow of death past the children at their May-quête, and wanders on, noting details of the growth of nature and driven back into memories. But he is still closed in himself. The net that the life around him and the associated memories weave is still one with the dead. Then he sees a wild cherry in bright bloom among yewtrees, and he is drawn outside himself: he feels his own darkness in the yews, and the unconquerable leap into beauty, into joy, in the cherry. He pours himself out into nature, accepting life and death, once more accepting struggle. Slowly he feels himself healed, is consciously one with 'sacred Reality.'

Hopeful of victory most
When hard is the task to sustain. . . .

Another fine poem is *The Thrush in February,* where Meredith makes a brave and moving affirmation of his faith in progress, in man's power to break through the obstructions and divisions of existing society into an earth of brotherhood. The poem opens with a felicitous account of the birdsong and the February landscape: then,

> *Remote, not alien; still, not cold;*
> *Unraying yet, more pearl than star;*
> *She seems a while the vale to hold*
> *In trance, and homelier makes the far.* . . .

> *He sings me, out of Winter's throat,*
> *The young time with the life ahead;*
> *And my young time his leaping note*
> *Recalls to spirit-mirth from dead.*

> *Imbedded in a land of greed,*
> *Of Mammon-quakings dire as Earth's,*
> *My care was but to soothe my need;*
> *At peace among the littleworths.*

He had listened merely to be charmed away from reality; but the song that revives his youth in wintry age drives him back to the hopes and aspirations of his youth. He regains his sensitiveness to the delicate and tremendous needs of life as the new births stir and break forth. He regains the rich insights that the simple song brings to common life. The song goes on forever, though the singer dies. Forever lasts,

> *For souls not lent in usury,*
> *The rapture of the forward view.*

The whole onward-movement of life, of men in their struggle, is something that cannot be broken, whatever the wrecks and setbacks. The goal of freedom and brotherhood, the new life, still gleams unquenched:

> *Glimpse of its livingness will wave*
> *A light the senses can discern.*

> *Across the river of the death,*
> *Their close. Meanwhile, O twilight bird*
> *Of promise! bird of happy breath!*
> *I hear, I would the city heard.*

The City 'of the smoky fray' is the place of enslavement, of the dehumanising cash-nexus; 'its Morrow no man's child; its Day a vulture's morsel beaked to bones.'

> *It strives without a mark for strife;*
> *It feasts beside a famished host.*

But this anarchic place of blind exploitation is also the place where are born the fighters for a different way of life. 'Yet thence our battle urges;

there spring heroes many,' for whom life is the bag of grain and death the harrow's tooth. With their far-reaching vision they 'give worn Humanity new youth.' They are song and star to lead men in the struggles of progress, to ever higher levels; and they reveal to men the earth as their true and only home. By accepting with love the material laws of development these men show the way to freedom.

Yet in this book of verse the imperialist confusion intrudes in a quatrain praising Gordon of Khartoum.

With 1889 he was working on *One of our Conquerors*. This year Frederick Jones, neighbour of Norbiton about a quarter of a century before, died; and so did Browning. Meredith attended the latter's funeral in Westminster Abbey.

He praises the Scots and the English of the North as 'the saving of the country,' yet goes on to talk of the country's 'close race with various and shrewd races.' His daughter was gadding much in London, and friends and foes, he says, keep sending him hostile notions of his poems. (His girl Marie, vivacious and pretty, was empty-headed; and had been aided in her social ambitions by Mrs Walter Palmer, of the biscuit-makers, who had chattered into sight in 1889. Meredith called her Queen Jean, and she did her best to lionise him—a photo shows him at one of her Reading house-parties in 1892, with Wilde, Irving, and Forbes-Robertson; Mrs Palmer in feathered hat leans loosely with a hand behind her head. Now, in 1889, she invited Marie to stay at a house she had taken in Bayreuth.)

In October *The Universal Review* published *Jump-to-Glory Jane*, a poem which dealt with a country-woman who became a Jumper. A Jumper was one of the odd sectarians who by continual jumping expressed their sense of salvation and glory and at the same time showed their repudiation of the unregenerate world. Meredith in his poem brings out clearly the idea of the jump as a blind reaction against an unjust world of exploitations, and makes us feel the act as the release of energies which the unjust world baffles and drives back on themselves. He begins:

> *A revelation came on Jane,*
> *The widow of a labouring swain:*
> *And first her body trembled sharp,*
> *Then all the woman was a harp*
> *With winds along the strings; she heard,*
> *Though there was neither tone nor word.*

Others join in, and the whole group express their rejection of the world outside shop, pub, and vicarage. Finally she jumps a prolonged defiance to the astounded Bishop, and jumps in a happy leap to death.

A lily in a linen clout
She looked when they had laid her out.
It is a lily-light she bears
For England up the ladder-stairs.

There is nothing difficult about the poem, which defines the Jumpers as the simple spontaneous repudiators of State and Church, of the cash-nexus. In their clean and happy jumping they have a certain harmony with the elemental flow and upward-movement of nature. What they lack is consciousness of the impulse or force that moves them; if they could gain that consciousness they would dominate the impulse and make it socially fruitful in a directed effort of revolt, changing the world. (I have seen a passage of the 1790's in which a Tory declares that the Jumpers of Wales were inspired by Paine's *Rights of Man*, a delusion which reveals the fear of an embryonic revolutionary emotion in the wild seizures.) Because of Jane's uncompromising resistance to the class-world, Meredith ends by saying she bears a lily-light for England, since in her have stirred the force which will in time turn into a true redemption.

Now hear what the editor, Quilter, who published the poem, says:

> The critics were puzzled, the public doubtful. Demands for explanation flowed in upon me by every post; clergymen remonstrated; not very clear as to their grievance these last, but 'doubtful of the tendency. . . .'
> The very artist I wished to illustrate the poem not only began, but continued, to make excuses, and finally confessed that he could not do justice to the verses. . . . Somehow this got abroad, and certain journals made themselves merry over the artist's incapacity to understand the text submitted to him. Then the journalistic word went forth that the poem was 'a satire on the Salvation Army,' and as such it was gravely characterised in several papers.
> 'Forced, feeble and vulgar,' was this 'tedious doggerel' according to one authority; 'silly and incomprehensible' growled a second; 'scarcely likely to add to the author's reputation' sighed a third, and so on throughout the list. If a kind word was spoken of Jane here and there, it was not written; my very publisher asked me privately what it meant, and friends and relations looked grave; discreetly avoided the subject, as one which was undoubtedly painful.

Quilter's own interpretation, however, was as stupid as anyone else's: he thought it a satire on Kingsley's Muscular Christianity.

In August 1889 Meredith gave some semi-sarcastic advice about illustrations:

> Whoever does it, should be warned against giving burlesque outlines. It is a grave narration of events in English country[-life]. Jane, though a jumper, is a thoughtful woman. She has discovered that the circulation of the blood is best brought about by a continual exercise, and conduces to happy sensations, which are to her as the being of angels in the frame. She has wistful eyes, in a touching, but bony face.

Next month he admitted that Jane derived from Mary Girling, the founder of the Shakers: the lines—

> Yes, they are a satire, but one of the pictures of our England as well. . . . The sensations of Jane, with her blood at the spin with activity, warranted her feeling of exaltation. An English middle-class Blavitzsky Maniac would also be instructive, though less pathetic than poor Jane.

He thus sees in Jane, in her pathos, an emblem of the way in which the people, the workers, have been twisted awry by oppression and alienation: her jumping is pathological. But at the same time it remains a revelation of the resistant energies which, properly directed, can transform England into a place of light. That is why Jane must be treated respectfully, unlike a middle-class neurotic, as 'one of the pictures of our England.' In fact it is not too much to say that Meredith is symbolising (sympathetically satirising) in Jane the spiritual condition of the working-class at the time, in whom there were elements of spontaneous revolt and resistance, often religious in idiom, and who were the hope of the future (the light on the stairs for England), but who lacked clear political understanding and method.

The poem appeared in a limited pirated edition in 1889: 'Whether issued by a lunatic or a profoundly speculative,' said Meredith. 'The reason why a poem of a writer whose verse is not popular should have been selected for fraudulent publication is not clearly seen.'

In 1890 he talks of the pudding-headed English who shuffle questions on without facing them. He now refused to send out any copies of the books of poetry which he was printing at his own cost, as he considered that he got only insults back. In May he wrote to Jessop that *One of Our Conquerors* was nearing its end. He felt a bit strained—'as I have condemned myself both to a broad and a close observation of the modern world in it, throwing beams both upon its rat-tides and its upper streams.' It is clear from that one statement that the public were not going to get another *Diana*.

In September Hardman died; and Arthur Meredith died nine days before him.

In 1891 he talks of his 'rather battered name,' and still refuses review-copies of his poems. In letters to Greenwood, that staunch imperialist, he reveals further his own inner conflict. He says that on all domestic or social matters he opposes Greenwood. 'But I share your feeling for the country, and am with you in your watchful outlook.' And later, 'The notion of stirring Englishmen with verse is comic. Foemen in the guts might do it. Or Brighton bombarded, or supplies of fresh meat failing.'

Himself, he is under the doctor, a man condemned to poverty by his love of poetry.

In April *One of Our Conquerors* had come out, a violent disappointment to *Diana's* public. It had the best send-off of any of his novels, serialised in *The Fortnightly*, *The New York Sun*, and *The Australasian*, though he received only £1,000 for six years copyright. The critics, even when not liking to be as rude as of old after *Diana*, declared the book's indigestibility. *The Daily Telegraph* admitted 'the last word of triumphantly analytic science,' perhaps all the more readily as the reviewer had no idea what was being analysed; but *The Daily Chronicle* groaned:

> Mr Meredith grows more and more trying. He seems to take a Satanic delight in wrapping simplicity in as many fantastic coverings as he can devise. Of course he doesn't mind you being cross; he enjoys it. You may take him or leave him; all's one to him.*

It wasn't all one to him; he detested his middle-class audience, but he desperately wanted an audience with political and poetic understanding, and asked nothing better than to submit his talents entirely to its demands. But it was true that there was a certain malice in the difficulties of *One of Our Conquerors*. *Diana* had been written in the full pangs of discovering that he was doomed to spinal paralysis and that his wife was dying; through it he tottered into renown by what was almost inadvertence and distraction. But because of his bitter hostility to the middle-class audience he wasn't going to play down to them and vulgarise his work. His sharp resistance took the form of a hard-hitting theme and an involved crisscrossed method of writing. Later he told Photiadès:

> I had discovered at the start of my career that nothing upset the critics so much as anything that was out of the common and required an extra need of attention. When I was about sixty, and I had inherited a small sum of money which made me independent, I took it into my head to serve those critics a strong dose of my most indigestible production. I presented to them, slyly, *Diana of the Crossways* and the novels which followed. But nothing drove them so crazy as *One of Our Conquerors*. The poor fellows knew not what to call upon or how to give an account of the accursed volume. It was necessary to commence by understanding it, and these blind men were groping in the thickness of their shadows.

---

* *The Athenaeum* found the 'vagaries of genius' in grammar and spelling; *The Pall Mall*, saying that much was masterly, denied the story any power to grip or move, and criticised eccentric diction; *The Spectator* found M.'s vogue inexplicable, since, 'in his misdirected cleverness,' he lacked even the qualifications of a second-rate novelist, he was of 'unique perversity,' his story 'slight, shapeless and very unattractive,' the narrative 'clumsily managed.' It was hard to find a 'simple, natural, unstrained phrase or sentence.' *The Saturday* thought the book a 'puzzle' with an intensification of M.'s usual faults of 'incoherence, prolixity, straining after epigram, seeking after the uncommon, lack of firmness in character-drawing,' Victor was a blatant cad, Nesta a mere characterless name.

Not that that was anything like the whole truth. The strain of his loss, of his advancing paralysis, can be read in the style; and something yet deeper. His effort to grapple with the nature of bourgeois man under imperialism —the new epoch which was now maturing with forms that had been present only embryonically in the days of Sandra-Vittoria and Beauchamp. His inner struggle in the effort to readjust his critical method to the new situation was extreme. He stumbled and sometimes fell down, as he was now doing with his paralysis; but for the most part he stood upright and maintained a clear human dignity, seeing the truth of what was happening.

26

One of Our Conquerors

VICTOR RADNOR has married an old woman for money. He then lives with Nataly for some twenty years, unmarried, and they have a daughter Nesta. Nataly is retiring in nature; but Victor, who has become a big City magnate with wide imperial investments, is pushing in the extreme. He forces the family into the open where they are in ceaseless danger of exposure, especially after his building of a big house and his resolve to enter Parliament. Nesta, who knows nothing of her bastardy, is wooed by an aristocrat Sowerby; also Dartrey Fenellan is in love with her, a soldier who resigned from the army in anger, and who, now in business, is saddled with an impossible wife. (She is separated from him, however, and soon dies.) Nesta, on a seaside holiday, meets a Mrs Marsett, who is the mistress of a Captain. Mrs Marsett, an overstrung romantic, tells Nesta of her position, and Nesta is pestered by a Major who meets her at the Marsett lodgings and who is chastised by Dartrey. On top of this, through the remark of a parson who hopes to marry her, she realises her own position. Nataly, with a supreme effort, tells the truth to Sowerby. Nesta, half-engaged, is repelled by Sowerby's smugness; and a sharp conflict thus breaks out between the daughter and the conventionally-minded mother who feels her smirched by the Marsett connection. That connection further upsets Sowerby, just as he has brought himself, aided by the thought of Nesta's fortune, to accept the unmarried state of her parents. Nesta begins to wake up, to become a rebel through her realisation of woman's predicament in her society.

Victor, undeterred, keeps on hoping that his old wife will die, and there is a painful scene when he and Nataly are forced to visit the dying woman. He carries on with his parliamentary ambitions, and is about to address his first public meeting when news comes that Nataly has died of a heart-attack. He breaks down, and when Nesta comes to him, falls into definite madness. She marries Fenellan, though Sowerby has belatedly brought himself to accept the situation, even the loss of Victor's money. Finally after a brief return to lucidity Victor dies.

The theme of the book is the breakdown of the great and audacious financier, Victor—his very name is emblematic; he is One of Our

Conquerors—one of the new ruling-class, the bourgeoisie in their imperialist phase. Early in the novel Meredith underlines the meaning of the name by digression about a supposed book, *The Rajah in London*, in which he defines the London Night as a revelation of the human wasteland brought about by the City's cash-nexus. 'For our pinched are here, the weedy, the gutter-growths, the forces repressing them. . . . London is at night a moaning outcast round the policeman's legs.' And he depicts the Indian wandering in this desolation. 'Behind his courteousness he is an antagonistic observer of his conquerors.' Victor, who embodies the forces that have conquered India, is also *Our* Conqueror, the conqueror and looter of *his own* people.

His story is made to represent the whole situation of his class. It is no argument against this point to say that statistically few of the great magnates of the day were in his particular domestic quandary. Here is a case where the apparently exceptional becomes the perfect example of the normal; for there is a difference between the exceptional as the bizarre and the wilful, and the exceptional as the extreme case of a general tendency. Don Quixote is statistically as unlike the majority of Spaniards of his day as he could well be; yet he represents the characteristic struggle going on in them, which looks to the future and becomes typical of human life. Victor's personal dilemma is exceptional; but the divided state of life and mind which it focuses is perfectly typical of his class. Again, not many magnates, statistically, go mad; but Victor's madness is the exact expression of what they are doing to society, the logic of their positions.

He is drawn carefully as a man who seems the exact embodiment of a class-ideal. With his gusto (as usual expressed through wines), his keen capacity for enjoyment, his boisterous good-humour and his quick shrewdness, he 'bids fair to become the idol of the English people,' says Lady Blanchington. Among the glittering rich, Colney the writer muses, 'He is their *Law*'; and then, 'the shallowness of the abstract Optimist exposed,' he sums up at the end.

The Abstract Optimist, in Meredith's terminology, is the man who sees himself bustling on to a worthy social goal—while in fact the goal is only the heightening of his own egoism. In such a man there is a widening gap between idea and actuality.

> Victor had yet to learn that a man with a material object in aim is the man of his object; and the nearer to his mark, often the further he is from a sober self: he is more the arrow to his bow than the bow to his arrow. This we pay for scheming: and success is costly; we find that we have pledged the better half of ourselves to clutch it; not to be redeemed with the whole handful of our prize.

That is the key-statement of the book's moral. By 'material object in aim,' Meredith means a material object without a philosophic relation, divorced from the struggle of man to become human. The object thus absorbs the man, who makes himself a thing; he is lost in the mechanism he has devised; the split deepens inside him; if he enters wholly into the object and thus 'succeeds,' he quite dehumanises himself and has no future but disintegration. He cannot disgorge the object, for *it is now himself*. Thus Victor, the representative of the victorious imperialist bourgeoisie, has no future but madness; his class has no future but destruction and disaster. And this is the truth hidden under his charming exterior, his Abstract Optimism which grabs the world.

His doom is prefigured on the first page of the novel. He is going over London Bridge and slips on some orange-skin, falling on the back of his head. A worker helps him up, and, after his comment on the way his white waistcoat is dirtied, an exchange of angry words goes on between worker and financier. The fall occurs at a moment of extreme 'optimism,' of an expansive mood when he feels within reach of the big political idea that he wants as the final expression of his power. As a motive it is repeated throughout the book; and Victor's mental collapse is preceded by memories of it, a throb in his head on the injured spot. A man who prides himself on his power of maintaining balance amid dangerous abysses, he feels the fall as an inexplicable flaw. ('Mother, we walk on planks,' Nesta says, and Nataly answers: 'You will grow used to it.')

Long before the strain wears through, his wife and daughter feel a premonition. After he comes home from the fall and tells of his housing plans, Nataly 'could have asked whether he was perfectly sane.' Later Nesta 'was arrested by the louder question, whether she could think such a man as her father irrational.'

He has displaced Inchling, who is shown as the older merchant-type; and he is determined to marry Nesta to one of the landed aristocracy. (He deliberately 'forgets' to tell Nataly that Dartrey's wife is dead. Dartrey, who knows all about the Radnors, would be a safe husband for Nesta.) His rôle as a colonial exploiter is stressed. 'Land-values in the developing Colonies, formed his theme.' . . . 'Victor's African room, containing large wall-maps of auriferous regions, were inspected; and another, where clerks were busy over miscellaneous Continents.'

He is an anti-Semite; and much of his great Idea revolves round the problem of reviving the adventurous vigour of the nation (which in his context means maintaining and extending imperialism). 'Is the Jew of the usury gold becoming our despot-king of Commerce?' He has caught this

attitude from the old-type merchant Inchling, his partner, but he has
applied it to the new situation:

> Ay, but brain meets muscle, and what if the Jew should prove to have
> superior power of brain? . . . Mr Radnor lighted on the tracks, by dint of a
> thought flung at his partner Mr Inchling's dread of the Jews. Inchling dreaded
> Scotchmen as well, and Americans, and Armenians, and Greeks: latterly
> Germans hardly less; but his dread of absorption in Jewry, signifying subjec-
> tion, had often precipitated a deplorable shrug, in which Victor Radnor now
> perceived the skirts of his idea, even to a fancy that something of the idea must
> have struck Inchling when he shrugged: the idea being . . . he had lost it again.

Victor thus stands for the new demagogy, which feels an ideology of
'national unity' is required to meet the danger within and without; he is
unsure what his Idea is, but he keeps fumbling round for it. He belongs
to the breed of Cecil Rhodes and Joseph Chamberlain—and of Hitler.
   Thus he dominates Inchling:

> Mr Inchling was a florid City-feaster, descendant of a line of City merchants,
> having features for a wife to identify; as drovers, they tell us, can single one
> from another of their round-bellied beasts. Formerly the leader of the Firm,
> he was now, after dreary fits of restiveness, kickings, false phophecies of ruin,
> Victor's obedient cart-horse. He sighed in set terms for the old days of the
> Firm, when, like trout in the current, the Firm had only to gape for shoals of
> good things to fatten it: a tale of English prosperity in quiescence. . . .

The anti-Semitism of Inchling, one of many reactionary attitudes, becomes a dynamic centralising factor in Victor, who groups round it his
demagogic ideas of national union based on the Empire.
   Let us look at his efforts to bring out the Idea into consciousness, since
on them, linked as they are with his 'fall' and his domestic strain, depends
his breakdown. He is in the odd position of being a foremost pillar of
society and the cash-nexus, while acting as a secret rebel against convention: this position underlies his urgent drive to find the Idea of national
(imperialist) salvation and yet begets in him an undercurrent of feeling
that all is not well with the society of which he is a figurehead. At moments he gets glimpses of a real revolt:

> If Society is to subsist, it must have the human with the logical argument
> against the free-flags, instead of presenting a block's obtuseness. That, you need
> not hesitate to believe, will be rolled downward and disintegrated, sooner than
> later. A Society based on the logical concrete of human considerateness—a
> Society prohibiting to Mrs Burman (his old wife) her wielding of a life-long
> rod. . . . The personal element again to confuse inquiry! . . . Victor clung to
> the theme because it hinted of next door to his lost Idea. He rubbed the back
> of his head, fancying a throb there.

His own anomalous position, while momently throwing up a wish for a
decently human society, works essentially as a pressure of anxiety driving

to find the way for safeguarding his repressive world against the demands
of human considerateness, the free-flags. If necessary some concessions
may be made; but the main thing is a new ideology of national union,
which must be built up if his society is to survive. 'A society opposing
Nature forces us to these murderous looks upon Impediments. But what
of a Society in the Dance with Nature? Victor did not approve of that.'*

Dartrey says to Nataly, 'Victor recognises what corruption that spread
of wealth is accountable for.' But Victor's recognition is merely the tremor
of fear caused by the premonitions of revolt among the oppressed (for is
not he himself torn between revolt and a mad optimism in regarding his
own position?).

> His lost Idea drew close to him in sleep: or he thought so, when awakening
> to the conception of a people solidified, rich and poor, by the common pride
> of simple manhood. But it was not coloured, not a luminous globe: and the
> people were in drab, not a shining army on the march to meet the Future. . . .
> Provide against the shrinkage of our Coal-beds; against, and for, if you like,
> the thickening, jumbling, threatening excess of population in these Islands, in
> Europe, America, all over our habitable sphere. . . .
> Our English require but the lighted leadership to come into cohesion, . . .
> and that astral head giving, as a commencement, example of the right use of
> riches, the nation is one, part of the riddle of the future solved. Surely he had
> here the Idea? . . . Only the vision was wanted. On London Bridge he had
> seen it—a great thing done to the flash of brilliant results. That was after the fall.
> There had been a fall also of the scheme of Lakelands [the house]. She
> [Nataly] was the one who sent him ahead at a trot under a light, by saying:
> 'You would found a new and more stable aristocracy of the contempt of
> luxury': when he talked of combating the Jews with a superior weapon. . . .
> He fancied an aching at the back of his head when he speculated.

The Idea comes to fruition in a situation which for one intolerable flash
reveals its imperialist basis. He is with Nesta at the Zoo:

> Over Southward, too, he would be addressing a popular assembly tomorrow
> evening. Between now and then there was a ditch to jump. He put on a sympa-
> thetic face of grief. 'After all, a caged wild beast hasn't so bad a life,' he said.—
> To be well fed while they live, and welcome death as a release from the
> maladies they develop in idleness, is the condition of wealthy people:—
> creatures of prey? horrible thought! yet allied to his Idea.

The rich, beasts of prey, who from their cages of self-alienation yet devour
the poor, are merged in his mind with Mrs Burman on her deathbed
preying on the life of himself and Nataly. Thus he feels a rending

---

* A radical pamphlet of 1889 (*Officialdom Rampant: The Primary Antagonist of Home Rule*,
by Richard Russell) declares, 'In 1886 . . . the false cry of "Unity of the Empire" was raised,
for the purpose of catching flats who were not in the underground secret of what was really
going on,' the consolidation of corruption.

sympathy for both beast and victim; but he suppresses the conflict and twists his anxiety back into the service of his Idea:

> Such anadyne as he could squeeze from the incarcerated wild creatures, was exhausted. He fell to work at Nataly's 'aristocracy of the contempt of luxury'; signifying, that we the wealthy will not exist to pamper flesh, but we live for the promotion of brotherhood:—ay, and that our England must make some great moral stand, if she is not to fall to the rear and down. Unuttered, it caught at the skirts of the Idea: it evaporated when spoken. Still, this theme was almost an exorcism of Mrs Burman.

And so when he breaks down, he returns to the moment of the fall on the Bridge (when he was picked up by a worker, who, exchanging abuse with him, used the word *punctilio*).

> He had 'a confession for his Nataly, for her only, for no one else.' He had 'an Idea.' His begging of Dudley to listen without any punctilio (putting a vulgar oath before it) was the sole piece of unreasonableness . . . [Then] Nesta came with a cry for her father. He rose; Dartrey was by. Hugged fast in iron muscles, the unhappy creature raved of his being a caged lion.

He is shut forever in the blind cage of self-alienation, unable even to prey.

Meredith subtly fuses the financial beast-of-prey in Victor with the ruthless 'husband' who thinks he loves his wife and who in fact drives her to death. Nataly is drawn with much power and insight. A woman of many strengths, she had been reduced to abject dependence on her 'generous' lover. She knows he is driving her to her death, but she has lost the capacity to protest, to explain, to do anything but follow fascinated in the track of his conquering. Her one independent act is when she tells Sowerby of Nesta's bastardy; but even that is an act wrung from her by the fear of the exposures that must come from an engagement with Sowerby. With great psychological force Meredith shows how the wretched woman has been so broken that when she finds out about Nesta and Mrs Marsett, when she discovers a spirit of decency and independence in Nesta, she is outraged; she sees only the repetition of her own 'sin,' her daughter brazen where she herself was sacrificed. Finally the scene where she is forced to confront the woman she has 'wronged' ends her demoralisation and leaves her only death. This scene is again a masterpiece (though drawing on the Miss Haversham and Mrs Clennam of Dickens): Mrs Burman is revealed as the insensate spirit of suffering hate, which wants to arrest life and finds its justification in religion. She is the other half of the society of which Victor is a part-representative; and so her confrontation of Victor and Nataly is the prelude to the death and madness which wipe out all three. None of the trio can face the truth which has been brought out.

'We are distracted, perverted, made strangers to ourselves by a false position,' says Nataly, who sees only the domestic issue. But what she says is the moral of the whole of Victor's position, of which the domestic issue is but a refracted fragment.

Against the doomed parents is set Nesta, 'a young woman educated for the market,' who grows slowly but steadily into a comprehension that sees beyond the domestic issue. She achieves her first step into freedom by realising the shackled and oppressed condition of women in her world.

> 'Women should feel for their sex. . . . There cannot be any goodness unless it is a practised goodness. Otherwise it is nothing more than paint on canvas. You speak to me of my innocence. What is it worth, if it is only a picture and does no work to help to rescue?'

But to Nataly her redemption appears as a moral collapse.

> She sighed: 'If one could think that a girl with Nesta's revolutionary ideas of the duties of women, and their powers, would be safe—or at all rightly guided by a man who is both one of the noblest and the wildest in the ideas he entertains!'
>
> Victor sighed too. He saw the earldom, which was to dazzle the gossips, crack on the sky in a futile rocket-bouquet.
>
> She was distressed; she moaned: 'My girl! my girl! . . . Nesta vows her life to it! Dartrey supports her!'

Nesta is far from a revolutionary; but she has broken something of her class-bonds and found the basis for the first steps in struggle. This novel ends with the loss of money, not the gaining of it: Nesta does not marry a poor man, but she comes right down out of high-society.

Dudley Sowerby is a fatuous Conservative, another of Meredith's upper-class youths who make an effort to be decent, but who are always too late. His slow progress into acceptance of Nesta, at first stimulated by her father's millions, ends in a love that can accept even the loss of her inheritance. But always too late. He is a mild example of what becomes tragedy in Edward Blancove, Richard Feverel, Lord Fleetwood.

Dartrey Fenellan is in the line of Austin Wentworth, a decent man with a measure of resistance to the worst trends of his society, but not seeing far. He realises the disintegrative movement. 'You've heard Colney Durance abuse old England. It's three parts factitious—literary exercise. It's milk beside the contempt of Dartrey's shrug. He thinks we're a dead people, if a people; "subsisting on our fat," as Colney says.' But he shows little signs of knowing how to struggle against the corruptions, though he whole-heartedly supports Nesta. His heart, however, is confusedly set against capitalism. When he hears some girls arm in arm singing so English a song as *Cherry Ripe*, he is drawn 'to the quick of an English tune.' He feels grateful, refreshed, and 'he had his thoughts upon the training of our English to be something besides the machinery of capitalists, and upon the country as a blessed mother instead of the most capricious of maudlin stepdames.' And he is deeply happy when he learns of Nesta's revolt; he draws back 'upon his natural brotherhood with souls that do.' He is 'often in the rebel ranks; he was dissatisfied with things as they are; was restless for action. . . .' Needless to say he is a Celt, an Irishman.

Colney is a writer with many of Meredith's attitudes as well as his characteristic of colliding with the critics. In him the negative criticism of England's backwardness is elaborated. He sees the 'succeeding Governments as a change of lacqueys—or as the purse-string's lacqueys.' England is held by 'a mercantile community guided by Political Economy [the cash-nexus] from the ledger to the banquet presided over by its Dagon Capital.' Looking at a party gathered by Victor, he sees 'a rich national pudding of the sycophants, the hypocrites, the burlies, the idiots; dregs of the depth and froth of the surface; bowing to one, that they may scorn another; instituting a Charity for their poorer fawning fellows to relieve their purses. . . .' At Brighton he looks at the blank-faced terraces staring on the sea. 'So these moneyed English shoulder to the front place; and that is the appearance they offer to their commercial God.' And he makes the Orphic pun: 'Capital!'

But he too is tainted with imperialism. He follows up his comment on the changing Governments as all lacqueys of Capital with the statement that 'Old England has taken to the arm-chair for good . . . and that, in the face of an armed Europe, this great nation is living in sufferance.' He follows up his picture of Dagon Capital over Britain with words of admiration for Victor: 'He is an active spirit . . . and his faults, short of ferocity, are amusing.' Nataly aptly answers, 'But the fits of ferocity?'

Meredith here uses twice his device of a novel within the novel: first *The Rajah in London*, where, through Indian eyes, we see the demented money-rush of London; then Colney's *The Rival Tongues*. In such inset-works Meredith always tries to treat his basic subject at a different level. *The Rajah* brings out the empire-theme by a direct view of the capitalist city through the eyes of an oppressed race. *The Rival Tongues* is a burlesque on the competition of imperialisms; it deals with the voyage of various savants of Britain, Germany, France, to Japan, where they hope to further their country's position by winning the Japanese to its language. This novel, which is being serialised, comes up every now and then in the narrative, to bring out the wider imperial rivalries that underlie Victor's progress to doom. Also it enables Meredith to poke fun at his critics, calling Colney's work pretentious and elaborate, and stressing the way in which the critics abuse it.

Attached to Victor is his clerk-messenger, Skepsey, an unpleasant little man, who is obsessed with the 'defence' of Britain and with physical fitness as a war-preparation. He boxes on all possible occasions—once even fighting and damaging his drunken wife. His wife dies soon after. 'He had buried his wife, he said: she [Nesta] feared, seeing his posture of the soaping of hands at one shoulder, that he was about to bewail it.' His harpings on the war-theme become monotonous, so often do they intrude on the story; and the war-theme is linked with the insistence that Germans and Americans are outdistancing Britain as an industrial and mercantile power.

Skepsey gets entangled with a girl of the Salvation Army; and Colney says, 'Look at your country, see where it shows its vitality. . . . You don't see elsewhere any vein in movement—movement.' (We have here a link with Jane the Jumper.)

There is little doubt, I think, that Meredith had been affected by General Booth's *In Darkest England* (1890). He could not but have been moved by the pictures there given of desperately hard-up women driven to prostitution and by the comparisons of the England of the lower-classes with Darkest Africa. 'The more the mind dwells upon the subject, the closer the analogy appears. . . . Talk about Dante's Hell, and all the horrors and cruelties of the torture-chamber of the lost.' This bitter picture of 'civilisation' is at the back of Meredith's mind in the concept of 'the rat-tides and the upper streams' of contemporary England in his novel. There seem even direct points of contact between the novel and Booth's book. Booth says, 'Go to Mudie's and ask for all the books [on social evil] that have been written on the subject, and you will be surprised to find how few they are.' In the novel, when Nesta says that women leading disorderly lives, but not men, are excluded from society, Sowerby replies, 'Oh! one reads that kind of arguments in books.' She answers, 'Oh! the worthy books, then. I would read them, if I could find them.' (That Meredith knew *In Darkest England* is proved by a letter of November 1890, which comments, 'General Booth's book has pricked attention to the case of the Poor, and the cry of the Poor is everywhere.')

In reading Colney's praise of the Salvation Army we must remember that in the Army's first days its soldiers did make a drive against vice which often led to them being stoned and beaten up, and that they admitted women to an entire equality in their ranks; and we are helped to understand such characters as Skepsey, or Colney himself, by realising how extraordinarily closely the Army was based on an imperialist conception. The missioners 'carried the war' into foreign countries, and planned their missions like war-campaigns; they held a naval demonstration in thirty-eight steamers in 1892 off Sweden; they talked all the while of Invasions; they were obsessed with the idea of 'Colonies', which they tried to set up at home but which they also wanted to carry out in a large way in the Colonies proper. They had a world-wide network for dealing with emigration and were closely connected with the exodus to the U.S.A. and Australasia. The Army almost got charge of an official Rhodesian scheme of settlement; and only the suspicions of the Australian Labour Party kept it from carrying out similar schemes in Australia.

S. H. Fitchett, a populariser of imperialism, wrote on *The Imperial Side of a Religious Movement*, and pointed out that Booth

> thought imperially in religion. . . . The structure of the Salvation Army is on this plan. It is not sectarian, but imperial. . . . One whole section of the Year Book is devoted to the subject of 'Emigration-Colonisation'—a composite phrase of ill sound, but of vast meaning. The section begins with a Credo: 'The Salvation Army believes that in the proper distribution of the peoples of the Empire lies the true source of strength.'
> It will be seen that in this Credo the imperial note is delightfully audible. General Booth was thinking, not of the sect, but of the Empire, and he undertook his emigration schemes not to serve the interests of his Army, but to advance the welfare of humanity in general and of the British Empire in particular.

Cecil Rhodes had the same ideas when he declared in 1895, 'If you do not want civil war, you must become imperialists.'

Oddly, Booth later carried out something of the work that the linguistic imperialists of Colney's novel attempted. In 1907 he visited the U.S.A. (as the linguists had done on their way) then went on to Japan, where he had an interview with the Emperor. Returning, he was made a Doctor of Laws at Oxford, and, paying another visit to the States, he discussed a University of Humanity with Theodore Roosevelt. After that, in Europe, he was received by four reigning monarchs. Colney's novel is generally less fantastic than Booth's triumphal progress, which has the same meaning as the movements of the savants—that of creating an imperial linkage and drawing Japan into Britain's orbit.*

---

* Booth in an appendix cites Carlyle's *Past and Present*, but says that he had never read it till a friend showed it to him and he was struck by the likenesses of his ideas to Carlyle's. His style can be very effective: 'Instead of Lord Mayor's Day why should we not have a Lazarus Day, in which the starving Out-of-works, and the sweated half-starved "in-works" of London should crawl in their tattered raggedness, with their gaunt, hungry faces, and emaciated wives and children, a Procession of Despair, through the main thoroughfares, past the massive houses and princely palaces of luxurious London.' (Meredith must have been moved by his Cab-Horses Charter—'every cab-horse has shelter at night, food, and work: why should the millions denied these blessings not claim the Charter?' For M. continually calls himself a cab-horse in his jogging toil.)

It must be admitted that there is a hectic, almost nightmarish note in this novel. This in part derives from the fact that Meredith has not wholly freed himself from his material, has not quite resolved his inner struggle in connection with the questions formulated by the book's theme. He is still himself to some extent torn by the confusions and illusions that dominate characters like Victor and Skepsey, and contaminate Colney and Dartrey. The harsh hectic note, however, also in part derives from the material itself, the mad world of Rhodes and Booth, in which as yet there is no fighting force born out of the common-folk and capable of politically changing the situation; and in the first chapters this note does bring about an extremely effective picture of London, rotting in the exhalations of mud and money, seen in strange penumbras of filthy gold. 'The English have hardened me outside,' he said as he wrote the novel 'and there has been a consequent process within.'

Meredith is confused; and yet, so deep is his creative impulse, in all essentials his criticisms of the epoch, his revelations of its inner struggle, stand authentic and moving. In his definition of Victor he gets at the root of the problem and the pattern of his drama remains securely true. It is only the edges that blur.

The style is at times strained and pompous, particularly in the first chapters. But even some of the phrases usually cited to show the cumbrous phraseology are not as bad as they sound. In the book's first sentence, Victor slips, not on orange-peel, but on 'some sly strip of slipperiness.' Yet, in reading the whole passage, we feel that the roundabout way of speaking derives from the fact that Victor can't see what has tripped him up: for him it is in fact 'some sly strip of slipperiness,' and the reason why we approach the fall through his reactions rather than through a more externalised picture is because of the terrific importance to him of this moment, which brings out his hidden fear, his deep fear and hate of the working-class.

No one can object to complaints about this book's tightness and stress; but the critics who raved about the diction quite ignored the meaning. One is forced to conclude that here as elsewhere complaints about the form have been used to evade the powerful issues raised by the content.

27

A Further Note on Politics, Maxse and Gissing

WE HAVE had continually to relate Meredith's thought and work to political events; but the world had changed so much since the 1850's and 1860's (in which *Sandra* and *Beauchamp* were rooted) that it would be as well to glance briefly at what had happened and was happening.

Emigration had speeded up. Between 1876 and 1909 some 4,147,007 persons emigrated; the peak period was 1881–90 when some 1,728,323 left England. And yet generally there was no fall in unemployment; indeed there was an increase from the mid-1870's.

The year 1873 had seen a crisis unprecedented in extent and duration. (*Beauchamp's Career* was published in 1874). The new industrialist countries intensified their competition, United Germany and the States freed from Slavery. England's world-monopoly had gone. With 1874, after a campaign against trade-unions led by the most reactionary employers, the workers began putting out their candidates for Parliament, backed by such radicals as Harrison, Beesly, Mill. The Liberals hurried to sap and placate the embryonic workers' movement with small reforms, and in 1886 two previous Labourites were under-secretaries in the Liberal Cabinet. There was no upsweep of socialist consciousness among the workers. The following passage states the negative aspects:

> The 80's and 90's of the last century represent the lowest point in the class-consciousness of the English workers: action, even in the shape of innocent Labour candidatures as in the middle 70's, was definitely abandoned; individual workers voted either Liberal or Tory, the very word 'revolution' elicited a scornful shrug of the shoulders, if not direct abuse, while drunkenness and betting became particularly prevalent. The last quarter of the last century stands out in the history of the Labour movement, not only of England, but of the whole world, as a period of unparalleled stagnation, decay, and complete absence of any vitality. [Rothstein.]

To this statement add the passages cited above from Engels. True, there were important movements in the lower depths, the strikes of the Dockers and the Matchgirls, the organisation of the unskilled or semi-skilled workers, which were in time to have important effects; but for the moment the picture was one of deadlock or obscure transition. One reason for the lack in militancy was the steady decline in prices after 1875, which went on till about 1905.*

We better understand *One of Our Conquerors* when we get this picture into our heads; and also better appreciate the profound integrity and penetrative powers of Meredith's intellect. Consider what was happening to other writers. On the one hand were the naturalists falling into pessimism, like Gissing; on the other hand were the aesthetes trying to keep some idea of beauty feebly glimmering by severing it from any active part in life. Hardy, though with naturalistic elements, was too big a man to be cut to the epithet; but he succumbed to pessimism and gave up writing novels when he was criticised sharply by the middle-class. Some young writers, like Shaw the Irishman or Wells of the English lower-middle-class, were struggling to escape the deadening dilemma of naturalism and arts-for-art's-sake; but they carried the marks of the 1880–1900 period into the following phase. Shaw in his wilful and individualistic note, which clashed with, and distorted, his original grasp of what capitalism was doing to men; Wells in his linkage with the new technological groups of imperialism and with the creed of big-business as the redeeming organiser. Meredith stood alone in striving to carry on the grand tradition of our Novel, realistically exploring the situation, creating types to embody social trends and conflicts, and preserving humanist faith in the outcome of the struggle—registering the shudder at the processes of capitalist alienation and yet building large-scale forms definitive of the key-patterns of the historical movement.

The Royal Commission on the Depression of Trade reported in 1886 that 'in every quarter of the world the perseverance and enterprise of the Germans are making themselves felt.' Britain's reply had been, not to develop her industries, but to speed up her grabbing of colonial areas. In 1860 she held 2,500,000 square miles with a population of some 145 millions; by 1880 she held eight million square miles with a population of some 268,000,000. Wars of imperialist expansion had gone on all the while. The Indians had been put down; campaigns were fought in Afghanistan and the N.W. frontiers; the Boer Republic was annexed; Egypt was occupied; Ireland was held down by force—with Gladstone's Coercion Act of 1881 as the worst example of oppression. This is the period of Seeley's exposition of the Expansion of England as a sort of somnambulist (and so innocent) land-grab and of Booth's religious Utopias of colonisation; of the revival of Chartered Companies in Africa

---

* To this very imperfect account add the thorough and detailed analysis given by Edward Thompson in his *William Morris* (1955).

and the swinging of sections of Radicalism and Labourism into imperialist championship.

It was also the period of rapidly developing monopoly: and this it is by which we define imperialism in its modern sense, as distinguished from previous cycles of imperial expansion. One example must suffice. J. and P. Coats, formed in 1890 with a capital of near £6 million, quickly absorbed other leading thread manufactures, and six years later had more than doubled its capital. Some large firms and a rival combine tried to fight back; they were crushed. The rival was brought under Coats' control, and Coats interlocked with the American Thread Company, the U.S.A. combine. At the same time they expanded with controls, or big shares, in large-scale organisations handling raw materials, collieries, French spinning firms, a Scottish and American combine dealing with linen thread, calico-printing, woolcombing, and so on.

With this powerful development in colonies and monopolies going on, the proletarian movement still lagged. But the fate of the Radical groups was settled: they had no future except to go over to the Liberals or to the emerging Labour movement.

Hyndman had founded the Democratic (soon the Social-Democratic) Federation in 1881; it began as a left-radical group. Even in demanding the nationalisation of the land, it wasn't going further than the extreme Radicals. But it attracted those who (as William Morris put it) considered that 'Radicalism is on the wrong line, so to say, and will never develop into anything more than Radicalism. . . . It is made for and by the middle classes and will always be under the control of the rich capitalists.' In a few years it declared for a Socialist policy.

But this was a splinter-group. The key-process was still in the Radical groups for a few years.

[As yet, 1886] the Socialists had not seriously tackled the problem of voicing and shaping in a Socialist fashion the rising doubts and discontents of the great mass of Radical working men. And under the conditions of the time the politically active and socially decisive sections of the working-class were Radicals to a man. It was obvious that here lay the line of advance for any revolutionary Socialist body that wished to become the unchallenged Party of the working men of England. To Engels alone belongs the credit for perceiving this vital fact. . . .

The working-class were taking a keener interest in politics. This was expressed in a rapid growth in the Radical organisations; of the 200 and more Radical working-men's clubs in London, for instance—which directly controlled at least one-fifth of the Liberal vote in the metropolis—no less than seventy-eight were formed in the four years from 1884. At the same time there was a profound process of differentiation under way in the Radical ranks. [A. Hutt.]

In February 1886 the anti-freetrade protectionists were meeting in Trafalgar Square; Hyndman organised a counter-meeting in the same place for the S.D.F., with the result of a wild march to Hyde Park down Pall Mall. Clubs were stoned and shops looted, and Hyndman, John Burns, with two others, were tried and acquitted. Engels noted that the majority of real workers were in the Square, that the S.D.F. audience was mixed (with much slum-proletariat, 'idlers, loafers, police-spies, and crooks'), and that the police were oddly absent till things were almost over. Hyndman's speech in the Square Engels described as 'rubbishy revolutionary bawling,' which 'discredited Socialism in the eyes of the workers.'

The bourgeoisie were very scared and thought the thing a real revolutionary uprising. Meredith at the time had a bad cold and wrote (February 11th) as if its blasts were the violent acts shaking the City:

> All is briny-foggy, mob-roar, smashing of windows, wrecking of shops, the head of the police in paralysis, the City prey to panic. My chalet shakes with sneezes, my nose is as the trombe of an elephant challenging his love.

There is no need here to deal with the complex details of the process by which the radical groups provided one of the most important bases of the new Labour Movement, or how the struggle for the socialist idea was waged in this development. But we may note one important moment, that of Bloody Sunday in 1887, when the police tried to keep the people out of Trafalgar Square. The wave of anger among the workers led to the first creation of a common platform between Radicals and Socialists of the working-class, the Law and Liberty League. An event very different in nature and results from Hyndman's pseudo-show of force.

What matters here is the significance of the Radicals between 1850 and 1890. In calling himself a Radical, Meredith (as we have seen) was affirming his solidarity with what was the only politically-conscious grouping of the working-class that had deep and wide roots in the country. Now that we have reviewed his main works we can reassert that as a writer he was truly Radical: that is, he truly defined the historical pattern of mass-experience as the bourgeois triumph terribly distorted the people and as new forces of resistance were built up, carrying on elements from Chartism and steadily looking towards the development of a separate working-class party with the power and knowledge capable of building a society of freedom and brotherhood.

Meredith's novels are the deep and rich expression of this critical phase of our national development.

It is a great pity that while Maxse stood in Meredith's mind as the Left Radical, Hyndman stood as the Socialist Leader. For Hyndman embodied everything most unreliably ambitious and superficially glib in the period of transition. He began company-promoting and directing, speculated on the Paris Bourse, worked as special correspondent for newspapers, and spent 1870 in Australia and the Pacific. At the age of about forty, near the end of the 1870's, he looked round for a political career. He approached Disraeli, then dissident elements of the Liberals and the Tories. Finding no encouragement he decided to form his own party on the basis of himself as an aristocratic tribune of the people. He now chanced to read *Capital* in a French edition and arranged to meet Marx, who found him 'self-satisfied, garrulous.' With the Federation he launched himself on his political career, which after many intrigues and twists landed him in the end in the imperialist camp in 1914. Engels saw him as 'a miserable carica-ture of Lassalle . . . an arch-Conservative and an extremely chauvinist-minded, although by no means stupid careerist . . . impatiently striving for a dictatorial rôle' (1883–5).

There could have been no one worse for educating Meredith in what socialism meant, or for helping him to see the alternative to imperialist war. In 1911 Hyndman wrote:

> Born into the stirring period when the armed uprising of oppressed Nation-alities was the most hopeful feature of European development, I have lived to see the day when pacificism has reached such a pitch among its more ardent votaries, that manful resistance to militarist aggression is resisted as a betrayal of democracy. This view is, to my mind, pusillanimous and contemptible.

And so he prepared to equate with the struggles of 'uprising or oppressed Nationalities' the imperialist clash between Britain and Germany, and called 'pacifist' and 'pusillanimous' the resistance, such as that led by Lenin, to the latter type of war.

But it was better, no doubt, that Meredith should get even a garbled version of Marxism through such works as Hyndman's *England for All* (1881) than none at all. And as his biographers tend to ignore as much as possible his relations with Hyndman, it is as well to note that they were fairly constant. After Seaforth and Italy, 'for years . . . I used to see Meredith frequently,' said Hyndman. He claims that he was first asked to write the review of *Beauchamp* for *The Pall Mall*, which he declined as being too close a friend and which Traill wrote. He took Traill down to Box Hill as Meredith was writing *The Egoist*. Meredith read out the Intro-duction, and noting Traill's expression, he said, 'You don't understand all that?' Traill stammered, 'I'll be damned if I do.'

> Many were my visits to Box Hill after my return from Australia, and we got to know Meredith's second wife very well: they staying with us in Devonshire Street and we with them down there. . . .

Many a pleasant day my wife and I passed with them at Box Hill, I taking long walks with Meredith during the day and playing duets with Mrs Meredith at night. The first of these walks I remember well was to Epsom and back, to see the Derby run . . . .

When I went in for my studies and writing on India, and afterwards on economic subjects and Socialism, I got much friendly encouragement from Meredith. . . .

He got Meredith to read Stepniak's *Underground Russia* for Chapman and Hall, and asked his advice about turning to journalism; Meredith advised against it. They met less after Hyndman gave up the Garrick Club (1874) and became more actively a politician; but Hyndman mentions one pleasant afternoon at Box Hill, interrupted by Haldane: Meredith at once began 'to strain for effect.'

It is probable then that Meredith read *The Summary of the Principles of Socialism*, which Hyndman wrote with William Morris in 1884; for we find his friend, Prof. York Powell, a fine progressive who used to visit Box Hill to read out Icelandic Sagas, writing to Hyndman about it:

I like it greatly, as the exposition, handy, clear and well-put, of your standpoint and the Marxists'. The poem also is excellent.

I wish we were safer from external trouble. Reaction will follow disaster inevitably if only for a time. The present parties without future, without talent, without faith are doomed of course. They are too ludicrous. I hope to see you here again and shall call sometime if I may on you at the 'House of Wisdom,' Queen Anne's Gate.

I sat up till two to finish your book, it interests me greatly to see the Marx position clearly put. [From Christ Church, Oxford, 1896.]

Behind *One of Our Conquerors* lies the financial crisis of 1890. The great banking firm of Barings, under Lord Revelstoke, tottered; and the Bank of England, with various City firms, had to raise £21,000,000 to save it. Hyndman's comment helps us to understand Victor Radnor's anti-Semitic fears: thus was smashed, he says, the City's satisfaction 'that a purely English house should stand so high at a time when German Jews held the leading place in nearly every great Continental city.' (Meredith could not have read Hyndman's book, *Commercial Crises of the 19th Century*, before writing his novel; for it appeared in 1892. It is typical of Hyndman's 'Marxism' that he declares in this book that limited companies are 'distinctly a step towards socialisation.')

We can bring out more concretely the points made above by looking at the development of two persons who had many elements akin to Meredith.

Maxse, we have noted, fell away from his Radicalism and joined the Tories. From the outset there had been various backward aspects in his thought. Thus, he resisted Woman Suffrage. His arguments are specious and merely veil a reactionary outlook. He says that the demand for women's votes comes only from the upper-class. The Women's Suffrage Society has put out the statement that women holding property are taxed and should therefore vote: this plea, he says, seeks to strengthen property and reaction. Also, if the women had votes, the clergy's influence would be politically enhanced, and that would be a disaster. He talks of the wilful ignorance of women, and points to what they have made of men. If women had the vote in France, he says, the Bourbons would be back. He then appeals to the 'physical weakness of women and their dependence on men.' Uneasily aware that all tyrants argue for their tyranny as preserving a natural order of things, he insists that here is a real case of a naturally-founded relation. He then attacks women (middle and upper class) for not being concerned with 'the struggling principles which determine the life of a nation,' such matters as universal education and the cause of the workers. Political government by women, he insists, conflicts with the ideal relations of men and women.

A man who could use such arguments in support of the workers' cause was clearly likely to revert to any reactionary position. And soon Maxse responded to the growth of imperialism by accepting the demagogic position that the Empire was necessary for Britain's standards of living and must be held at all costs—the unfaced contradiction being that the exploitation of the Empire and the raising of the levels of the colonial peoples could not go on side by side, and that the maintenance or bettering of the levels at home must also conflict with the needs of monopoly: so that the causes of the colonials and of the home-masses were indissolubly linked.

As the question of Home Rule for Ireland came up, he broke away from Left Radicalism. At the April meeting in 1887 of the Council of the National Liberation Federation which passed a resolution against the Government's coercive measures in Ireland as 'tyrannical, vindictive, unjust, unwise, unwanted and disastrous,' he was howled down for his protest. He declared that if Ireland was let go, the Empire would break up; Scotland and Wales would demand separation: anarchy and insurrection would be stimulated; and England would be ended as a great nation. When Parnell in 1881 appealed to Victor Hugo to make a declaration on behalf of the oppressed Irish, Maxse rushed over to Guernsey to persuade Hugo to keep quiet. He admitted the sufferings of the Irish peasantry through the 'pernicious land-system,' but argued that without the Coercion Bill there would have been chaos. Parnell, he says, doesn't want land-reform as it would quiet the demand for separation; and England must hold Ireland for imperial purposes or herself go down.

Finally by 1894 he had fallen in solidly behind Joe Chamberlain. His *Judas* attacked T. P. O'Connor for calling Chamberlain *Judas*, vilified Morley for his support of Home Rule, and sneered at 'men who aid the projects of the enemies of this country—the men who whine over the fall of Lobengula, but denounce British officers as murderers.'

It is hard to believe that this savage backwoodsman was the man who sacrificed a high political career out of disgust over the Crimean War and enthusiasm for the 'cause of the workers.'

Such a collapse enables us to assess the moral resistances of Meredith to the imperialist infection; and we can gauge his noble insights and deep faith in man by considering the failure of George Gissing, the writer who, with Hardy, could have carried on his work. Born in 1857, and dying in 1903, Gissing was the son of a pharmacist of Wakefield who died when his son was about thirteen. He managed to get a fairly good education, but he suffered dire poverty made more difficult by the adolescent idealism that led him into jail and marriage to a prostitute. This marriage set the key of his first two novels: *Workers of the Dawn*, 1880, which also deals with the escape from religious belief through the study of Darwin, Strauss, Schopenhauer, and *The Unclassed*, 1884, in which two girls are rescued from whoredom. In *The Unclassed*, and his next work, *Isabel Clarendon*, 1886, he had the aid of Meredith, as we have noted.*

Gissing's knowledge of life in the East End (or in Lambeth) and its infinite squalor, his ability to enter into the yearnings of sensitive workers and lower-middleclass youths for a better sort of life, enabled him to widen the scope and material of the English Novel. But though he tried at moments to link the lonely yearnings with the struggle of a whole class to raise itself out of the mire, he could not sustain faith in any real change of society. He fell back on pessimism and naturalism.

The Unclassed deals with two young men, poor and lost, one a shophand who has been a pharmacist, and one a school-master, who have literary ambitions. Waymark is torn between love of a prostitute (who in the end comes into money and has a social conscience) and a refined religiously-repressed young woman with a semi-mad mother; Casti

---

* Meredith's influence carries on throughout his work (especially obvious in novels like *A Life's Morning* and *Our Friend the Charlatan*), able to give him much, but not the final insight involving faith in man.

Of *A Life's Morning* Gissing says, 'Meredith tells me I am making a great mistake in leaving the low-life scenes; says I might take a foremost place in fiction if I pursued that.' So he next wrote *Demos*. His excitement at the contact appears in his letters to his sister. 'It is an excellent thing to have got his good word. His own novels are of the superlatively tough species.' He continued his admiration. 'It is incomprehensible that Meredith is so neglected. George Eliot never did such work, and Thackeray is shallow in comparison': (of the first Uniform Edition). Again, 'For the last thirty years he has been producing work unspeakably above the best of any living writer'—and yet few read him.

marries a wretched and morbid wench, a relative, who succeeds in destroying him. *Isabel Clarendon* deals with the struggles of religious doubt and the pangs of jealousy.

Here under Meredith's direct influence he makes an effort to control his pessimism. Waymark, for example, begins with a burning desire to strike a blow in defence of the oppressed masses; then he twists into a cynical disbelief in progress and a conviction that only art matters; but as he begins to solve his personal problems, he loses his abstract idea of art:

> 'Yes, I will write again,' Waymark returned, with a wrinkling of the brow. 'And it shall be something savage.'
> There was coming back upon him this old desire to battle with the rampant monsters of the world. After all, perhaps art for art's sake was not the final stage of his development. Art, yes; but combat at the same time. The two things were not so incompatible as some would have us think.

There speaks Meredith's voice. Waymark fuses his two earlier opposed attitudes on a higher level of unified purpose.

But Gissing could not sustain this position. *The Unclassed* draws attention to the warm sources of comradeship in the workers, the dead greedy life of the petty-bourgeoisie. But it seemed to Gissing that the latter were the dominant force in his England; and that what was called Progress or Democracy meant the furthering of their vile way of living, their dehumanised and philistine attitudes.*

And so he sank deeper and deeper into depression. *Demos, a Story of English Socialism*, 1886, is a bitter attack 'on working-class aims and capacities,' and reveals how he saw political action of any sort as building up the world of the cash-nexus in its drabbest form. The main character, Mutimer, is a socialist worker who comes into money, tries to run his mines with good working-conditions and earmark the profits for the socialist cause, and is forced by capitalist competition into acting like other masters. He weakens, then loses the estate when a new will is found, and becomes a 'professional agitator.' He founds a co-operative society, takes risks, finds a deficit, and is accused of fraud at a meeting, where in the

---

* *Isabel Clarendon* is much more mature in its characterisation, but lacks the definite theme of *The Unclassed*. Isabel Clarendon and Ada are well done: the decent but rather helpless woman who can't break from her class-values, and the girl who feels wholly up against things. There is much of Meredith in the picture of the egoist bourgeoisie; and his influence appears in the optimistic touch at the end (the suggestion that the two misfits, Ada and Kingcote, will come together—contrast with Ada, Constance of *Our Friend the Charlatan*, and with Kingcote, Peak of *Born in Exile*). Gissing makes a brave effort, but cannot give his misfit-rebels the basic social focus (of opposition to bourgeois values) that Meredith can. See Ch. 27 for a quotation showing the Meredithian anti-imperialist.

The sisters in *Thyrza* owe much to *Rhoda Fleming*; *Denzil Quarrier* re-uses the theme of *One of Our Conquerors* (a sort of slight Victor threatened with exposure on the eve of election), etc., etc.

tumult he gets knocked on the head. Into this story is woven the motive, continuous in Gissing's work, of the desire for a refined wife: Mutimer jilts his working-class girl Emma and marries the genteel Adela, who can't bear him.

Gissing was unable to see that his story had no bearings on the issue of socialism, since, even if its picture was accepted, it merely demonstrated that in capitalist society capitalist values were ubiquitous. But it shows the vicious-circle of depressed reasoning that went on in his mind, tying him to a class he detested, and making him feel more lost and useless with every deepening spasm of rage and revolt. And so he drifted from misery to misery, till in *Henry Ryecroft* (1903) he has blindly identified Democracy with the Bourgeoisie and decided that 'every instinct of my being is anti-democratic, and I dread to think what our England may become when Demos rules irresistibly. . . . To think that at one time I called myself a socialist, communist, anything you like of the revolutionary kind!' Correctly, he sees that this thing he calls Democracy is going to issue in a militarist tyranny, and he foresees the world-wars coming in a burst of barbarism. 'There has but to arise some Lord of Slaughter, and the nations will be tearing at each other's throats. . . .'*

Yet he had the experience and power to have carried on Meredith's work in terms of the middle-class and proletarians of the imperialist epoch; and he began with much of the will to do so. Even in his work as it stands he has given us an invaluable document of many aspects of late-Victorian society; a document not without its brighter and gentler colours as in *Thyrza* (1887). But the lack of anything resembling a strong and coherent socialist force in the proletariat convinced him in his formative years, in the decisive decade of his work, the 1880's, that the middle-class were the 'democratic movement. They set the tone in politics: they are debasing art and literature' (*Born in Exile*). 'Only a consuming fire could purify the places where they dwell.' He wanted that consuming fire, but

---

* *The Whirlpool* (1897) shows how close Gissing's material is often to Meredith's, and yet how lacking in the organisational centre provided for M. by his realisation of the nature of self-alienation. Rolfe weakly seeks culture; his wife Alma is the daughter of a failed financier who committed suicide. She is vain and selfish, subordinating all to her career as a violinist; and is at a millionaire's Wimbledon bungalow when he is murdered. Her guilty secret haunts her, and she is tortured with jealousy of her old friend Sibyl (who, she thinks, was the millionaire's mistress). She can't help trying to ruin Sibyl, is outwitted by a society procuress, and humiliated by Sybil; in the end she is driven to poison.

Rolfe wavers between liking and disliking the brutalising programme of Kipling, 'the voice of the reaction,' the revolt against 'the softness and sweetness of civilising,' while realising in it 'the tongue of Whitechapel blaring lust of life in the track of English guns.' He prophesies the awful consequences of our imperialism.

How close is all this to *One of Our Conquerors*, and how far. Compare also his *Denzil Quarrier*. (Cecily and Mrs Travis in *The Emancipated* repeats the motive of Nesta and Mrs Massett.)

lost any faith that the proletarian masses could kindle it. So, by a strange process of inverted logic (common in our own day) he ended by colouring the revolutionary forces with the discords and contradictions of the thing they opposed.

But what concerns us here is the revelation that his work gives of the terrible pressures bearing on any writer sensitive enough to feel what was happening to our people in these cruel years. By assessing Gissing's tormented failure we can better realise Meredith's resistances.* And similarly, by assessing the despairs that lay behind Hardy's abandonment of the novel, we can better realise Meredith's deep defiance. Even before the attacks on *Jude*, the Bishop of Wakefield publicly burned one of Hardy's novels—only because he could not burn the author, the author commented. 'If this sort of thing continues, no more novel-writing for me.' Meredith's attitude always was: If this sort of thing continues, it is necessary all the more to penetrate the egoist core of the evil thing.

---

* Hardy escaped the full hell of Gissing by returning to Wessex, to the countryside; but he remained as pessimistic. It is interesting to note how the split forms of naturalism and aestheticism both deny the moral basis of art, its social responsibility, in the name of Truth or Beauty. But in true art, as Keats knew, Beauty is Truth, Truth Beauty—i.e. both are aspects of the unified life-process.

Note too how often Gissing's formulations are like Hardy's; 'man, in some inconceivable way, may at his best moments represent a Principle darkly at strife with that which prevails throughout the world as known to us,' *Ryecroft*. '. . . till the farce is played out? There is something flattering to one's vanity in the careless playing with one's fate. . . . Freedom! What a joke the word must be to whoever is pulling the wires and making us poor puppets dance at his pleasure,' *The Unclassed*.

28

Ireland and the Enamoured Sage

A work that had better be treated here is *Celt and Saxon*, published in 1910. Its date is uncertain, and Meredith probably worked at it at the time of Gladstone's Irish Coercion Bill; but its tone has most affinities with *One of Our Conquerors* of all his other works. In its unfinished state it is hard to say how he was going to develop the story and the characters. There are many Irish actors in it; and it opens with the visit of young Patrick O'Donnell to Mr Adister in North Wales. Adister is a reserved hard man, whose daughter Adiante had been in love with Patrick's brother, Philip, but, thwarted by her father, has married a Danubian prince and is trying to sell her Welsh property so as to finance a *putsch* and regain her husband's principality. The O'Donnells are friends of Captain Con, a voluble rebellious Irishman, who has married Adister's sister, the incarnation of chilly middle-class respectability. There are also the Mattocks, who have inherited a fortune: John is a big landlord with political ambitions as a Liberal, and Jane, to get rid of her social conscience, has started a steam-laundry to employ poor women. Rockney, a journalist, is another Colney-Meredith character. 'He did not so much write articles upon the health of his mistress as deliver Orphic sentences.' He is defined as generally progressive and humane:

> Deeds of valour were noted by him, lapses of cowardice: how one man stood against a host for law and humanity, how crowds looked on at the beating of a woman, how a good fight was maintained in some sly ring between two of equal brawn: and manufacturers were warned of the consequences of their iniquities, Government was lashed for sleeping upon shaky ordinances, colonists were gibbeted for the maltreating of natives: the ring and fervour of the notes on daily events told of Rockney's hand upon the national heart— with a faint, an enforced, reluctant indication of our not being the men we were.

That coming-to-rest on a note of imperialist fear is what links the work with *One of Our Conquerors*. In making such statements as that we aren't the men we were, Meredith is reacting correctly enough to the stagnation of the 1880–1890's discussed in the last chapter; but he is also to some extent being taken in by the Colney-Rockney idiom.

Patrick O'Donnell and Jane Mattock seem the two characters whose development into something of social rebellion and decency he meant to show. What part Adiante was to play it is impossible to tell. In the novel as it stands, the positive aspects revolve round Captain Con.

The harpings on problems of war, defence, trade-competition with Germany and the U.S.A., panics of the middle-class, have the same note as *One of Our Conquerors*; even such a matter as horse-breeding is seen in relation to military needs. And Jane's Laundry suggests the work of the Salvation Army. The violent attack on John Bull, bourgeois England, which is linked with Rockney, has elements of the war-fear, though it goes further in denouncing the lack of uprightness and imagination. Yet it too returns to the war-theme. After beginning with promise:

> India, our lubber giant, had ceased to kick a leg, and Ireland, our fever-invalid, wore the aspect of an opiate slumber. The volcano we couch on was quiet. . . . Once more the personification of the country's prosperity [Bull] had returned to the humming state of roundness. Trade whipped him merrily, and he spun.

(India and Ireland are joined again as the examples of imperial oppression: 'Bad news from Ireland came upon ominous news from India.') But the diatribe sinks to the level of the falsifications of *Maud*, which equate Peace with Profits, with Decadence and Hypocrisy.

> Your Frenchmen are revolutionising, wagering on tentative politics; your Germans ploughing in philosophy, thumbing classics, composing music of a novel order: both are marching, evolutionising, learning how to kill. Ridiculous Germans! capricious Frenchmen! We want nothing new in musical composition and abstract speculation of an indecent mythology, or political contrivances and schemes of Government, and we do not want war. Peace is the Goddess we court for the hand of her daughter Peace, and we have won that jolly girl, and you are welcome to the marriage-feast: but avaunt new-fangled theories and howlings: old tunes, tried systems, for us, my worthy friends.

Meredith is there, of course, trying to burlesque Tory notions; but he shows a dangerous confusion as to their basis. He ignores the difference between the subjective attitudes of individual exploiters and the dynamic of the total system. When we recall the part played by the section claiming to be the most progressive of the bourgeois parties, the Liberals, in the secret preparations for the 1914 war, the stupidity of Rockney's formulations is manifest. He mistakes the fact that the young imperialism of Germany at this phase seems more vigorous and militaristic for a proof that Britain, hugging her vast gains of loot and oppression, is averse from war, whereas in the total system the two imperialisms are equally driving

towards 1914. Meredith is setting out the sort of stuff that he had heard
only too often in office and dining-room; but his method suggests more
of personal implication than is artistically valid for objective depiction.

Still, this book holds many caustic and rousing passages. Captain Con
is a splendid creation, with his restless poetic speech, his warm heart, his
relentless opposition to the oppressors:

> But will Philip O'Donnell tell me that Ireland should lie with England on
> the terms of a traveller obliged to take a bedfellow? Come! He hasn't an
> answer. Put it to him, and you pose him. But he'll not stir, though he admits
> the antagonism. And Ireland is asked to lie down with England on a couch
> blessed by the priest! Not she. Wipe out our grievances, and then we'll begin
> to talk of policy. Good Lord!—*love?* The love of Ireland for the conquering
> country will be the celebrated ceremony in the concluding chapter previous
> to the inauguration of the Millenium. Thousands of us are in a starving state
> at home this winter, Patrick. And it's not the fault of England?—landlordism's
> not? Who caused the ruin of all Ireland's industries? You might as well say it's
> the fault of the poor beggar to go limping and hungry because his cruel master
> struck him a blow to cripple him. We don't want half and half doctoring, and
> it's too late in the day for half and half oratory. We want freedom, and we'll
> have it, and we won't leave it to the Saxon to think about giving it.

Patrick, who wants to farm in quiet, admits that when he's in Ireland his
feelings and a part of his judgment take that line; Philip wants agreement
for the strengthening of Britain; Rockney is anxious (like Maxse) for
'sharp measures in repression, fair legislation in due course.'

Again Con exposes the nonsense of the talk about peace when in fact
the Empire is waging war all the while:

> 'There's hardly a day in the year when your scarlet mercenaries are not
> popping at niggers.'
> Rockney had the flick on the cheek at his manhood now, it might be hoped.
> 'Our what?' asked Mr Rumford, honestly unable to digest the opprobrious
> term.
> . 'Paid soldiery, hirelings, executioners, whom you call volunteers, by a
> charming euphemism, and send abroad to do the work of war while you pro-
> pound the doctrines of peace at home.'

Philip says the question is what we fight for:

> 'You fight to subjugate, to enslave,' said Con; 'that's what you're doing,
> and at the same time your journals are venting their fine irony at the Austrians
> and the Russians and the Prussians for tearing Poland to strips with their
> bloody beaks.'

Somebody says of him, 'He thinks and he feels, poor fellow,' and Rockney
adds, 'That shall pass for the epitaph of the living.' Con replies, 'Inscribe
it on the dungeon-door of tyranny.'

There is once more a tribute to the industrial North as having the best English, and a vague reference to the coming worker's movement:

> Nor did those worthy guides (popular books) to the pursuit of wealth contain any reminder of old John Mattock's dependence upon the conjoint labour of his fellows to push him to his elevation. As little did they think of foretelling a day, generations hence, when the empty heirs of his fellows might prefer a modest claim (confused in statement) against the estate he bequeathed. . . .

Whether Meredith could have resolved the conflicts stated in this work in an understanding of the full rôle of imperialism, we cannot say. Probably the fact that he did not finish it is evidence that he could not master the energy of insight needed for the task. But it is of interest that he at least began such a work.

A passage in Gissing's *Isabel Clarendon* (1886), written with the close aid and advice of Meredith, is worth citing here:

> There happened to be diplomatic difficulties with Russia, and Mr Lyster—much concerned by-the-by, with Indian commerce—was emphatic in denunciation of Slavonic craft and treachery, himself taking the disinterested honesty, of principle in politics.
>
> 'We shall have to give these fellows a licking yet,' remarked Colonel Stratton, with confidence inspired by professional feeling.
>
> 'I should think so, indeed!' put in Frank Stratton, the eldest son. 'And the sooner the better.'
>
> 'What I want to know,' exclaimed Mr Lyster, 'is whether England is a civilising power or not. If so, it is our duty to go to war; if not, of course, we may prepare to go to the——'
>
> 'Don't hesitate, Mr Lyster,' said Mrs Stratton good-naturedly, 'I'm sure we all agree with you.'
>
> 'Civilisation,' proceeded the politician, when the laugh had subsided: 'that is what England represents, and civilisation rests upon a military basis, if it has any basis at all. It's all very well to talk about the humanity of arbitration and fudge of that kind; it only postpones the evil day. Our position is the result of good hard fighting, and mere talking won't keep it up; we must fight again. Too long a peace means loss of prestige, and loss of prestige means the encroachment of barbarians, who are only to be kept in order by repeated thrashings. They forget that we are a civilising power; unfortunately we are too much disposed to forget it ourselves.'
>
> 'The mistake is,' remarked Frank Stratton, 'to treat with those fellows at all. Why don't we take a map of Asia and draw a line just where it seems good to us, and bid the dogs keep on their own side of it? Of course they wouldn't do so—and then we lick 'em!'
>
> His mother looked at him with pride.
>
> 'I respect our constitution,' pursued Mr Lyster . . .; 'but I've often thought it wouldn't be amiss if we could have a British Bizmarch'—so he pronounced the name. 'A Bizmarch would make short work with Radical humbug. He would keep up patriotism; he would remind us of our duties as a civilising power.'
>
> 'And he'd establish conscription,' remarked Frank. . . .

We can certainly hear something of Meredith's voice here—and read some sixty years after its publication the passage does remarkably illustrate the continuity of imperialist policies.

In January 1892 there came out a reprint of *Modern Love* with some extra poems, of which *The Sage Enamoured and The Honest Lady* was the most important. 'A piece to provoke our Social Conservatives,' he called *The Sage*; and said, 'You will find it, when you run in the vein of the meaning, a poem with more sustenance. . . .' By March, 'it has caused everybody to take up the old cudgel "Obscurity" for my incorrigible nob. However, on we go.' *The Sage*, based on his relations with Hilda de Longueil, is in fact a difficult poem in that it must be read very carefully; but its meaning is quite clear.

A gracious and lovely girl attracts the Sage even more than he could have imagined in hot youth. She, to cure him, tells him her life-story: a romanticised version of two lovers mating, driven by outraged society, pledged more deeply by the threat of being parted. She'd like to tell the simple truth, but the habit of prettifying reality is too much for her. He listens in silence, and she thinks him the condemning male. But after a while she hears the hollowness of her own words echoing in his critical silence, and speaks the plain facts. A living contact springs up, and he gratefully recognises in her breaking-down of 'modesty' for his enlightenment an act more delicate than any rosebud of maiden innocence.

Now he speaks. Passionate love, a force that, garnered, would serve for a lifetime, has been recklessly reduced to a few 'not quintessential drops,' and thrown off by the girl and her lover. Not that he holds any brief for puritanism that attacks only the woman: such sexual experience is neither devilish nor divine. Either conception equally perpetuates the split in the spirit, and accepts as eternal:

> The chasm between our passions and our wits,

between mind and sense. We must see the evolutionary ascent of man,

> the blind progressive worm
> That moves by touch, and thrust of linking rings,

developing an ever more complex grasp of time and responsibility for the future. The notion of pleasure changes with each stage, till man realises a higher joy burning and directing the present. At this level many old desires fall away and are superseded. Sex-passion is, however, unique, since it is needed at all stages; it raises issues that can be solved only when men and women live in absolute equality.

Yes, he is talking in abstractions; but his generalising of the subject

shows more, not less, sympathy with the girl. Till equality is won, a deep
tenderness of understanding aid is the

> *step to right the loaded scales*
> *Displaying women shamefully outweighed,*

and this tenderness is not the old chivalric attitude based on the division
of the sexes.

The girl is now released from her prison of isolation. She feels in step
with her fellows, taught to hear the heartbeat of the world. No more she
shrinks and slurs over the facts of experience. She accepts her past as a
phase in her movement towards this awakened sense of comradeship and
of the laws of human development. She is at peace with herself and feels
a new relation to the masses:

> *The peace, the homely skies, the springs that welled:*
> *Love, the large love that folds the multitude.*

Her reward is the quickened and deepened concept of beauty. The struggle
against the forces of division still goes on, but now she has a new sense
of truth and fraternity to arm her. The conversation ends with a quiet
realisation of a common purpose:

> *He needed her quick thrust*
> *For renovated earth: on earth she gazed,*
> *With humble aim to foot beside the wise.*
> *Lo, where the eyelashes of night are raised*
> *Yet lowly over morning's pure grey eyes.*

In January he read Hardy's *Tess* and commented on Maupassant's
wretched end. 'The crash with Maupassant comes from avenging Nature
—heredity helping. A moderated youth would have given him life. In
reality, for a man of his powers, he produced little. And already he had
begun to work upon himself. I regret. He was one of the few living whom
I read with satisfaction on the handling of his matter.'

'Work in upon himself.' Meredith's aim always was to work outwards
from his intense inner struggle till he found the social basis which gave
breadth and centrality to his figures.

He now could not stand for long. In April, St Andrews conferred its
LL.D., but he was too ill to go and receive it personally; and he wrote to
Sandys, who was expected for a Sunday visit, 'I never hear a laugh. A
club of parsons with one carnal Curate among them would exhibit ten
times the levity.' In June he was operated on by Buckston Browne for
stone (and again in December 1895, and March 1899). Browne remarked
the alarming precipitancy with which in his ataxic condition he threw

himself into a chair, and that however ill he was, 'his welcome was always cheery and often rollicking, and I do not remember a single frown.'

In October his son Will married a Daisy, 'an extremely sweet good girl' (said Mrs Leslie Stephen), 'rational, but of no disturbing intellect' (said Meredith). Will had some talent as an artist, and gave up engineering for publishing, going into Constable's as a director.

The same month saw a new book of poems, *The Empty Purse*, which included the much-bewildering *Jane*.

There are here nature-poems of his best vintage: with the stoical faith tempered by the springing sense of renewal and of the living edge of contact between man and nature in the productive act—*Tardy Spring*, *Night of Frost in May* (which looks back to old Copsham days and hears its nightingales as the indomitable force that breaks through into beauty), *Wind on the Lyre* on the moment of singing and exalting union:

> *The breast of us a sounded shell,*
> *The blood of us a lighted dew.*

There are two Odes, one in which he conjures up *Youth in Memory*, hails the young, and sets out the ceaseless struggle for progress, and one in which he restates the thesis of his lecture on Comedy. *The Comic Spirit* dispels irrational terrors: where the peasant heard witches aloft,

> *He, from the rub of minds dispersing fears,*
> *Hears migrants marshalling their midnight train;*
> *Homeliest order in black sky appears. . . .*
> *A cry that is our common voice; the note*
> *Of fellowship upon a loftier plane. . . .*
> *. . . sweet singing keynote of the wise,*
> *Laughter—the joy of Reason seeing fade*
> *Obstruction into Earth's renewing beds,*
> *Beneath the stroke of her good servant's blade.*

These are excellent phrases, but nothing substantially is added to the lecture.

On the debit side there are poems which reflect the theme of war-defence found in *One of Our Conquerors*. But the long poem that gives its name to the book keeps to the social issues of decay and renewal. It is addressed to a rich young man who has squandered his money and who now in poverty has a chance to see the truth of life and make himself a human being. It describes his early years, and the way they were perverted by class-values which told him of his superiority to the common-man because of his money-power. Thus blinded, the young man went his bestial way with parasites and slaves; but now, bankrupt, he is released from the spell of the sorcerer gold, 'clean rescued from beast,' and the

poet appeals to him to recognise his chance of freedom. The lesson of
Earth is set out. 'Go into thyself, strike Earth.' Then come up, Antaeus-
like, out of earth's embrace into a realisation of the lies that enfolded,
throw off all cynicism about men and women:

> May brain democratic be king of the host!
> Less then shall the volumes of History tell
> Of the step in progression, the slip in relapse. . . .

He is told to find his place in the struggle for progress. He will be able to
distinguish the difference between demagogy and truth by asking, 'Is it
accepted of Song?' For Song is the touchstone of sanity and active reason,
of true Measure, 'It embraces or mortally bites.' The means that genuinely
lead to the extension of brotherhood and the equality of the sexes ring
harmoniously with the Song.

The moral is a sense of responsibility towards the future:

> Keep the young generation in hail,
> And bequeath them no tumbled house.

And an understanding of all that is implied by the love of earth.

> Who gives is the man-loving Nazarene,
> The martyrs, the poets, the corn and the vines.
> By my faith in the head, she has wonders in loom;
> Revelations, delights. I can hear a faint crow
> By the cock of fresh mornings, far, far, yet distinct;
> As down the new shafting of mines,
> A cry of the metally gnome.
> When our Earth we have seen, and have linked
> With the home of the Spirit to whom we unfold,
> Imprisoned humanity open will throw
> Its fortress gates, and the rivers of gold
> For the congregate friendliness flow.

For union with earth is union with men, and 'new ground, new skies
to appeal,' and the ending of the idealist inversion of reality with its split
of body and soul, 'a mind and a body no longer inversed.'

> The sense of large charity over the land,
> Earth's wheaten of wisdom dispensed in the rough,
> And a bell ringing thanks. . . .

These long didactic poems of Meredith are not very successful; they
are tough fare, with much grit in the home-ground wholemeal. But
though they cannot be called important poems, they are good reading.
We feel the very wrestling of Meredith's mind as he strives to grasp and
define his thoughts. The difficulties are on the surface. And every now and
then the lines kindle and flash into true song. He himself admitted that

The Empty Purse failed as a poem, 'but I had to convey certain ideas that could not find place in my novels.'

Watts wanted to paint him and give the portrait to the nation. Meredith declared himself sceptical about posterity's interest in his 'grizzled mug'— a touch of bitterness. But he surrendered. Mrs Watts found him attractive, 'better than his work. He gives himself out more *simply* and with as fine a touch when he talks.' This year Sergeant also made two drawings of him. And in October, while busy at novel-writing, he had to waste time 'about an American investment that has gone crazy.'

Deafness was badly on him by 1894, and he had ulcerated eyelids. Morley, after not having seen him for some time, was shocked at the change. 'His disabilities in movement were painful, and he is very deaf. . . . Less turbulent and strained than he used to be.' Blunt, whose sonnets *Esther* Meredith had admired when they came out in 1892, visited him about the same time; and in August came a young French writer, Marcel Schwab, with a son of Daudet. Eight months later Henry James brought along Daudet himself and wife. Madame Daudet wrote a journalistic account, admiring Mrs Palmer's curl-crowned head as she graciously inclined to Meredith in her Piccadilly mansion, and explaining to the French public that Meredith was the English Mallarmé—presumably because both poets had been accused of obscurity, since in many respects two more unlike poets would be hard to find. Meredith saw the Daudets off at Victoria; and he was almost pulled off his legs, his fingers and Daudet's entwined in a rheumatic knot.

June 1894 had also seen the publication of his novel *Lord Ormont and his Aminta*. Next month Marie was married; and Meredith went on with his last novel, *The Amazing Marriage*, which he had begun some fifteen years earlier, with Stevenson (Woodseer) as one of the chief characters. In 1893 he had picked it up again, and now despite his disabilities he was hard at work on it, driving 'two dozen characters as two, making all run together.' This year too he broke with Chapman and Hall, as he found that they had been putting out *Diana* two years after their contract expired. He wrote in regretful anger to his old friend, Fred Chapman, 'It is a pitiful tale you reveal. I will not recall incidents, which pluck from you the mask you choose to wear in decency.'

In November 1894 he became a grandfather.

In July 1895 Clodd brought the Omar Khayyám Club to Burford Bridge. Meredith came at the close of dinner and made a speech. Hardy and Gissing were both present. In November *The Amazing Marriage* was published after serialisation (condensed) in *Scribner's*.

29

Aminta is Not the Lord's

LORD ORMONT is a slight work, as though Meredith is taking breath between the hectic fury of *One of Our Conquerors* and the lyrical intensity of his last novel. He worked eight hours a day to complete it in 1893, when it was serialised in *The Pall Mall*.

Aminta and Matey Weyburn have known one another in schooldays when Lord Ormont was a hero for the youngsters. He turns up later to work on the Lord's library-catalogue and finds her in the house. She has been married in the Embassy at Madrid to Ormont, who, irritated at not getting what he considers the treatment due to his army-merits, has become averse from English society. His desire for seclusion, which leads him to let the family-estates, gives the effect that Aminta is not really his wife; and she is pestered by attempts at seduction, particularly by one Morsfield.

Ormot's sister Lady Charlotte is one of those who refuse to believe that Aminta is married. Finally, after Aminta has been humiliated, Ormont sets himself to show 'society' that she is really his wife; but she has fallen out of the spell of his army-glamour. She discovers her true mate in Matey; and they go off to live unmarried in charge of an advanced school in Switzerland. Ormont finds out too late what he has lost.

The basic theme is thus once again the failure of a man tied to the world of the ruling-class, even when in a state of pseudo-revolt (as Victor Radnor also was), to move at the right pace of growth if he is to learn the reality of love, of fellowship. The presentation is mild, and the tragic element is not stressed, though it is gently brought out in the scene between Ormont and his sister when he learns that Aminta is gone. But Ormont belongs to the series that stretches from Richard Feverel to Lord Fleetwood.

Aminta, however, is no Lucy to wilt into brainfever, no Diana to be beaten by the money-forces, no Clara to meet guile with guile. When she is disillusioned of her Lord, she slips off with her young lover to find a place in the world of work. The opposition of the world of work, where personal integration is possible, to the world of privilege and wealth, where class-values distort the human essence, is made explicit in this book, and that is what gives it its slight place in the Meredithian gallery.

Ormont is based in part on the Earl of Peterborough, whom Macaulay called the last of the Knights Errant. The Earl was disgruntled at his treatment after success as a general; and he lived with the singer Anastasia Robinson, whom he 're-married' after falling ill in 1735—dying in a few months. But he is fused in the novel with the Earl of Cardigan, who led the light brigade at Balaclava and who was a keen duellist. Cardigan in his later years posed as an ignored hero. He married his second wife Adelina at Gibraltar; and this Adelina, like Aminta, excited comment when riding in Hyde Park at her husband's side.

Ormont needs war. His sister says:

> 'Ormont has no chance of employment unless there's a European war. They can't overlook him in case of war. He'll have to pray for that.'
> 'Let us hope we shan't get it' [says Matey].
> 'My wish; but I have to think of my brother. . . . All he wants is to serve his country. If you won't have war, give him Gibraltar. . . .'

Thus Meredith brings out the cold callousness of the ruling-class, who, like Squire Belsham, take a family-view of the nation. Ormont himself, who wants only 'to serve his country,' coldly considers serving a foreign power.

> Angry evaporations had left a residuum of solid scorn for these 'English' who rewarded soldierly services as though it were a question of damaged packages of calico. He threatened to take the first offer of a foreign State 'not in insurrection.'

Later he advises Matey to take to foreign service. 'A young man of military tastes should take service abroad.' (We are reminded how Wilfrid's entering the Austrian army is made in *Sandra-Vittoria* to serve as the emblem of a total lapse from the responsibilities of love and truth; and how in *Celt and Saxon* Adister strongly advises Patrick to take a lot of Irishmen in a kind of private enterprise of filibustering imperialism into South America.)

Matey and Aminta in their adolescence admired Ormont's exploits in India; and an argument at that time brings out the first statement of the contradiction inside such gallantry:

> 'We are a civilian people; we pride ourselves on having civilian methods.'
> 'How can we be if we have won India with guns and swords?'
> 'But that splendid jewel for England's tiara won . . ., we are bound to sheathe the sword and govern by the Book of the Law.'
> 'But if they won't have the Book of the Law!'
> 'They know the power behind it.'
> 'Not if we knock nothing harder than the Book of the Law upon their skulls.'

Matey and Aminta grow up; and part of their growing pains is the discovery that the hero Ormont remains adolescent.

> Lord Ormont was discoursing with racey eloquence of our hold on India: his views in which respect were those of Cuper's boys.

A Day of trial, a Devil of a Day, is come upon England. 'My lord connected our day of trial with India.' He sets to work drawing up his plan of defence and does nothing about it.

He knows the physical woman, and nothing else of womanhood, 'like many of his class and kind.' And this oppressive insensibility, which destroys him in the end, is linked directly with England's fate—the fate of his class. His sister thinks after the crash:

> He said of his country: *That Lout comes to a knowledge of his wants too late.* True, old England is always louting to the rear. . . . But what if the words were flung at him in turn? [Meredith's italics.]

And shortly after we find 'diatribes against the burgess English and the pulp they have made of a glorious nation.' The failure of consciousness to keep time with events, which is one aspect of the split between theory and practice, of egoism, is thus generalised from Ormont to his class; and the England of his class, doomed, is explicitly defined as the England distorted and dehumanised by the bourgeoisie. Ormont's little peevish rebellion has only intensified his class-position, his inner discord, just as Victor's defiance of the ruling marriage-conventions works out as making him supremely an exemplar of the pervasive class-frustration.

Lady Charlotte is well-done as one of Meredith's arrogant *grandes dames* (such as Lady Caroline Maxse in real life), who is so sure of herself that she can be roughly kind, with no nonsense about her: 'large-heartedly charitable to the classes flowing in oily orderliness round about below it [her class]—if they did so flow.' When told that her tenants are restive and have their case, she answers, 'But we've got the soil, and we'll make a fight for it.'

Critics with their usual blank inability to enter into Meredith's political intentions have asked what there is about Ormont to alienate and disillusion Aminta. Like all the characters of this slight book, she is sketchily developed; and her growth has to be inferred from the kind of thing I have cited above. Matey too comes out as a pleasant unassuming young man, who only gains strength of character as he detaches himself from the illusions that have bound him to Ormont and his world. This detachment includes a scorn of that world's notions of honour: he feels no compunction about hiding from Morsfield in a pub and has no intention of fighting duels. As if to set himself in full contrast with Victor Radnor and his anti-Semitism, Matey protects a young Jew at school, and in fact owes his job to the good offices of his friend's father. (Lady C. asks him when she first meets him if he is a Jew. He says no. She asks if he'd be ashamed to tell the truth if he was. He says no.)

What Matey wakes up from is the delusion that men like Ormont are heroes and that they have any independent contribution to make to England's development.

> In the England of that period original or unknown ideas were a smoking brimstone to the nose, dread Arabian afrites, invisible in the air, jumping out of vases, armed for the slaughter of the venerable and the cherished, the ivy clad and celestially haloed. . . . A step with them, and we were on the Plegethon waters of the French Revolution. For a publication of simple ideas men were seized, tried at law, mulcted, imprisoned, and not pardoned after the term of punishment; their names were branded: the horned elect butted at them; he who alluded to them offered them up, wittingly or not, to be damned in the nose of the public for an execrable brimstone stench.

> Lord Ormont broke through his shouts or grunts at Aminta's reports of the secretary's *ideas* on various topics, particularly the proposal that the lords of the land should head the land in a revolutionary effort to make law of his crazy, top-heavy notions, with a self-satisfied ejaculation: 'He has not favoured *me* with any of these puffballs of his. . . .'

> This idea, proposing it to our aristocracy to take up his other ideas, or reject them on pain of the forfeiture of their cast and leadership with the generations to follow, and a total displacing of them in history by certain notorious, frowsy, scrubby pamphleteers and publishers, Lord Ormont thought amazingly comical. English nobles heading the weavers, cobblers and barners of England!

So Matey turns to his co-educational school, which includes pupils from many countries—a kind of Utopian world in miniature, of international brotherhood and equality between the sexes. An image drawn from Meredith's memories of Neuwied.

Ormont and his war-roots, the State that is founded in the Ormonts, fade out in the minds of the lovers. 'It's not scaling Alps or commanding armies.' 'It may be better,' said Aminta and thought as she spoke. Then as the idea matures, she breaks her class-bonds and reaches out to common humanity.

> Aminta ceased to recline in her carriage. An idea that an indolent posture fostered vapourish meditations counselled her sitting rigidly upright and interestedly observing the cottages and merry gutter-children along the squat straight streets of a London suburb. Her dominant ultimate thought was, 'I, too, can work!'

And so, in due time, she breaks through:

> 'Once I did desire that station—had an idea it was glorious. I despise it: or rather the woman who had the desire.'

'But the step down is into the working world.'
'I have the means to live humbly. I want no more, except to be taught to work. . . .'
'You have faith in the power of resistance of the woman living alone. . . .'
'It means breathing to me.'

Here then is a women who has won the freedom that Diana could not gain, and she can therefore turn to her lover in equality.

All the ingredients of Meredith's thought and expression are thus present in this novel; but they are not drawn together in the intense focus which he needs to define the shattering impact of capitalist self-alienation. The book is consequently slight, but we can all the more easily analyse the structure, the motivation for clues to Meredith's method.

The Press made its usual comments, but good-humouredly. *The Saturday Review* said that you 'could scrawl yourself, if bitten by the asp of metaphor, loving the wrong word in the improper place,' English as difficult. *The Athenaeum* liked Ormont and his sister, and saw Meredith as 'a rather flippant Zeus, hurling thunderbolts with his right hand and letting off squibs with the left.' *The Bookman* commented on Meredith's intellectual agility. Henry James in a letter denounced the work: 'Not a difficulty met, not a figure presented, not a scene constituted—not a dim shadow condensing once into audible and visible reality.' *Lord Ormont*, as I stated above, has a slight texture; the effects gained do not warrant the length taken to gain them; but what James is raging against is the way the difficulties *are* met, the figures presented, the scenes constituted, with a degree of social insight that he finds intolerable.

Meredith himself felt antipathetic to James's introspective manner. *The American Scene* he found 'not a revisiting of America, but a tour of James's own inside'—with a few odd glimpses into the outer world from 'a little window in his anatomy.'

The theme of the old man and the young girl keeps cropping up in these years. We have just seen Aminta unsuccessfully married with old Ormont and in the previous chapter we considered the poem of the Enamoured Sage. Directly or indirectly the problem of youth and age often touches the later poems. Meredith's unfinished play *The Sentimentalists* was to deal with the young widow of a thinker. She had been married two months; and two years later, wooed by a younger man, Arden, she struggles to stay true to the memory of her marriage. An unfinished novel, *The Gentleman of Fifty and the Damsel of Nineteen*, written in alternative chapters narrated by He and She, has the theme of an oldish man long faithful to his love for a Frenchwoman who has married a rake (the Renée theme); he now finds himself drawn to a young girl who falls in love with him, but tries to hide it, while his Frenchwoman is becoming available again as a widow. This is a trivial work, which, in the extant chapters, shows no signs of a Meredithian conflict. Perhaps the theme was so close to his emotions that it baffled his efforts to link it with any deep social meaning and therefore became unmalleable. As it stands, it has an amusing opening—the man discovers the rector discoursing up to his waist in a stream and soon joined by his wife: the pair have fallen out of a boat, but the explanation is not at first sight clear. The daughter, the She of the tale, comes out and gives the laugh that the man, the He, has politely stifled. This laugh, it seems, is what links them.

After his wife's death the education of the daughter, Mariette, was Meredith's main care. He took much trouble to find a small school or governess. One woman he interviewed told Alice B., 'I am rather frightened at the many things he will not permit his daughter to do.' He wouldn't let the girl travel the short distance from Box Hill to Ewell without a maid. But otherwise he was an indulgent father—though it is perhaps something of a criticism of him that Mariette grew up such a shallow creature and his son Will had no particular purpose in life.

30

The Amazing Marriage

MEREDITH HAD begun this novel some seventeen years before; for in April 1879 he told Stevenson he was about a quarter through it. He may have looked at it again in the early '80's; but he took it up seriously again only in 1893; and after being serialised in *Scribner's*, it was published in November 1895—a second edition being printed in the following January. After discovering what he considered Chapman's bad faith, he had changed his publishers again, going to Constable; and there were comments on his book's having met 'a somewhat wintry welcome' from Chapman and Hall and then gaining an offer of a thousand pounds down, plus royalties, from another firm. He replied temperately that a wintry welcome was excuse enough.

The Amazing Marriage has a long and charming prologue in the tale of the elopement of a married Countess with an old man, the Old Buccaneer. They live happily in Switzerland; and as she soon becomes a widow, he marries her. They have two children, a son who enters the British army, and a daughter Carinthia who lives in the mountains with her parents till they die within a few days of one another.

The son, Chillon, comes to fetch his sister away, and they walk across the mountains. On the way they meet Woodseer, a penniless nature-lover (based on Stevenson). He has had a fall and Carinthia talks with him. Lord Fleetwood, a very rich aristocrat in an unstable state of emotional revolt against his world, also comes on Woodseer and sees in his notebook phrases scribbled about Carinthia. Deeply stirred—for he too has his nature-cult and feels in Woodseer's descriptions a girl in whom he can meet his own rebel-self securely free—he chances to encounter Carinthia at the resort to which she and her brother have gone. Carried outside himself, he proposes marriage that night in the ballroom, though he has exchanged only a few words with the girl. She who lives in her own wild dream of herself sees in him the reflection of her resolute integrity, and accepts. He departs the next morning.

Her brother and her uncle agree to push her into the marriage, which Fleetwood repents in a recoil against all entanglements; also he desires Henrietta, who loves Chillon. The latter knows he is sacrificing his sister to a man who doesn't want her; but he is hard-up and uses Carinthia's engagement to further his own marriage-plans. The uncle, with whom he is in a business-partnership to make gunpowder, is a miserly old man, who simply wants to get rid of any encumbrance. So Carinthia is sacrificed, not being told of Fleetwood's insulting message.

She marries him, and he drives straight off with her to a boxing match in which a man of his is fighting. Then he deposits her at an inn, leaves her coldly, and returns in the night up a ladder to lie with her.

She, at a loss to understand, goes off with Madge, the girlfriend of the boxer, who, careless of her reputation, has been trying to save the latter from booze. She stays at the greengrocery of Madge's family, and gradually realises her desertion. But she is with child and wants to tell Fleetwood. Now begin a series of clashes and misunderstandings, as she frankly seeks to meet him and he twists every impulse of decency in himself into a fresh basis of antagonism to her. His pride-rotted soul wants to surrender, as he feels afresh the strange integrity of her being; but he can never do it when the time comes. The marriage becomes a cruel duel, in which she learns to harden herself and to meet an unsuspected world of oppressive hatreds.

At last she goes to Fleetwood's estate in Wales, where he has a mine, and there bears his son, whom he does not repudiate. She is loved by the miners, with whom she feels an immediate kinship. Fleetwood has to come down to deal with a strike, which he treats arrogantly. She goes off to a country-house of his nearer London, escorted by a Welshman Owain, a small mine-owner who lives on man-to-man terms with his workers, and who has been linked with her by his dying wife.

Fleetwood from time to time has taken up with Woodseer in a tormented effort to find some basis of truth in life; but he always drives himself deeper in the net of revenge and bitterness. At last, however, he is abruptly sobered by the suicide of one of his gambling set. He has been toying with Catholicism as his failure to find a steady root in 'nature' through Woodseer is forced home on him; and now he has a sharp recoil of self-disgust. He is able to go to Carinthia and express repentance. But she has now finally learned to stand on her own feet—or at least to break any sense of dependence on her husband. She will have nothing to do with him. Her balance is, however, still imperfect; her fiasco as a wife has thrown her passionately back on union with her brother.

He meanwhile has gone financially from bad to worse, changing his military allegiance as Meredith's upper-class 'patriots' are always ready to do at the pressure of the cash-nexus. He tries to sell himself into the Austrian service, and then engages in the Carlist expedition into Spain.

Carinthia, needing somebody or something beyond herself to which she can attach her energies, obstinately fights to go with him as a nurse. (Here she is close to the tenacious Sandra—and also to Merthyr's sister.) Finally she does go. Fleetwood enters a monastery as a monk, and soon after dies. Carinthia, returning from Spain, marries the Welshman Owain and finds her place in common life.

This novel resumes the themes with which Meredith began in *Feverel*: the breakdown of the bourgeois man who reluctantly is forced to realise something of love and its obligations, but who does so by a distorted process that ensures his failure. Fleetwood is too late, like his predecessors. He is the most powerful study of tragic element of self-alienation in the class-world that Meredith made, outside *The Egoist*; and in this fact alone we see that there was no flagging of Meredith's creative powers right to the end.

Fleetwood is a profoundly-realised creature of evil, for whom there can be in the end only the choice of total renunciation of life or collapse into sheer malice and hate. He wants to break any integrity he meets; and under his gust of desire for Carinthia in the mountains there is the smothered wish to possess her in order to wreck the spirit of freedom in her. That is why he is compelled to the declaration of marriage, and why, in his involved fear and desire, he fights to arrest their union. He no sooner gets to know Woodseer and recognises in him some free element that defies his class-power than he wants to see him tainted, to bring him down into a gambling mania and then to enmesh him with the corrupted Livia, one of Meredith's women of evil fascination in the line of Mrs Lovell. He has desired Henrietta, and to free himself from her image he plots to prove her polluted like the others.

He constructs in his mind the concept of the world as a madhouse, in which only a sense of bitter irony and contempt saves a man from being overcome by the manias of the others. Prove yourself as mad as the others, but do it deliberately, standing above and outside yourself.

> Fun, at any cost, is the one object worth a shot in such a world. And the fun is not to stop. If it does, we are likely to be got hold of, and lugged away to the altar—the terminus. That foul disaster has happened, through our having temporarily yielded to a fit of the dumps and treated a mad world's lunatic issue with some seriousness. But fun shall be had with the aid of His Highness below. And the mixing in it of another element, which it has to beguile us— romance—is not at all bad cookery. Poetic romance is delusion—a tale of a Corsair; a poet's brain, a bottle of gin, and a theatrical wardrobe.

Above all he dreads a serious and responsible human relationship; and to hide from the nature of his fear he summons up these notions of tragic irony, of an ultimate mystery in men that cannot be plumbed:

Glimpses of the picture his deeds painted of him since his first meeting with this woman had to be shunned. He threw them off; they were set down to the mystery men are. The degrading, utterly different, back view of them teaches that Life is an irony. If the teaching is not accepted, and we are to take the blame, can we bear to live. Therefore, either way the irony of Life is proved.
. . .

Having established Life as the coldly malignant element, which induces to what it chastises, a loathing of womanhood, the deputed Mother of Life, ensues, by natural sequence.

Thus the 'division between the young man's pride of being and his warmer feelings' goes on. Woodseer tells him that he really hates Nature despite his pretence at sensibility. 'You hate Nature unless you have it served on a dish by your own cook. That's the way to the madhouse or the monastery.' And he notes the Lord's behaviour, 'Glints of the devilish shot from him at the gaming-tables. . . . He could be magnificent in generosity; he had little humaneness. He coveted beauty in women hungrily, and seemed to be born hostile to them.'

He is ready to make magnificent gestures. He sets up one of Madge's family in a fine shop in the West End because of Carinthia's sheltering in Whitechapel; but he refuses to meet the demands of his Welsh miners, despite the huge sums of money he wastes:

He passed through the heated atmosphere of black-browed, wiry little rebels, who withheld the salute as they lounged: a posture often preceding the spring in compulsorily idle workers. He was aware of an instinct abroad, an antagonism to the proprietor's rights. They roused him to stand by them, and were his own form of instinct, handsomely clothed.

Thus Meredith gets at the key-point. Fleetwood's responses are everywhere distorted because his property-sense has become 'his own form of instinct,' his deepest emotional response.

Woodseer, discussing titled wealth with Owain, considers:

Objects elevated even by a decayed world have their magnetism for us unless we nerve the mind to wakeful repulsion. He protested he had reason to think the earl was humanising, though he might be killing a woman in the process. . . . 'Imagine a devil on his back on a river, flying a cherub.'
Owain sparkled from the vision of the thing to wrath with it. 'Ay, but while he's floating, his people are edging on starvation.'

And so we come back to the lie of 'mystery' in which the corrupted man veils and excuses the corruptive process.

Men uninstructed in analysis of motives arrive at this dangerous conclusion, which spares their pride and caresses their indolence, while it flatters the sense of internal vastness, and invites to headlong intoxication. It allows them to think they are of such a compound, and must necessarily act in that manner.

They are not taught in the schools or by the books of the honoured places in the libraries, to examine and see the simplicity of these mysteries.

The duty of the poet or novelist is to strip the veil of the lie of mystery.

He should arrest all the characters of his drama to spring it to vision and strike perchance the chord primarily if not continually moving them, that readers might learn the why and how of a germ of evil, its flourishing under rebuke, the persistency of it after the fell creative energy has expired and pleasure sunk to be a phlegmatic dislike, almost a loathing.

His repentance comes too late and can only complete his self-destruction; but then he does realise the part played by money-power in his doom. 'I see the beast I played. Money is power, they say. I see the means it is to damn the soul, unless we—unless a man does what I do now.' But it is too late. He cannot control the power; he can only surrender to it or flee into solitude, out of life.

Carinthia, reared in the mountain loneliness by her father, has all the resources he lacks. For she has learned the union with nature which purifies the union with man because it totally ignores and denies the money-power, class-values. 'Listening, storing his [her father's] words, picturing the magnetic, veined great gloom of an untasted world.' She has no class-consciousness at all at the outset—a point brought out by her friendliness to the disabled Woodseer as opposed to her brother's stiff awareness of nothing but the latter's shabbiness. When she holds Madge's hand at the boxing-match in tense fellow-feeling she annoys Fleetwood and establishes her own future course, her movement away from Fleetwood's world into that of the commonfolk. She becomes the Whitechapel Countess, at home in a little greengrocer's shop. Among the miners she feels an immediate fellowship. They are fighting their proprietor lord. 'She, too, dealt with a lord.' She begins learning Welsh, sings the people's songs, mingles with them as one of them. When the strike grows stronger, they cannot forget she is Fleetwood's wife, but it makes no difference to her.

> Carinthia walked over the hills to her staring or down-eyed silent people, admitted without a welcome at some doors, rejected at some. Her baskets from the castle were for the most part received as graciously. She continued to direct them for delivery where they were needed, and understood why a charity that supplied the place of justice was not thanked. She and her people here were one regarding the master, as she had said. They could not hurt her sensitiveness, she felt too warmly with them.

What other Victorian novelist could have written that? She 'understood why a charity that supplied the place of justice was not thanked.'

Meredith does not specify exactly the period in which the novel is set but it is at least intended to be much earlier in the century. This point must be grasped if we are to see the rather dim and gentle figure of Owain as he is meant to be seen. Meredith understands, even if not clearly, that the days when a capitalist-entrepreneur to some extent did live in a world of his own making had long since passed away. In speaking of Fleetwood's intervention in the strike he says, 'in our younger days a lordly owner still might come to an agreement with the men by small concessions and the physical influence.' His whole statement implies that such econ-omic relations no longer apply.*

Carinthia feels a longing towards the poor. She thinks, 'Children of the poor have happy mothers.' And the act riveting her sense of solidarity with those mothers comes when she saves a child from a mad dog with disregard of her own safety. Her calm realistic courage is then underlined by her desire to cauterise the wound of another bitten child, which Fleetwood, with his horror of contact, prevents. (The child dies.)

The way in which she clings to her brother in the latter part of the book is at times irritating. She is given the same blinkered obstinacy as Sandra-Vittoria. And yet the picture has its rightness. She is returning on her bases, her family-bond, after the long misery of her conflict with Fleetwood, in order to gain a sense of worth, an active place in the world. But Meredith seems tiring here: all his strength goes into showing the breakdown of Fleetwood. We feel that Carinthia must proceed to realise the shallow selfishness of her brother and discover with renewed depth of meaning what her going back to Wales with Owain means. However, Meredith scamps the dénouement. No doubt, tired, he feels that his long book cannot be made any longer, and that he has shown enough of Carin-thia's inner drive to convince us that she will go on struggling through any veils, lies, class-distortions to the naked human truth. However that may be, the book tails off with several blurred contours.

The other positive character, though on less generous and powerful lines, is Woodseer. He too has broken through the class-barrier to some extent, though he tends to dissipate his energies in a slouching enjoyment of nature, in goodwill without an aim.† Fleetwood manages to deflect

---

* After 1832 the Welsh miners' unions were savagely repressed, and the men set up a secret organisation, Scotch Cattle, which terrorised bad employers and blacklegs. With the depression in the 1850's a more general militancy grew up which in the early 1860's crystal-lised in the Amalgamated Association, a national body, which crashed after a hard struggle of five months in 1875. For some fifteen years there was regression during which the sliding-scale principle supplanted trade-unionism proper. Meredith was to some extent drawing on his own recent visit to Ferndale in Wales.

† Woodseer had possibly been meant to play a more active part in the first conception: 'Woodseer, perpetual bather in morning, who begins life with an old head, but with springing blood, and falls from many a fiery chariot, to feel at home and put his fragments together when he touches earth.' M. to R.L.S. in Oct. 1884.

him to some extent, especially towards the worldly-corrupt Livia, but cannot destroy him. His lowest point is reached when he submits to Livia and betrays the trust of a dying man; but he breaks away and turns again towards Carinthia. In the simpler devotion of Madge, a working girl, he finds a stable support, and he marries her. Madge says:

> 'I think her face . . . I can't describe . . . it flashes.'
> 'That's it,' said Gower, delighted. . . . 'When it flashes, it's unequalled. There's the supremacy of irregular lines. People talk of perfect beauty: suitable for paintings and statues. Living faces, if they're to show the soul, which is the star on the peak of beauty, must lend themselves to motion. Nature does it in a breezy tree or over ruffled waters. . . . Artists prefer repose. Only Nature can express the uttermost beauty with her gathering and tuning of discords. . . . I remember my impression when I saw her first on her mountains abroad. Other beautiful faces of women go pale, grow stale. The diversified in the harmony of the flash are Nature's own. . . .'
> 'You teach me what's meant by poetry.'

Thus Meredith states his concept of beauty as in its highest always involving motion and the clash of opposites fused in the flash of realisation. And, in the Keatsian sense, Carinthia is Beauty because she is also Truth: she reflects always the world of men and nature about her in terms of her own struggle forward.

Woodseer of course is Welsh (and so is Madge). His father, a clear-minded minister struggling to do his best for the poor, represents the good stock from which he springs, the virtues he has to carry to a new level—finding in Nature what his father found in God, and then going on to rediscover his social devotedness on the new level. (The fact that Fleetwood is driven into a conflict far beyond the comprehension of most of his class is also linked with the fact of his Welsh blood.)

Two more points. The strike-motive persists in the book, as if Meredith was saying that a key to a man's character can be found in the way he reacts to a strike. Owain treats his men as friends, not in a vague patronising way, but fraternally; Fleetwood fights them with hatred; Chillon manages to stop violence against strikers in the Midlands and comes to terms with his powder-making workers; the miserly uncle opposes the men and dies—there is an explosion at his works. In all this there is certainly the reconciliation-formula, but there is also something more, which comes out in Carinthia and her entire solidarity with the miners.

Meredith uses ballads (in the first section) and the device of Dame Gossip to gain an extended social focus, a variation of planes of vision.

This last novel then is worthy of him, despite its tailing-off. It states once more his championship of women in their fight for freedom and equality; it defines with profound insight the nature of the alienating process of bourgeois egoism; it makes a devastating criticism of its society and sees salvation only in fraternal union with the people, the workers.

The critics generally were now ready to accept Meredith as a grand-old-man, with muted grumbles. *The Athenaeum* recognised his brave philosophy and the way in which he always showed man as responsible for his own fate, and admitted that the style was 'not so obscure as it is often represented to be.' *The Westminster Gazette* saw the novel had Meredith's two great qualities 'movement and fulness' to a superb degree. *The Saturday Review* thought his 'indirect method' often carried to excess and agreed that he must puzzle 'a decent public nourished on good healthy marionettes' (a morally cannibalistic public, it might indeed have said); but it excellently remarked that Fleetwood and Carinthia were set about with 'the *eyes*, the wonderful chorus of characters which Mr Meredith uses so persistently and with such amazing effect.' *The Pall Mall* recognised delicate intricate analysis, passionate energy of imagination, and a style that gripped the mind. *The Spectator*, while admitting wit and shrewdness, found the book 'terribly hard reading for the natural man,' and deprecated the New Euphuism. But no reviewer showed any awareness of what the book was about. *The Athenaeum* thought Fleetwood failed through having no clear plan in life; *The Pall Mall* took Meredith's fierce attack on egoist man as 'a romantic rare refinement of attitude towards the world.'

Not that attacks on his style were lacking. Gosse, unable to deny that in earlier works the onward movement of Meredith's powerful mind overcame stylistic contortions and produced a result, not always simple, but often vehement and noble, went on to say that the later works were marred by the 'increasing extravagance of his artificial diction,' so that 'it is difficult to enjoy and sometimes impossible to understand what he writes.'

V

Conclusions

31

Last Poems and Opinions

THE EVENTS of his last dozen years are not of much importance to us. There were no more novels, and only a handful of poems of any importance. These were the years when his reputation as a grand-old-man automatically increased, and every odd literary aspirant wanted to visit Box Hill and write an article on his impressions, so that his biographies are overweighted with such trivial stuff. Meredith himself persisted in asserting that he was not popular, that he had no audience. Chapman and Hall had issued an edition of eleven novels, with *Shagpat* and *Farina*, in the years 1885–95—i.e. following *Diana's* success. Then, after Will Meredith went into Constable's, there came the édition-de-luxe of thirty-two volumes, poems and prose; but limited to a thousand copies. The Library edition, 1897–1910, of eighteen volumes, had a wider circulation, as did the Pocket Edition, 1901–6. (After his death came the Memorial, Standard, and Mickleham editions.) His works thus in his lifetime, and in fact up to the 1920's, steadily expanded in their issues. But he always maintained that he had no public. We can therefore only consider that he did not hold the middle-class public he had reached as constituting a serious public at all.

In 1896 he attended his last public function, an exhibition where Sandys' portrait of Mrs Palmer was shown. He stayed with Lady Battersea at Cromer this year and the next, but he was getting past such visits. When he stayed for the last time at the house of Alice (now Lady Butcher), he hurt himself rather badly by slipping on the stairs. An anecdote of this year brings out well his difference from the aesthetes:

> I met Meredith the other day. 'What shall we talk of,' said he, 'politics or art?' 'Politics I never think of,' said I, 'and art I never talk of.' 'Let's begin on Epps' cocoa,' said he, and so we started and had a fine time of it. [Byrne Jones.]

In 1896 he printed in *The Daily Chronicle, The Warning,* a sonnet fiercely attacking the aggression of the Jameson Raid in South Africa. He speaks of 'mighty men ballooning high,' then falling with a bump out of their élite-fantasies.

> *Concerns it most ourselves, who with our gas—*
> *This little Isle's insatiable greed*

329

> For Continents—filled to inflation burst.
> So do ripe nations into squalor pass,
> When, driven as herds by their old pirate thirst,
> They scorn the brain's wild search for virtuous light.

As usual, put to the test, he sheds his confusions and sees clearly.

On his 70th birthday, in 1898, he was presented with an address from thirty leading writers telling he had 'attained the front rank in literature after many years of inadequate recognition.' He maintained his interest in Italy, sent his 'constant love' to Swinburne, and said that 'an Imperial must be an armed England.' His *Odes in Contribution to the Song of French History* were published in October.

He was being something of an enamoured-sage with Lady Ulrica Duncombe, a Girton girl, daughter of a Yorkshire peer, to whom he told the tale of the old Devon lady. But her serious-mindedness wasn't proof against the snobbery of a Durbar. 'It is a matter of surprise that she who was placed high as the celestial blue above the Smart Set should on her return from India have adopted their tone and style.' And she married the Viceroy's military secretary. This was the sort of person to whom he wrote wise counsels, 'Have you a mind for political affairs? I trust you not to shun them: they brace the mind, are open air to it. I may help you, if you direct me as to the way.'

He wrote to Walter Jerrold who wished to write a book on him:

> . . . a dislike to being made the subject of a book. . . . I might claim that an unpopular author should be held exempt from exhibition. And again, the book of which he is the theme can hardly be expected to succeed. [1899.]

In the summer of 1900 Maxse died. 'The loss to me is beyond all count.' But he was staunch in his disbelief of personal immortality, and was more friendly than ever with the freethinker Clodd.

> Stern wrecker of the Established Faith!
> From whom the parson shrinks appalled. . . .
> Then into Nature's entrails peer'st,
> Not finding there the Christian's God. . . .
> A bearer to thy fellows, Clodd.

When the Boer War broke out, he knew the British wrong, though he didn't much like the intolerant and biblically-minded Boers. In October 1899 he wrote to Hyndman:

> I regard your article on Justice with full approval. This hateful war tears me in two. I have to wish for the success of our men in the cause that I condemn. The Demon is that mount of Gold. I had always the dread that the first steps of Imperialism would be bloody. . . . The tide of Brummagen [Birmingham: Chamberlain] policy was too strong, Cairo to the Cape a mighty hunger.

He sees the imperialist reality; but his inability to grasp starkly the nature of the State prevents him from understanding that he can best show his sympathy for 'our men' by fighting uncompromisingly against the drive to war. In December 1901, 'The Boer War (he detested it) was dragging lamely on, and he belaboured the English with the vigour and bitterness of a disillusioned patriot' (D. MacCarthy). In his sonnet *At the Close* he prophesied doom on the ruthless conquerors, and in letters to two newspapers in 1902 he pleaded for a humane treatment of the Boers. In May of 1901 his book of poems, *A Reading of Life*, appeared.

Leslie Stephen died in 1904; and Watts too. He himself had been dangerously ill in the later months of 1903. 'My friends are dropping, to right and left, and I ask why do I remain,' he wrote to Janet, who was about to visit him. And so the years dragged on. In 1905 he accepted the Order of Merit. 'A title would have sunk me.' He refused a Baronetcy, which would have inferred an acceptance of the social hierarchy; but he accepted the Order, because O.M. could signify no more than Old Man. And he was deeply stirred by the baffled Russian Revolution. The fashion of interviewing him on various matters in the news had grown up, and reporters joined the sightseers come to admire the crippled grand-old-man. In 1908 his 80th birthday saw addresses and a swarm of journalists. But he felt undeceived, and considered himself unpopular and unread. 'This 80th of mine comes but once, thank the Lord! . . . letters naming plays from novels, begging letters, letters of great gush, idiotic letters; one from a piteous-voiced bankrupt clergyman!'

In 1905 he had fallen and broken his right leg. He now went for his daily airing in his chair, pulled by a donkey named Picnic, with Cole the gardener and Bessy Nicholls his nurse in attendance, while his dog Sandie ran about. 'I don't think he knows one little thing about women,' said Bessy. Occasionally he went for a motor drive. In January 1906 he made a resolute expedition to register his vote against the Tories at the General Election, having to travel six miles to Leatherhead and be carried into the booth. The summer of 1905 and 1906 saw him in a cottage at Aldeburgh, —'a place without charm, like Crabbe's poetry; only grandeur of Sea. It lifted and steadied me to its own dead level.' He liked to be near Clodd; and there he sat on the old quay talking with the fishermen. (He liked also to chat with the donkey-boys at Box Hill.) 'I'm going quickly down,' he told Morley and reaffirmed his certainty of no other-worldly existence. On the first day of 1906, he wrote this letter to Swinburne, 'All flowers of earth on you both for this year and the many to follow.'

In April 1909 Swinburne died. 'The blow was heavy to me. . . . Song was his natural voice.' He wrote his last letter to express his regret. Then in May one Friday he caught a chill, but drove out next day. Facing the dawn, he died on Monday, the 18th, amid an exceptionally blossomy spring. Denied Westminster Abbey for his attacks on religion, he was buried at Dorking, with sprigs of his favourite white bean and lilac-flowers on his coffin, beside his wife. Hardy commented to Clodd that the Abbey needed 'a heathen annexe.'

Now for his last poems. In 1896 he wrote three more odes to go with that he had written for France in 1870—dealing with the French Revolution, Napoleon I, and Alsace-Lorraine. 'It is History—my view; and I make History sing!' Next year he remarked less confidently that he had had to embody 'gross matter' to be true to his subject, and had had to fight the temptation to be rhetorical. The book of 1898 was dedicated to Morley.

The new Odes do not add much to the first, and there is much heavy going in them. He expounds at more length the dream of brotherhood on a happy earth that burned in the French Revolution. France before 1789 lies drained by 'jewelled flies . . . in a glistening spray'—an image fused with that of a frozen body 'beneath a hoar-frost's brilliant crust.' Then the mass-forces break through into the new life of the revolution, and

> For them that hungered, she was nourishing food,
> For those who sparkled, Night.

The union of heaven and earth Meredith uses as a symbol to express the ending of the old division in man, the spiritual and social division, and the ushering-in of the great day of fecund brotherhood, proclaimed at the Feast of the Pikes. Treachery from within and attack from without beget the Terror. But the peasant soldiers turn the tables on the leagued kings and hunt the hunters. So far there has been hope: such matters as the Terror and the War, however ugly in themselves, have been the necessary retort of the patriots to the violences aimed against the revolution. But now the old divisions return in a new and established form as the revolution ceases to struggle for freedom and equality, and greed resassumes its sway. Napoleon represents the new phase, in which some of the revolutionary virtues are carried on, but in which the oppressions are riveted. The fall of Napoleon brings no betterment, but substitutes for his tyranny that of the Holy Alliance.

Then comes the Ode of 1870, followed by *Alsace-Lorraine* which rather weakly appeals to France to drop any ideas of a *revanche* and to set an example of a peaceful way of life. The Ode is weak because to complete the sequence it needed to link its appeal with a call for the recreation of the spirit and the acts of the Great Revolution; and this it does not do.

Meredith's image of the Marriage of Heaven and Earth deserves a glance. Drawn from Greek ritual-myth, it is used by him to express the ending of the class-split, the ending of the division of mind and body, head and heart, the ending of egoism, the delighted union of man and woman in equality, the achievement of an earth of peace and plenty. In *Wind on the Lyre* it stands for the creative moment, the union of opposites, that wings 'our green to wed our blue.'* Green is there earth and blue heaven. And as Trevelyan says of the Ode on the Revolution,

> The central idea of this piece, as also of those that follow, is that in 1789 France rose midway to heaven to meet her bridegroom, descending from 'the blue.' This heavenly lover represents the true liberty, equality and fraternity.
> . . .
> The marriage of Heaven and Earth is a favourite metaphor of Mr Meredith's.

Heaven thus represents the ideal, the dream, the future, the spirit, which only the unbetrayed revolution can unite stably with the earth of the present.†

'Not the kind of poetry we read for pleasure,' said *The Academy*; 'Had better have been left unattempted,' *Saturday Review*; 'A devil in it,' Francis Thompson; 'Carlyle turned metrist,' *The Athenaeum*; 'A strange irony of fate that the lucid genius of France should be sung in such desperately tortured and turgid strain,' *The Bookman*.

A Reading of Life has the *Night Walk* which we early discussed. The title-poem deals with Artemis and Aphrodite, the balances of discipline and enjoyment which are necessary to a full life. Both goddesses are good

---

* He responded deeply to music. Beethoven was his great love. (Jenny plays Beauchamp a piano-version of part of the 9th symphony—in the first version the whole! When Jane begins to like Patrick, she thinks, 'He might be taught to appreciate Beethoven and work for his fellows,' she asks if B. doesn't touch him more than Italian music, and he replies: 'There's a forest on fire in it.') In May 1864 he says he is working on an Ode to Beethoven (lost).

In later years he was much interested in Wagner, whose influence to some extent pervades works like *One of Our Conquerors* with its complex interlinkings of motives. Dartrey talks about the way he's stricken the Italians (xiii): 'I held out against Wagner as long as I could.' Victor too has been won over (xxiii)—cf. his Lakelands concert (xx), F. Jameson (who suggested the retaking-up of *Amazing Marriage*, was a devoted Wagnerite and translated part of the *Nibelungen Ring*. Frau Cosima thought him the reincarnation of Wagner and things became a bit complicated between them (he used to sunbathe in the Tyrol). M. comments that all will be well with J. as he has 'legal assistance and the most innocent of souls.'

He learned the violin at Neuwied; in 1907 he thanked a Welshman for a song-setting, 'I have done my best to read the music, enough to see that it is excellent. . . .'

† *Modern Love* has, 'The grace of heaven seems holding earth in its embrace.' In *The Amazing Marriage* he says of the mated woman, 'She brings us to the union of body and soul; as good as to say, earth and heaven. Secret of all human aspirations, the ripeness of the creeds is there.'

in their proper place, aspects of Mother Earth; they become Tempters when they claim the whole of life. The happy and fulfilled life is a fused trinity of blood, brain, spirit, 'glassing her [Earth] in union.'

Foresight and Patience forcibly sets out his belief in democracy as the sole pledge of culture, the development of the masses as the sole basis on which art can survive and expand. Foresight looks to the future, Patience accepts the present; in the struggle between the two the full movement of progress is brought about. 'When they do meet, it is our earth inspired.' Foresight is horrified at the gross egoist lives of the millions feeding and breeding on the earth. Patience admits much of the charge; in fact at this moment 'locust hosts' of destruction are being drilled by the great powers for war. But civilisation has met grave challenges before and has survived. It will survive again if men can meet the issues without succumbing to fear. Indeed the basis of hope for the future lies in the very masses that Foresight has accused.

> To strengthen the foundations is the task
> Of this tough Age; not in your beams to bask.

Men only face problems when the maturing clash has arrived:

> 'Tis not in men to recognise the need
> Before they clash in hosts, in hosts they bleed.
> Then may sharp suffering their nature grind;
> Of rabble passions grows the chieftain Mind.

Effective leadership, 'shaping strength,' emerges only out of mass-experience.

Foresight sees what is true and loses his despair, his Utopian haste. He sees that in the contemporary world, because of the mass-development of which he earlier complained, there is a cultural basis not existent at any previous stages when the low levels of economic development necessitated an élite.

> That rings of truth! More do your people thrive;
> Your Many are more merrily alive
> Than erstwhile when I gloried in the page
> Of radiant singer and anointed sage.
> Greece was my lamp: burnt out for lack of oil;
> Rome, Python Rome, prey of its robber spoil!
> All structures built upon a narrow space
> Must fall, from having not your host for base.

Patience (i.e. close contact with actuality and confrontation of immediate tasks) alone can clear or bank the flood of problems with the aid of Reason. Idealist philosophers, on the contrary, are grieved to see 'your

Many nourished, starved my brilliant few,' and so they leap into the void of subjectivity, 'dive down the fumy Aetna of their brains.'

Aye, says Patience, the philosophers thus destroy themselves, but Philosophy remains to be truly developed.

Foresight agrees. Philosophy—man's power of clear thinking, of staying true to his own essence and despising nothing but fear—alone can achieve 'passage through our slough.' It alone can make man master of fate. It will 'light us in the shade, warm in the frost, make Good our aim and aid,' perpetually 'renewed, unconquerable.' For its security lies in its goal, 'Advantage to the Many.' Away with Irony and the Satire, when they are the refuge of the intellectual who cannot face his task in the development of life, his need to make his art a servant of the Many. Satire and Irony of this sort

> . . . crack a childish whip, drive puny herds,
> Where numbers crave their sustenance in words.
> Now let the perils thicken: clearer seen,
> Your chieftain Mind mounts over them serene,
> Who never yet of scattered lamps was born
> To speed a world, a marching world to warn,
> But sunward from the vivid Many springs,
> Counts conquest but a step, and through disaster sings.

(In February 1904 Meredith wrote to the dying Leslie Stephen: 'We who have loved the motion of legs and the sweep of the winds, we come to this. But for myself, I own that it is the Natural order. There is no irony in Nature.')

In those last lines of *Patience and Foresight* Meredith proves how ready he was to submit his talents to the needs of the masses and that his defiance of the 'public' referred only to the middle-class readers. He writes for an audience not yet ready to read his works. And what is astonishing is the perfect application of his lines to the post-1917 situation when in widening areas of the world the audience that he wanted has come into existence, *the vivid Many*. His demand that the intellectual should turn from mere irony and satire, from personal bitterness and petty retreats-into-self, to serve the numbers who 'crave their sustenance in words,' had only a vague reference to the situation of 1900; it seized the potential of that situation, which became actualised in 1917. Today his lines sound with a trumpet-loudness, fiercely relevant to our scene. 'To speed a world, a marching world to warn.' That is the function of the intellectual, recognised in the Soviet Union, in the New Democracies, in the People's China, in countries like France where poets such as Éluard and Aragon have a mass-audience to hearten and warn. It is the diametric opposite of the function of the intellectual as conceived in the countries where society is regressing and only the locust-hosts are thriving, where existentialist 'irony' and Orwellian 'satire' are the refuge of the lost and regressive intellectual.

In *The World's Advance* (1893) Meredith had defined the movement of history as spiral, and jestingly compared it to a drunkard's involved progress. Now in *Forest History* he traces the development in the woodland, the first taming of things, the monastic centre, the feudal castle, then the rebel Robin Hood, and folk-tales of fairies. Shakespeare resumes all this process of growth, but merges the forest-bases with his urban consciousness. In him 'the city over forest flowered, the forest wreathed the city's drama-mart.' He then has shown us how to fuse the life of nature and of man, and we must keep reachieving his work. For in that reachievement of the unity of man and nature lies 'our conquest.'

In 1905 Meredith wrote a poem to Russia which I shall consider when I come to his interviews on the same subject. And in 1908 he composed for the Milton Tercentenary organised by the British Academy his last poem, *Milton*, which, in Miltonic idiom, nobly celebrates the poet-champion of Freedom. He echoes Wordsworth in saying, 'We need him now.'

> For Belial the adroit is in our midst;
> Mammon, more swoln to squeeze the slavish sweat
> From hopeless toil.

But in this call against the wage-exploitation which stands in our age for what feudal tyranny stood in Milton's, he goes on to speak of Moloch as now imperialist: 'aggrandised, monstrous in his grinning mask of hypocritical Peace.' He means that the reality is the war-drive under the fine pretences; but his words could be taken in the regressive *Maud*-sense.

In 1909 *Last Poems* came out after his death. The two poems just mentioned are included. There are also a tribute to Garibaldi and some pleasant nature-pictures as well as some 'defence' poems in which he edges over to the theme of 'national unity' along imperialist lines.

Now to his opinions of these last years as set out in letter or interview.

He held fast to the vital basis of art in ethics, in its relation to people. 'Real greatness must be based on morality,' whereas 'many of the famous are only clever interpreters of the popular wishes' (i.e. of the bourgeois public). 'I preach for the mind's acceptance of Reality in all its forms.' 'A frank acceptance of Reality is the firm basis of the Ideal.'

Typical of his many statements on Death is the following made to Stead:

> I was a very timid and sensitive boy. I was frightened of everything; I could not endure to be left alone. But when I came to be eighteen, I looked round the world (as far as a youth of eighteen can look) and determined not to be afraid again. Since then I have had no fear of death. Every night when I go to bed I know that I may not rise from it. That is nothing to me. I hope I shall die with a good laugh, like the old French woman. The *curé* came wailing to her about her salvation, and things like that, and she told him her best improper story, and died. The god of Nature and human nature does not dislike humour, you may be sure, and would rather hear it in extremity than the formless official drone. Let us believe in a hearty god—one to love more than to fear.
>
> There is Pan. You know something about Pan, too. He has always been very close to me. He is everywhere—so is the devil, who was framed on the model of him by our medieval instructors. Just now the devil is more thought of in England than the Christian god. He is more popular. The time will come for the mind of man to see the veritable god. Nature goes on her way, unfolding, improving, always pushing us higher; and I do not believe that this great process continues without some spiritual purpose, some spiritual force driving it on. Change is full of hope. A friend of mine was lamenting over the sadness of autumn. 'Are you sad when you change your coat?' I asked him.

A statement that shows his great virtues of courage and hope that had carried him through a vile epoch and extreme personal misery, and also the elements of vagueness that he had not been able to eliminate from his thoughts.

Other examples of his courage are worth citing:

> People talk about me as if I were an old man. I do not feel old in the least. On the contrary, I do not believe in growing old, and I do not see any reason why we should ever die. I take as keen an interest in the movement of life as ever, I enter into the passions of youth, and I watch political affairs and intrigues of parties with the same keen interest as of old. I have seen the illusion of it all. But it does not dull the zest with which I enter into it all, and I hold more firmly than ever to my faith in the constant advancement of the race. . . .
>
> If I touch anything, however slightly, I am afraid that I shall fall—that is my only loss, my walking days are over. [1904.]
>
> I still look on life with a young man's eye. I have always hoped I should not grow old as some do—with a palsied intellect, living backwards, regarding other people as anachronisms because they themselves lived on into other times and left their sympathies behind them with their years. [1903.]
>
> People say the brain grows jaded. Don't believe them. The brain never grows weary. It's one's stomach that overrides feeling, and I, unfortunately, was born with a weak stomach. [To Schwob.]

He went on to say of the dark pine-coppice opposite on the slope, 'The brain needs darkness so that thought may spring forth and grow freely,' and he mentioned that he hated bells even if they rang only for the king's death.

He remained true to his keen championship of women for equality in many statements, including the letter to *The Times* (Nov. 1, 1906) in which he supported their claims to the suffrage; and, while deprecating acts of hysteria, pointed out that males could act in the most hysterical way, as Mafeking Night had shown.

An interview of 1903 had established him as an oracular source for the press. He declared that 'we have a Parliament that is brought together too much on the old lines.' The Australians (with their working-class representation) were doing better. Let the English working-class drop their political apathy and take 'a livelier, steady and constant interest in the affairs of the country.' He attacked the clergy's control of education and demanded immediate Home Rule for Ireland. The Liberal party was doomed 'unless it opens its arms to the Radicals'—i.e. continued radical changes of the prevailing system.

He watched the rise of the Labour Party with interest. In February 1906 he writes, 'The list of Labour Members rejoices me in one way, rather alarms in another. Will they be open to large questions?' That is, he welcomed the advent of a working-class party, but was doubtful, as he well might be, whether the leaders as yet knew what they were fighting for or how to fight for the larger issues of social change. His crippled state had made him unable to take part in the political developments leading to the Labour Party or to meet the new leaders coming up from the working-class. But he admired John Burns because without knowing much of him he saw him englamoured with such struggles as the great Dock Strike. 'There is hope for British democracy while it can produce such men as he.' And he wrote to Hyndman in 1908 at the time of his 80th birthday:

> And now you are among the foremost in the fray, while I do but sit and look on. I am accused sharply by myself, and yet am helpless. You can imagine, therefore, what my thoughts are when congratulations come showering under the note of 'happy returns.' Cheerfulness has not forsaken me, but Nature has cast me aside, and I do not like this mere drawing of breath without payment for it. However, I take pride in those who fight gallantly with honest conviction of the justness of their cause. . . . Very warmly yours.

He was looking on Hyndman, it must be remembered, as a fighter for socialism.

His attitudes to imperialism continued to the end to show the confusion already analysed. He had advocated conscription in 1878 at the time of the scare over Tsarist Russia in Asia. Now he approved of it again. And here his weaker aspects coincided with the jingoist element in Hyndman's sectarian 'socialism.'

I was pleased to see you and Blatchford in union for a national army. A poem of mine, 'The Call,' in the *Oxford and Cambridge Review* raised the same cry. One may fear that a landing of foreign artillery on our shores alone will rouse the mercantile class. Doubtless, also, there is an apprehension as to the prudence of schooling the toilers in the use of arms. We are not yet a people.

That is, in advocating conscription, he is thinking of a Citizen Army that would act for righteousness and at a pinch turn into a revolutionary force. But his inability to grasp that in the existing situation such an army in Britain could only act at the State's will makes him in fact (as Hyndman later did) support an imperialist policy.*

Where he was right, as against the pretenders that all was well in the best of possible worlds, was in his clear awareness that things were heading for war. He stated to a Welshman in 1909 that he was by temperament an optimist and that he believed in the future of the race, the progress of man; but he was a pessimist in that he saw looming ahead the Armageddon of Europe, a generation of thunder and lightning. He himself would not live to see it, but it would come. Britain was limp and fearful, while militarism in Germany would beget a barbaric courage dead to higher aims. War waged by such a nation would be terrible indeed. In 1903 he had written in *The Telegraph* on Pan-Germanism, but he then thought War and German expansion held back by inner conflicts and the problem of finance.

And yet from time to time he sees deeper. Reading Bury's *Later Roman Empire* he grasps the nature of Justinian's State as none of the bourgeois historians including Bury himself, had done—

> a man of judgment, yet he would vindicate Justinian's Imperialism at the cost of the people's misery under grinding taxes to furnish means for war, by pointing to Italy recovered, etc., etc.:—and, as the result of the Emperor's death, Italy, Africa, Gaul (Provincia), Spain, fell away from the East Empire, the state of the Imperator was loathed by the people, despised by the barbarians. No, not a step should Imperialism take before it has cleansed and fortified itself within. [1903, to Morley.]

The problem is what that inner cleansing involved. But, set against the facts, Meredith is always right in his political sense: as in the grasp he shows of what the State of Justinian meant. Again in 1907 he said:

---

* The radical idea of the militia as a people's army capable of revolutionary action and of a standing army as an inevitable instrument of tyranny is well set out in *Greece in 1823 and 1824* by Col. L. Stanhope (1824) who went from the Greek Committee in London to help the insurgent Greeks. He fought hard on the issue. 'Never let the Greeks tolerate a standing army, or foreign troops. . . . The whole nation should be, at all times, armed, ready to protect their property, their persons, their liberties, and their country.' On the way-out he studied the Swiss system as useful for 'the cheap defence and liberties of nations. I consider that even the Landwehr of Prussia is a power that may one day overthrow despotism in that quarter.' These radical conceptions of the armed people could only be realised under socialism.

I take a hopeful view of the progress of civilisation, in general; but not so much of Great Britain, at least in the near future. She has been too greedy for power, empire, wealth. She has seized more than she can hold or administer.

In 1906 he wrote: 'We have not had clean hands in China.—Never attempt to dissociate your ideas from the real of life. It weakens the soul; and besides it cannot be done. . . . Look for the causes of evil.'

When the Russian Revolution of 1905 came, he supported it with all his might. After Red Sunday he told *The Sunday Chronicle*:

> Russia cannot, it is certain, long escape the spirit of Liberalism that has swept over Europe. The sympathy of the British people with the brave fellows who are fighting an uneven, almost hopeless, battle, as it seems, is very great. And it should be practical. . . .
>
> Everybody should spare what he can, and the money should be telegraphed at once to one of the leaders who are not in prison. We must help them, and this is the only way. They cannot expect much help from Germany. Germany ever since 1870 has been an armed camp. . . . But no doubt the German people will sympathise with these poor fellows. . . .
>
> [In France] people were attracted by the undeveloped riches of Russia to invest their money in that country. And France has her bondholders to consider . . . but she has a great spirit of humanity . . . and the French people also will have much sympathy with the aims of the Russian revolutionaries.

He uses the term Liberalism simply for progressive ideas; we have seen how sharply he criticised in the past the actual personages or ideas of the Liberal Party.

That he was effective in his appeal for funds for the revolutionaries is shown by a passage from Blunt's *Diary*: 'George Meredith has been appealing for funds for the revolution in Russia, and I have subscribed £10, and yesterday came news that the Grand Duke Serge has been blown up with a bomb, so I am subscribing again.'

His poem, *The Crisis*, declares his faith in the Russian people and his belief that they will take neither a course of blind violence nor one of Tolstoyan non-resistance, but that they will achieve a disciplined revolution:

> *Spirit of Russia, now has come*
> *The day when thou canst not be dumb.*
> *Around thee foams the torrent tide,*
> *Above thee its fell fountain, Pride.*
> *The senseless rock awaits thy word*
> *To crumble; shall it be unheard? . . .*
> *Thy land 'twixt flame and darkness heaves,*
> *Showing the blade wherewith Fate cleaves,*
> *If mortals in high courage fail*
> *At the one breath before the gale.*
> *Those rulers in all forms of lust,*

Who trod thy children down to dust
On the red Sunday, know right well
What word for them thy voice would spell,
What quick perdition for them weave. . . .

What is important in this poem is the way in which he sees the deep courage, the humanity, the sources of renewal in the Russian *masses*, who are neither Tolstoyan visionaries nor brutish hordes, he insists.

Those who bind
Thy limbs and iron-cap thy mind,
Take thee for quaking flesh, misdoubt
That thou art of the rabble rout
Which cries and flees, with whimpering lip,
From reckless gun and brutal whip;
But he who has at heart the deeds
Of thy heroic offspring reads
In them a soul; not given to shrink
From peril on the abyss's brink;
With never dread of murderous power;
With view beyond the crimson hour.

And it is these masses who will say to their land, 'Let there be light.'

It is in such responses that we see the deep vein of revolutionary passion in Meredith. Where true-blue Liberals draw back at such a moment, produce all sorts of qualms and look anywhere except to the masses for the solution of the crisis, Meredith acclaims the mass-force as the significant aspect of the situation, the source of all renewal and hope.

In an interview for *The Westminster Gazette* he repudiated Tolstoyan ideas of non-resistance to evil. 'Submission to evil is a distinct evil in itself. But I am not prepared to say that a bloody resistance is required, unless, as in this case, when a nation may be compared to a man with another holding a knife at his throat. In such a case, not to resist is a grave error.' He recognised Tolstoy's power and nobility, but couldn't follow him as an ethical or religious preacher. Tolstoy was a fanatic in the last resort; all men who hated sexuality and looked on 'extinction as a saving grace' were the foes of Nature; the evil they feared was 'the perpetual recurrence of beast-like tendencies. Those we may hope to exorcise; but we cannot depart from the founts of our origin, our links with the world of Nature. As to Death, any one who understands Nature at all thinks nothing of it. . . . We go that others may come—and better, if we rear them in the right way.'

He had been steadily moving from Left Radicalism to a socialist viewpoint. In 1886 he wrote in *The Pall Mall Gazette*, 'We are to have a House of Commons incapable of conducting public business,' and in his last years he spoke strongly against the party-system. That did not mean that he wanted any ruling-class dictatorship of the form we now call Fascism; it meant that emotionally (without any clear idea of the working-out) he was recalling Harrison's analysis of the Commune and its council (soviet) system as opposed to the bourgeois parliamentarianism of Versailles. Harrison had then made to some extent the mistake of thinking the formal difference the vital one, whereas the real contrast lay in the class-basis of the opposed organisational forms. What is significant is that Meredith did not consider the existing form of party-conflict as the eternal form for the development of democracy. He always held the 'conflict' of Tory and Liberal to be a feint, a lie, a mere shadow-boxing for positions between two sections of a single party, the capitalist party; and the logic of his position is that the development of a single party uniting the mass of the people for the overthrow of capitalist relations would be more democratic than the existing system.

In October 1887 he wrote to Chapman on a manuscript of essays that the author tended 'to enlarged modern views on politics: so far socialistic that he is for Nationalisation of Land: the putting of much into the hands of the State—which is opposed to English feeling, although there are signs of English reason awakening to some idea of the necessity.' We see there the usual confusion about the State, the avoidance of the key-question: what kind of State is to gain the new powers? one that centralises and strengthens monopoly-controls, or one that socialises production and puts the workers in charge? But Meredith's phrasing shows his friendliness to the socialist approach. Later he wrote, 'I am thinking of becoming a socialist, and then I shall have been everything, except a curate.' The play-ful tone, aimed at the disapproval which he knows the avowal will beget, does not lessen the seriousness of the words.

But he was a crippled man, cut from action; and there was no party, not even any individual, to whom he could turn in Britain for enlighten-ment. He kept to his old term Radical, which for him meant the man or party aiming at radical, not partial, change—ready to accept the world's pace if there was genuine and steady movement forward, but ready also to meet any effort to clamp reaction down with such responses as those of the Chartists, Mazzini, the Communards. On his 80th birthday he said that he wished to be remembered as one who had written works 'of very radical sentiment.'

He remained steadfast about his unpopularity. In 1908 he tried to deter Galland from writing on an author who had 'no claim to popularity in England.' He told Trevelyan, who had written a book on his poems, that the reviewers would keep their 'hereditary opposition' or disappoint him. (Though to another who had praised him he says that he is not the first poet cursed as obscure and the others have won abundant praise on gaining 'a full hearing.') He told Photiadès, 'My name is celebrated, but no one reads my books,' and 'the Press has often treated me as a clown or a harlequin.'

He still liked to suggest novels and improvise themes. Once

> he outlined a new story, to be called, perhaps, *The Benefactor of the Race*, or some such title, which should deal with the efforts of a man who wanted to improve humanity and was for ever getting into quarrels in endeavouring to do so, and who would not marry the lady he desired to in fulfilment of his System, etcetera.
>
> 'Why don't you write it yourself?' . . . Meredith broke into that genial torrential laugh of his that electrifies everyone who hears him, and which someone has said is the merry brother of his serious voice. 'They would want me to cut out the excrescences,' he replied. 'No, no! Somebody else must write it. I give them the idea.'

Such an idea, however, belonged to the *Feverel*-level, with its exposure of the contradictions besetting every bourgeois effort; it was contrary to Meredith's deeper views, which was no doubt a reason why he didn't want to write it. And anyhow the recounter has possibly missed the main point. Chesterton says:

> He asked me to write one of the stories for him, as he would have asked the milkman, if he had been talking to the milkman. It was a splendid and frantic story, a sort of astronomical farce, all about a man who was rushing up to The Royal Society with the only possible way of avoiding an earth-destroying comet; and it showed how even on this huge errand the man was tripped up by his own weaknesses and vanities; how he lost a train by trifling or was put in gaol for brawling. That is only one of them. I went out of that garden with a blurred sensation of the million possibilities of creative literature.

That is more in the key of Meredith's own later novels. The man trying to avert 'cataclysm' (a term used in *Beauchamp* for revolution) and getting 'tripped up' could have been turned by Meredith's method into another Victor Radnor.

The theme in fact haunted him. In 1887 he spoke of a story about 'a Knight of Perfectibility'; and in May 1904 he at length fixed on Wells as the Author most likely to understand and carry out the project. He asked him down to Box Hill and outlined his ideas in detail; Wells loudly enjoyed the recital; but nothing came directly of it—though after-effects may well have tinged the later Wells novels like *Tono-Bungay*, where, however, the essential Meredithian grasp is lacking.

In passing we may note an interesting use of the image of trodden orange-peel in a letter of 1902: here Meredith says that the revolutionary struggles of his early years may have seemed to fail at the time, but they were in fact laying the basis of a new world. 'Looking back at the blows and rebuffs of the old days, I am instructed to see that we may draw the hope of living juices from street orange peel in the mire. We were as that trodden castaway of times.' When we recall the orange-peel that brings down the empire-financier, we can claim that this passage reveals the image's under-associations. The *trodden castaway* that trips Radnor is for him the struggling underdog—the worker who picks Radnor up and with whom he exchanges abuse. The 'downtrodden' has answered back, and that is why the financier is so enduringly shaken. (Women, in *One of Our Conquerors*, are described as 'trodden underfoot.')*

The last bit of literary counsel he wrote was in March 1909, to a minor author who sent him a drama on Joan of Arc. In the trial-records, Meredith pointed out, 'at times the peasant springs out in a retort on her tormentors. Such realism you avoid. . . . It would have been salt in the drama.' And so his last comment is in commendation of realism, as his last letter was in praise of the poet, Swinburne, who stood for him as the mouthpiece of the European movements of national-liberation in the mid-century.

---

* M.'s favourite image of himself as a driven cab-horse is the same as that used by Mayhew's factory cabinet-maker (*London Labour and Labour Poor*) to define the nature of exploitation.

32

The Vexed Question of his Form

WE HAVE now followed the movement of Meredith's mind through his works; and in these last two chapters we shall consider his Form and Content. The concentration of his society's hostility in attacks on his Form make a further scrutiny of that aspect of his work necessary, though in the last resort Form and Content cannot be separated.* That there were many vices in his style cannot be denied; and yet in the full historical view we can see how even those vices in some degree originated from the positive aspects of his work, both in its achievement and its intentions— though in turn they limited and partly frustrated those positive aspects.

He began as one of the New Poets, seeking to work out a dialectic of development rooted in earth and society. He took from this grouping an emphasis on the dynamic word, the concentrated image of action; and much of both the energy and the constriction of his writing derive from this fact. Driven back on himself with the failure of the mass-movement after 1850, he tended to use poetic images sharply standing up out of the flow of narrative or exposition, jagged, as if he needed thus to knit hard tense thews of resistance in a world going in the opposite direction. In his struggle against that world of the extending cash-nexus, he released his energies of expression; and the concentrated sharp image was a weapon of counter-attack, swiftly and brightly moving, against and across the enemy-positions.

The situation is complicated by the fact that he is inevitably penetrated and controlled by the enemy-forces at certain points; and his work, both in form and content, reveals throughout the furious battle that goes on as he seeks in turn to repel and control the invasion.

I have already noted the opposed, yet mingling influences of Richter and Peacock. Carlyle too was pointed-at as affecting Meredith both in

---

* Browning had similar attacks: *Men and Women* is 'a book of madness and mysticism . . . power wantonly wasted, and talent deliberately perverted . . . nothing but a set purpose to be obscure, and an idiot captivity to the jingle of Hudibrastic rhymes,' *Sat. Rev.* (24 Nov. 1855). The same journal in 1855–6 highly praised Longfellow and Patmore (*Angel in the House*) and wanted Whitman's *Leaves of Grass* thrown 'instantly behind the fire.' But Browning's pietistic retreat from all radical positions broke down the opposition to his vital qualities, and he became the object of a cult.

thought and style; and his impact, akin to that of the New Poets in many ways, needs a more detailed investigation. H. D. Traill remarks on the shock of Carlyle's method on all the middle-class canons. 'It was naturally *The French Revolution* which dealt the rudest blow. . . . *Sartor Resartus* could be neglected as mere subjective rhapsody; but the grave or professedly grave history of one of the gravest of modern events was another matter.' The pundits objected even to using the word style for 'this hotchpot of vocabular montrosities, this witches' caldron of disjointed sentences, outlandish compounds, fantastic nicknames, extravagant metaphors and obscure allusions.' But the imagery and rhythm which embodied a powerful sense of the period's revolutionary upheavals could not be ignored. The young were conquered. 'The fascination which he exercised over them was extraordinary; one despairs of ever making it intelligible to the youth of a generation for whom Carlyle's proportions though imposing are no longer heroic.'

Take the following typical passages from *The French Revolution*:

> Maternity awakes, to hear children weeping for bread. Maternity must go forth into the streets, to the herb-markets and Bakers'-queues. . . . But instead of Bakers'-queues, why not the Aristocrats' palaces, the root of the matter? [VIII, iv.]
>
> . . . when dumb Drudgers staggered to the King's Palace, and in wide expanse of sallow faces, squalor and winged raggedness, presented hieroglyphically its Petition of Grievances; and for answer got hanged on a 'new gallows forty feet high.' [VII, vi—also II, ii.]
>
> History, looking back over this France through long times . . . confesses mournfully that there is no period to be met with in which the general Twenty-five Millions of France suffered less than in this period which they name Reign of Terror.

It is a style of *action* and *impact*. The clipping of definite or indefinite articles gives a breathless directness; the personifications generalise the particular and thus underline the historical moment, its deep significance; the pictorial sharpness adds to the sense of participation in the event.

Thus *Maternity* instead of *Mothers* gives an effect of mothers in the mass —all mothers, all women in their rôle as mothers. *Maternity*, the source of life, is opposed to *Palaces*, which thus become deathly things; and the feeling of the rejection of the aristocracy by the very life-principle is accentuated by the use of the word *root*. Similarly in the second passage *Drudgery*, the mass of toilers, is opposed to the *King*, and the image of the rags fluttering out like wings suggests the aspirations of the people, the future that they hold despite their misery in contrast with the mighty but doomed monarchy. The wing-image is given an ironic overtone by the addition of the gallows treading-on-air. That is the retort of power to the aspirations. In the third passage *History* is used instead of the Reader or some such term, and gives the reader the feeling of being himself History.

It is this kind of effect at which Carlyle is an adept, and in which he so proliferates that he may be said to have brought a new quality into prose, a quality based in action and participation. What Meredith responds to and develops in his own way is that new element.

It is significant that when in 1887 asked for admired passages in prose and verse, he cited of contemporary prose only Charlotte Brontë's description of Vashti (Rachel) acting:

> She stood locked in struggle, rigid in resistance. . . . To her what hurts her becomes immediately embodied: she looks on it as a thing that can be attacked, worried down, torn to shreds. Scarcely a substance herself, she grapples to conflict with abstractions. Before a calamity she is a tigress; she rends her woes, shivers them in convulsed abhorrence.

What he reacts to in this passage is its statement of struggle, its picture of the woman grappling with torment and abstraction, conquering and embodying them—that is, transforming them, making the evil thing serve life. Vashti is here for him the poet in the world of the alienating process at its climax. *Rigid in resistance.* That phrase suggests the best and worst in Meredith's own style. Like Vashti he fights ceaselessly against an omnipresent evil force; and without certain rigidities he would crumple up. (We have here, perhaps, the clue to his nervous tensions and breakdown.)

Already in *Feverel* he realises that the middle-class audience will never face the exposure of their true motivation:

> At present, I am aware, an audience impatient for blood and glory scorns the stress I am putting in incidents so minute, a picture so little imposing. An audience will come to whom it will be given to see the elementary machinery at work: who, as it were, from some slight hint of the straws, will feel the winds of March when they do not blow. [xxv.]

It was not that he did not recognise the need for directness and simplicity in the expression of emotion. 'English verse . . . is forced, in dealing with Nature, to lean on the simple natural words most imagerially expressive. Our Latin and Norman French are rejected in the tongue of emotion' (1883). But this simplicity must not be an evasion of the truth, a mere superficiality that avoids the depths. The tale without realism, he says,

> does not advance, 'tis true; it drives the whirling circle round and round the single existing central point; but it is enriched with the applause of the boys and girls of both ages in this land; and all the English critics heap their honours on its brave old Simplicity:—our national literary flag, which signalises us while we float, subsequently to flap above the shallows. [*One of Our Conquerors.*]

For in such unrealistic work there can be no definition of development. The bourgeois want the false, the veiled, the superficial. Victor says: 'If I read fiction, let it be fiction. . . . I can't read dull analytical stuff or "stylists" when I want action—if I'm to give my mind to a story. I can supply the reflections. I'm English—if Colney's right in saying we always come round to the story with the streak of supernaturalism.' And Nesta, before she fully wakes up, prefers 'the tale of slaughter' to Colney's satires.

By Analysis Meredith does not mean introspection or naturalistic detail. He means the realistic power to relate action to the consciousness of its social implications, which involves showing how people really act, not how they think they act—or rather showing the relation, when necessary, between the split thought and action. The audience 'impatient for blood and glory' have got to be slapped in the face by a true realism.

The reader in turn must be ready to take pains.

> Thought is tough, and dealing with thought produces toughness. Or when strong emotion is in tide against the active mind, there is perforce confusion. Have you found that scenes of simple emotion or plain narrative were hard to view? . . .
>
> In the Comedies, and here and there where a concentrated presentment is in design, you will find a 'pitch' considerably above our common human; and purposely, for only in such a manner could so much be shown. Those high notes and condensings are abandoned when the strong human call is heard. [1887.]

On the one hand this leads to his incorporation of the type of poetic imagery gained from the struggles of the New Poets into the prose narrative. And the philistine opposition to such imagery is seen as part of the mechanistic philosophy with its basis in the cash-nexus.

> The language of metaphor was to Mr Adister fool's froth. He conceded the use of it to the Irish and the Welsh . . . [but it] aroused an irritability that speedily endued him with the sense of sanity opposing lunacy; when, not having a wide command of undecorated plain speech which enjoyed his approval, he withdrew into the entrenchments of contempt.

On the other hand Meredith's anti-bourgeois position leads him in quest of a new realism able to grasp simultaneously the inner and outer world, the individual and society, and to show the struggles going on between the united opposites. Thus, Sowerby as a hidebound Tory detests metaphor. Note the terms in which Meredith describes this reaction, since they show how he conceived his style of allusion and image as directed at illuminating the process of alienation:

> The internal state of a gentleman who detested metaphor as heartily as the vulgarest of our gobble-gobbets hate it, metaphor only can describe; for the reason that he had in him just something more than is within the compass of

the meat-markets. He had—and had it not the less because he fain would not have had—sufficient stuff to furnish forth a soul's epic encounter between Nature and Circumstance: and metaphor, simile, analysis, all the fraternity of old lamps for lighting our abysmal darkness, have to be rubbed together that we may get a glimpse of the fray.

In *Beauchamp* he uses the image of 'thongmen' or overseers beating at galley-slaves to express what he feels of the critics who use the whip 'to terrorise us from experiments in imagery.'

Meredith amusingly sets out in *Diana* the two methods of description. The subject is Dacier; and Diana is the writer:

> *Old Method:* His eyes are pale blue, his features regular, his hair silky, brownish, his legs long, his head rather stooping (only his head), his mouth commonly closed; these are the facts, and you have seen the same in a nursery doll. Such literary craft is of the nursery.
> *New Method:* He lends an attentive ear when I speak, agrees or has a quaint pucker of the eyebrows dissenting inwardly. He lacks mental liveliness—cheerfulness, I should say, and is thankful to have it imparted. One suspects he would be a dull domestic companion. He has a veritable thirst for hopeful views of the world, and no spiritual distillery of his own. He leans to depression. Why! The broken reed you call your Tony carries a cargo, all her manufacture —she reeks of secret stills; and here is a young man—a sapling oak—inclined to droop.

It is not, as critics have said, that he turns from the external to the internal characteristics. He supplants the *mere description* of either with the *definition of impact*, of two persons impacting on one another.

And so when he talks of Realism, he is not intending the mere externalisation of narrative. He called *The House on the Beach* 'a Realistic Story,' and *The Athenaeum* was puzzled. 'Unluckily realism in the higher sense,' it said, 'absolute fidelity to nature and to probability, is not within Mr Meredith's province. This story is as much realistic as *Bleak House*.' Precisely! *The Athenaeum* took realism to mean naturalism. Meredith meant that the tale truly exposed the cash-nexus and found an effective image, psychologically penetrative, for doing so.

In the story itself he lightly and sarcastically indicates his meaning of the term: an art-form which truthfully shows the origins of things treated:

> If a sagacious impulse directs them to discountenance realistic tales, the realistic tale should justify its appearance by the discovery of an apology for the tormented souls. . . . They are the sons and victims of a desperate energy, alluring by cheapness, satiating with quantity, that it may mount in the social scale, at the expense of their tissues. The land is in a state of fermentation to mount, and the shop, which has shot half their stars to their social zenith, is what verily they would scald themselves to wash themselves free of.

His Realism is thus not in any sense a naturalistic transcript. But he has no systematic aesthetic, and so in hurried comments he uses the term to cover both the full realistic grasp, which includes the definition of social types, and the naturalistic fidelity which tends to wallow in details usually ignored or hidden. Though he does not approve of this naturalism, he sees in it a diverted element of rebellion, which has its passing use in clearing the ground, in attacking bourgeois inhibitions, in breaking down false romanticism. He wrote to Henley:

> The rude realism of your verses *In Hospital* has braced me. And with this breath of the darkness of life you give a note—'Out of the night that covers me'—which has a manful ring to clear and lift us, whatever the oppression that may have been caused. No realism frightens me. At its worst, I take it as a correction of the flimsy, to which our literature has a constant tendency to recur. Even the lowest appears to me more instructive than Byronics.—But when, out of hospital, you cry out in ecstasy of the 'smell of mud in the nostrils,' you strike profoundly—beyond the critical senses.
>   I thank you for the volume. It has the tone of a voice in the ear—as near to life as that. You have not aimed at higher. Do so in your next effort. [1888.]

In *One of Our Conquerors*, where he keeps recurring to problems of the novel, Colney refers to 'the custom of our period (called the Realistic) to create, when casual opportunity offers, a belief in the narrative by promoting nausea in the audience.' And later Meredith relates this naturalism to the 'audience impatient for blood and glory.' He says, 'popular [i.e. bourgeois] artists, intent to gratify the national taste for effects called realistic, have figured in scenes of battle the raying fragments of a man. . . .' And in the opening of *Diana* he sees Naturalism and Sentimentalism as two sides of the same coin.

> Worse than that alternative dirty drab, your recurring rose-pink is rebuked by hideous revelations of the filthy foul; for nature will force her way, and if you try to stifle her by drowning, she come up, not the fairest part of her uppermost! Peruse your Realists—really your castigators for not having yet embraced Philosophy.

Naturalism, with its excesses, is thus the tit-for-tat retort to the bourgeois lie; but the situation cannot be left at that kind of negative revolt, which reverses but does not transform values and is thus in the last resort as alienated as the prettifications. Meredith defines true art as Realism plus Philosophy. Such an art has its roots in earth, in common experience; but it owns the power to generalise, to create types, to relate present with past and future, to achieve poetic vision as well as realistic impact.

So he advises a young Russian writer in 1885: 'Set your mind on Earth and Life, the two perpetually intershuffling. Observe; write but to tear to strips, for a time.' And in *Earth's Secret* he wrote of 'close interthreading

Nature with our kind.' In *Beauchamp* he declares, 'My way is like a Rhone island in the summer drought, stony, unattractive, and difficult between the two forceful streams of the unreal and the over-real, which delight mankind' (i.e. the middle-class public). He thus believes that he is rescuing the classic components of the novel in the situation caused by the sharp development of the forces of self-alienation; and writes in 1892 ironically to a young writer, 'I would advise you strongly to renounce all classic components in a novel. They puzzle readers, irritate reviewers.'

Realism with a vision of the future is the only way that grand art can be built in such a world. Without the vision, expression must fall to grubbing naturalism, shocked by the ghastly egoism and cruelty of the best of all possible bourgeois worlds. With the vision it can own the courage to penetrate the horror in quest of the struggling forces that reveal already the ways and means by which the society of self-alienation can be overthrown.

He is tempted in such a society to 'write his best in perversity' (*Diana*); but though his involved resistance to the lures does have a contorting effect, he continually breaks through into clear and vital statement. All the while, however, he is aware of the maleficent public which can hate but which cannot understand anything.

> Our critics appear to be fascinated by the quaintness of our public, as the world is when our beast-garden has a new importation of magnitude, and the creature's appetite is reverently consulted. They stipulate for a writer's popularity before they will do much more than take the position of umpire to record his failure or success. . . . [*Comedy*.]

They have no sense of human values.

Meredith desires another audience, and believes that he will one day have it; but he is weighed down with an angry awareness of the actual public. In this sense, his vices of style, which register his bitter resistance, are wounds in the struggle, testimonies of his virtue—though they gain this quality only because of the continuous effort which issues in triumphant clarities.

We saw in his *Patience and Foresight* his magnificent call into the future to the mass-audience he desired. This position he keeps setting out in his poems. *The Discipline of Wisdom* asserts:

> *Who sweats not with the flock will seek in vain*
> *To shed the words that are ripe fruit of sun.*

In *The Woods of Westermain* he warns against 'that sly temptation of the illumined brain,' a feeling of superiority to the masses:

> *For be sure the bravest wing*
> *Preens it in our common spring,*

> *Thence along the vault to soar,*
> *You with others, gathering more,*
> *Glad of more, till you reject*
> *Your proud title of elect.*

And *The Garden of Epicurus* says that the remote philosophic garden may
breed gentlemen, but cannot change the world:

> *Our world which for its Babels wants a scourge,*
> *And for its wilds a husbandman, acclaims*
> *The crucifix that came of Nazareth.*

The more one considers, the more remarkable one finds the steadfast
way in which Meredith keeps his faith in the masses and orientates himself
towards mass-struggle. For in his world the signs were confused and sub-
terranean. But he holds unshaken a sense of mass-action drawn from
Chartism and 1848, and across his bad epoch looks unblinking towards
the mass-forces that were to move in organised forms against the alienating system in the next century.

I have admitted that he falls into a twisted and over-tautened style; but
most critics write of his work as if it is homogeneous in texture, whereas
in fact the difficult elements are never equally present even in the same
book, and the books themselves vary in an extraordinary way. *Shagpat*
has a buoyant poetic verve; but *Feverel* keeps on being thrown back on
itself, alternating lovely lyricism with dry detachment. *Evan Harrington*
is as readable as Dickens, and its sustained account of the Countess's fight
against odds is satirical humour at its highest. *Harry Richmond* has so
flowing a narrative that it has been pointed out as the workshop at which
Stevenson learned much of his skill; but the opening part of *One of Our
Conquerors* has a blurred raw quality as if Meredith wanted to convey the
very contusion and disintegration from which Victor is suffering. The
first half of *Vittoria* is magnificent broad drama, and Beauchamp's election-
fight is depicted with a masterful marshalling of political types. Renée in
her youth is shown with a mixture of mature psychological grasp and
lyrical sweetness; and the breakdown of Nataly is defined with an unslackening control of power. And so on. The variety in Meredith is
extreme; and no single judgment can cover it.

Let us take even what may be called a Meredithian cliché:

> His ladies never walk; they swim. Mrs Doria swims to meet Richard
> Feverel; Mrs Mount swims 'wave-like to the sofa'; Lady Rosely swims
> 'sweetly' into the room; Mrs Lovell swims 'into the general conversation';
> Madame d'Auffray swims to meet Beauchamp; Diana is always swimming—
> on one occasion she swims 'to the teatray.' [Newman in *Free Review*, 1894.]

Here it is true we meet an overdone formula, which began in an effort to find an elemental image to express feminine movement—the woman one with the element through which she moves. It appears in a strained form in the first version of *Love in the Valley*: the girl 'swims to me on a tear'—i.e. she blurs and seems undulating to him when seen through the orb of a tear. And the undine of *Farina* sets out the whole aesthetic of woman-as-wave, woman-swimming. The image then continues throughout the novels—but not always so mechanically as Newman suggests. Thus the Countess de Saldar 'swims in the pleasure of a nobleman's compliments'—an image that excellently suggests her physical dilation and expansion in the englobing warmth of her triumph.

Nesta, after feeling a considerable stress in Sowerby's presence, enters to the Misses Duvivier. 'She swam up to Dorothea's lap, and dropped her head on it, kneeling.' Meredith there means to convey her distracted movement, her sense of moving through a solid element of obstruction —in the previous paragraph we have the phrase 'the wall of social concrete' to express the blank element in Sowerby against which she feels foundered. But the term is too bluntly mechanical; it does not stir us.

In *Diana*, however, again at a moment of stress for the heroine, we find the image effectively used:

> 'If I had begun life in a cottage!'—when really a big storm-wave caught her from shore and whirled her to mid-sea, out of every sensibility but the swimming one of her loss of self in the man.

And in *Ormont* we have the long swimming scene, when, having stripped the veils and bonds of the cash-nexus world with their clothes, the lovers realise their need of one another. Here the metaphor comes right out into the open, as action, and we see what it means to Meredith.*

Thus even the irritating elements in Meredith can be shown to be not at all wilful tricks of style; they are often the unsuccessful residuum of his poetic effort to define struggle and renewal, earth-contact and development.

---

* The swimming-together of Bagarag and Noorna in *Shagpat* brings out the idea of participation in rhythmic and significant action against (and in) the elements. Meredith wrote of Lady Duff-Gordon, 'She cut her way through the accustomed troops of adorers, like what you will that is buoyant and swims gallantly.' Clara in an emotional crisis is 'swimming on the wave in her bosom,' and then 'she swam for a brilliant moment on tears, and yielded to the overflow.'
An allied image is thus of the woman-as-ship. Jenny walks 'like a yacht before the wind.' Constantia Durham is 'The Racing Cutter.' Cecilia 'loved the sea, and the stinging salt spray, and circling gull and plunging gurnet, the sun on the wave and the torn cloud'—and it is after leaving her that Beauchamp feels the yacht as the symbol of luxury-beauty. (Two of the best scenes of young love are linked with water: Renée at Venice, Richard and Lucy— compare his dream of floating with Bella.)

But the critics, because they dared not look into the meaning of his novels, could not separate the good from the bad in his style, his method, and realise the way in which his method as a whole expressed a deep resistance to the existent world. We have had many examples of their desperate opacity already, but some more will do no harm, since it is essential to understand how Meredith's work was resisted by middle-class society and its mouthpieces.

Henley said that much of his writing was tediously amusing: the pen of a great artist in the left hand and the razor of a spiritual suicide in the other. Meredith was the master and victim of a monstrous cleverness, and so on. J. M. Robertson in the *Yellow Book* attacked him for preciosity resulting from 'individual self-will, defiance of censure . . . and self-absorption in isolation.' (Thus was ignored his demand for a mass-basis in art; and thus his crippled end at Box Hill was used to blot out his earlier energetic contacts.) William Watson in *The National Review* (1889) denounced him in an essay *Fiction, Plethoric and Anaemic*, taking *Rhoda Fleming* as an example, 'an ill-constructed and very unequally written story, having some fine scenes and clever, if equally unattractive, character studies . . . a certain not too great abundance of material lying loose about in various stages of disorder.' Again:

> This perversity is not a natural bent towards the artificial. . . . He can be crispness or curtness itself at need, often indeed wonderfully vivid, sometimes within and sometimes without and sometimes on the verge of the confines of taste. [Brownell.]

Thus any praise was used to stress his errors and 'obscurities.' Henley, remember, was one of his 'admirers.' Even the defenders generally admitted the enemy's case. A writer in *The Temple Bar* of April 1893 saw in him 'a large and penetrating observation,' but declared that he shared with Richter 'a certain tortuous obscurity of phraseology' based in a horror of the simple and the commonplace; and Arthur Symons tried to explain him as a poet struggling 'against the bondage of prose.'

> A style conceived in verse, and brought up on Arabian extravaganzas and German fantasies, could scarcely be expected to adapt itself to the narration of the little colourless facts of modern English Society. [*Fortnightly*, Nov. 1887.]

There is a shred of truth in that, but it ignores that the poet is one with the radical revolutionary and that the littleness he abhors is the dwarf-nature of alienated man.

Let us turn then to his poetry itself. Here there is often crabbedness mixed with overloaded diction, e.g. the inversions of the following picture of the eagle, shot down by an arrow and hung up near the fold:

> *Hung the hooky beak up aloft the arrowhead*
> *Reddened through his feathers for our dear fold.*

But there is another type of unusual syntactical organisation which is quite clear and which does achieve its emotional and pictorial effect:

> *And he the wind-whipped, anywhither wave*
> *Crazily tumbled on a shingle grave*
> *To waste in foam. . . .*
> *When the renewed forever of a ken. . . .*
> *Weak out of sheath downy leaves*
> *Of the beech quivered lucid as dew. . . .*
> *Flutter-huddled their twigs to a crowd,*
> *The beam of them wafted my sight*
> *To league-long sun upon seas:*
> *The golden path we had crossed. . . .*

'The wind-whipped anywhither wave'—there the syntactical tangle gives extremely well the movement of water. 'Weak out of sheath downy leaves' again gives finely the effect of the young leaves that have just slipped open; 'flutter-huddled' is another way of concentrating a pictorial effect; and 'league-long sun upon seas' yet another—the league-long trail of light on the heaving waters. Taken all together the various twists and strains there put on language are vindicated by the richness of the movement communicated—the opening leaves, still frail, which are blown into a bright mass and stir like the waters he crossed with his wife. A bridge is established between his present agony of loss and the shared past, and the light-motion both intensifies and relieves the pang.*

He is capable of the plainest of statements, made effective by the sweet wrench and leap of the rhythm in a line like, 'The young time with the life ahead,' or by the breadth of vision: 'Fair Mother Earth lay on her back last night . . .'; or in sustained character-definition in poems like *The Old Chartist*:

> *I'm not ashamed: Not beaten's still my boast:*
> *Again I'll rouse the people up to strike.*
> *But home's where different politics jar most.*
> *Respectability the women like.*
> *This form, or that form,—*
> *The Government may be a hungry pike,*
> *But don't you mount a Chartist platform! . . .*

---

* This expressive use of new syntactical forms, allied with an effort to develop more dynamic rhythms, links Meredith with Hopkins: though he could not have known Hopkins's work, and the sections of his poetry closest to Hopkins's method were written after Hopkins had stopped writing. The similarities derive from a shared resistance to bourgeois trends.

But I can best bring out his contribution by taking one of the units of *Modern Love* which defines the final breakdown of the relationship:

> *Mark where the pressing wind shoots javelin-like,*
> *Its skelton shadow on the broad-backed wave!*
> *Here is a fitting spot to dig Love's grave;*
> *Here where the ponderous breakers plunge and strike,*
> *And dart their hissing tongues high up the sand:*
> *In hearing of the ocean, and in sight*
> *Of those ribbed wind-streaks running into white.*
> *If I the death of Love had deeply planned,*
> *I never could have made it half so sure,*
> *As by the unblest kisses which upbraid*
> *The full-waked sense, or failing that, degrade!*
> *'Tis morning: but no morning can restore*
> *What we have forfeited. I see no sin:*
> *The wrong is mixed. In tragic life, God wot,*
> *No villain need be! Passions spin the plot:*
> *We are betrayed by what is false within.*

First, note the elemental force of the pictorial image: wind and water in a wild wrestle. The water is seen as a heaving body—broad-backed, tongued, with ribbed streaks. The wind presses in embrace. But the contact of love is changed into a deathly thing: the wind is a wounding spear. The living body becomes a skeleton shadow, disintegrates. The place of such bridal mating becomes a grave. Thus the vain embraces of the night, the unblest kisses, are merged with the sea-scene; the outer desolation and unending conflict are the scene within as well as without.

The effect is gained partly by direct statement, partly by the force with which the elemental movement is merged with the struggles of the lovers. There is no question of the sea-image being used to define or explain the emotion of the poet. The ceaseless movement of nature into decay and renewal is one with the human struggle.

For the same reason as his syntactical inventions he often makes unusual word-combinations, e.g. *poppy-droop, swan-wave, circle-windsails.* Here the effects gained are generally clear and vivid, and he enriches our language. In rhyming he tried to widen the prevailing systems; and for this too he was blamed. He wrote to Hilda on a complaint of his way of rhyming, calling it 'French heresy or bluntness of ear':

> The ear of the boor in fact demands the hard consonantal smack of an exact similarity of sound, together with the repetition *ad infinitum* of the one rhyme to people, being steeple:

In this matter as in most of his innovations he has been vindicated as having realised the lines along which our verse-forms could best attain increased strength and freshness.

Alice Meynell objected to the use in his verse of quantity, saying that accent was sufficient for poetry 'which is read in repose.' Here are some examples of the remarkable way in which he could put together clanging accents, with an effect of quantitative lengths of sound:

> Lárge, and smóky réd the sún's cóld dísk dróps.
>
> Up lánes, woóds throúgh, they troóp in jóyful bánds.
>
> Stréaming like the flág-réed Soúth-Wést blówn.

The third line has five consecutive stressed strong syllables.

These effects come off: but it is true that in other cases the sound-length of various syllables jars and disturbs the rhythmic movement intolerably. Alice Meynell's complaint, however, betrays the wrong line of protest: Meredith didn't want to write to be 'read in repose.' He wrote to be read outside the quiet armchair. Confusedly he was seeking to beget a new kind of poetic action and active poetry. While this impulse gives his verse many of its best qualities, it also produces its main weakness, its textural insensitivity. There is often, in revulsion from Tennysonian harmonies, a harshness in which syllables jolt and crackle without emotional and artistic justification. He wanted rocky poetry; but many of the jagged edges are ugly and prevent his poems from reaching the highest rank. He was right in resisting the Tennysonian solutions, but his 'rigidities in resistance' often went too far.

And yet he has a definite place in our poetry; and it is hard to deny an important rank to the poet of *Love in the Valley*, *Hymn to Colour*, *Modern Love*, *Skylark Ascending*, *Earth and a Wedded Woman*, and many another earth-poem. In the last resort, however, too much of his poetic impulse went into his novels for him to make of his poetry the key-expression of his vision of life. Mainly it was the imagery of man-mating-earth that went into his verse: the full definition of social struggle went into the novels.

The Spectator in 1887 wrote of *Ballads and Poems* that Meredith's verse was for the most part inarticulate: not meaningless, but unable to say what it wants to say. Yet, 'what a pure and lucid strain of lyric sweetness, what floods of passionate eloquence, are to be found side by side with his crudest and most repellent verse.' As in so many of the attacks on his work, there was a measure of truth in this evaluation. But since the criticism never went on to show what he was trying to do, it misfired, and he resented it. He was not trying (as Symons said of the same book) to show

Nature as a source of joy and healing in opposition to the tragic tangle of human existence. The human existence he dealt with was that of a society in which the process of self-alienation was reaching its limit, and the nature to which he turned derived its meaning from human activity, the transformative energies of production. But all that was far out of the ken of the critics, the public.

Meredith always thought of himself as a poet; and Blunt pleased him by saying that that was how he always considered him—though in fact Blunt was trying to hide the fact he hadn't read the novels, or didn't like them. But it was in the novels that the main working-out of his poetic faculty is to be found. The method which we saw at work in the lines from *Modern Love* is the typical method of his prose, though naturally on a more extended scale, a less concentrated system. We have noted in passing many of the ways in which he links man and nature—the mountain setting of Mazzini and his followers that opens *Vittoria*, or the pure alpine air that is part of Carinthia's spirit. And that sort of thing, in large and in little, might be indefinitely exemplified.*

Here is one passage, which must serve, from near the end of his writing days, from *Lord Ormont*. It describes Aminta's country-journey in a carriage, and is felicitous in its details, finely bracing in its general movement, and, in its fusion of woman and landscape, expressive of the expansive impulse of freedom that stirs within her:

> She had rocked in a swing between sensation and imagination, exultant, rich with the broad valley of the plain and the high green waves of the downs at their giant's bound in the flow of curves and sunny creases to the final fling-off of the dip on the sky. Here was a twisted hawthorn carved clean to the way of the wind; a sheltered clump of chestnuts holding their blossoms up, as with a thousand cresset-clasping hands; here were grasses that nodded swept from green to grey; flowers yellow, white, and blue, significant of a marvellous unknown through the gates of colour; and gorse-covers giving out the bird, squares of young wheat, a single fallow threaded by a hare, and cottage-gardens, shadowy garths, wayside flint-heap, woods of the mounds and the dells, fluttering leaves, clouds: all were swallowed, all were one unworded significance.

There the dynamic word of the New Poetry is put fully at the service of

---

* In *The Fortnightly*, June 1868, he declared that the lyric impulse could easily be attenuated. 'A large and noble theme has a framework which yields as much support as it demands. Lyrics yield none; and when they are not spontaneous, they rob us of a great deal of our strength and sincerity. . . . A great lyrist (and we have one among us [Swinburne]), inflamed by the woes of an unhappy people throbbing for fulness of life and freedom, sings perforce; but he has a great subject, and we do not see that it is his will which distinctly predominates in his verses.' Even Heine, who, with an 'irritant exile', breathed irony' into his lyrics and shaped them into true form and significance, makes himself his constant theme and ends by wearying.

human purposes. Such a passage suffices to refute those who talk of
Meredith as a writer of epigrammatic gibberish.

This chapter may be fitly ended with two passages from the letters to
Hilda. First, he complains that his faults are picked out to the exclusion of
his positive and more characteristic qualities.

> It is because I do not pass among reviewers that they treat one who is so
> little a favourite with the public, and who courts no favour, with this form of
> politeness. I am termed a harlequin, a performer of antics. I choose, when I
> write, the expression seeming to my imagination just, and if it is not conven-
> tional, they denounce it. When there is stress of emotion, my speech is neces-
> sarily simple, in harmony with the common human element. They admit it,
> yet cannot allow that at other seasons the writer's fancy (if he have any) should
> be allowed to play.
>
> So they pursue their course, treating each new book of mine to blows, and
> me to reluctantly lessening contempt confirmed in dislike, while gradually the
> submerged volume comes back to the surface, is demanded, and spoken of
> respectfully. I am told that my first volume of poems, written when I was a
> minor, will now sell for ten pounds. All of them go for double the original
> price. Yet after close on forty years of honest work, I present myself to receive
> the certain lash. . . .
>
> I know my faults. I know too that all writers have some. The unfairness
> consists in reviewing favourites on the lines of their good things, and the
> unfavoured in examples of their weak or unappreciated.
>
> I suppose I shall not publish very much more, and to be lashed up to the end
> is wearisome, if but for the monotony.

In a later letter he comes to grips with the problem, both of his own
shortcomings and the hatred his work stirred:

> Looking back over history will help you to look forward, above and beyond
> the tumble of the waters. What you do is to begin a flight with your mind,
> and quickly relapse on your sensations, with a sigh and a cry for a capable
> crowned Man to come and settle affairs. And if he came, he would but passingly
> smooth them.
>
> For permanent work, the people must be active. Already it is perceptible
> that they are everywhere thoughtfuller than they were. Can you truly deny
> it? Rather let my dear Lady ask herself whether she does too unresistingly
> weary of even the sight of struggle. Her cry for the capable Man is one of the
> errors of democracy too. It means the cry for the Sword to cut the difficult
> knot. And that, as we observe in history, represents a fracture which has to be
> mended by many decades of labour. Democracy nevertheless is learning.

He is not speaking specifically of literature, but his words apply there as
elsewhere. *For permanent work, the people must be active.* They had been
active in the period from which he derived, that of Chartism and 1848,
and he knew that they would be active again, that they were stirring—
though in comparison with the 1840's they were still quiescent. Out of

Memory and Hope he built many permanent elements in his writing; but in the deadly quiescent present he was thrown too much back on himself, into an explosive shortcircuiting of his powers, with the result of many unstable and impermanent elements. But in the last resort, because he always fought the deathliness, his work belongs to the future of his Hope, where the people are active and build for permanence, for humanist universality. And for this reason he was attacked by the critics who guarded the deathly values of the bourgeoisie.

In the words of James Thomson, here are words that if you prick them, bleed. In Meredith's own words: 'You will find by and by, that when taken altogether I am clear.'

33

The Ignored Question of his Content, and his Influence

After the first crude moralistic attacks, on *Feverel* and *Modern Love*, the onslaught on Meredith almost entirely concerned itself with his form, and so there is little to say about distortions of his meaning. Interpretations of his themes, if made at all, were uniformly so imperceptive that they require no consideration. Except in one matter, the theme of Earth in his poetry and his novels. A certain depth of intelligence, and above all a capacity to detach oneself from the circle of bourgeois preconceptions, were needed to get inside works like *Sandra* or *One of Our Conquerors*; but one had to be very stupid indeed not to see the materialist basis of many of the poems.

H. S. Salt in his 1895 essay in *The Free Review* shows the degree of awareness on this matter among the more independent-minded readers. He recognises Meredith as 'at once the sanest and the humanest of English novelists, the strongest brain and the most feeling heart of his literary generation, he will be read and studied with increasing attention when the great ethical and social movements that are now at work shall have rendered antiquated the larger part of contemporary fiction.' And he grasps something, from a simple rationalist angle, of Meredith's creed of Earth. Small as this perception of Meredith's virtues was (for it failed, like all others, to grasp his penetration into the processes of self-alienation), the reactionary forces had to fight against it.

'Cleverness' had been the objurgatory term long-used to remove attention from what Meredith was talking about. It at once suggested unscrupulous and tricky superficiality, artificial remoteness. The attempt of men like Salt to exalt him as an ethical teacher, and the criticisms of the Henleys who saw him as a subtle but rather wrongheaded psychologist, shifted the problem of distorting his meanings on to a new level. He was made the novelist of the Fine Shades that he had mercilessly exposed in the Pole sisters and Wilfrid, of Subtleties for their own sake, and his social views were treated as if concerned with purely sectional issues such as Equality for Women, without reference to his critique of bourgeois society as a whole. He was seen as intellectualist, rationalist, lost in somewhat thin abstractions, and rather pathetically noble.

The clear element of materialism in his verse had to be deodorised. R. Colles in *The Author* (1 May 1895) showed the way. Call him Wordsworth's successor and the High Priest of Nature. F. Melian Stawell took things a step further in *The International Journal of Ethics* (April 1902), twisting plain statements with spiritualistic interpretations. (J. Moffat in *Hibbert*, July 1905, was a little more honest and rebuked Meredith for his 'disparagement of human personality'—which, translated from its parsonical vagueness, means that he saw the idea of personal immortality as a shameful form of egoism.) In *The Fortnightly*, December 1907, L. Magnus described him as the reconciler of Darwin and Wordsworth, and sought to blur Earth out in the God from whom Meredith essentially laboured to redeem her. After this, a commentator like G. H. Trevelyan might make a slightly more truthful analysis; but his failure to get at the core of the problem (the revelation of self-alienation and the struggle against it) meant that the pious smell thickened. Meredith had been respectabilised.

When then of his real achievement, the real Content of his work? In dealing with his Form we had inevitably to move over to his Content, since in any deep analysis the two are one.

There is no need here to repeat what has been said of Egoism in our inquiry into his political and spiritual positions. His work, as we have seen, from first to last is concerned with concretely grasping the ways in which the society of the cash-nexus distorts the human essence. He drew largely on Carlyle's idiom in this effort, but he remained true to the struggle against the dehumanising forces while Carlyle became their great mouthpiece. From Bagarag's fight to destroy the Identical to Carinthia's struggle to understand the outrage of her society which has been canalised in the egoistic fear and fury of Fleetwood, there is a clear line of unbroken development.

Meredith, despite the unsystematic and often confused nature of his thinking, forged steadily ahead towards a dialectic of process. From the outset of *Poems* 1851 and *Shagpat* he realised to a considerable extent that if he was to struggle against the divided-man of the cash-nexus (who, in striving to make men into things, dehumanises and splits himself) he must struggle against all the philosophic and religious abstractions which cut men into body and spirit, and reality into this-world and another-world. He understood that the struggle for a philosophy of the unity of process was also a social struggle against the forces of greed and ego-power that ruled his world. He saw, though not with complete vision, that the philosophy he wanted must base its notion of an active relation to nature, to earth, on the productive activity of men which changed nature and themselves.

Hence his use of *Earth* as the rallying-point of his resistance to the divisive forces of society. Hence the vast advance he made on the romantic rebels who could not reach the concept of the unity of process without losing their grasp on the struggle against existing divisions, or who, at their best, clung to the hope of a revolutionary change but could not sustain a realistic approach to the issues.

In our analysis of Meredith's work we have sufficiently discussed the strengths and weaknesses of his concepts, his applications of those concepts. For some fifty years he maintained his struggle—in the darkest and deadest half-century of our history. His courage and insight in such a resistance to the pressures of the seemingly-triumphant bourgeoisie cannot be overpraised. But the fact that he had for the most part to base his work emotionally on a mass-audience that wasn't there, an audience of the future, left its mark on his style in the odd mixture of constriction and expansiveness discussed in the last chapter, and in an inability to grasp stably the nature of the class-State. From these weaknesses derived the confusions in *One of Our Conquerors* (present in a considerable degree also in *Beauchamp's Career*), and the fantasy expressed in several of his later poems that a free citizen-army could be built in his England—an army which would refuse to be the instrument of imperialist policy.

And yet, as we have noted abundantly, at a pinch his good human sense always saw him through. He responded to the 1905 Russian Revolution in a way which showed the depth of his belief in the masses. We can perhaps express the confusion and the deep feeling for the human truth in his mind by saying that if he had lived till 1914 he would most probably, with many heartburnings, have supported the war against Germany, and that if he had lived on till 1917 he would most probably, with many more heartburnings, have supported the Soviet Revolution.

We have also seen in our discussion of his works how he seeks from the outset to create a positive hero who is set against a world of corruption and self-alienation. From Bagarag onwards—through the many types such as Austin Wentworth, Evan, Sandra-Vittoria, Robert Armstrong, Beauchamp, Nesta and Dartrey, Matey Weyburn, Carinthia and Wood-seer—he seeks to define the individuals who fight against dominant bourgeois trends. Harry Richmond and Diana are uncertain strugglers—and that is why the books in which they appear were the two most popular of his works; while in *The Egoist* and *The Tragic Comedians* the main focus is on the disintegration of personality in those who cannot fight or who betray the fight.

This creation of the positive hero is an achievement no less remarkable than the unerring perspective of bourgeois self-alienation. It is something quite new in world-literature. Scott's heroes are amiably lost between two worlds; Balzac's are in the midst of the hurlyburly of the cash-nexus and are only decent in so far as they recede from the capitalist pressures; Flaubert has no heroes in our sense of the term. Zola gets a glimpse of heroism in *Germinal*, but cannot sustain the vision except in Utopian terms. Tolstoy and Dostoevsky in different ways are intensely sensitive to capitalist self-alienation and to the need of some regenerative way of life; but they turn to religious solutions, even though Tolstoy far outgoes Dostoevsky by his feeling that in work and brotherhood lie the main clues —Dostoevsky thus tending to fall under the domination of the very processes of self-alienation that he thinks he is denying. Even Dickens is not strong in his heroes; for he bases his feeling of the transformative forces at work in his whole picture of the common-folk, not in his heroes.

Gorky was the first writer of world-stature who broke through all hesitations, confusions, compromises, fears, and in works like *Mother* showed directly the political struggle of the proletarian masses to change life at the core. But though Gorky did not know Meredith's work, we cannot refuse to Meredith the title of his precursor. Meredith strives always to show the heroic individual becoming aware of the need to revolt, to fight the process of dehumanisation and division, to achieve personal fulfilment by self-identification with the forces in his society struggling for a new life. That is his tremendous virtue. What he cannot do is what Gorky does—turn concretely to the working-class for his hero and define directly the battle for socialism.

There is no need to explain further why he suffers from these limitations, which have their basis in his bad epoch. Rather than ask why he could not write a *Mother*, we should wonder how he maintained such creative integrity as to write a *Vittoria*, a *Beauchamp*, an *Egoist*.

And while defining his positive heroes, who are real because they struggle against the real forces of social destruction and decay, he is never Utopian—or only marginally, as with a character like Merthyr. He keeps his realistic grasp, so that he shows the point at which his Vittoria, his Beauchamp, his Alvan, are unable to sustain the struggle and succumb to the class-forces they have been resisting. Vittoria is broken down by a false pride in her own intuition, which ends by attaching her to the King; Alvan more crudely finds that vanity brings him to the level of the class-enemy; Beauchamp does not fall so badly—but his death, while in one sense representing his need for union with the working-class of the future, also expresses the way he declines upon an act of individual heroism instead of playing an heroic part in the movement that has gripped his life. And always the definition is made within a total focus which throbs with belief in the fraternal future, in the common-man's capacity to overcome the throttling divisions.

He can depict individual figures of the common-folk like Mrs Berry or Madge, Rhoda or Old Gammon; but the industrial workers are outside his ken. Only in the Welsh miners on strike in *The Amazing Marriage* can they be said to enter his work, and then it is as an undifferentiated group—though drawn with all sympathy and shown in a significant relation to his heroine. And indeed we may say also that the working-class is the real hero of *The Tragic Comedians*, since that novel utters the conviction that they in their party will triumph where Alvan failed—they appear directly only as the background of Alvan's musing morning: the power behind him, he thinks, but in fact the power that has left him behind. Meredith praised the industrial workers of the North of England but never showed them. The nearest he got to a worker as a hero was Robert of *Rhoda Fleming*, with his defiance of the gentry; but Robert, though a labourer in the tale, comes of small-farmer stock and becomes a small farmer.

There is a further characteristic that results from their basic positions. Meredith in all his main characters is simultaneously aware both of what a man or woman is, and what he or she might be. This kind of perspective no doubt is to be found one way or another in all great art; but with Meredith it moves to a new and decisive level of consciousness. He is able to achieve this level because in the last resort he sees his people always in terms of struggle and because the struggle he sees is real—that is, he does not abstract aspects of life as psychological, moral, artistic entities. He sees the various aspects as aspects of a total process which, in his world, always involves the pressures of capitalist self-alienation and the struggle to change the world so as to extend freedom and brotherhood.

And so oddly, he is the precursor of Socialist Realism—to the rear of Gorky, but still well within view. For Socialist Realism is expression concretely based in actuality, in immediate struggle, in the existing positions of people, and yet always fusing its realism with a vision of the transformative process, of the future within the present.

There could then be no more one-sided judgment than the following:

> The people who are wrong in Meredith's novels are more arresting than the people who are right, not merely because the Comic Spirit singles them out and magnifies them to us, but because they have actually more of Meredith's own self in them. . . . Meredithian Comedy ends by making us examine ourselves, because it is the creation of a man who began by examining his own secret self. [J. B. Priestley.]

Meredith began in no such way. He began by examining the relation of individual and society, in the specific historical situation in which he found himself. Such comments as the above, all too typical, derive from a consideration of *The Egoist* (and Stevenson's comments on it) and ignore the fact that *The Egoist*, though without a strong positive character, derives its sharp focus from the directly political work which has preceded it. Sir Willoughby is possible as a creation only because of Bagarag, Sandra-Vittoria, Beauchamp.

Meredith said in *Beauchamp* that the superhuman beauty of the conventional novel-hero had destroyed the public belief in any heroes at all. By restoring a content of struggle, soundly based, he restored reality to heroism.

Throughout he tests his heroes by their relation to women. For in the love-relation he feels that the man's attitude to Earth and to Fraternity can best be gauged. From Shibli and Noorna onwards this method prevails.

> Meredith's ideas, in which love and the reactions of different personalities form the groundwork, are developed in his novels through the behaviour of his characters in society. Consequently, it would be impossible to imagine a novel of Meredith's without women. For example, the revolutionary ideas of Nevil Beauchamp find their chief expression in his relation to Cecilia Halkett and Jenny Denham. In *Sandra Belloni* and its sequel *Vittoria* the struggle for freedom of the Italian people is figuratively presented in the heroine's vindication of her personality. But her personality could only be unfolded in the experience of love, which she learned at last, after a fiery ordeal, to understand. [Bierig, a German critic.]

True, except that the phrasing is a trifle abstract. Love-relations are not the 'chief expression' of Beauchamp's revolutionary ideas; there is also the election-fight, the projected newspaper and so on. The struggle for Italian freedom is not simply 'presented figuratively' in the heroine's vindication of her personality; it is also presented as a plain struggle for freedom, and it is through her participation that Vittoria vindicates and develops her personality. But the general point of the remarks is correct enough, and important.

Meredith is right enough in making the love-relation a test of truth and understanding; but he makes it so pre-eminently the test because of the general political situation we have discussed. The lack of mass-struggles drives him back on the love-relation as the test of devotion to fraternity, and the issue of women's equality becomes the primary mode by which the struggle to change society is viewed.

> The love-season is the carnival of egoism, and it brings the touchstone to our natures. I speak of love, not the mask, and not the flutings upon the theme of love, but of the passion; a flame having, like our mortality, death in it as well as life, that may or may not be lasting. Applied to Sir Willoughby, as to thousands of civilised males, the touchstone found him requiring to be dealt with by his betrothed as an original savage. [*Egoist.*]

Once again there is no need for us to recapitulate here. We have seen how Meredith's work from first to last is permeated with the notion of woman's equality with man, the incompleteness of man as of woman in a situation where women are ranked as inferior and stunted by an education based on such attitudes. He set this position out in *Shagpat*, and he kept it up throughout the years when he saw the struggle of middle-class women gathering and uttering itself till its climax in the Suffragette Movement.

He had here to weather the opposition of many of the women who thought themselves advanced, as well as of the novel-reading public in general. Thus a novelist (Adeline Sergeant) protested in *The Temple Bar* of June 1889 that his 'heroical feminine type' was false, as women differed from men in powers and temperament, and that he saw women as lesser men.

> There is scarcely a woman in his books who is not, righteously and grandly, in revolt, at war with herself, or with society, at war with the ignorance, the cowardice, the want of candour, want of judgment, want of sense, which a bad education, rather than a bad disposition, has made characteristic of women, at war with society for its narrowness, its harshness, its want of humour and tolerance, and its impenetrable stupidity.

Even a woman-novelist of the day, sure that woman's goal wasn't to be the equal comrade of man, kindles at the recital.

We saw how the first person to appreciate something of Meredith's method was the poet James Thomson. Then came the young men, Hardy and Stevenson and Gissing, who drew deeply on his work, whether or not they wrote about it. Critics like Henley and Arthur Symons praised certain aspects, and at least appreciated that here was a man of rare quality. But these commentators were rather the exception; and often when something true was said, it was said in order to be turned against him: Henley put a laurel-crown on his head, Meredith said, then buffeted him in the stomach.

> Each book is the elaboration of an idea, the working-out of some theme taken on its intellectual side. . . . The book is a series of deductions from it. Its essential unity, therefore—in spite of excrescent detail—is agreeably unmistakable. But it is hardly necessary to point out that it is not the unity of a sympathetic image of life immediately beholden in its entirety. It is a mathematical, that is to say artificial, unity. [Brownell.]

The idiom of such a denigration is drawn from the notion that Meredith is coldly intellectualist because of his insistence on brain-stuff, on clear thinking. But the fundamental idea in any one of his books is not intellectual in the narrow sense; it is an idea that is also a life-image. Each book has the unity of a deep grasp of social process and struggle—but not a 'sympathetic image of life' immediately likely to please the bourgeoisie (who are here identified with humanity). The notion of Meredith as a detached analyst came mainly from *The Egoist* with its lack of strongly positive characters and engaged struggle, but, as we have seen, the whole furious force in the novel's analysis came from the works that preceded it with their 'image of life sympathetic' to all persons struggling against the egoist world.

Even the more intelligent critics, who have seen that there is a revolutionary passion at work, have left the matter vague:

> Mr Meredith grew up in the high hopes fed by the revolution of the mid-century, and the most heroic figure in his books is Mazzini, the 'Chief' in *Vittoria*. He has a moral and spiritual afflatus of the nobler order, peculiarly and traditionally English, in that line of the great English prophets, which come down from Langland and Sir Thomas More to Carlyle. His creed does not depend, visibly, on formal doctrine for its force, but neither does it rest on any preoccupying enmity towards doctrine. His inspiration plays in various moods —strenuous, ethereal, ironical—rarely serene, over his vision of 'certain nobler races, now dimly imagined'; and casts a new interpreting light, above all, on the rarer forms of love and patriotism. [Elton.]

Much of that is true; but it is vitiated throughout by the muffling of the sharp impact of Meredith's definitions, his precise statement of the enemy and of the desired future of the Vivid Many.

Must we then say that Meredith's work miscarried because we seem to find nobody who grasps his intentions? Not at all. If we are to decide a writer's merits by the degree of understanding about them that we find in bourgeois critics, what writer will survive? Without going back to more distant times such as the Elizabethan, consider the ineffable opacity of the critical reactions to Balzac, Dickens, Tolstoy. . . . The fact that the resistance to Meredith took the form of attacks on his style does not mean that he was failing to get home with other irritants than abstract nouns. It is only to be expected that the full political analysis of any significant past writer should have to wait till the present, when the world-situation makes it at last possible to view culture from the angle of the struggle for full freedom from the alienating process, the struggle for humanist universality which includes the brotherhood of man and the equality of woman.

A brief consideration of Meredith's influence will elucidate this point.

First, though he did not much influence Wilde, it is perhaps instructive to take the latter's two main criticisms, the first on the conventional lines, in *The Decay of Lying*, the second, which goes deeper, from *The Soul of Man under Socialism*:

> Ah! Meredith! Who can define him? His style is chaos illumined by flashes of lightning. As a writer he has mastered everything except language: as a novelist he can do everything, except tell a story: as an artist he is everything except articulate . . . always breaking his shins over his own wit. . . .

This passage sees him 'a child of realism not on speaking terms with his father,' a romanticist who has closed himself in thorny hedge of wonderful red roses. The second passage has abolished the hedge:

> One incomparable novelist we have now in England, Mr George Meredith. There are better artists in France, but France has no one whose view of life is so large, so varied, so imaginatively true. There are tellers of stories in Russia who have a more vivid sense of what pain in fiction may be. But to him belongs philosophy in fiction. His people not merely live, but they live in thought. One can see them from myriad points of view. They are suggestive. There is soul in them and around them. They are interpretative and symbolic.

Wilde aspiring to be a Socialist has supplanted Wilde content to be a witty Liar.

Hardy's profound debt for the liberation of his own best qualities we have already touched on; and Gissing's debt to his encouraging example. Hardy's and Gissing's pessimism represented the decline of our cultural situation; but both writers sought in weakened and restricted ways to carry on the tradition of fearless truth, of penetration into the human situation, which Meredith had founded as the necessary next stage of our novel after the phase represented by Dickens (with its immediate basis in the vitalising mass-struggles of the years 1830–48).*

R. L. Stevenson drew on a different aspect of Meredith's work. He loved his broad adventurous flow in *Harry Richmond* and his minutely

---

* Priestley stupidly calls *Rhoda* 'that curious novel which always suggests a Meredith masquerading as a Hardy,' instead of seeing that the roles were reversed! Baker sees that 'the difference between him and M. goes so deep that it is like the break between two literary epochs, one reacting against its predecessor,' (*Hist. of Eng. Novel*, ix), but does not grasp the organic link. R. Peel writes of 'the gloomy splendour that ought to be in *Rhoda Fleming* and is in *Tess*' (*A Victorian Pagan*). Why ought it be there, except that the critic is prejudiced in favour of pessimism? Instead we may ask: the sturdy faith that sees beyond tragic irony, why isn't it in *Tess* where it ought to be?

The sense of a close link between Hardy and Meredith, despite the differences, can be traced well back in the criticism of the 1890's, e.g. W. Wharton, *Free Review*, July 1894: 'It is the peculiar glory of novelists like G.M. and T.H. that they have redeemed English fiction from the reproach of provincialism.' The critic goes on to compare *Tess* and the Meredithian heroine for their opposed qualities, one the victim of fate, the other the moulder of her own life.

scrupulous analysis in *The Egoist*. He responded to the bold 'blow for life' in *Rhoda Fleming*. His love of the open-air, his dislike of the hypocritical, his desire for adventure—all these elements of his character found nourishment in Meredith's writing. But Hardy could not re-apply Meredith's concept of progressive development while carrying-on his work of penetration into the concrete issues of human conflict and suffering, into the living relation between man and nature; Gissing could not add Meredith's breadth while carrying-on much of his analytic insights; and Stevenson could not hold fast to an understanding of the political bases of conflict while carrying-on with the vital impulse into action, into a discovery of kinship with nature, into stoical resistances.

> I am a true blue Meredith person. I think George Meredith out and away the greatest force in English letters, and I don't know whether it can be considered a very encouraging thing that he has now become popular or whether we should think it a discouraging thing that he should have written so long without any encouragement whatever.
>
> It is enough for instance to disgust a man with the whole trade of letters that such a book as *Rhoda Fleming* should have fallen flat; it is the strongest thing in English letters since Shakespeare died, and if Shakespeare could have read it he would have jumped and cried, 'Here's a fellow!' No other living writer of English fiction can be compared to Meredith. Of course, I would give my hand to write like Hardy. I have seen sentences of his that I don't think can be bettered in any writer or in any language. Still, I serve under Meredith's colours always.*

Hardy in 1909 refused to write a critical estimate of his work:

> I have known Mr Meredith for so long a time—forty years within a few months—and his personality is such a living one to me that I cannot reach a sufficiently detached point of view. . . .

Meredith's effect on Hardy, Gissing, Stevenson—a mixture of action and reaction—is fairly easy to see; but in the confused mixture of trends that show up with the turn of the century, the matter is not so simple. However, up to 1914 (i.e. including writers who had gone through their formative period by that date), his influence remains strong. In a general way his work had cleared the ground for writers like Wells and Galsworthy. It was not the only factor making it possible for novelists to begin now with certain realisations of the dialectics of individual and society, which were lacking or confused before his day; but it was certainly a primary one.

---

* In 1894 Henry James calls R.L.S. 'this too apt pupil of Meredith.' Among the writers who became friendly with him was William Sharp (Fiona Macleod); and Yeats was reading him with admiration. The poems 'are certainly very beautiful, and have far more serenity and suavity than I had expected.' *Love in the Valley* 'is full of a curious intricate richness.'

Literary history will note the influence of his ideas on a popular novelist like H. G. Wells, who has vulgarised them, or on an artist like Galsworthy, who has elaborated them. For confessions of this influence see *The New Machiavelli* of Wells and *The Patrician* of Galsworthy. [Galland.]

His influence, however, was indirect as well as direct, operating in many ways through lesser writers who were affected by him in the post-*Diana* period.*

We can see the impact of his ideas and methods on a writer like Henry James, who had many insights into the inner struggle of his society, but who feared to grasp the core of it as Meredith did. James read *Evan Harrington* in early life, as it appeared serially in *Once a Week*, and it left a deeper impression than he was aware. Meredith puzzled and fascinated him; and when he read the *Letters* in 1912 he poured out his genuine response mixed with his shrinking-away from the deepmost creative elements in Meredith's personality and work. 'I catch the emanation of something so admirable, and, on the whole, so baffled and tragic.' Such an observation goes deeper than those concerned with Meredith's intellectualism or his 'ethical teaching' in the abstract; but it shows the fundamental inability of the man who accepts alienation as an eternal condition of humanity to enter into the rebellion which, however blurred at moments, is always seeking a way out of the cash-nexus dilemma. There were baffled elements in Meredith, but what James feels as such is his noble inability to rest on an artistic exploitation of a given (reasonably-safe) perception of existing contradictions. The tragedy is in James's own fear of the full artistic and moral task, not in Meredith's throwing-out of fear. Unless one sees in Meredith *the conscious defeat of tragedy*, one sees nothing.†

James then notes correctly the bad editing of the *Letters*, 'the absence of

---

* J. Oliver Hobbes (Mrs Craigie) uses a Meredithian method, in the superficial sense, to confuse the issues, e.g. in *Robert Orange*, 1900: he strongly disapproved of her. Mary Webb drew from him for her treatment of nature. Barrie sentimentalised such of his analytic method as he could imitate, e.g. *Sentimental Tommy* (where the Meredithian and anti-Meredithian struggle, at a feeble level, can be seen). C. E. Montagu in *Fiery Particles*, 1923, states that his method was developed 'under the stinging shower-wit of sparkling spray from Meredith's astringent wit.' A writer like Kathleen Mansfield shows the action-and-reaction at work. 'I lay and read the *Egoist*. It seemed to me marvellously good in its way. . . . But when I read *Richard Feverel*, and that seemed so false, so preposterous—one could only groan for it —and it's so odious. . . . But he is a big man, and he *can* write wonders.'

G. Lowes Dickinson depicted M. as Geoffrey Vivian in *A Modern Symposium*, a novel showing many Meredithian influences.

† James was one of those at whom Meredith flung ideas for novels, which had a highly stimulating effect: see *The Notebooks* (1947) for 16 March and 19 April, 1894, and 10 Feb. 1899. Prof. Stevenson says well of the early reading of *Evan*: 'it served as a catalyst to make him conscious of his own nascent impulse to be a writer.' We may add that it had a powerful effect on his whole vision of life. It is this deep pervasive influence that mattered rather than the more direct effects on tales like *The Death of the Lion*, *The Pattern in the Carpet*, *John Delavoy*. James says that in his personal intercourse with Meredith he saw him as 'a charming, a quite splendid and rather strange Exhibition' before which he simply sat.

any attempt to project the Image of character, temper, quantity and
quality of mind, general size and sort of personality that such a subject
cries for: to the shame of criticism. For such a vividness to go a-begging!'
He seems stirring with a grasp of Meredith's significance, but he smothers
it by saying that Meredith didn't live in the 'world of art.' He notes the
'poorness of range' in the correspondents; only in writing to Morley, and
in a lesser extent to Maxse, he thinks, was Meredith able to say 'a certain
number of rare and fine things, many beautiful felicities of wit and vision.
. . . He was *starved*, to my vision, but the more nobly pathetic.' Meredith's social side, but not his artistic is illuminated.

Again there is a half-truth here. Meredith's letters indeed show how
cramped he was for companionship; but this loneliness was the expression
of his consistent opposition to the social and political processes of the
Victorian bourgeoisie; he could only utter half-himself to his friends, because none of them shared his deep revolt except in partial ways. If he had
concentrated more on 'art' in James's sense, he would have quite failed as
an artist, because he would have slackened in his intense opposition to the
ruling cash-nexus and its egoisms. It was that opposition which gave
unity to his art and his life, his thought and his action; and it is precisely
this unity which troubles James. Instead of seeing its central importance
both for the understanding of Meredith and for the art-problems of
James's own world, and *then* investigating it for flaws and weaknesses, he
blames Meredith for his virtue.

Later in the same year, 1912, he returns to the subject. Meredith was
'an admirable spirit, if not an *entire* mind,' who threw out

> splendid great moral and ethical, what he himself would call 'spiritual' lights,
> and has again and again big strong whiffs of manly tone and clear judgment.
> The fantastic and the mannered in him were nothing, to the intimately sane
> and straight; just as the artist was nothing to the good citizen and the liberated
> bourgeoisie.

Again James exposes his own split-mind, which he attributes to Meredith.
For Meredith the fantastic and the sane, the artistic and the socially-
significant were one. (He was not a 'good citizen' in James's sense of the
term, which implies an acceptance of the system, plus a creed that a little
rationalist tinkering can get things all straightened out.)

And yet the element in James which did reach out to what was humanly
and artistically true in Meredith enabled him to pay the magnificent
tribute, 'He did the best things best.'

Thus, Gissing, Hardy, James and Stevenson can all be said to have been
vitally affected by Meredith; and though variously drawing on him for
certain important aspects of their own work, one and all essentially failed

him—that is, they failed to carry on the key-tasks set by his novels and poems. An even more dramatic failure appears in D. H. Lawrence, whose formative years were strongly affected by Meredith and Hardy—and Gissing too. Even without having any external evidence for this—as one has—one could not doubt it if one read, say, the storm-scene in *Feverel* and then turned to any of Lawrence's passages where a strong emotional relation between man and landscape is defined. In such passages we touch the heart of Lawrence's creative impulse; but the road he took from about 1914 was the betrayal of the truths learned from Meredith. We can indeed put our finger on the moment when Lawrence swings definitely from humanist bases to the demented formulas that characterised his cornered-animal efforts to escape what seemed a mad world. In February 1914 he comments on the criticisms that see some value in his prose, none in his verse. 'How I hate them [the English]. I believe they are still saying that of Meredith.' His interest in Meredith reawakes; but when in June he got a copy of the poems, he found himself now out of key with them. 'Very glad to get them—and a bit disappointed. They aren't what I need just now, I suppose. I have been interested by the futurists.' He had learned much from Meredith of the self-alienating process of his society; but as the crisis breaks with the 1914 war, he loses all faith in man—seeing only bourgeois man, and turning in various mystical ways to the primitive who has not yet arrived within sight of bourgeois alienations. Thus he inverts the position of Meredith, drawing on his earth-imagery but using it to deny 'brain democratic.'

After the 1914–8 war the influence of Meredith, as far as any serious effects are concerned, fades out. Only now, as a true literature of social struggle and transformation can at last be born on a broad basis, is his significance discoverable.

But I should like to cite one more example of his pre-1914 impact, since it pleasantly shows how some of the younger folk were beginning to respond to him. Charley Sorley, who showed some promise as a poet, was killed at the age of twenty in the war, in 1915. In 1912 he called Tennyson and Swinburne 'rotters' who educe the effeminate in man. Next year he described how Tennyson 'vulgarised' the return-to-nature.

> A paltry poet in general, Tennyson is most pre-eminently paltry and super-ficial when he sings about nature and earth. He was not long on hedging her in with the shapely corsets of alliterative verbiage. Meredith was the first to break through this barrier and discover her in her truth. England, however, was so busy reading Tennyson that they thought Meredith a clever novelist but too smart for them; and no poet at all.

Meredith would have appreciated that metaphor of his having broken through the barriers of the corsets into the truth of mother-earth! But, though he was over-simplifying, Sorley had the right feeling. In 1914 he expressed his 'hatred' of Browning as the Lost Leader of his own poem, a 'bigoted theist,' and added acutely, 'I always feel that if less people read Browning, more would read Meredith (his poetry, I mean).' He contrasts the 'dusty intellectualism' of a poem like *Rabbi Ben Ezra* with the 'windy elemental strength' of many Meredithian poems. (But he failed to get inside *The Egoist*.)

The Sorleys died out in 1914-8 or failed to make themselves heard in the breakaway 1920's; but Charles's young voice may serve to remind us that true works of art continue, even if only partially, to carry out their function of stirring people to revolt and deepened consciousness, however bad the times. They do something essential in maintaining the continuity of spiritual and social struggle.

And now for our final glance at Meredith's achievement.

He was a man of 1848 who remained true to the principles of that tumultous year of mass-struggles that ushered in the modern world. In a period of unprecedented spiritual decay, the period when British imperialism was giddily expanding and the mass-struggle against it was in its infancy, he remained true to those principles. He was a Radical Revolutionary—that is, he emotionally carried on the revolutionary hopes of 1848, while at the same time keeping close to such political organisations of the people as were at all effective and representative, those of the radicals. Not that his position was static. It steadily developed, despite certain confusions, towards a deeper grasp of what was politically and culturally at stake in the changes going on in Britain in the years 1850–1900.

He did for our culture what Flaubert and Zola did for French, what Tolstoy, Dostoevsky and Chekov did for Russian, what Ibsen did for Scandinavian. In him our novel becomes fully adult, realistic; he adds to the previous gains a new sense of the relation to political struggle, to the whole moving historical structure. Without philosophy, he said, 'history is the skeleton-map of events. Fiction a picture of figures modelled on no skeleton anatomy. But each with philosophy in air blooms and is humanly shapely.' He called always for struggle. 'Our faith is ours, and comes not on a tide.' And for an art based in the needs of the common folk who produce and reproduce life:

> Until from the warmth of many breasts, that beat
> A temperate common music, sunlike heat
> The happiness not temporary sheds.

A critic has said that he would have gone deeper if he had been German or French, Norwegian or Russian, 'but he never forgot the gaunt spectre of the Philistine convention behind him.' That, however, is untrue. The other countries, like England, had their bourgeois Philistine, but, for varying historical reasons, they also had resistances, however chaotic and unstable, acting powerfully against the invading cash-nexus. Meredith is the *English* expression of the social crisis which in its world-reach is defined by such writers as Tolstoy, Ibsen, Zola.

There is no point in comparing these men, each with his strengths and his weaknesses. Meredith, if he has many faults, has one supreme virtue: from first to last he sees the forward-movement or regression of people, their development in resistance or submission to the alienating processes of capitalism, as a political issue. That is, he sees it steadily and sees it whole.

On the one hand, there stand the constrictions and over-condensations of his style, which can be generally reduced to the pressures of the historical situation in which he found himself: in which he loathed the only existent audience, the British bourgeoisie, and felt driven back on to himself, with the audience of his hopes removed obscurely into the future. The negative aspects of his form-content thus make him the forerunner of various formalist or over-stylised methods of writing, of the abstraction of moral attitudes or problems into a kind of psychological no-man's-land: methods or positions which proliferate in the period of advanced imperialism. On the other hand, we find him unslackening in his struggle against these negative aspects, which he clearly understands as Decadence; he looks in his innermost being always to an integration of art and life in which creative activity and the needs of the Vivid Many are one; he strives above all to define the kind of characters who will bring about this 'radical' change in society, in people. Thus he anticipates the conflicts and disintegrations that overtake art in the imperialist epoch; seeks to grapple with them and to find the true resolution in struggle, in the building of the new man. Both his strength and his weakness derive from the fact that in his historical situation he tries to define its deep conflicts and reach forward to the necessary resolutions, while lacking the active mass-relations that his ideas imply and need for their full application. His struggle becomes too much a 'one-man show'; at the very heart of his effort to define a revolutionary integration of man and society, to define a new type of man and woman born out of uncompromising struggle, elements of inflated individualism persist and even gain renewed strength. Much more might be said of this sort of contradiction in his work; and yet the last word lies with the struggle for the true resolution. That is why the decadents have been unable to use Meredith, to claim him as their precursor; they have on the contrary been forced to forget him altogether, to blur him away from any effective rôle in our literature.

The writers who followed him, from Hardy to D. H. Lawrence, gained certain key-aspects of their creative insight from his work, but sank below the level of consciousness he defined and demanded. Now, amid the fully-emerged conflicts of imperialism in its final phases of decay and destruction, we can realise thoroughly at last what that level of consciousness was and how it relates to our own efforts to grasp the political and cultural resolutions (ultimately a single resolution, a human resolution) required for our salvation and advance. Meredith assumes a remarkable significance as the all-important link between our problems and the great tradition of our literature. Our task is not in any sense to continue directly the form-content of his work, to take over his stylistic methods and purify them, and so on. His form-content is indissolubly linked with the period which he defined. Our task is rather to penetrate the struggle in his work, to understand how far he was defeated by intolerable pressures, how far he succeeded in finding the new active relation of art and life which his deepest ideas postulated. By so doing we can more fully and concretely enter into the life-process of our people at a most difficult moment of growth, realise how the distorting pressures operated, discover with a new breadth and intensity our relation both to the great tradition and to the situation (political and cultural, politico-cultural) in which we live and struggle.

In the last resort the form-content of Meredith's work is everywhere based in the experiences of our people in the years when imperialism was consolidating its grip, when the old forms of popular assertion against the rulers of the class-state had largely broken down and the new forms were embryonic. The tensions of resistance (often as rigid as the muscles of a wrestler locked in life-and-death grapple), the unslackening pangs amid the terrible pressures making for isolation and alienation of the individual from his fellows, and the unconquered regathering of strength for the renewal of struggle on a wider mass-level—all these elements which go to make up the total form-content of his work are deeply expressive of what was happening among our people, among the producing masses; and they stand sharply opposed to all that was happening among the ruling-class, who were tightening the imperialist controls. That is why we can claim that Meredith defines and embodies the life of our people in the dark and difficult first-stages of imperialism, warily tense with the immediate resistances to what seems an overwhelming force of 'egoism,' and yet blithely and powerfully knitting energies for the next large-scale extension of struggle.

This man, who had thrilled with the cries and hopes of 1848, lived on to write *The Crisis*, hailing the Russian masses in revolt. He who had known Dickens and worked for him, lived to write a poem that belonged to the world of Gorky. He bridged the epochs of Mazzini and Lenin, even if in the latter case he merely approached the verge of the new territory.

We cannot do better than come back to some more of the words of James Thomson. 'George Meredith has constantly devoted himself to his ever-fruitful fields of real living nature and human nature.' Sandra-Vittoria is the 'sovereign character of our modern fiction; in her he has discovered *a new great nature*, which he has endowed with *a new great language*' (my italics). That is, he discovered the clue to the heroic, to the creation of the positive hero in our world.

There are many flaws indeed in his work. But I think that we must accord without reservations the name of greatness and a secure place in our literature, in world-literature, to the man who wrote *Shagpat, Evan Harrington, Sandra-Vittoria, Beauchamp's Career, The Egoist, The Tragic Comedians*—not to mention *One of Our Conquerors* and *The Amazing Marriage*. The public for which he hungered is now being formed, in Britain as elsewhere; and once we grasp the nature of his aims and struggles, it is not hard to take his faults in our stride as we read.

Notes

1

Cabrals. Louisa's husband had a brother Silva: hence the Count's name in *Evan.* In 1881 Guglielmo wrote, pushed by his sister who had found out that their cousin was an established writer. But that seems all the contacts.

Welsh. He became hon. president of the Cymmrodorion Society in 1908, and in his letter calls himself half Irish, half Welsh. See other letters of 1864, 1877, 1881, 1908, etc., with the discussions in the novels, especially *Sandra, Celt and Saxon, The Amazing Marriage.* He could fancy descent from Meredudd ab Owain (b. 999) or M. ap Bleddyn, prince of Powys (d. 1132).

2

Portsmouth. Walter Besant was born there (see *By Celia's Arbour*). And note how Nelson intrudes in *Harry Richmond* for both Harry and Ottilia. *Crossby* tells us that the houses of Southsea, built on the common, were to be thrown down without compensation 'if the enemy should land.' The closed-in fortress-town of Meredith's youth may have helped to build his later concern with the possibilities of Invasion.

Crisis. Dipwell Farm of *Harry R.* may represent a farm where George was left awhile.

Ossian. What he later tried was to merge Ossianic union-with-nature with Homeric distinctness of human character. For the Ossianic moment in adolescent experience, see H.R. (x): the ride in the mist. 'I forgot the existence of everything but what I loved passionately, and that had no shape, was like a wind.' The rider is one with the changing rack of the world he dominates (as yet with no coherent purpose). In 1889 George still recalls Ossian: the letter to Mrs G. Stevenson on a night of storm and 'ancient battle': 'drenching vapour sailed, and Scotia bled and Ossian wailed!'

3

All his life he studied the German historians, Niebuhr, Harnack, Mommsen; used German editions of the classics, German philologist works; learned to know Grillparzer, Giebel, Uhland, Heine, etc. He early read the prose-writers like Tieck, Brentano, Kerner, Zschokke, and Richter (who deeply affected him).

Back in England he found Goethe's influence strongly at work in writers ranging from Bailey to Carlyle or Emerson. The Idea of Goethe was powerful even among writers who had never read him.

4

Charnock. Hippias in *Feverel*; not the solicitor (xvi) who merely embodies George's boredom with the law, though Ripton T. behaves in the office much as George must have done. Charnock's works included: A Glossary of the Essex dialect, a work on ancient Essex manorial customs, Local Etymology, *Ludus Patronymicus, Nuces Etymologicae, Cornish Surnames* (a copy exists inscribed to G.M.), books on words derived from proper names and the origin of the main Christian Surnames in G.B. and Ireland—and even meddlings with Etruscan, the Walloons, the Transylvanians, the Woolwa and Mosquito Vocabularies, etc. He wrote a Guide to the Tyrol (including Carinthia) and edited *Bradshaw's Illustrated Handbook to Spain and Portugal* (34 vols., 1865–99), not to mention having a finger in *Anthropologia.* (None of the works mentioned were published in 1846.) He was a Dr. of Philosophy of Göttingen as well as a Fellow of the Society of Antiquaries.

Aretchid Kooez is not A Wretched Quiz, as Galland takes it. The phrase comes from the *Anti-Jacobin* (xxxiii) 25 June 1793. (Stevenson also errs here.)

Money. We may summarise George's money-position in early years thus. When he was only two, an Act cut interest on bank annuities to 3½ per cent and brought his mother's income down to £35 a year. She died three years later and according to the marriage indenture the money had to be applied solely to maintain and educate the boy. The solicitor of her family kept a strict eye on the carrying out of these provisions. It was this £35 a year that took George to St Paul's School. April, 1840, his aunt, Miss Anna Maria Macnamara died, leaving £1,818 12s. 11d., divided equally between George and her brother; George now had £1,909, with yearly income £66 12s. 6d. This enabled him to go to Neuwied, where money stretched further than in England. (Augustus had accepted the Macnamara solicitor as sole trustee.) The Charnoch articles provide for him, lodging, instruction, and £20 a year. There is no evidence of Chancery approval of the articles of clerkship.

The Monthly Observer. George's verse is mainly translation from the German: Heine, Goethe, Von Eichendorff. Note that he did Goethe's: 'Happy alone are the souls that love.' (Galland sees the link of a 1851 poem with Tennyson's *Love and Death,* and thinks *La Mort* may have drawn the latter in.) For the changes in *Chillianwallah:* M. B. Forman in *The Athenaeum,* 24 Aug. 1912. Horne's encouragement made him try *Chambers.* George also tried *The Standard,* interviewed the editor, but got no pay for his first contribution. (He once said he wrote two articles for *The Manchester Guardian* before he was 22.)

How much George was affected by Mary's poem is shown by his own *The Two Blackbirds* and *Feverel,* xxvi. Of another poem in the same issue (anon. but perhaps by Mary), *The Pilgrim of Life,* he says, 'Nothing so sweet as suggestive poetry. Nothing so likely to be spoilt by interpretation. In these cases the heart is the best interpreter.' And refers to the Author(ess). The comments reveal his state of heart rather than his intellectual position.

He mentions an anon. contribution on the great Lisbon earthquake: 'it exposes no cause and develops no meaning, but is hopeful.' (Later he remarked, 'I wrote verse before I was 19.')

Personalia. Ned Peacock married and left a son who was later often at Lower Halliford as a playmate of Arthur.

There was strain between Ned and his father through the marriage, so that George does not seem to have met Peacock for some time.

5

Personalia. Emilia's other sister was Giulia (the name also appears in *Sandra*). Note the discussions of Murat as a cavalry-leader in *Ormont*.

Ollier, born 1786, set up shop as publisher with his brother, wrote novels, was connected with *The New Monthly Magazine*, contributed to many magazines, acted as literary adviser to Edward Moxon and was reader to R. Bentley; he had a keen humorous mind and loved art and music as well as poetry; died 1859.

When he wrote to Tennyson, he was at Mrs Ned P.'s place at Southend.

Poems. He also had a poem in *Fraser's* (introduced by Peacock). The last poem in *Household Words* was *Monmouth*, 1856, with the theme of the Pretender, who is king of day, crowned by the sun. 'He claims and he shall have his own.' Imagery of sense-fusion appears in 'And hopeful as the springing morn, they glisten down the curves of Tone': song and light in one. Generally, however, the poems were weak, Crimean-patriotic, 'Oriental,' Tennysonian—an Ode on the Duke of Wellington and a tale of a Californian Gold Rush lynching of a woman. (To *Chambers's* he sent 2 sonnets on English Kings, saying he had lots more.) But he was studying the Border Ballads.

When W. Matz found twenty poems attributed to M. in the contributors' book of *Household Words*, Meredith's son tried to throw out all but three. But a letter to Parker (publisher of *Poems*) and a version of two of the poems in a copy of *Poems* in M.'s script refute the latter.

A letter to Parker (Dec. 1850) encloses the selection; he thinks *Cassandra* best, though unfinished (and not published till 1862) and the *Pastorals* the most original; he accepts Parker's verdict as to inclusions, but mentions that Horne spoke favourably of those he saw. He says that he expects nothing but loss. 'A name must be successful before a book can.' But he hoped 'to gain a certain position among those who best appreciate good poetry. Tennyson, whose name you quote, had, if I hear aright, but a doleful beginning.' (In 1899 he says the book is of value only 'for the curious in youthful struggles to express.') We know of at least one review in *Fraser's* and an article (£4) in *H.W.*

Terms. I throughout use the term *idealist* in its strict sense of a system of thought in which there is a basic division between body and spirit, man and nature, and which must look to an otherworldly basis (whether God is transcendent or immanent) for values, meanings, unity. I use *materialist* for a system which seeks to overcome this split. A system which sees man as both united with the rest of nature and yet opposed to it, since his active relation, born in labour-process, in art and science, has given him his own peculiar consciousness of separation as well as union. (This position of man, in nature and of it, and yet in a sense 'above' it in so far as he masters it, has provided the basis on which one aspect or another can be abstracted alone as the essential or real thing.)

Not that the terms in question can be used in any absolute way. Each system must be analysed in its specific historical situation. An *idealist dialectic*, such as Bruno's or Hegel's, may then be found to have materialist elements, in so far as it helps men to grasp the nature and structure of process, development —while a *mechanical materialism*, by being unable to compass the fulness of life, may stimulate a dualistic approach to body and spirit. But in the period with which we deal—the post-Hegelian period—the development of *dialectical materialism*, a philosophy which overcomes all the weaknesses of mechanical materialism and is capable of defining human and natural process with a progressive elimination of the idealist split, becomes possible; and this possibility determines the fruitful lines of thought. The system for which poets like Horne were groping was this new and adequate materialism.

Tennyson. A letter of April 1857 deprecates imitation of Tennyson. In 1861 he finds Tennysonian influence in the idealistically namby-pamby *Tannhauser* (Fanc and R. Lytton). In 1870 he describes the *Idylls* to Morley as 'dandiacal fluting. . . . I read the successive mannered lines with pain—yards of linen— drapery for the delight of ladies who would be in the fashion.—The praise of the book shuts me away from my fellows.' Later in the same month he noted happily, 'I see the *Quarterly* deals rather firmly with the "Holy Grail"—something in these days.' (In Dec. 1869 he had commented on his boyish admiration of T. and the latter's lack of any real philosophic basis.)

In July 1875 he was kinder about *Queen Mary*, though he thought it lacked any trace of power—and as for the songs, ' "Milking the cow" smells of milking the brain. Mary's "Low-low" is an instance of public consciousness—before Victoria's people.' In Dec. 1885 he jokes at T.'s snobbery before titles.

To Jessop in 1867 he said the *Idylls* were 'to poetry what Vestments are to Religion.' Browning had faults, but not those of 'a mannered trickster airing a leg with love-knots.'

Compare his remarks to Swinburne, 'I believe the Essay (on Byron) will do much towards restoring a great name its proper rank, even in a day when the drawing-room and tea-table are Imperial in Britain.'

He despises the Laureateship, and as the Boer War nears asks if the Boers have a Laureate. If so, it will set their cause back.

(From Palgrave's *Reminiscences* it seems that Tennyson did not approve of the rewriting of *Love in the Valley* after it had received the imprimatur of his praise.)

South-west wind. This wind recurs in his poetry as an emblem of invigorating struggle, of meeting earth and sky. Also in his Letters: and *Egoist*, xxvi.

New Poets. In Dec. 1856 he was interested in the news of a pension for Bailey. 'Will that £100 per ann. chain him to earth, or only give him firmer spring into the empyrean.' Note also the reference to *Festus* in *The Monthly Observer*.

In November 1882 he writes of a relation of Dobell he had met, who 'thinks Dobell too soon forgotten by an ungrateful public.'

The passage in *One of Our Conquerors*, 'Even to the shore of that strange sea, where the maid stands choosing this one man for her destiny, as in a trance,' is a memory of Massey's *Babe Christabel*, 'Last night . . . she trembled o'er her

mirror'd charms. . . . The unknown sea moans on her shore of life: she hears
the breakers roar: but, trusting him, she'll fear no more. . . .'

Positivism. Comte was known to M.'s world by the works of H. Martineau, 1853;
Lewes (on Comte and Science) 1853; J. S. Mill, 1865—see M. in a letter, March,
1864. Not many studied Comte's vast works. Comte, note, was fiercely opposed
to the equality of the sexes.

6

Peacock. Note his essay on the Bottle of Cratinus in *Fraser's,* 1857 (the comedy-
lawsuit between Comedy and Booze over the Poet, who says he needs his
mistress Booze to love his wife Comedy). Meredith recalled it twenty years
later.

Peacock's belated return to fiction, *Gryll Grange,* is best explained by his need
to expel the irritant that had been George's argument on behalf of the New
Poetry, etc. (Mary, born 1821, was 7 years George's senior.)

Lucy Duff-Gordon: admired Goethe, Molière, Peacock, *Arabian Nights;* her influence led M. to see Rachel in London in Racine, to admire de Musset, write
profiles of St Beuve and St Marc Giradin.

Arthur: probably named after Arthur Ellis, George's cousin, then adjutant at
Woolwich and available as sponsor.

7

Vathek is mentioned in a late 1874 letter. The Oriental idiom was no doubt
stimulated by such works as Goethe's *Divan* and Thackeray's pastiches in *Punch,*
as well as Lane's version of the *Nights,* 1839–43.

Southey's *Curse of Kehama* has also contributed to the theme, and the whole
concept of struggle in the New Poets, which is resolved here and in *Orion* alone.

There are eastern tales in *Household Words,* e.g. the fable *The Dealer in Wisdom*
(23 Aug. 1851) where the narrator is a Cairo barber and aphoristic phrases guide
the hero. Note the name Bagarag (suggesting a rough worker) and compare
Teufelsdroech's Bags of disordered notes. When Hyndman asked why a woman
was described as like a palmtree, M. replied, 'The hair falling over her shoulders
and her slender shape.'

See Carlyle's *Model Prisons* for a typical attack on Egoism as the spirit of
capitalism. For M.'s steadfast admiration of Mazzini: letters of April 1902.

8

Fitzgerald: in 1867 published versions of *Euripides* and *Theocritus,* that won his
uncle's approval. His father said he must marry the girl chosen for him or be
disinherited (maybe this tale helped to build Feverel); but in the end (1873) he
married secretly. Once his father got in the same railway carriage as Fitz and
his wife, and Fitz had the nerve to scribble a note on his newspaper, which he

passed politely to his wife. In 1877, mortally ill, he arrived home, and his father promised anything he wanted. Fitz asked for his wife and gained her acceptance by the expedient of dying.

George Eliot: also recommended *Shagpat* in a letter (18 Jan. 1856): her own first novel appeared 1857. Meredith was rather sarcastic about her in table-talk. 'Her more pretentious literary methods failed to impress him,' says Carr; and he hailed a phrase used by a friend ('Panoplied in all the philosophies,' she 'was apt to swoop upon a commonplace'). He said unkindly that she 'had the heart of a Sappho, but the face, with the long proboscis, the protruding teeth as of the Apocalyptic horse, betrayed animality.' But he also called her 'the greatest of women novelists.'

Farina. The theme comes from a legend to which Coleridge refers in a poem printed in *Friendship's Offerings:* 'In Köln, a town of monks and bones . . . I counted two and seven stenches. . . .' A note refers to Necessity the Mother of Inventions and the way Extremes beget one another: the stinks begot 'the most fragrant of spirituous fluids, the Eau de Cologne.'

Influences detected are Thackeray's extravaganzas; La Rochefoucauld, Molière, Peacock.

Farina was reprinted eight years later at 1s. In December 1856 George wrote to Chapman for £25 'to sum the £70 requested in advance of Feverel.'

9

Art. Wallis's Chatterton shows Meredith in 1855, though he was probably wearing a beard by then. Wallis lived till 86; didn't show at the Academy after 1877 and became a landscape-painter, also an authority on the ceramics of the Near East, where he lived many years. He was two years younger than M.

Meredith had come to know the best of contemporary art—the academics like Ward, Frith, Egg, Wallis; the old Turner and the young Watts; the dissident pre-Raphaelites, with whom he felt much sympathy. A letter to Janet in May 1861 on the Academy says of Leighton's *Paolo and Francesca,* 'the sole English picture exhibiting passion that I have seen. I have the delight to stand alone in my judgment of this, and I shall see the world coming round to my opinion, and thinking it its own.'

In Italy he came to admire Giorgione, Titian, Veronese.

Married Love. For a while he had something of a revulsion from women: in a letter to Wyse he says he hopes never to love again, women are morally no better than animals and so in a chemical sense beneficial to men. Compare *Feverel,* xii; also the tinker's praise of a pipe as against a wife; and a passage, later suppressed, comparing woman and wildcat. By the time of *Rhoda,* xxviii, such views are handed over to the types he most disliked, here Edward Blancove.

We must recall that Mary had earlier given him the impact of high sensuous delight that went into *Love in the Valley* and the love-scenes of *Feverel.*

On his second marriage he had to give his father-in-law a detailed account of his life and situation. He wrote of Mary, 'The separation was her own doing, though not regretted by me, save for my boy's sake.'

Prof. Stevenson has a theory that on George's return from Neuwied he went to Hampshire and had a frustrated love-affair with a country-girl (reflected in Lucy Desborough, Dahlia Fleming, Mabel Sweetwinter and the girl of *Love in the Valley*). He notes the 'bad taste' of making the distracted Mrs Peacock help the valley-girl at her toilet, and the lines of *Modern Love* 'An early goddess was a country-lass' . . . Maybe, but I feel rather that the valley-girl is Mary pastoralised and no doubt merged with country-girls that George had admired in Hampshire and the Rhineland. The same with Lucy.

10

The setting of *Feverel* is the country south of the reach of the Thames between Shepperton and Chertsey; Raynham Abbey is Woburn Park and Belthorpe Farm is Ham Farm; the tryst of the lovers, the Old Lock at Shepperton.

The Abbey is in a sense a Crochet Castle; and Hippias (based in Charnock) suggests the hypochondriac Hippy of *Melincourt*. Richardson's influence has also been suggested; Miss Richardson (xxvii) appears more in the original version. Kingsley is mocked-at by Adrian as Brawnley, 'rank radicals all of you, base materialists,' he is addressing Austin W.

The cuts affected secondary characters: Mrs Doria, Benson, Ripton Thompson, the old doctor, Mrs Grandison. The first version brought out at length the anti-feminist motives round Sir A., e.g. Benson's grip comes from having suffered like his master; Austin W. is denied the bringing-up of Richard through his slip.

The weakness in Richard is expressed by his loss of the wedding-ring when he meets Mrs Doria, Clare, Adrian; he turns to the plebeian Mrs Berry for a ring in his need, but is unable to sustain this 'compact' with common life. The class-division in his spirit is thus symbolised.

Note the use of the 'liberating laugh' at a decisive moment of Richard's development out of childhood: the sudden realisation of the truth of relationships that sees through the previously dominant falsity. (The 'laugh' is not just a sense of humour, as the critics take it!)

Prof. Stevenson takes *The Fair Frankincense* to be *Farina*, but Meredith describes it as having two Prophets 'and altogether a new kind of villain, being Humbug active—a great gun likely to make a noise, if I prime him properly.' (Christmas 1856). This can hardly fit *Farina*. (For 1856, only 2 poems in *H.W.* are known.)

He also points out that *Feverel* may have derived from Sir G. T. Staunton's memoir of his father who had an abstract educational 'system.' Staunton had been M.P. for S. Hants or Portsmouth through most of M.'s boyhood. For contemporary works with something of a mixture of Sterne-Peacock there were Lytton's *Caxtons* and *My Novel*.

Austin Wentworth. He brushes aside the rationalisations of fear, the lies, and goes straight to the point. The others fail for months to bring Lucy and Sir A. together; as soon as he hears what is wrong, by nightfall Lucy is accepted. He brings Bessie Berry's truant husband back. At the end Lady Blandish entreats his presence in the desolated scene so that faith may be rekindled in the others.

Contrast Adrian's ironic evasions. The boy's fate is being decided now? 'So is everyone's,' he yawns.

The split of theory and practice in Sir A. is stressed. 'The direct application of an aphorism was unpopular at Raynham.' When Richard breaks loose, his father does not question his system, but blames human nature. All that section of the novel is a subtle indictment of the class-system of which Sir A.'s system is a refracted form.

Welsh. Note the alliance of the Feverels with the Ap Gryffyth. (Even in *Farina* Wales appears in a roaming craftsman who has made the Siegfried design that dominates the heroine's fancy.)

Attacks. He wrote diffidently to Kate Vulliamy (Oct. 1863), 'On consideration, I thought the 'The Ordeal' could not do you harm: I can only trust that it will not offend. It deals with certain problems of life, and is therefore not of a milky quality. I am afraid that it requires stout reading. If you weather it, unshocked, you will find my other works less trying.' But he didn't want to upset the Huguenot susceptibilities of a family that he was to marry into.

Marie V., his second wife, told of a relation who, on hearing that she was to be married, wrote in mixed encouragement and discouragement, remarking how she'd read in a forgotten book how kissing won't last but cooking will. (She told this to Hardman in the drive-home after a dinner at which a widow chaffed George about having been prejudiced against him by *Feverel*. The sort of stupid insolence he had to put up with at dinner-parties.)

Carlyle. In a late letter (Jan. 1902) he mentions C.'s constant recommendation to him of the study of Goethe.

II

Esher: in the main street between the Post Office and the Bear: once the Grapes coaching-inn, with low narrow rooms. (Near was the house where Jane and Anne Porter lived; the Howitts stayed at the Cedars for a while and the novelist Samuel Warren was buried near the new church.)

Meredith met some of the French exiles: Prince de Joinville and Comte de Paris: 'I never felt attracted,' he says, 'by the Comte's vague mind.'

Maxse. In May 1863 Meredith tried to divert Maxse from vegetarianism, but later himself was converted. In October he jeers at Maxse's notion that every girl 'is conscious that she should never trust herself alone with a man, etc.' And he mocks his genteel taste for Tennysonianly-false poems, his inability to grasp Carlyle's inner meaning.

He protests in 1865 against Maxse's individualistic notions of revolt and insists that the right moment must be found for action. He wants education and organisation to be built effectively up—though he admits that rebellious action of any sort is justified against any effort of reaction to assert itself. (He is speaking of matters of religion, but his line of argument applies to his whole political position.)

Maxse married in 1862. 'The bride was almost beautiful. . . . Lady Maxse and the daughters are pleasant people in their way, with aristocratic vices well under control.

13 (36 pp.)

Burnand. Meredith used some tales told in chat by Burnand, in *Once a Week.* When B. laughingly remonstrated, he introduced him to the editor. (*A Story-Telling Party,* 1860, Garner 5 gns.)

Janet. She says of Kinglake and M., who disliked one another, 'Both were shy in different ways, and both were at their best when alone with one or two friends. My Poet, in the early days when I saw so much of him, was a delightful companion when he knew he was liked; before strangers his shyness took the form of asserting himself rather loudly, and trying to be epigrammatic and witty; he gave one the impression that he was not quite sure on what footing he stood.' (Kinglake is probably the P.G., the Perfect Gentleman, of M.'s correspondence.) The Rosses lost their money through being involved in Egyptian finances. Janet supported Ross. When later at the Val d'Arno, she farmed someone's estates and often entertained the Duke and Duchess of Teck at a villa lent by a Count: they were fleeing their creditors, and ate and drank her out in long carousals. Arthur once called on her at Florence. Ross died in 1902. (He had been with Layard at Nineveh, and wrote *Letters from the East.*) She met M. at Box Hill in 1904, a resolute old lady, 'white-haired, erect, stern and eagle-eyed' (as her great-nephew said).

She wrote two books of reminiscences and two cookery books; and developed her fierce glances, her crushing phrases; a champion of songbirds against Italians with guns: selling vermouth to her friends; routing the unemployed in 1919 when they came to 'loot' her house and facing armed Fascists at the age of 80, indomitable and futile.

Evan Harrington. The serial was illustrated by Keene. The Dickensian influence is strong in all the lower-class characters, such as the Cogglesbys, Raikes, the Lawyer Perkins (the Perker of *Pickwick*).

In diction the writing is mostly direct, but at times we meet touches of the new-poetry: 'Without phrasing a word, or absolutely shaping a thought in her head,' she slanted across the sun to Mr Raikes.' But there is little of lyrical nature-imagery.

Miss Current was Miss Louisa Courtney, an old friend of the Duff-Gordons; Pat the retriever pup was Janet's Peter, given when broken-in to Arthur. Mrs Morton, chased by her husband, briefly appears.

The settings: Beckley seems Fair Oak Lodge, some fifteen miles from Petersfield (Fallowfield) with the river Rother running through its grounds. The Green Dragon was probably the Anchor; the Dolphin, the Folphin.

Augustus. A South African friend calls him a handsome man of medium stature, well educated, very obliging in business, who said that in England he had often walked several miles a day. In his mid-sixties he climbed to the top of Table Mountain. A clergyman said, 'I am very interested in the career of your distinguished son,' but Augustus turned away in silence. To one friend, however, he lent *Farina.*

He returned to England about 1863, and settled near his old Portsmouth home, finally in a house that belonged to his second wife. George paid an occasional duty-visit (e.g. Oct. 1870). Augustus died in 1877 at the age of 79; his wife, dying 1885, aged 65, was buried at Southsea in the same vault. George went to his funeral and inherited a few effects and portraits never shown prominently at Box Hill.

Short tales. For Christmas *Once a Week* (1860) he offered two projects: King Arthur listening to stories of the modern world, or tales told by a group stranded at a lonely inn. Soon after, he writes asking for higher rates than usual, 'I'll give you some very good stories, but I must have money.' (With regard to Evan's U.S. rights he had written, 'I'm horribly poor, and £30 or £40 is a windfall.') In Feb. 1861 *The Highwayman* appeared renamed *The Parish Clerk's Story* (5 gns.) A village-girl is wooed by the squire's son, who, disowned, turns highwayman; the heroine's cousin is also thought seduced by another youth; all ends well. A poor tale, but showing some of the ideas of *Rhoda* in schematic form. (A tale, *The Friend of an Engaged Couple*, unprinted, exists in ms., with Lucas' notation.)

12

Jessop: wrote *The Trials of a Country Parson*; a successful headmaster, he wrote also on medieval England; was later rector of Scarning, Norfolk.

Wyse. His father, of Watford, was ambassador at Athens. Wyse chanced on Provencal in the shop of the poet J. Roumanille: his own books were *Parpaioun Blu*, 1868, and *Li Piado de la Princesso*. He introduced the work of Aubanel and Mistral to Meredith, who made a version of part of Mistral's *Mireio*.

Venetia. He wrote also, 'Viennese crinolins and the tyrant white coat do their best to destroy the beauties of St Mark's. Charming are the Venetian women. They have a gracious walk and all the manner one dreams of as befitting them. Should one smile on a Whitecoat, she has the prospect of a patriotic dagger smiting her fair bosom, and so she does not. . . . I made acquaintance with a tough Baronne, who has brought two daughters of immense circle. How quietly the pretty Venetians eyed them.'

Poems. Rossetti tried to get M. to interest Chapman and Hall in reprinting Wells' *Joseph and his Brethren*. When M. went to Rossetti's studio and was given a copy of *Early Italian Poets*, his admiration was acute.

Rossetti promised to illustrate *Cassandra*, 'which poem has taken his heart.' No drawing is known. In March 1862, 'My book hangs a little. I am sick at the sight of it.' His friends argued much about the *Rosanna*, addressed to Maxse and advocating the marriage of the spirit of the Alpine rainbow with the London cabman: a humorous statement of his creed that the poetic realisation of nature must be united with the everyday life of men, the world of work.

Thrice he tells Maxse that *Spirit of Earth Ode* will please him. *Modern Love*, he says, 'requires thought, and discernment, and reading more than once.' He also inquired about battle-uniforms, no doubt for Grandfather B. The lowest to which he ever fell was *Martin's Puzzle*, 1865, with its conventional pious consolations of the sort liked by Browning. Yet even this was rejected by the *Cornhill* as too free thinking and liable to offend.

Of *Modern Love*: 'Rossetti says it is my best.' T. H. Huxley liked it very much.

Twenty-five years later Arthur Symons wrote, 'It is an altogether new thing; we venture to call it the most "modern" poem we have.'

There are pre-Raphaelite elements in the book (mixed with imitations of the German Ballad) developed out of the New Poetry; but a poem like *Margaret's Bridal Eve* falls far below Rossetti. *The Spectator* said that M. 'mistook' for courageous realism, 'poetic Pre-Raphaelitism.'

13

Arthur. Burnand tells a tale of 1859. Meredith, he and Fitz were dining at Esher. Arthur, then six, kept asking for wine. Meredith, irritated, said, 'If you will have it, you shall.' And pushed a tumblerful on the child, who was ill for days. But generally father and son were happy together.

Hardman. Met M. at Littleworth Cottage, Esher. His wife was a daughter of James Radley. He was a would-be epicurean, who had his *Role of Cookery* accepted by *Household Words* in 1848. The routine of M. and H. was a long furious walk, a meal of bread and jam (or honey) back in the cottage, then more walking; in the evening M. read out his latest work. H. sat in 1858 to Frith for a picture of Henry VII; a photo of him in the costume shows well he suited the part. M. chaffed him for his likeness to Cobbet, whose biography he wrote till he heard Morley was doing the same. (M., in a letter of Dec. 1862, gives a German citation showing how Cobbet terrified even the German reactionaries.) M. introduced H. to Rossetti, whom H. found a 'very jolly fellow.' After a studio-party at R.'s, he retaliated with a club-dinner. 'I flatter myself they never sat down to a better selected meal.' At 12.30 he took M., rolling drunk, home down the Haymarket. He mentioned that at this time M. was given to furious felling of trees and sawing of logs to promote circulation and digestion.

Maxse: had two sons, two daughters, one of whom Lord Edward Cecil married in 1894: Meredith and Wilde attended the wedding.

Sentimentalists. Put aside till 1870, some scenes added. In 1893, listed in forthcoming publications. 1895–1900, the first five scenes rewritten. Produced in March 1910. It is slight and fragmentary.

Rossetti. His head of M. as Christ in his Mary Magdalene drawing (*c.* 1860) is a fine definition of M. at this time. 'My brother was wont to say,' wrote Michael, 'this Meredith bore a rather marked resemblance to the busts of the Emperor Hadrian; I think he improved upon them.'

In the house M.'s sitting room was on the hall's right, also to be used as dining room; his bedroom was on the top floor, small, with a river view. 'We were all to dine together, if present together in the house.' There were many tales about the break: Swinburne flung a poached egg at M. for running Hugo down; Rossetti resented a breakfast remark of M.'s, said he'd throw a cup of tea in his face if the words were repeated, whereupon M. repeated and R. threw; the others substituted good boots for the cracked pair left outside M.'s door, so he left that day and sent a cheque for a quarter's rent, etc. (Clodd's Notes settle the matter: Meredith found Rossetti's Fanny too vulgar.) Whistler and

Sandys both told a tale of M. being witty at the expense of R.'s pictures before his patrons. As late as October young George du Maurier talks of 'the Rossetti lot' (Swinbourne, G.M., Sandys) 'as thick as thieves;' though R. in August wrote, 'Meredith has evaporated for good.'

Swinburne. Letters exchanged 1867-8: S. visited M. at Kingston, 1867. After the break M. still termed S. the finest poet and truest artist of the new generation, apart from his erotic obsessions. At his death he said, 'He was the greatest of our lyrical poets—of the world, I could say, considering what a language he had to wield. Song was his natural voice.'

In 1898 Gosse persuaded S. to sign the Address to M., who asked S. and Watts-Dunton to lunch at Box Hill. M. is said to have asked why S. had made no comments on his last novels, and S. replied he couldn't read them. M. resented the remark, says Watts-Dunton.

Bawdy. In 1861 he writes with delight of Swinburne's *La Fille du Policeman*, especially of the chapter where the Bishop of London rapes the heroine, 'the funniest rampingest satire on French novelists dealing with English themes.'

Emilia. There were many important Italian exiles or their relations in England, e.g. Vendati, Mrs Venturi (Emily Ashurst, secretary and translator of Mazzini): Mazzini's *Letters to an English Family. Sandra* is a fusion of Emilia Macirone and Emilie Venturi. Meredith knew the latter as well as her sister Mrs. James Stanfield; the two chief English friends of Mazzini. He proof-read the first volume of Mazzini's collected writings which Mme-Venturi was seeing through the press.

M. never met Mazzini. Once he was on his way to meet him and news came of some disaster that made the Italians drop all engagements and throw themselves into work.

Letters (1862). To Maxse in Italy he writes about the horrible accounts of sea-fighting (the Monitor and Merrimac). 'Science, I presume, will at last put it out of our option whether we will improve one another from off the face of the globe, and we must decide by our common sense.' He praises Mill's *Liberty* as a protest against the tyranny that 'society' begins to exercise. (Contrast the 1867 poem where he sees 'society' as the Class-State against the People.) Also he protests against some too-simple comments by Maxse on 'pagan sensuality' (after seeing Pompeii?). He mocks Maxse's liking of the 'cherubic chastity' of the Fane-Lytton *Tannhauser* and says the hero was right to turn to the earth goddess.

In June he is on *Sandra.* 'What works I could throw off if I had the digestion of any of the creatures that hope to be saved. I am fretted with so much in my head that my hands can't accomplish.' He finds the International Exhibition poor. 'Fancy the Poet Laureate in the line of march.' A few days later, '*Emilia* goes slowly forward,' rewritten.

In Feb. he told Janet he was writing for *The Morning Post*, 'which pays your Poet.'

His rawness about the treatment of his work shows in his giving the Vulliamys *Feverel* to read; he wanted no false pretences.

In March he wants to go 'to the Monday popular concerts, to hear Joachim,

and music.' In May, 'The nightingales are at their best.' In July Edward Peacock
and his boy are at Copsham; Rossetti and Swinburne are expected. To Mrs
Jessop he remarks that he has cut up four printed chapters of *Sandra*, 'who
begins to dissatisfy me totally, as do all my offspring that have put on type.' He
is exercising furiously with beetle, an iron-tipped staff tossed in the air and
caught. He dreads Christmas. 'I shall be ridden all night by a plum-pudding-
headed hag: shall taste the horrors without vacuity of Death: we will hope
better things for our grandchildren.' (He wrote a madrigal of dyspepsia to
Hardman from St John's College. 'Fire is wet and water dry: Candles burn
cocked hats awry: Hope her diamond portal shuts, Grim dyspepsia haunts my
—Ahem!')

Hugo. To Maxse, June 1862, he says, 'Read "Les Misérables," if you can get it.
. . . It is conceived in pure black and white. It is, nevertheless, the master work
of fiction of this century—as yet. There are things in it quite wonderful.' (In
August 1861 he praised *Les Cymbaliers du Roi.* 'The alliteration is really so persistent that the ears feel as if they had been horribly drummed on.') In April
1866 he speaks of the 'miraculous descriptive power' of *Travailleurs de la Mer.*
'The Storm is amazing: I have never read anything like it. It is next to Nature
in force and vividness. Hugo calls the sea and sweeps the heavens; the elements
are in his hands. He is the largest son of his mother earth in this time present.
Magnificent in conception, unsurpassed—leagues beyond us all—in execution.
Not (nur Schade!) a philosopher. That's the pity. With a philosophic brain, as
well as his marvellous poetic energy, he would stand in the front rank of glorious
men forever. His occasional dirty speech is just a part of his grotesque greatness.
It costs me nothing to overlook it—especially in this age of satin.' Note how
here as in the estimates of Tennyson, drapery is used to represent all most false
and conventional in Victorian society.

In March 1866 he wrote to Swinburne, 'How true it is what you say (in
Essay on Byron) of overleaping idyllic details and striking the pure elements!
This fairly accounts for your admiration of Hugo, who can do the same, when
he will not insist upon being French.'

In Jan. 1868 he asks S. for Hugo's poem. (He has asked for Baudelaire in
March 1867, and now mentions receipt of S.'s Blake.) In *The Fortnightly*, June
1868, he sarcastically contrasts Hugo's clean imaginative realism and B. Lytton's
pseudo-philosophising (*Chronicles and Characters*, 1867). Hugo does not look on
evil with the same reposeful sentiment. (See later his reaction to Hugo in his
France ode.)

In 1883 he writes to Maxse who had visited Guernsey, 'I want to hear of
Hugo. . . .'

He felt akin to Hugo in the fusing of social and elemental imagery with (at
best) an historical realism that Swinburne for instance lacked. (Swinburne condemned *Les Misérables*.)

Balzac. Passages copied into George's and Mary Nicoll's Commonplace Book include (as well as things from G. Sand, Dickens, Dumas, Miss Mitford) some
Balzac. He had *Mignonne, A Tenebrous Affair, Lily in the Valley* in his library at
death; and he agreed with Alice Brandreth in her enthusiasm for *Lost Illusions*.
Note the vicious attack by Leslie Stephens in *The Fortnightly*, 1871, which

describes Balzac's novels as masquerades of devils tormenting a few lost angels, a nightmarish dream, a collection of monstrosities—though the tearing of the veil from corruption and greed is admitted.

Stendhal. He wrote in 1861 to Maxse on *L'Amour*; advised a young novelist in 1864 to read Stendhal and Zschokke; in Feb. 1906 notes two essays on S. in the *Revue des deux mondes* as worth reading. He had *Rouge et Noir* and *The Abbess.*

Marie. She spoke with a pretty French accent and translated French books and papers for Chapman and Hall; played the piano well, especially Chopin. Her sister Kitty married shortly before her. There were three brothers, two kept on the factory in Normandy; the third started a new one at Montigny. About 1885 they sold out and retired to England. A fourth sister married a French officer. (The Norman valley of the factory, rich-pastured with a river twisting between lines of poplars and willows, appears in *Beauchamp*.)

M.'s attention now begins to turn more to France: see *Rhoda*, xxii, *Beauchamp*, *Ode to France*. He said, to a Frenchwoman, 'Latin eyes are the only ones which can gaze. English eyes only stare.'

Letters 1863: (summer) 'Now that Emilia's off my mind, alas! Poetry presses for speech! I fear I am, unless I make a great effort, chained to this unremunerative business for a month or so. I am getting material for the battle-scenes in "Emilia in Italy." But, I have an English novel, of the real story-telling order [*Rhoda Fleming*], that must roll off soon and precede it. Minor tales, too, and also an Autobiography [?*Harry Richmond*].' December: He expects *Sandra* for January, 'a contrast between a girl of simplicity and passion and our English sentimental, socially-aspiring damsels.'

He tried to get Janet a job: the translation of Renan's *Life of Jesus*, but Chapman and Hall funked the book. Thackeray's death 'startled and grieved' him. (He does not seem to have met him; considered him capable of discarding 'puppetry' and animating his characters 'with the flesh of positive brainstuff,' but let the bourgeoisie get him down.) He himself was furiously tossing the beetle. With reference to Thackeray's death he says, 'And I, who think that I should be capable of eyeing the pitch-black King if he knocked for me in the night! Alas for those who do not throw the beetle!'

Letters, 1864. Comments on *Sandra*. 'Poor little woman! What will the British P. say to a Finis that holds aloft no nuptial torch.' By July he records that *Vittoria* gets on 'swimmingly.' Also, he expects editorship of a new magazine. By August *Vittoria* 'does not proceed fast.'

In October he hopes to have *Rhoda Fleming* out by January in one volume.

To a woman writer he writes sage counsel against 'the exclamatory style,' and bids her study George Eliot in this matter.

He is not afraid of calling himself materialist. In relation with sports he says, 'Let men make good blood, I constantly cry. I hold that to be rightly materialist —to understand and take nature as she is—is to get on the true divine highroad' (the word divine is a concession to Jessop, whom he addresses).

(See Sencourt, iii, for humorous letters on sport in the *Wykhamist*, June 1872.)

Poems. In March 1864 he wrote a war-song in support of the Danes against German aggression.

One morning soon after his marriage he woke at 3 a.m. and wrote *Cleopatra*, which was to be illustrated by Sandys. In *The Cornhill* of Sept. 1866 a poem on Cleopatra by Swinburne appeared, with a drawing by Sandys that both the poets thought poor. What happened to M.'s poem isn't known.

14

Naturalism. In 1887 he writes with revulsion of a book by Mendès. 'It is the monsterisation of Zolaism . . . sheer Realism, breeder at least of the dung-fly! Yet has that Realism been a corrective of the more corruptingly vapourous with its tickling hints at sensuality. It may serve ultimately in form of coprolite to fatten poor soil for better produce.'

Sentimentalism. Peacock's anti-romanticism (sentiment as 'canting egoism in the mask of refined feeling,' *The Four Ages of Poetry*) merges with Carlyle's political analysis of the egoist cash-nexus to beget *Sandra*. Meredith calls sentimentalism the modern monasticism to mortify poor humanity: thus the *Farina*-theme moves into the contemporary world. Both A. Symons and F. T. Blanchard (1926, *Fielding the Novelist*) noted the close spiritual kinship between M. and Fielding as democratic Anti-sentimentalists.

Personages. Merthyr suggests Byron in the brother-sister bond and as the aristocrat-turned-patriot. I think Meredith uses Georgiana to imply the ingrown bond-of-the-past which Merthyr cannot outgrow; that is, he cannot achieve the move-ment into the new life-centre as Sandra the democratic and girl-of-the-people can. The Georgiana-bond thus means the backward-looking element, the feudal fantasy, which for all his genuine self-dedication to the same cause as Sandra, he cannot break from.

Lady Gostre is a slight version of Lady Duff-Gordon. Lady Charlotte is well-drawn; one of M.'s bold hard upper-class women, though coldly balanced in her refusal to show jealousy or be vulgarly excited; her tact, however, becomes cynicism. Mrs Chump is detested by all the critics, presumably because she so excellently wrecks the Pole world.

Swinburne had stirred M. with his *Song of Italy*: he had 'a thousand spirits of fancy about it,' March, 1867.

Brainton in the theatre scene suggests Guppy, *Bleak House*, xiii.

Setting. Based on Copsham. By a pollard-willow of his Black Pool he kills off Purcell; the scene of the second-last chapter is what he sees from his window, the space by the mound (where he told Janet of Emilia Macirone) with moss and frost for flooring. (He bade Maxse note this scene, and thirty years later recalled it in the poem *Night of Frost in May*.) Purcell, crushed by the unrealised parental hand, is a meek Richard Feverel, with something of Arthur Meredith.

Method. Note the diverse uses of indirect approach, to get a rich focus of reality, a more socialised perspective: e.g. Georgiana's disjointed account of the scene of Wilfrid's exposure in Devon, the double account of Sandra's crisis, the discussion with Tracy of her Opera (to generalise the situation and bring out the idea of political meanings in personal relations), the intrusion of the Philosopher. *Sandra* like its two predecessors ends with a letter.

It is of interest to compare Swinburne's two novels, which carry the indirect method to an extreme. In the desire to merge poetic and realistic elements there are many links with Meredith's work; and a character like Lady Midhurst comes close to a Meredithian exposure of bourgeois egoism. But Swinburne fails to break through the obsessional imagery that keeps reducing the world's evil to the whips which he hates and yet desires in masochistic challenge; and so he falls into pessimism. The struggle against the alienating processes weakens into an acceptance, even a glorification of evil as necessary for the masochistic test or ordeal; and the test itself becomes narrowly stoic, limited to the single suffering-desiring body.

Yet there are many powerful elements which show how Swinburne could have linked his work with Meredith's. To do so, he would have had to move from Mazzinism to a grasp of what the Paris Commune meant. Instead he reacted with blind fear and horror to the Commune and ceased to develop as an artist; above all he was unable to carry on his novel-writing. The political characters in *Lesbia Brandon* show his inability to merge realism with any deep political understanding. But there is enough virtue and force to make us hazard a guess as to what might have happened to our culture if Swinburne had effectively struggled through to a full realism and had joined Meredith in his attack on the bourgeois process of self-alienation.

In *Lesbia* (Ch. iii) he has a discussion of the novel and shows a reminiscence of *Sandra* by calling Carlyle a puritan on a hippogriff. Meredith praised the picture of Leonora (based on Rossetti's Fanny). *Love's Cross Currents* did not appear till 1877 when it was anonymously serialised; but Meredith may have read it in MS. He would certainly have been fascinated and repelled.

France. Perhaps some touch of Stendhal in the novel's notion of Passion. Note that *Sandra* was condensed by Forgues for the *Révue des deux mondes* in 1864, autumn, and Forgues' note compared M. with Stendhal.

Responses: even in the worst of societies something of a vital art-work gets through to the young: Henry Sidgwick wrote, 'Beg, borrow or steal "Emilia in England"'; it had such an effect on me that I employed my spare cash in buying up the man's other work.' Feb. 1865. Justin McCarthy (*Reminiscences*) says that at this time M. 'had a small circle of enthusiastic admirers scattered here and there. Wherever you happened to go you were sure to meet a man or woman to whom G.M.'s genius was an obvious and a positive fact.'

15

Sandys: in 1865 did a picture of Bhanavar for a new edition of *Shagpat*. A letter from M. in May 1863 rambles about the Garrick Club Sweepstake for the Derby. Several years later Sandys won with a ticket given him by M. 'I expect a dinner. But let me order it. There's a dry still Champagne I know of.'—Sandys was a great borrower from his friends.

Work. The Altschul Collection has a 31 pp. manuscript, *The Friend of the Engaged Couple,* 1862; and M. seems to have written for *Once a Week* in 1861 *The Lost Highwayman* and *Paul Bentley.*

Saxon-Norman. These race-terms of conflict (used as terms of class-struggle in the Cromwellian period) are used in *Rhoda,* xviii, in the class-sense. Compare Disraeli's *Sybil.*

Personages. 'Don't you love Dahlia more? I do,' said M. to someone who admired Rhoda. Edward is to some extent based on Ned Peacock who studied as barrister and was addicted to boxing in chambers, and who roused his father's wrath by marrying a girl 'beneath him.' Mrs. Sumfit has a link with Mrs Crickledon. Col. Barclay may be based on an officer seen at Lords in June 1863 and mentioned in a letter as to go into a book.

The Farm seems Byfleet Manor House near Queen Anne's Hill; Greatham is Cogham; Fairly Park is Beaulieu where M. stayed on his honeymoon while writing this part.

M. tended to minimise the book's merits, perhaps because of its flat failure— Letters, Jan. 1865 and 1883. 'I wrote in saddest spirits, rare with me. Stomach, my friend.' Also, he wanted to get on with *Vittoria.* The novel's original title was *A Woman's Battle.* (Clodd's Notes, June 1895, say he offered *R.F.* to Hurst and Blackett, 'who accepted, Blackett assuring M. he could secure good review in *Times.* M. was disgusted at this "log-rolling" and took away MS.')

Adam Bede and *The Heart of the Midlottian* influenced the novel (and perhaps *The Scarlet Letter*).

16

Ipswich Journal. Acquired by the Jackson in 1739: a widow married Foakes, a friend of Charnock, in 1858. Foakes and M. were later neighbours in Surrey; F.'s stepson, who played with Arthur, became an historian. When Dolman tried to examine the *I.J.* files to find M.'s work, M. called him a ghoul and prayed that the commination service be thundered in his ears.

Pall Mall Gazette: started 1865 by G. Smith of Smith Elder and Co., who also started the *Dict. of National Biography.* (Greenwood gave the Government the information that led to the buying of the Suez Canal shares; he died poor.) *The Journalist* dealt with Greenwood, W. T. Stead, and Morley; the MSS. seems to have been burned.

M.'s hatred of the journalism of his day appears in *The Tragic Comedians,* vii.

Chapman and Hall. In 1864 he offered to spend three afternoons a week at the offices. One odd event was his being drawn into a libel case against a book by his cousin, Lieut.-Col. A. B. Ellis (who wrote some works of factual value on the natives of West Africa); he does not seem to have been aware of the relationship.

Hardy. At the Burford Bridge Hotel in July 1895 Hardy said that M. had called his first MSS. *Very Wild.* Meredith interrupted: *Promising!*

A letter of July 1886 asks Hardy to visit. If the S. West wind is blowing, 'then, as you know, the cloud of one hour is the golden curtain of another.'

M. thought *The Dynasts* would have been better in prose. In his letter of March 1909 he evades saying anything definite. 'The book was welcome all the more as a sign that this big work was off your mind,' etc.

Shaw. Of *Immaturity* (1879) he says, 'George Meredith shared the guilt of its refusal with John Morley, who read for Macmillans. I fear he repeated crime with the other four (novels)—certainly with *Cashel Byron's Profession*.' Salt and others had a plot of taking Shaw to Box Hill, where he was to talk so fast that M. couldn't get a word in; but it all fell through.

Shaw says, 'I valued Meredith as a poet and as a cosmopolitan *bel esprit*' (apparently this refers to his sympathy for all the European liberation-movements) 'of a certain mid-Victorian type (represented by Dilke, Laurence Oliphant, Hyndman, etc.); but politically he was a Rip Van Winkle in the Socialist movement; and the literary life in the Surrey hills was contrary to all my rules of conduct: even as gifted a man as Meredith could not live it as long as he did without becoming a walking anachronism. *Diana of the Crossways* is fifty years behind *Our Mutual Friend*; its social values were all out of date. That is why so many people who, like myself, have a very high opinion of his natural power, can read nothing of his except the poems and *Shagpat*.'

Typical Shavian wisecracks, with a few home-touches and a basic superficiality. Why does he speak of *Diana*, and not of *Sandra-Vittoria, Beauchamp, The Tragic Comedians, One of Our Conquerors*? And the comparison to men like Dilke and Hyndman shows an eye for the obvious and a blindness to the truth—while there is no hint that 'literary life in the Surrey hills' was the late result of physical incapacity.

Talk. He called Hardman's mother the Great Mother of the Pantagruelians and worked out a theory that she was Venus in disguise and her son a big burly Cupid.

S. M. Ellis says he drawled in 'the manner now associated with Lord Dundreary, but which had been the prevailing habit of speech among gentlemen, especially officers, in the days of his youth.' But Morley calls his voice, 'strong, full, resonant, harmonious.' Eva Gordon said it'd be a treat to hear him recite the Alphabet.

17

Sandra. The episode of the 'spy' at the beginning, her utter contempt for a spy or traitor, sets the key for her own unconscious betrayals. Her intense belief in herself is expressed by her belief that her voice can force a spy to recognise his own baseness.

Meredith stresses her pagan virtue. The Countess Ammiani laments her pride of revolt that makes her refuse to pray. (She prays only at the bedside of the wounded Merthyr.) 'But she has no religious warmth,' Anna von Leckenstein thinks with satisfaction after hearing her sing.

Revolt. Note how Ch. ix, with its account of how the girls trap the Austrians, echoes what he saw during his previous trip to Italy. Note also how Angelo reveres Mazzini, though with aristocratic focus. 'I revere him. It's odd; I always fancy I hear his voice from a dungeon, and see him looking at one light. He has a fault: he does not comprehend the feelings of a nobleman. Do you think he has made a convert of our Carlo in that? Never! High blood is ineradicable.' Vittoria answers, 'I am not of high blood.'

The split with the King is foreshadowed in Ch. iv. Carlo says the king is their instrument. Agostino mutters, 'Yes, if we were particularly skilled in the use of that kind of instrument.'

Barto has much of Meredith's favourite attitudes. 'It [the letter] was worth the attempt to get possession of it, for anything is worth what it costs, if it be only as a schooling in resolution, energy, and devotedness:—regrets are the sole admission of a fruitless business; they show the bad tree.' Laura is based on Princess Belgiojoso, and Luciano Romara on L. Manara (cf. *Egoist*, xii).

The Novel. The earlier parts written at Mickleham, summer 1864, were copied out by Marie. Lewes and Sandys encouraged M., having heard chapters in MS. The book drew M. and Swinburne together; Swinburne stayed for a few days at Kingston Lodge, March 1867 (M. was bothered by the near church-organ).

In Ch. ii, he says the 'tale is not partisan.' 'The wisdom of means employed, or of ultimate views entertained, may be questioned and condemned; but the men themselves may not be.' He means that the subjective values of men on both sides must be given truthfully; but the total picture, of inner and outer life, should be in terms of a basic judgment of history. That is, the method is profoundly partisan, but that does not conflict with a devotion to the truth.

About 1850 there were many reunions of exiles, French, Poles, Russians, Italians, which Mazzini and Kossuth attended, and at which Tambuli sang *Italia O Italia* till they wept (D. Masson, *Memories*).

Mazzini himself loved the Alps, 'No one knows what poetry is, who has not found himself there, at the highest point of the route (St Gothard Pass), on the plateau, surrounded by the peaks of the Alps in the everlasting silence which speaks of God. There is no atheism possible in the Alps,' (1848). Contrast Meredith's image of lofty thoughts based on earthy fact. The detached elusive way in which Mazzini is presented suggests an idealist aloftness from the rough-and-tumble.

18

Fortnightly: he did several reviews and a poem *Phaethon* in galliambics. Swinburne protested at too small a payment for a poem in the period when M. was editing. (There is a tale of their meeting at the Garrick, which made things worse according to Sandys.)

Letters, 1866: M. (still at Kingston, now invaded by speculative builders) defends prayer for children, and for adults as long as no gifts are asked for (cf. Shrapnel in *Beauchamp*).

Harry Richmond. The Squire has a strike of miners, which he ends by direct discussion and conciliation. Meredith remarks that the best of the workers are migrating to the States. The war-theme comes in with Major Dykes on the scent of a new weapon of destruction in the hands of the French. Heriot, as an army officer, writes, 'We want a war. . . .'

The 'autobiography,' *The Adventures of Richmond Roy*, outlined as a proposed serial for *Once a Week* five years before be began *Harry Richmond*, had been of a picaresque nature. Young Roy, in quest of a fortune in London encounters Contrivance Jack, a Dickensian bravo. Roy works as secretary to a blind gentleman while Jack runs through various jobs. Then Roy is articled to a solicitor by his aunt; Jack, innocent, is entangled in a murder and amorous of a racetrack-tout's daughter. Then Roy meets a lovely girl at a country-house; she is in some enigmatic peril and he undertakes to see her secretly to London.

So far our knowledge of the novel goes. Some details were taken into *Harry Richmond*. Roy goes to a London mansion which he imagines his father's home —and finds his father a mere singing-master there. Jack is once employed by a man who thinks himself Dauphin of France. (We must not forget that Wyse was in fact the grand-nephew of an emperor; and two sons of a naval officer about 1842 assumed the name of Stuart and achieved good marriages. At the time of M's novel they were still in London, very hard-up but using royal insignia and orders of chivalry.)

Germany. No doubt Lewes's *Life*, 1855, made him think afresh of Goethe; Morley stirred him, 1877, with *Das Göttliche*. Note that he sent Arthur to be educated in Germany (but in Lord Ormont the advanced school is set in Switzerland).

Some points of contact with Goethe. Richard Feverel's learning that he is a father and *Wilhelm Meister*, VII, viii; Hamlet discussion in *Tragic Comedians* and *W.M.*; *A Gentleman of Fifty* and *Der Mann von fünzig Jahren*; Ottilia, a ballad-name in *Farina*, is the heroine of *Elective Affinities* and a step-daughter of Goethe; the thesis of trial marriages in *E.A.* and in *One of Our Conquerors*, xxiv, and *Daily Mail* interview 1904. (He lent *E.A.* to Ulrica in 1901, borrowing Eckermann's *Conversations*.)

Wilhelm Meister is the story of a young man's education like *Harry Richmond*; both books are concerned with the power of romantic illusions. (*H.R.* refers to *Zigeunerlied* and Ottilia's liking for Goethe.) See generally M. Krusemeyer, *Eng. Studien* (lix, 1925).

The professor was perhaps inspired in part by Milnes' essay on Von Humbolt at the Court of Berlin (*Fraser's*, Nov. 1860). There the freethinking old man ('I who remember 1789') is shown scorning the court and connected with Goethe's Bettina, an unconventional person. But if so, Meredith, by omitting the antagonism of the professor and the court, lands himself in the falsity of the whole Ottilia-concept.

Kiomi: based on a gypsy artist's-model used by Sandys, e.g. in his *Judith*.

19

Events. A daughter Marie (Mariette) Eveleen was born in 1871. In November 1872 he was in a carriage accident in France: the horse bolted and he was hurt but not badly, though his brother-in-law was knocked senseless and Betty V. was bruised. His wife and children were in another vehicle.

Alice. Once she scandalised her godmother in London by going on top of an omnibus with George to the Tower—though the presence of Arthur consoled the old lady. Janet looked after Arthur when George was in London and coached him in London, and she translated a book from the German, at George's suggestion, for Chapman and Hall, though her mother's better-known name had to appear as that of editor.

Dickens. June 1870: 'Dickens gone. The "Spectator" says he beat Shakespeare at his best, and instances Mrs Gamp as superior to Juliet's nurse. This is a critical newspaper.' No doubt he is part reacting against anything said by his foe, *The Spectator*, but he had been drifting away from Dickens's influence—to a certain extent protecting himself against it as he hammered out his own method; for he had clearly absorbed so much of Dickens that he could have carried on his work at the *Evan Harrington* level. (Cf. his letter to Stevenson, June 1878, and his late remarks to Clodd.) But an essay by Alice Meynell brought him partly back to a recognition of Dickens's merits.

Comments on poetry. He disliked Morris's *Love is Enough* (Jan. 1873): 'Our public seems to possess the fearful art of insensibly castrating its favourites. The songs are of the species of Fitzball's Gossamer Tree: charming in melody, but there is no such thing as a gossamer tree.' This is a valid criticism of the abstract approach to Love; but unfortunately M. does not seem to have known Morris's work after he turned to socialism.

He still admired Swinburne ('finest poet; truest artist—of the young lot— when he refrains from pointing a hand at the genitals') but now never sees him, fears he has offended him. 'All states of life have their privilege, and mine is to be behind the scenes of many illustrious and ringing names, and to laugh.' In August 1874 he asks Maxse to read S.'s *Bothwell*.

In Oct. 1872 he wrote to Swinburne hoping 'none of you worried of that Buchanan attack. Criticisms in England are usually an expression of the writer's personal likes and dislikes—what do they matter?' (In 1866 he had written, 'I have heard "low mutterings" already from the Lion of British prudery; and I, who love your verse, would play savagely with a knife among the proofs for the sake of your fame.' Asks about Buchanan. 'Lewes sends him up I don't know how high. My feeling is that he is always on the strain for pathos, and would be a poetic Dickens.')

He sent Greenwood an imaginary review of poems 'Armageddon, etc., dedicated to Dr Cumming of Scotland,' and got proofs, but that seems all (1870).

Maxse. Other works of his were *Our Political Duty* (2nd ed. 1870); *A Plea for Intervention*, Jan. 1871; *Objections to Woman Suffrage*, 1874; *Whether the Minority of Electors should be represented by a Majority in the House of Commons*, 1875; *National Education and its Opponents*, 1877; *Woman Suffrage, the Counterfeit and the True*; *Reasons for opposing both*, 1877; *The Irish Question and Victor Hugo*, 1881; *The Speech of Admiral Maxse on the Irish Crimes Bill which was howled down at the meeting of the Council of the National Liberal Federation . . .* April 6th, 1887; *The French Press and Ireland*, 1888; *Home Rule*, 1889; *Judas*, 1894.

Beauchamp's Career. Maxse identified thus: Timothy Turbot, Falsey; Cougham, Moffat; Oggler, Alfred Pegler (who nominated Moffat); Shrapnel, Dr Hearne;

Romfrey, Grantly Berkeley; Killick, G. Kill, a bootmaker; Austin, Russell Gurney—also Lord Palmet as Lord Rosslyn.

Grantly Berkeley was a maternal uncle of Maxse: younger son of the 5th Earl of Berkeley. He assaulted James Fraser for a libellous review of his novel *Berkeley Castle*, which deals with family history. (Fraser was the publisher of *Fraser's Magazine*: beaten savagely with a heavy gold-headed whip, he died.) B.'s brother Craven was present: Meredith uses the name twice in reference to the Romfrey Castle and accurately describes Berkeley Castle (in Gloucestershire).

Meredith told Maxse that he himself too could be seen in the mirror of this book. Henry Murray saw him as Shrapnel, with the same obstinate tuft of grey hair bristling over his brow, 'the tall old man whose extreme leanness made him appear of more than actual height . . . the face of more than feminine delicacy with an almost angelic softness of expression.'

'You have discovered my likeness to women,' says Beauchamp to Palmet. Meredith told Gissing that poets had much of the woman in them or weren't much good as poets. Compare *Tragic Comedians*, Ch. vii. (To Stevenson he wrote, 'My Diana is out of hand, leaving her mother [himself] rather inanimate.' And when asked how he understood women so well, he said, 'It's the mother in me.') A young American, J. Hawthorn, saw him at Box Hill: 'quick and precise as a beautiful bird,' but really shy and embarrassed. 'He would have been happier as a beautiful and brilliant woman, the queen of a salon. He played at masculinity and extolled it, but masculine men don't do that.'

Cecilia, daughter of a colonel, was the wife of Maxse. Alice Brandreth claimed to have contributed to the girl of the novel in her aspect of strict conventional training.

Renée: some twenty years later M. said to Schwob, 'Was she not a sweet girl? I think I am a little in love with her yet.' Her Norman landscape is that of the Villiamies, visited in 1872.

All Beauchamp's love-relations reflect his inner conflicts, Renée is linked with his romantic relation to her brother whose life he has saved; Cecilia, when he turns to her, is seen through the glow of what her money can do to help the cause; Jenny is approached through convalescent gratitude and the spell of her uncle's character. Hearne's polemical bent is shown in the very titles of his pamphlets, e.g. *Thoughts on Medical Education, and the Importance of Relieving Mental Labour from Legal Restrictions; Cholera Non-contagious, and the Absurdity of Quarantine Restrictions.*

Lydiard, something of a self-portrait, is set out as the man who has the balance lacked by Beauchamp; but it is a sign of M.'s essential identity with Beauchamp-Shrapnel that Lydiard in fact contributes nothing to the novel.

Odd details. The History of the Inextinguishable *Sir Harry Firebrand of the Beacon, Knight Errant of the 19th century*, finished by Christmas 1870, may be a brief first version. But Clodd's Notes (April 1895) say that M. 'outlined plot of unwritten *Firebrand of the Beacon*.'

The enclosures appear again in Ch. xxxix; the theme of the best workers migrating to the States in Ch. xv; the illusion of aristocratic leadership again in Ch. xxviii; Shrapnel sees prayer as dedicating the world to God; he makes a devastating attack on the Liberals in Ch. xxvii, 'an army of bastards, mercenaries

professing the practicable for pay,' compromisers with a pendulum-swing.
Shrapnel is a vegetarian.

Note two points where the money-theme appears. When B. sails off with
Renée, he is pulled up and crushed by the realisation of his lack of money. And
later when he spoils Baskelett's marriage with a rich widow, the family is united
in resentment: it was an 'unwritten crime against blood' to hinder the money-
accretion.

On 2 March, 1880, M. wrote to Maxse, 'Your letters on the Commune
greatly pleased me.' I cannot find where they were published.

The novel was later admired by Symons, Justin McCarthy, T. P. O'Connor.

As examples of the kind of idiot things written of Meredith, take S. M. Ellis
on *Beauchamp's Career*: he thinks the book a warning for a time of national crisis
when clarity of reasoning and stability of character are needed. He utters in-
credulity of 'the seemingly impossible behaviour (though founded on fact)' of
the 'gentlemen' reading out and ridiculing a private letter, that of Shrapnel to
Beauchamp.

The French Scare. Palmerston whipped up a panic by declaring that 50,000 French
might land any night. The Militia Bill was passed. The funeral of Wellington
was used to intensify the war-drive—see Morley, *Life of R. Cobden* (II, Ch. v).
(The Colonels-episode occurred actually in 1858.)

Praise of Bright as a friend of the poor is meant to express Beauchamp's resistance to Romfrey. But M. is always ready to praise anyone (even Cardinal
Manning) who seems to take up the cause of the workers. This generosity,
however, shows vagueness as to the full workings of the class-conflict.

20

Morley: something of Dacier in him, the need to bridle a vigorous animal. He
wrote on many famous men, with an inclination to the rationalists, Lucretius,
the Encyclopedists. In 1875 M. was specially struck by his *Rousseau*, which
probably helped him to grasp the inner split of bourgeois man and write *The
Egoist*. Morley's *Robespierre*, 1876, sent him back to Carlyle.

Note how many of M.'s friends were positivists, agnostics, free-thinkers—
Morley, Stephen, Maxse, Morison, Harrison, Hardman. (The Sunday Tramps
visited Darwin as well as Meredith, a fitting combination.) Stephen died of
cancer: his first wife was a daughter of Thackeray.

There was a period of sharp break with Morley that seems to have started
with G.M's ridiculing of Buchanan's *The Book of Orm*, which Morley admired.
(There had perhaps been a slight strain when Morley was persuaded earlier by
Lytton and Forster to get G.M. to modify a review of 'Owen Meredith's'
verse.) Morley wrote saying that G.M's conversation for the past six months had
made him painfully unhappy with all its 'opinions, ideas, and likings.' In May
1874 Maxse and Greenwood brought about the first steps of a reconciliation, and
in a year the old intimacy was resumed.

Hardman: fading out as a friend, as M.'s physical energy goes. The letter of Dec.
1870 on the Kingston Pantomime, *Tuck Transformed* (into Mayor) has, however,
the old hearty ring.

Friends. Dr Gordon was well-read, had lived at Weimar and known Goethe, and had served in the Austrian Army! Among the wretched snobs whom M. tolerated were the sisters of Sir Trevor Lawrence (Our Affable M.P.), one a pug and one a terrier, both fools. After they visited Marie lying speechless near death, she wrote, 'Elles sont repoussanets.'

Alice he mocked for her old-man admirers and warned against predatory pleasures. Later when her daughter Dorothy wanted to leave home and work among the East End poor, he supported her. (Alice mentions his capacity for abrupt rages.)

Frederick Harrison, who saw a fair amount of Meredith though they were not intimate, mentions that the M.s used to attend George Eliot's Sundays.

Wagnerian friends with whom he later went to concerts were Dr Plimmer (Bacteriologist and F.R.S.) and his amiable German wife.

Politics. He is often confused when the imperialist issue looms up, e.g. on Disraeli and India, March 1876. He is anti-Turk in August, 'A nation cancered by the Harem must be extinguished.' The Russia-in-Asia scare makes him say Conscription must come, the sooner the better, March 1879. In 1877 he jeers at the 'Black Christian of the Bloody Cross,' and expresses faith in France's power to progress. (In July 1874 he had protested against a pessimist essay by Morison on France.)

Foote. M. promised if possible to contribute to F.'s magazine. 'I am naturally doubtful, considering the public we have, but of many failures comes the final victory,' Dec. 1878. In May 1879 he advises the working-out of the 'Philosophy in controversial Radicalism.'

Thomson reviewed *Beauchamp* in *Cope's* and *The Secularist*, 1876: the *Egoist* in *Cope's*, 1880.

When Foote was in jail (1883) for blasphemy, M. sent him an autographed copy of his latest book of poems; a decade later he sent a cheque to a testimonial fund for him, and, learning that Foote hesitated about printing his name in the list of subscribers for fear of getting him into disrepute, he insisted on being included among men who were making 'recognition of high and constant courage.'

He went with Maxse to a meeting addressed by Bradlaugh during his fight for the right of atheists to testify without a religious oath, and after his newspaper had been recently prosecuted for blasphemy and sedition; and was deeply impressed. He tried to make Greenwood see that B. was 'neither to be laughed nor sneered down, nor trampled.' He also much exasperated the 'Parsonry' of Box Hill neighbourhood with his sharp arguments.

Chloe. Welsh, see the reference to her *rhaiadr* of childhood in the fine vision of Ch. ix. Her last act is prefigured throughout: the Beau calls her the Fair Suicide, the Ghost of one who died for love; she has the Silken Cord in her hands, etc.

Poems. Attila's refrain perhaps imitates Horne's *Delora* ballad, 1846. Victor Radnor hums an *Attila* tune; and Sept. 1906 M. writes of 'fearfully sweet visions of him [Haldane] in an Attila charge of horse with the staff of the fiery (emperor) William.'

Earth laughs in the Autumn Ode, but M. later cut the passage.
There are fragments extant of a play with a Spanish setting that seems of this
period.

Comedy. The Spectator (missing the distinction of Comedy and Humour) argued
that the English had the Comic Spirit, and discussed if such Comedy could
succeed on the stage: a discussion typical of the abysmal lack of understanding
of M.'s thesis.

See Carlyle's *Essay on Richter*, 1827, for the Laugh.

Meredith may have taken a hint from Richter's *Introduction to Poetry*, which
sees the reader's knowledge, fused and contrasted with the thoughts and actions
of characters in a novel or play, begetting an 'infinite incongruity.' But M.'s
concept of exposure and liberation is hardly there.

The Public that M. discusses is the existing bourgeois public, but he compli-
cates his argument by shifting to the public he wants, an anti-bourgeois public
not yet in existence. When he said to York Power, 'Thank God I have never
written a word to please the public,' it was the bourgeoisie he meant, not that
a writer should be individualistic. On the contrary he considered that his whole
responsibility lay in making his art serve a popular (anti-bourgeois) public.

To Horne he wrote, 'I publish and find my head in the pillory, am battered
with bad eggs, and am suffered to withdraw promptly. So the task of forgetting
the world is not so difficult. I have ceased to care what it thinks about the
matter of my contribution to light literature, and aim only at the satisfying of
my own taste. It is the happiest of all states for an author, and the best for
inspiring good work in time to come.' But that is only making the best of a
bad job.

21

Meredith was annoyed at Kegan Paul for selling serial rights over his head to *The
Glasgow Herald*, where the title was changed to *Sir Willoughby Patterne, the
Egoist*. Henri Davray, who translated *The Egoist*, was told the preface was a
series of imitations of various writers; M. read it out, imitating each style with
astounding effect. (Sutro later wrote a synopsis of the novel as a play, com-
missioned by Forbes Robinson.)

The jealous man who shaved his wife's head in *Gryll Grange* underlies a remark
by Adrian in *Feverel*. Memory of Peacock's May Day rite at Lower Halliford
appears in *The Egoist*, iv, and *One of Our Conquerors*, xix.

The setting here is Ranmore and Box Hill.

Henley's remark on the 'perfect good breeding of high comedy' shows how
little he grasped the novel's point.

Meredith gets a hit at Mudie's in xv. 'The ancients were not decorous: they
did not, as we make our moderns do, write for ladies.' In vii he contrasts
'romances' and the living world. The Alps-image beckons Clara as freedom, 'a
visioned loophole of escape.'

Clara thinks, 'I could follow a soldier, like poor Sally or Molly. He stakes his
life for his country. . . .' This opposition of the soldier to the egoist recurs in
M.'s writing—cf. Hopkins's sonnet on the soldier. But the emotion, genuine
enough, becomes a cheat when applied to the 'defence' of ill-gotten gains.

The Ellises, already annoyed at *Evan*, suspected another insult in Crossjaye Patterne of the Marines, though he is quite a pleasant character. His son is said to come from Capt. Ellis's son George, but probably also has hints from Will Meredith who was now just the boy's age.

The style has a conversational flavour unlike that of the other novels, gained by unfinished sentences and repetitive phrases. No doubt this comes partly from M.'s growing trick of extemporising tales about acquaintances (strengthened by his reading chapters aloud to friends with all his declamatory devices). But there was also something in the theme that made him use the method, The dialogue in general has more of the crisscrossing of thoughts than is usual in novels, though common in life, as each person pursues his own train of ideas. This self-absorption is specially stressed in Sir Willoughby. The style thus echoes the content.

Stevenson: see *A Gossip Romance* for Burford Bridge (where Keats also stayed).

22

Hélène-Clotilde. Lassalle's killer, Yanko von Racowitza, a Rumanian prince, died five months after the marriage. Hated by the people and disinherited by her parents, she went on the stage without much success but with many lovers. She married an actor. After five years came a divorce. She then in the States married a baron who had lost his estates in Russia through association with Nihilists. They went to Munich and lived on precarious journalism. He died in October, 1911, and a few days later she poisoned herself. To the last she kept her titian-red hair in its splendour.

Tragic Comedians. Note how the Pompey-Caesar motive (which helps the lovers to come together) also prefigures the end, and suggests at the same time the power-passion in Alvan. The interview with Ironer (Bismarck) is an example of the slight historicity; but Meredith's statement of faith (that the working-class movement would win and B.'s triumph of reaction was temporary) is worth noting, written at the height of that triumph.

England is described as behind in the power-race. The English have 'gone to fat,' they 'have gained their end in a hoard of gold and shut the door upon bandit (i.e. rebel) ideas.'

Alvan sees Mazzini as the deep dreamer, Bismarck as the rigid power-ruler, himself as uniting the dream of brotherhood and state-power.

The Dark Tree, which appears here ominously (Chs. vii and xiv) can be found in *Shagpat.*

Reviews. The Daily News was friendly: 'fateful and tragic is the story as an old Greek play.'

23

Diana. Dedicated to one of the Sunday Tramps. Copsham suggested the Copsley of Lady Dunstane (Lady Duff-Gordon); Arthur Rhodes is a weak picture of Meredith himself; Westlake is Kinglake; Braddock, to whom Rhodes was articled, is Charnock. The Crossways Farm near Abinger, Hammer, was Diana's Crossways—note that the name is also symbolical: woman at the Crossroads of choice.

Mrs Norton, in winning the case that coupled her with Lord Melbourne, and in the long court-fight that followed, did involuntarily much to better the laws and conventions dealing with women. The secret-sale was that of the coming repeal of the Corn Laws: it was blabbed by Sidney Herbert who had just joined the Cabinet, and Lord Aberdeen told Delane. Meredith's putting-into-print of the version that credited Mrs Norton with the act almost caused a rift with the Duff-Gordons; in 1896 he inserted, at the demand of Lord Dufferin and Ava, a note saying that he had not meant his heroine's original to be saddled with the scandal.

The Norton-Melbourne case was parodied in Dickens's case of Bardell versus Pickwick—it is interesting that the same material occurs importantly in Dickens's first novel as in this late one of Meredith's.

M. was undoubtedly feeling also affinities of his theme with the tale of Mrs O'Shea, whom he had got to know well at her aunt's house. Separated from her husband and linked with Parnell, she was in something of a Diana position.

Evolution. In 1862 he wrote to Jessop, teasing him about the 'dogma of Genesis and the mild facts of Geology' (adding that he doesn't consider the Old Testament can do young people any good. 'I try to make him [Arthur] feel compassionately to the Devil.')

When he told Clodd, 'I back your Huxley throughout,' he merely meant that he backed science against religion, not that he accepted Huxley's interpretation of evolution.

Poems. R.L.S. wrote to Yeats in 1896 that ten years earlier he had been haunted and drunken with lines from *Love in the Valley* near Hyères. In 1907 M. protested to Mrs Sturge Henderson against the charge of precosity in this poem.

He told Clodd, 'Chiefly by that in my poetry which emphasises the unity of life, the soul that breathes through the universe, do I wish to be remembered; for the spiritual is the eternal. Only a few read my verse, and yet it is that for which I care most. . . . I began with poetry and I shall finish with it.'

24

Some friends wrote notices of *A Reading of Earth*, e.g. Foote in *The National Reformer*, and W. Sharp in *The Scottish Art Review*. Sharp stressed that M.'s verse is used for abstract or concrete definitions which M. felt he couldn't put in his prose.

Note that M. loved the paintings of Corot.

25

1887. Janet asked him to go to Florence in May, and to Tarentum; two years later he discusses her memoirs, necessarily 'skeleton-cupboard and desk-drawer prattle.'

He met Frank Harris at *The Fortnightly*, who tells of his high loud voice and says his eyes flitted all the while.

In May he writes on the impossibility of doing good writing under the influences of drink except 'flashy trashy stuff . . . wildness or grotesque conceit.'

1888. Characteristic expressions about death: to Gosse, May 17 (and to Mrs Jones, Feb. 1889). About the need to liberate women, 'the most heavily burdened' of all, so that their independence may beget 'great and blessed changes,' Nov.

1889: against immortality as 'priest's opium' to Foote (Feb.).

One of Our Conquerors. The original title was *Conqueror in Our Time.* Dartrey may have been suggested by Col. Fred Burnaby, who wrote *The Ride to Khiva.* The Rev. Barmby is Jessop, at least as to voice.

The two ancient maiden ladies, the Duvidneys, are done with biting satire in their lost and pious respectability. The way in which the night spent with their excreta-smelling dog breaks down their resistance to having Nesta stay with them is fine subtle comedy. They fail to drench the stink out with scent, and are tortured into a recognition of *fact.*

Victor has his Alps vision of pure victory (xix): this is the part of himself he cannot attain. Note his temptation by Lady Halley when he dallies with the idea of union with her: 'The Society, lured with glitter, hooked by greed, composed a ravishing picture. . . .' The settling of a strike by man-to-man methods again appears as an emblem of social reconciliation. He is touchy about finance as gambling.

Celt and North-of-England are praised (xi).

I have had no space to deal with the many lesser characters, Caddis, M.P., and so on, who fill out the picture of the knavery and idiocy of upper-class society. Mrs Marsett is a coarse example of the Mrs Lovell-Mary Nichols type (she admires Byron): her mixture of feverishness, looseness, decency is well brought out.

The journey motive derives from the extemporised fantasies M. had built up round Alice Brandreth's visit with her father to a philological congress in Russia (1876).

The central fall-motive was no doubt suggested by Meredith's own physical tendency now to fall. Cf. Woodseer's fall that opens *The Amazing Marriage.*

Attacks. J. M. Robertson in *Yellow Book* (April '97) found it the hardest novel he knew to read, save *La Terre,* which was difficult for different reasons. J. Payne (*Humouristica*) calls M. a 'cramp jargoneer' and depicts him sporting amid the ruins of language.

Anti-Semitism. Meredith often uses the term Jew for money-lender, creditor—reflecting the colloquial usage which can help to stir anti-Semitism. But his care to make Matey friendly with a Jew in his next book gives the effect of making sure that his own personal attitude is dissociated from that of Victor's here. (His treatment of Alvan shows that he was both personally free from anti-Semitism and aware of it as a political force.)

Style. 'You mention "One of Our Conquerors" with revulsion. It is a trying piece of work. I had to look at it recently, and remembered my annoyance in correcting proofs. But strange to say, it held me. A doctor of the Insane wrote . . .

that the opening chapter showed all the intimations of incipient lesion of the
brain, and he wondered whether I had studied the disease. . . . The novel has
value, for containing the character of Nesta Radnor, little Skepsey, and Dartrey
Fenellan (and) an Irish Gentleman, of a Type different from Colonel de Craye,
of the "Egoist." Also I found in it much that is now [1906] manifest of the
malady afflicting England.' The malady can only be the incipient lesion that
brought Victor down. (The statement shows that he liked Skepsey, the small
man gone almost as mad as his master—though what is plain aggression for
Victor is 'defence' for Skepsey. The (and) is surely a misprint—the brackets are
mine. The Irishman is Dartrey.)

26

York Powell. His vigorous mind shows in such comments as these (to Elton):
'Balzac and Meredith will represent the century. Do not mention such a person
as George Eliot. She did much good work and much bad. She meant well, and
she and Mrs Grundy quarrelled, and made it up over filthy Ghetto piety.' And
he adds, 'W. Morris says, "A clever man, not an artist." He can't rise above the
naive melodic'—true enough of Morris's middle period. Morris himself so hated
the bourgeoisie that he disliked also the realistic novels that dealt with them;
Dickens was as far as he could go. For the heroic he turned to the Norse. (Only
in The Wood Beyond the World, in a contorted archaic style, he tackled the theme
of alienation.)

Defence. For the later confusions of M. on war, note here the idea of Britain as the
world's champion of liberty throughout the world, and the fear that the 'despots
of the world' may overcome rivalries and unite against her. Hence a further idea
of Britain waging just wars, 'Let not any Government seek to support itself by
foreign aid against its people, or we will aid the people' (the 1857 allegory cited
in Ch. 7).

27

1892: comments amiably on Shaw's criticism of him; sends love to Swinburne in
March. Some good glimpses of M. in 1892, 1895-6, can be found in Michael
Field's Works and Days (M.F. was Katherine Bradley and Edith Cooper). They
see his daughter as a spoiled girl with blonde hair in masses, steel-blue eyes, full
curved lips, elegant but ungracious—though later they found her nice after all.
The Le Galliennes were there—Mrs Le G. 'a boneless heap of green Liberty
smocking' and her husband 'delicately set apart.' Meredith always lunched at
three o'clock, and brought out old hock. On the last visit a woman journalist
tried to make him accept a model of the Dresden bridal cup. The ladies were
huffed because he was too taken up with this Hortense.

This year he became president of the Society of Authors after Tennyson.

1894: in June he was at the wedding of Maxse's daughter and Lord Edward Cecil
in Chelsea: with Lord Salisbury, Chamberlain, Balfour, Morley, Asquith,
Wilde, Hall Caine, Mrs Humphrey Ward, and Blunt. (Hall Caine's book on
Rossetti infuriated him.)

The Empty Purse. Even here we find the bad confusion over Peace (social struggle blurred with war, so that one fails to notice when war takes over from social struggle, which it represses). 'Peace, our lullaby word for decay.'

Empire Wars. Harrison has a good essay in *The Fortnightly* of Feb. 1879 on *Empire and Humanity*: as usual his positive side is weak, his attack on imperialism excellent. Meredith wrote two essays in 1886 on Gladstone, one strongly urging Home Rule: cf. letter, Oct. 1906.

Personalia. Alice tells us he was upset by young girls laughing at the smutty jokes in a French play; she said they didn't understand, he said they knew French better than their mothers.

The Butchers got Will a job in the Telegraph Construction and Maintenance Co.; he worked at Greenwich, and M. visited him there in the lean-to corrugated-iron hut where he worked. Alice cites M. speaking of Death as 'the friend without whom life were impossible.'

28

Rockney is based on Greenwood: see J. W. Robertson Scott, *The Story of the Pall Mall Gazette* (1950). Greenwood's attitude is shown in his article, 'Britain, *Fin de Siècle*' in the *Contemporary*: he predicted 'national troubles and perils before the end of the nineteenth century-domestic abarchy and defeat in a great war' (1890). The same year the *Review of Reviews* noted that G. had for 15 years prophesied English armaments 'had become so gigantic that war was imminent.' In 1902 Meredith writes of an expected visit by him, 'I shall have another melancholy feast of forebodings.' Yet Greenwood showed 'courage and independence at the time of the Boer War . . . (But he who) took his place among the critics of the Unionist Imperialist mood of those days, played an important part in creating that temper' (J. L. Hammond). There we touch the inner conflict and the contradiction of such characters, which have many links with the people and problems of M.'s novels.

The Journalist, which was to depict Morley and Stead as well as Greenwood, was much rumoured in the newspapers; and Meredith told one friend that it was not to be published till after his death. A tale says that he in the end made his friend Dr Plimmer burn it in his presence.

29

Lady Charlotte in her bluntness sees the middle-class virtue of the Mean as a form of Egoism.

Matey Weyburn cannot but be a name taken from *Our Mutual Friend*— Wreyburn, the lost young intellectual who finds salvation in the love of a working girl, and who has as foe Headstone, the worker perverted by bourgeois education. (But note Waymark, the schoolmaster hero of Gissing's *Unclassed*, who saves a prostitute and in the end marries her.)

Sport appears in the praise of pugilism among the workers and the long swimming episode (set at Felixstowe where M. had stayed with his first wife some forty years earlier). Robertson, in a general attack on M.'s style, particularly abused this episode as impossible.

Prayer is praised (xiv), but linked with Earth. 'We do not get to any heaven by renouncing the Mother we spring from; and when there is an eternal secret for us, it is best to believe that Earth knows, to keep near her, even in our utmost aspirations.'

In sending Chillon to fight in Spain, M. is following his common pattern of showing the 'patriotic' upperclass youth as ready to enlist under any foreign banner; but he is also recalling Carlyle's *Life of John Sterling*. Sterling was an ardent Carlist, and though he did not go on the 1830 expedition, R. C. Trench did. So, to some extent, Chillon here appears as a Merthyr: and like Merthyr, with a devoted sister.

30

Setting: a return to earlier scenes, round Portsmouth and Petersfield, also Hindhead, Richmond and the like.

Old Buccaneer: derived it seems both from Trelawney (and his Adventures of a Younger Son) and Thomas Cochrane, Earl of Dundonald, 1775–1860. Lord Feltre stands for the worldly corruption of Catholicism; Fleetwood's conversion is one of spiritual disintegration.

It is possible that the first eight chapters were the ones written early (Sassoon). Conan Doyle visited M. in 1894, and had the first two chapters read out: he claimed credit for encouraging M. to go on.

The novel came out about the same time as *Jude the Obscure*, and the joke went that the titles should be *The Amazing Jude* and *The Obscure Marriage*.

31

In 1908 he wrote enthusiastically on vegetarianism. In 1906 he praised Holyoake as 'one of the truly great Englishmen of our time. From his earliest days as worker he spoke for the poor. . . .' He overstates Holyoake's sincerity; but his eagerness to praise a worker who carried on the free-thinking fight shows where his heart lay. (In a letter of Nov. 1906 he mocks at the Genesis text on Light, considering Harlequin with his transformation-act superior to God.) And jests about 'fifteen merry Prelates, inveterate in malignity' to Clodd in Feb. 1908.

Hyndman. To Morley in 1906 he spoke of H.'s attack on the English in India as liable to do 'mischief.' Hyndman was always unbalanced (true enough): it's a wonder 'he has not appeared waving a torch in the streets.' But 'a good fellow.' Blunt's pamphlet on Egypt is, however, knowledgeable, and though it too may do mischief, 'a subject for meditation.' (We must not forget that M. is bringing these anti-imperialist works to the view of the compromiser Morley. In 1909 he wrote to the Tory Burnand, 'there is Hyndman wielding the Socialist baton, to ravishing discords! What will be uppermost eighty years hence? Upon that I muse.')

He wrote stupidly to Nevinson in 1907, 'I am with the Revolutionaries, but not to the extent of declaring war on Russia. Moreover, I think that Stolypin . . . is doing his best.'

He wrote in 1903 a message to a conference discussing a North Sea Squadron and a naval base on the East Coast; apologised in 1906 for not being at the dinner of the Liberal Colonial Club; and in 1905 in *The Observer* advocated conscription. He wrote in 1908 a poem for the Union Jack Club's Album! Worst, he wrote to *The Times* in 1908 praising Queen Victoria's Letters—contrast his earlier scornful remarks on her writing.

Work. In a 1906 letter he says *The Egoist* comes nearest of his books 'to the proper degree of roundness and finish'; that *Diana* was 'felt' in him as he wrote; that he doesn't care much for *Rhoda*; *Feverel* was 'earnestly conceived, and is in some points worthy of thought.' *Beauchamp* does not probe so deep but is 'better work on the surface'—showing how he was falling from his deeper perceptions.

In May 1907 he explained the Venus-image in the *Hymn to Colour*: at dawn the planet is 'full of silver' with darkness round. She seems to 'fly on dark wings.'

In one of his last notes he cautions a reader that his Odes must 'be read twice —and that is much against them in this country.'

Writers. He liked *The Shropshire Lad*, 'revelry of naturalness' (1903); he supported a petition on behalf of John Davidson, a memorial for Henley, a donation for H. Kingsley's widow; and wrote one of his last letters (Jan. 1909) to correct an account of his relations with Rossetti in Chelsea. In 1906 he told of knowing Whistler well, without a quarrel. Whistler once visited him in the country. They had 'merry bouts,' and W. was a 'lively companion.'

He once called Gray's *Elegy*, 'The Undertaker's waltz.'

Blake. M. knew Gilchrist's life and edition. He was discussing Blake with Alice one day and she went on to say she was interested in the Devil. He cut in, 'I am so fond of his Songs of Innocence.' He may well have been stirred by Blake to develop his own thought thus: 'We must have poetry to hallow this and other forms of energy. Better say life is holy. . . . We know that every form of energy, even this flimsiest, as you esteem it, should minister to growth.'

Personalia. In his last days, with a plaid on his knees, greenish lights quick in his deep-blue eyes. With Titian's *Sacred and Profane Love* in reproduction opposite.

He had four grandchildren: George and Margot M., Joan and Dorothy Sturgis. In 1908 Mariette broke her nose in a taxi-accident but had it well set. Meredith was mostly cheerful, but we hear of him saying to a visitor in hospital, 'Do not speak to me.'

In 1899 he was given an hon. Doctorate at Oxford; in 1905, the gold medal of the Royal Society of Literature.

32

'I use the metaphorical to avoid the long-winded.' Also he made the plea: 'One fancies that a cultivated man might perceive in a writer a turn for literary playfulness, when strong human emotion is not upon him. To find this taken seriously, as an example of my "style", is quaint. But we will admit that there is too much of it' (1892).

For condensation see further *Beauchamp*, xxviii; against journalistic cliché, *One of Our Conquerors*, xix; ideas distorted by romantic fiction, *Beauchamp*, xlviii.

In *The Tragic Comedians* metaphor is said to be good if 'not like the meta-
physician's treatise on Nature,' not 'a torch to see the sunrise.'

Note also, 'We will make no mystery about it . . . listening to my own voice
more than is good.' He mentions he tried dictation, but it prevented him from
putting his whole self out into the novel.

In 1877 Swinburne named M. and George Eliot as conscious artists whose
work owes more to will than inspiration, and thus holds them back from the
front rank.

Verse: part of the harshness comes from the leaving-out of connectives and relative
pronouns, inversion of conditional clauses, use of adjectives as substantives or
vice versa. (*The Athenaeum* on *A Reading of Life* said, 'He has harmony, without
melody,' follows the French 'in seeking after rarity of rhyme.')

Critics. 'The office of critics is now, in fact, virtually extinct; the taste for tickling
and stripping is universal and imperative, Rhoda. Have you ever met a Reviewer? It is curious to see how small the thing that stings can be.' May, 1864.

Vashti (from *Vilette*): The selection was made in 1887: he cited *Iliad*, xxiv, Keats's
Grecian Urn and *Autumn*, Tennyson's *Oenone*, Coleridge's *Kubla Khan*, Shakespeare's *Henry VIII* (IV, ii), Dido'a lament of *Aeneid*, iv. In prose, Hamlet to
the players, Saint Simon on the Regent Orléans, and the Vashti-picture.

Personalia. Haldane brought at various times Asquith, Grey, Dillon, Lloyd George,
Lord French. The latter argued with M. about tactics at some battle till he (F.)
went off in a fury. Roseberry was found antipathetic.

M. stayed with Haldane in London and at Cloan where an old Presbyterian
minister would listen to him, pat his arm, and say, 'Ye're still but a laddie.'
Once at a country-house Curzon, back from his Viceroyalty, diverted the
billard-room with tales of his Eton birchings. Everyone smiled but Meredith,
who said, 'If I had a son at Eton and I thought he had to put up with such
indignities, I'd take him away at once.'

One of the tales he told Ulrica was about a spinster of sixty who, asked what
she wanted from poetry, replied over her shoulder with a shout, 'Passion!'
Among the lady-friends of this period was Lady Grandby (later Duchess of
Rutland) who drew pretty portraits of the women he admired.

33

The Amazing Marriage says that the novel must make everything unroll to the
understanding like legal proofs, and by the revelation of character. The *Diana*
introduction is the main place for the thesis of brainstuff in fiction—and has the
comments on Thackeray's powers and cowardices. (In *Vanity Fair* T. spoke of
the Fair as the place of 'all sorts of humbugs, falseness and pretensions.' But he
feared to show the Humbugs as integrally rooted in the nature of bourgeois
society: he tried to attack them as mere excrescences that could be eradicated.)

The theme of the split of head-heart comes into *The Amazing Marriage.*

G. R. Swann (*Philosophical Parallelisms*) sees the dialectical movement of
character-growth in Meredith's novel, but in abstract terms.

Unpopularity. 'I take it from all alike as the cab-horse takes the whip.'
'Stomach bad, and the English will not let me probe deeply into humanity.

You must not paint either women or men: a surface view of the species flat as a wafer is acceptable. I have not plucked at any of the highest or deepest chords.'
To N. MacColl, Feb. 1902: 'My name counts for nothing with the public. So I withstand it, as often as I can.'
He writes July 1908 to Hueffer, on the project of a new magazine, of 'our public more than usually frivolous.'
'I have at present a feeling of the Fates in conspiration with a frowning country to forbid further action of my pen. And, by the way, if the run against this novel (One of Our Conquerors) should put my present men out of pocket, I shall feel bound to give them a chance of indemnification with the offer of a more generally readable. But they may have become incredulous on this point': to Shorter, May 1891. Was the easy but rather flat Ormont thus conceived?
He told Legouis in July 1905 that England had 'little criticism beyond the expression of likes and dislikes, the stout vindication of an old conservatism of taste.' So far he had not seen 'one criticism of my books in prose or verse.'
When Alice was asked for an article on him, he repeated, 'Never write anything about me. Never! My books are never read, so why should anyone want to know about me? no, my dear, don't do it!' She said she'd only write if she read untrue things about him after his death. 'He shrugged his shoulders.'
'There are more Merediths than one,' he said in these late years; but though he had steadily developed, the continuity of his ideas is extraordinary.
'He is one of those personalities who need fear no comparison with their best writings,' said James Thomson.

Stevenson. See Life for Prince Otto and Meredith. Gosse tells tales about Stevenson's odd hat, etc., which show a close likeness to the careless Woodseer. James recognised the central importance of M. for R.L.S.; Gosse scolded R.L.S. for it.

Hand List of Meredith's Publications

Poems, 1851 (J. W. Parker and Son, 5s.).
The Shaving of Shagpat. An Arabian Entertainment, 1856 (Chapman and Hall, half a guinea; Dec. 19). Reissued 1865 with engravings after Sandys (and from the same types as the second edition in 1872 with new Bhanavar drawing on cover).
Farina: A Legend of Cologne, 1857 (Smith Elder & Co., half a guinea). Second edition, with title-page engraved by Linton after Crane's design, 1865, a shilling. Third edition, with Crane's design on wrapper, in 1868 by C. & H. at same price.
The Ordeal of Richard Feverel, 1859 (C. & H., 3 vols. at 31s. 6d.: June 20). Revised edition, 1878, by Kegan Paul & Co., in one volume (after appearing in 2 vols. of the Tauchnitz series). A sixpenny edition in 1899 by Newnes; again in 1900 by Constable. Everyman Lib., 1935.
Evan Harrington; or, He would be a Gentleman, 1860 (Harper and Bros., New York, at one dollar 50 cents). In England, 1861 (Bradbury and Evans, 3 vols., at 31s. 6d.). Second edition in 1866, one vol., with Keene drawing; a sixpenny edition by Constable, 1911.
Modern Love and Poems of the English Roadside, with Poems and Ballads, 1862 (C. & H., 6s.: April 28). American edition, 1891.

Emilia in England, 1864 (C. & H., 3 vols., 31s. 6d.: April). As *Sandra Belloni*, 1886, one vol., 6s.

Rhoda Fleming, A Story, 1855 (Tinsley Bros., 3 vols., 31s. 6d.: October). Sixpenny, Constable, 1901.

Vittoria, 1867 (C. & H., 3 vols., 31s. 6d.: Dec. 20).

The Adventures of Harry Richmond, 1871 (Smith, Elder, 3 vols., 31s. 6d.: Oct. 26. Second impression, Dec.); sixpenny (Constable) 1901 and 1912.

Beauchamp's Career, 1876 (C. & H., 3 vols., 31s. 6d.: Nov.).

A House on the Beach, A Realistic Tale (Harper, N.Y., 1877).

The Egoist: A Comedy in Narrative, 1879 (Kegan Paul, 3 vols., 31s. 6d.: Oct.). One-volume edition, 1880, 6s.

The Tragic Comedians: A Study in a well-known Story, 1880 (C. & H., 2 vols., 12s.: Dec.). Reissued by Ward, Lock & Co., 1881, at 2s., one vol.—in Tauchnitz, same year; reissued with note by C. Shorter by Ward, Lock, Bowden & Co., Jan. 1892 at 6s. (reprinted July 1892; changes in intro., June 1892; reprinted Dec. 1893—and in Warwick House Library). Penguin Lib. 1947.

Poems and Lyrics of the Joy of Earth, 1883 (Macmillan & Co., 6s.: July 7). Reprinted through errors; third edition, March 1894; fourth, March 1895.

Diana of the Crossways: A Novel, 1885 (C. & H., 3 vols., 31s. 6d.: Feb. 16). Second edition April; a third in May.

Ballads and Poems of Tragic Life, 1887 (Macmillan, 6s.: May 10). Second edition, March 1894; third, May 1897.

A Reading of Earth, 1888 (Macmillan, 5s.: Dec. 20). Second issue, Jan. 1895.

Jump-to-Glory Jane: A Poem, 1889 (pirated). Then, edited and arranged by Harry Quilter (Swan, Sonnen-Schein & Co., 5s.: Oct.).

The Case of General Ople and Lady Camper, 1890 (J. W. Lovell Co., N.Y.).

The Tale of Chloe: An Episode in the History of Beau Beamish, 1890 (Lovell, N.Y.). English edition (Constable, 3s. 6d.: Sept. 1900).

One of Our Conquerors, 1891 (C. & H., 3 vols., 31s. 6d.: April 15); reissued same year. (1891, in English Lib. of Heinemann and Balestier, of London and Leipzig, printed in Leipzig.)

Modern Love: A Reprint to which is added The Sage Enamoured and The Honest Lady, 1892 (Macmillan, 5s.: Jan. 26). Second edition, March 1894; third, June 1895.

Poems: The Empty Purse With Odes to the Comic Spirit To Youth in Memory and Verses, 1892 (Macmillan, 5s.: Oct.). Second edition, Jan. 1895.

Lord Ormont and his Aminta: A Novel, 1894 (C. & H., 3 vols., 31s. 6d.: June 18).

The Tale of Chloe, The House on the Beach, The Case of General Ople and Lady Camper, 1895 (Ward, Lock & Bowden, 25s.: Jan.). Small paper in Feb.

The Amazing Marriage, 1895 (Constable, 2 vols., 12s.: Nov. 15). One volume edition, May 1896.

An Essay on Comedy and the Uses of the Comic Spirit, 1897 (Constable, 5s.: March).

Odes in Contribution to the Song of French History, 1898 (Constable, 6s.: Oct. 21).

Poems, vol. xxxi in *Works*, 1898 (Constable): has several new poems, some from magazines.

Essays, vol. xxxii in *Works*, 1898, has *Comedy* with 2 reviews.

A Reading of Life, 1901 (Constable, 6s.: May); second impression, 1909.

Twenty Poems, 1909 (privately printed: contributions to *Household Words*).

Last Poems, 1909 (Constable, 4s. 6d.: Oct.).

Poems Written in Early Youth (mostly the 1851 and 1862 vols.), 1909 (Constable, 6s.: Jan.).

Miscellaneous Prose in *Works*, vol. xxxiv, 1910.

Letters . . . edited by His Son, 1912 (Constable, 2 vols., 21s.: Oct.).

The Poetical Works . . . (edited) by B. M. Trevelyan, 1912 (Constable, 7s. 6d.: Oct.).

Various small prints of small collections of letters—to Clodd and Shorter, 1913; to R. H. Horne, 1919; to Swinburne and Watts-Dunton, 1922; to Alice Meynell, 1923.

Up to Midnight, reprinted from *The Graphic* (J. W. Luce & Co., Boston, 1913)—misses out the last 8 pars. of last contribution.

Collected Editions: Thirteen vols. (C. & H., 1885–95); Edition de Luxe (Constable), 32 vols., 1896–1912; The Library Edition (18 vols.), 1897–1910; The Pocket Edition, 1901–6 (15 vols.); The Memorial Edition (1909–11), 27 vols—with the Standard and Mickleham editions after 1914.

(The C. & H. set had *Diana, Evan, Feverel, Sandra, Vittoria, Rhoda, Beauchamp, Egoist, Shagpat and Farina, One of Our Conquerors, Lord Ormont*; simultaneously with it Roberts Bros., Boston, began a U.S.A. copyright series.)

*

U.S.A. editions: *Evan Harrington*, 1860 (see above); *Rhoda* (1888: 2 vols. in Seaside Lib. Pocket Ed.); see above for the 3 short novels; *Egoist* (1879 in Franklin Square Lib., and 1888 in Seaside Lib.); *Diana* (with only 26 chapters, in Seaside Lib. 1885); F. Square Lib. 1885—3 cols. to page), both pirated; *Ballads and Poems*, 1887; *Modern Love*, 1891 (400 copies only); *Lord Ormont*, 1894; *Essay on Comedy* (n.d.).

A Note on His Reputation

Before Meredith's death the following books or booklets on him were published:

George Meredith. Some Characteristics, R. Le Gallienne, 1890 (5th issue 1900, with new material)—with *Some Notes in regard to G.M. in America* by W. M. Fullerton.

G.M., A Study, Hannah Lynch, 1891.

G.M., Poet and Novelist, M. W. MacCallum (Sydney), 1892.

G.M. An Essay towards Appreciation, W. Jerrold, 1902.

Browning and Meredith, M. W. Abbott (Boston), 1904.

The Poetry and Philosophy of G.M., G. M. Trevelyan, 1906.

G.M.'s Allegory, J. McKechnie, 1906.

Bibliography, A. Esdaile, 1907.

On Some of the Characteristics of G.M.'s Prose-Writing, T. S. Short, 1907.

Some of G.M.'s Poems, A. Woods.

G.M. Novelist, Poet, Reformer, M. Sturge Henderson, 1907.

Aspects of G.M., R. H. P. Curle, 1908.

The Novels of G.M., E. J. Bailey, 1907 (N.Y.: London, 1908).

Forman records under *Notices and References in Books*, one item of the 1850's (and that by Horne in Australia), one of the 1860's (McCarthy), two of the 1870's (both Swinburne), four in 1880–4 (one McCarthy, two J. Thomson, one Sharp)— then, between 1885–95, thirty-two; 1896–1914, one hundred and twenty-four.

Under *Notices and References in Periodicals*, one of the 1860's (McCarthy), four of the 1870's (one by Morley, one Henley), two 1880–4—then, 1885–95, one hundred and twenty-eight; 1896–1914, six hundred and forty-two. (These figures exclude reviews.)

A rough glance at some of the aspects of Meredith discussed in articles and essays between 1886 and 1909 will be instructive.

Courtney in *The Fortnightly* makes a schematic discussion of a conflict of analytic power and constructive genius in him. *The Saturday Review* says he 'goes into retreat with a problem of character, of conduct and of fortune, which he has to solve,' writes for himself, yet under the cold hard surface is original thought and true characterisation beyond the reach of other contemporary novelists. *The Spectator* fears that Meredith Cult is going to rise (1886).

Barrie in the *Contemporary* asks why he isn't popular. Because he has too much wit (1888).

A. Sergeant in *Temple Bar* and W. Watson in *The National Review*—see in text (1889).

Le Gallienne replies in *Time* (1890). He says that M. is in disgrace with the public, not because he can't tell a story well, but because he won't tell those the public wants. His book came out this year.

Dowden makes an academic defence: 'Difficulty is a relative matter.' In the *Novel Review* Le G. writes on Meredith for the Multitude, saying that he has passion and humanity, the great qualities—with his own poetic elements, humour, wit, wisdom: the result highly complex (1892).

The Temple Bar says his people illustrate 'wisdom gained through a large and penetrating observation of humanity'; there is something of Richter in a 'certain tortured obscurity' of phrase. Fear of the commonplace appears in style and minor characters, so that the latter often seem unreal through a touch of caricature (1893).

The Free Review has Newman's attack and a discussion on his poetry's picture of man, nature, sex-relations. Discussions of his attitudes to Nature now begin to thicken. (1895.)

The Edinburgh Review admires his work up to *Evan Harrington*. G. S. Street in *The Yellow Book* discusses his 'manipulation of words to express complexity of thought.' R. Colles sees him as succeeding Wordsworth (*Author*). G. Smith in the *Fortnightly* analyses the divergence of his women from mid-Victorian types and the possible conflict of M. as moralist with M. as artist. Salt goes into his Nature Lessons in the *Free Review*. Max Beerbohm parodies him in Christmas number of the *Saturday* (1896).

Shaw discusses M. on Comedy in the *Saturday*; Robertson attacks in *The Yellow Book*; the *Quarterly* thinks his 'judgment is not equal to his genius'; the *Saturday* decides that his poetry is not 'in the true sense poetry at all'; the *Bookman* finds him robust but often maddening in syntax; A. Symons sees him as poet struggling with prose, dramatist writing novels: (1897).

The Academy asks why *Shagpat* isn't popular, and has articles on his nature-poetry, his early poems. *Blackwood's* calls him 'the great psychologist of comedy' (1898).

The relation of Hardy is discussed in the *Bookman*, where also H. Lynch re-states her views, finds him too ruthlessly intellectual—like Wagner but incapable of 'depths of simplicity and poignant naked passion' of the *Tristan* end. She compares him with Stendhal and praises his landscape-powers (1899).

The Academy makes a plea for his verse-obscurity as fathomable and fruitful; Gosse goes into Hardy's relation to him in the *International Monthly* (1901). Now articles increase, but are largely repetitive, and there is no point in citing them (except maybe, *MacMillan's*, March 1902, on M. and Richardson, and E. Dick in *The Alpine Post* of January 1908).

Meredith Outside Britain (till 1914)

FRANCE. E.-D. Forgues gave a condensed version of *Feverel* in *La Revue des Deux Mondes*, April–May 1865; in the previous year, Nov.–Dec., he had done the same with *Emilia in England*, which appeared in book-form, 1866, with a note comparing Meredith and Stendhal. In the *Revue*, June 1867, Forgues treated Meredith, with Trollope, Mrs Browning, and Alfred Austin; he mainly considered *Vittoria*, in which he said the characters moved dizzied and breathless through a mist.

A version of *The Egoist* appeared in 1896; the *Essay on Comedy* in 1897; *Chloe* in 1908; *The Tragic Comedians* in 1911; *Gen. Ople* in 1913. A. Fontanes attempted various poems—the *Hymn to Colour* in 1909, *Modern Love* and *Love in the Valley* next year.

In 1896 Mme Daudet with her sketch had begun discussion afresh. C. Legras opened a series on English writers in the *Journal des Débats*, 1900, with Meredith. A. Chevrillon gave a brief statement of Meredith's faith in the *Revue de Paris*, 1902, and E. Legouis lectured on *The Egoist* in 1905—his text published in the *Révue Germanique*, as was an essay on M.'s women by H. Cordel in 1906. In 1910 came the little book of Photiadès; and Galland was working on Meredith. (There were comments on Meredith in works on the English Novel by Blaze de Burg, 1900; Chevrillon, 1910; F. Roz, 1912.)

We must add the interest in Meredith of M. Schwob, expressed in *Spicilège* (1896).

Not much, but far more than elsewhere. See in general M. E. Mackay, *Meredith et France*, 1937.

GERMANY. Germany saw an essay on Meredith in *Das Literarische Echo* in 1899, which appealed for attention to 'this pure and enlightened source' when so much trash was translated; and a brief note in *Deutsche Rundschau*, Sept. 1904.

In 1904 an authorised translation began, with *Feverel*, *Harry Richmond*, followed by *The Egoist* and *Diana*; then by *The Tragic Comedians* in 1909.

Not till 1910 and thereafter did any body of critical evaluation grow up, beginning with E. Dick, B. Fehr, E. Wrage, etc. Meredith thus did not particularly affect the pre-1914 novel. Samples of the criticism of his work can be found in Guy B. Petter's *G.M. and his German Critics* (1939)—not very impressive.

ITALY. 1873 saw *Feverel* in a popular series at Milan; and *Diana* came out in a magazine in 1906, in book form in 1909 (Milan again).

OTHERS. Prague produced *Feverel* in 1902. Russia had a version of *The Egoist* in 1894—the first translation of this book made. Holland saw *The Amazing Marriage* in 1896 (condensed).

A. Raffalovich, a Russian *littérateur*, contacted Meredith in 1881 and wrote of his work (as also of Stevenson's) in the *Revue de St Petersbourg*; and in July 1895, *Vestnik Europy* had an essay by Z. Vengerova. (Raffalovich, son of a Russian banker in Paris, also wrote in *Le Gaulois*.)

Index

417